THE PRACTICE OF DIPLOMACY

In the post-cold-war world the role of diplomacy has visibly expanded in the face of far more unstable international conditions. This is partly because of the emergence of complex relationships between a larger number of power centres, including non-governmental organizations as well as states. These developments are adding to the machinery of diplomacy, expanding the number of topics of negotiation and modifying the established character of diplomacy in significant ways. This book explores the historical development of diplomatic practice from the earliest times and shows how it has grown and adapted to the needs of changing international environments. It follows these developments into the late twentieth century and concludes that while diplomatic techniques have altered in response to new needs and have taken in technological advances in communications, the activity itself is inevitable and has never been more important.

The authors have brought together their wealth of research experience to provide a broad approach to diplomacy that is both coherent and accessible. *The Practice of Diplomacy* will be essential reading for undergraduates and graduates in international relations and international history as well as for those training as diplomats.

Keith Hamilton is Editor of *Documents on British Policy Overseas* in the Historical Branch of the Foreign and Commonwealth Office. Formerly he taught international politics at the University College of Wales, Aberystwyth. **Richard Langhorne** is Director and Chief Executive of Wilton Park, FCO, and was formerly Director of the Centre of International Studies, University of Cambridge. He has also taught at the universities of Exeter and Kent.

For our parents

THE PRACTICE OF DIPLOMACY

Its Evolution, Theory and Administration

Keith Hamilton
and
Richard Langhorne

Routledge
Taylor & Francis Group

LONDON AND NEW YORK

First published 1995
by Routledge
2 Park Square, Milton Park, Abingdon, Oxon, OX14 4RN

Simultaneously published in the USA and Canada
by Routledge
270 Madison Ave, New York NY 10016

Reprinted 2000

Transferred to Digital Printing 2005

Routledge is an imprint of the Taylor & Francis Group

© 1995 Keith Hamilton and Richard Langhorne

Typeset in Baskerville by
Ponting–Green Publishing Services, Chesham, Bucks

British Library Cataloguing in Publication Data
A catalogue record for this book is available from
the British Library

Library of Congress Cataloging in Publication Data
A catalogue record for this book has been requested

ISBN 0–415–10474–2 (hbk)
ISBN 0–415–10475–0 (pbk)

CONTENTS

ACKNOWLEDGEMENTS

This book was conceived in the late 1980s as a brief history of diplomacy for students of international politics. Since then the enterprise has expanded in scope and content, and recent political developments in eastern and east-central Europe and the apparent end of the cold war have led us to revise the later chapters to take account of changed perspectives and newly emerging practices. Our purpose has, nevertheless, remained much the same, and we hope the resulting volume will provide a useful introduction to those seeking to understand the ways in which diplomacy has evolved and the work of its practitioners.

We should like to thank for their advice and assistance Professor Derek Beales, Mr Richard Bone, Dr Eleanor Breuning, Mrs Glyn Daniel, Miss Jane Davis, Dr Erik Goldstein, Dr Ann Lane, Dr Frederick Parsons and Dr Moorhead Wright. The finished product remains, however, wholly our own responsibility and it should not be taken as an expression of official government policy.

Keith Hamilton
Richard Langhorne
St David's Day, 1994

INTRODUCTION

Diplomacy, the peaceful conduct of relations amongst political entities, their principals and accredited agents, has rarely been without its critics or detractors. Sometimes regarded as necessary but regrettable, at other times with deep respect, it has seldom, if ever, had a more significant role to play in human affairs than it has at present. The necessity for organized dialogue in an era when the relative certainties of a bipolar states system have so recently given way to a disorderly, confused multipolarity is witnessed by the frenetic pace of contemporary diplomatic activity. The collapse of long-established hegemonies and the re-emergence of long-neglected enmities have placed a high premium on the work of those skilled in mediation, negotiation and representation. In the meantime efforts to restructure and revive existing international institutions have tended to focus public attention as much upon the execution as the administration of foreign policy. More than thirty years ago, Lord Strang, a former British diplomat, remarked: 'In a world where war is everybody's tragedy and everybody's nightmare, diplomacy is everybody's business'. The end of the cold war has deprived the aphorism of neither its pertinence nor its validity.

If diplomacy is important, it is also very old. Even the most ancient and comparatively most primitive societies required reliable means of communicating and dealing with their neighbours. The process was generally considered worthy to warrant a general agreement that the safety of diplomatic messengers be assured by divine sanction. And while our knowledge of the earliest diplomacy may be limited, we know enough to see that it existed widely, that its results were sometimes recorded in highly public ways – on stone monuments, for example – and that rules of the game had been devised and developed.

The diplomatic process, its machinery and conventions, has grown steadily more complex, usually in fits and starts. Its growth has been a response to the interconnected developments of more complicated governing structures in human societies and the consequentially more complicated things they have wanted to negotiate with each other, or represent to one another. As states began to evolve in Europe at the end of the Middle

1

Ages, and by the mid-twentieth century became, in only mildly differing forms, universally accepted structures, much greater clarity emerged about what sources of authority might legitimately send and receive diplomatic agents. Their precise relationship to these authorities then became so significant that establishing it could lead to disputes which could prolong wars for years at a time, until during the eighteenth century such stultifying disputes were abandoned as inherently impractical.

It had always been clear that diplomats enjoyed special privileges and immunities while actually engaged in diplomacy, though it was often a matter of dispute as to when a person was genuinely a diplomat, and sometimes as to what their privileges and immunities were. These arguments tended to disappear during the eighteenth century and a more or less general agreement about their extent and nature emerged. With the emergence of continuous diplomacy in the seventeenth century, diplomats themselves increasingly became a recognizably professional body. This led to a series of disputes about exactly which persons in a diplomatic household were entitled to privileges and immunities and about what status embassy buildings and compounds should be given. In practice most of these questions were resolved by 1815, certainly most matters of precedence were regulated then and additionally in 1818. It was not until 1961, however, that a general agreement about the legal bases of diplomatic relations was arrived at and codified into a treaty. This agreement was principally fuelled by the arrival of large numbers of new, post-colonial, states who had no experience of the essentially *de facto* rules operated by the older states system. It was also partly the consequence of deliberate breaches of those rules which had occurred during the early cold war.

This kind of pressure was a modern example of what has always been an important factor in the development of diplomacy. As the machinery of diplomacy has responded to changes in the entities it represents, most obviously with the evolution of states and most recently with the emergence of power centres not located in states, so it has also responded to the needs of successive international environments. Development has occurred most significantly during periods when war, for one reason or another, has been regarded as a particularly ineffective means of pursuing interests, and diplomacy has become its principal substitute. The institution of the resident ambassador was partly a response to this situation in Renaissance Italy, and the completion of the web of foreign ministries linked by permanent embassies was the consequence of the intense diplomacy of the late eighteenth century. Later on, when the prevention of warfare became a principal objective of diplomacy after 1815, the consequences included the development of the peacetime conference in the early nineteenth century and the subsequent construction of both the League of Nations and the United Nations in the twentieth century.

In the contemporary world both kinds of pressure are plainly and simultaneously visible. There are changes occurring in the global distribution of power which follow from changes both in the nature of power itself and from consequential changes in its location. Such changes bring the risk of conflict in multifarious forms and raise the profile of diplomacy. There are changes, too, to be seen in the character of the state. The state has been, since the seventeenth century, the principal and sometimes the only, effective international actor. Now there are more states than ever before, differing more widely in type, size and relative power, and this factor alone has greatly increased the quantity of diplomatic activity and the range of topics that are discussed. Some of these topics are now derived from economic, financial and technological issues which transcend the traditional role of the state and operate on a global, horizontal basis disconnected from the essentially vertical state structure. Dialogue between old and new sources of power and old and new centres of authority are blurring the distinctions between what is diplomatic activity and what is not, and who, therefore, are diplomats and who are not. Such dialogue is also creating an additional layer of diplomacy in which non-state actors communicate both with states and associations of states and other non-state actors and vice versa. The effect has certainly been an explosion of diplomatic and quasidiplomatic activity. This book gives an account of the way in which diplomacy acquired its characteristic structure and discusses the forces which are quite sharply modifying that structure for the purposes of the contemporary world. Nevertheless, it also shows that the history of diplomacy demonstrates continuity. The exigencies of dialogue between communities, rulers, states and international organizations over time has brought the development of perceptibly similar structures.

In writing this book the authors have borne in mind particularly the needs of international relations and international history students and the work is also intended to provide valuable background material for the foreign service trainees of any state or organization engaged in learning the art and practice of diplomacy.

PART I

FROM THE BEGINNINGS UNTIL 1815

1

THE OLD WORLD

And Israel sent messengers unto Sihon King of the Amorites, saying,
Let me pass through thy land: we will not turn into the fields or into
the vineyards; we will not drink of the waters of the well: but we will
go along by the King's highway, until we be past thy borders.

(Book of Numbers 22, vv. 21–2)

Despite the fact that Sihon did not accept this request for a *laissez-passer*
and suffered dreadfully for not doing so, it is often and correctly observed
that the beginnings of diplomacy occurred when the first human societies
decided that it was better to hear a message than to eat the messenger. If
that has been agreed then there have to be rules which assure the safety of
the messenger, and if there are rules, there has to be some sanction for
them. This must have been true from times before we have any record at
all, and from early recorded history, when the evidence is derived almost
entirely from epigraphic sources – often frustratingly broken just at the
crucial point – it is clear that diplomatic exchanges were quite frequent,
that they led to what were evidently treaties, that good faith and en-
forcement were even then perennial problems and that the sanction for
the safety and general good treatment of ambassadors was divine. It was
no doubt the more effective in a world where the local pantheon would be
expected to intervene regularly in daily life and to be the source of sudden
and nastily effective retribution in the case of wrongdoing, either directly
or by human agency.[1]

What is also clear is that there is not enough evidence for us to form other
than a shadowy view of what truly ancient diplomacy was really like.
Certainly it was intermittent and generated no permanent institutions; and
how far rulers recorded transactions or negotiations and to what degree
they differed in their practices, we can know only patchily. With rare
exceptions, it is likely that the lack of evidence does not hide sophisticated
diplomatic structures which have been lost. For most of the state structures
took the form of large, loosely formed empires, with porous boundaries,
slow communications and little need to deal on any continuous basis with

7

any other entity which had to be treated as an equal. Such conditions did not give rise to the development of complicated diplomacy nor to the devices required to pursue it. We have an idea of the kind of attitude that must once have been general. It arises out of the survival of the Chinese Empire from ancient times into the modern world. When Lord Macartney attempted to open diplomatic relations with the Chinese Emperor in 1793 on behalf of King George III, he encountered the response of a diplomatic dinosaur. The Chinese reply was as follows:

> As to the request made in your memorial, O King, to send one of your nationals to stay at the Celestial Court to take care of your country's trade with China, this is not in harmony with the state system of our dynasty and will definitely not be permitted. Traditionally people of the European nations who wished to render some service at the Celestial Court have been permitted to come to the capital. But after their arrival they are obliged to wear Chinese court costumes, are placed in a certain residence and are never allowed to return to their own countries.[2]

Of course this reply was as much evidence of a particular world view as of diplomatic practice, but it did illustrate one aspect of the oldest kind of diplomacy, as did another Chinese example of its administration, this time from the nineteenth century. One of the reasons why the Chinese had such difficulty coping with European inroads was the absence of a central office or officer for co-ordinating diplomatic responses. For some purposes, provincial governors at the edges of the Middle Kingdom held responsibility for reacting to the outside world; for other needs different holders of influence at Peking might intervene capriciously, and yet other matters would be dealt with by the Barbarian Tribute Office. Even after foreign missions in China had been forced on Peking, there was little urgency about sending reciprocal Chinese missions abroad.[3] Some of these characteristics were to be found in the Roman Empire, with similarly insignificant consequences – but only for so long as it was not necessary to deal with another party as an equal. Faced with that, such systems collapsed.

ANCIENT GREECE

The first diplomatic system of which there is not only reliable but copious evidence was also one whose evident complexity was derived from the need to communicate among equals, the reverse of the submission or revolt situation which normally obtained on the peripheries of loosely controlled empires. In ancient Greece, a collectivity of small city-states emerged, separated by a sufficiently rugged topography to ensure their independence, but connected by sea routes and relatively short, if difficult, land journeys, thus compelling regular intercity communication. This diplomatic

8

traffic was made more necessary by the fact that, for a substantial period, no single city was powerful enough to establish an empire over the others, nor were they overwhelmed from outside. This ensured that they must deal with each other as equals. And, of course, it was easier to do so, since they shared a language and a largely common inheritance of culture and religion.[4] The practice of frequent diplomatic exchange was probably increased by the marked Greek tendency to be intensely quarrelsome internally and bellicose externally. Greek diplomacy was propelled by these characteristics and did little, if anything, to relieve them. What developed out of this situation was not a clear-cut and fixed system of behaviour, nor did any kind of administrative structure appear, but there is no doubt that a pattern emerged, some of it extremely surprising to the modern eye.

The Greeks knew three kinds of representative: the *angelos* or *presbys*, the *keryx* and the *proxenos*.[5] The first two, meaning messenger and elder respectively, were envoys used for brief and highly specific missions; the second was a herald, having special rights of personal safety; and the third was resident and informal, perhaps akin to a consul, though so different as to make any detailed comparison impossible. Before about 700 BC, what we know is confined to Homeric descriptions, and they certainly include one fine example of an embassy – that of Menelaus and Odysseus to Troy, revealing also a certain level of accepted immunities, to be flouted only with serious risk of retribution. In this case, Antimachus had proposed that the two ambassadors should be murdered, a fact later learnt by the Greeks, who took eventual revenge for the suggestion: Agamemnon had the two sons of Antimachus beheaded after they fell from their chariot in battle.[6]

Thucydides is the outstanding source of information about the later period.[7] Greek ambassadors were chosen with care, usually by the assembly of the city, and sometimes, in order to get the right men, in contradiction of existing regulations, for example, that men might only have one state job at a time. Their qualities were not necessarily those of suave or confidential negotiators, for one of the more surprising elements in Greek diplomacy was its open and public nature. Policy in the sending state was frequently debated at length in public, and the arguments to be used by ambassadors openly determined. They were often issued with extremely restrictive instructions and very rarely were plenipotentiary powers given. Such openness also had the effect of excluding the collection, recording and subsequent use of military or diplomatic intelligence. This exclusion was not complete, but to the modern eye, the diplomatic exchanges of the Greeks were marked by an astonishing ignorance.

On arrival in the host state, where the treatment was expected to be reasonably hospitable in a physical sense, though unaccompanied by any grandeur or ceremony, the ambassadors were conducted to the assembly, where their oratorical abilities were foremost, as was their nimble-footedness in answer to questions or subsequent debate. It was rather as if the principal skill expected of a British ambassador to the United States was to produce a fine forensic performance before the Senate Committee on Foreign Relations. This aspect of the work may account for the tendency of Greek cities to criticize returning ambassadors, often sharply, sometimes even to prosecute them.[8] Taken together with the lack of payment, a marked tendency to question expense accounts and the lack of any *douceur* in the way of life, it is quite remarkable that ambassadors could be found to serve. These disadvantages were no doubt mitigated by the relative brevity of the missions undertaken. Greek embassies were strictly *ad hoc*. Their credentials were valid for one negotiation only and appointment as an envoy was always a brief tenure.

A second aspect of Greek diplomacy which would have surprised even a high-Renaissance embassy was the number of ambassadors involved in a mission, which could be as many as ten. This was mainly intended to increase the weight of the case being put in another state's assembly, but large numbers were also used to represent different strands of opinion in the sending state, and as such could cripple an embassy's effectiveness. The outstanding example of this was the vitriolic abuse exchanged between Demosthenes and Aeschines when serving on an Athenian mission to Macedon in 346 BC. Demosthenes would not sit at the same table or sleep in the same house as his colleague.

This lack of consistency, lack of continuity and lack of confidentiality rendered the pace of Greek diplomacy extremely slow, as it staggered between shifting domestic public opinion and the ignorance which the absence of any kind of administrative process and record keeping imposed. Yet the constant flow of missions, the understood immunities which kept them relatively safe, the treaties and alliances which resulted and the often high standard of public debate give a picture of highly sophisticated, if not always effective, diplomatic activity. It is to be remembered for example that the Athenians succeeded in creating a league of over 200 members drawn from states over a wide area and in maintaining it for most of the fifth century BC.

In this kind of achievement, the *proxenos*, that other Greek diplomatic figure, played little part. A *proxenos* acted for another state while remaining resident in his own state. The office could be hereditary, but was more generally derived from a sympathy developed by the *proxenos* for the political method or culture of his adoptive state. It would be notable Athenian sympathizers with Sparta who might be appointed as the Spartan *proxenoi* in Athens, for example, Cimon and Alcibiades. The logical consequence of this appeared from the fourth century BC onwards when *proxenoi* were often granted citizenship of the state they were representing. The principal duties of the *proxenos* were to offer hospitality and assistance to visitors from the state that they represented, and this usually included the accommodation of their ambassadors. It also included giving advice on the current domestic political situation, and *proxenoi* were often the leaders of the political faction which was best disposed towards the state they represented; but it did not include the handling of negotiations, nor did it carry any other contractual duties. Moreover, there was no suggestion that the *proxenos* was expected to carry his external sympathies to the point of damaging the interests of his own state. In bad times there was probably little a *proxenos* could do; in good times, however, in commerce, culture and politics, his influence could be substantial. Athens came to regard the office as important enough to justify the grant not only of citizenship, but also of protection and political asylum, if need be. The post was generally regarded as one of distinction, commonly to be found among senior statesmen in a Greek city-state. Martin Wight said of it:

> The modern system is weak in giving expression to the sympathy of individuals for foreign peoples, exemplified by the concern of many Victorian Englishmen for United Italy, of R. W. Seton-Watson for the central European and Balkan nations, of C. A. Macartney for Hungary, of T. E. Lawrence for the Arabs, of Denis Brogan (honorary citizen of La Roche Blanche, Puy de Dôme) for France as well as the United States. Such sympathies in the modern world are eccentric, slightly suspect, and mainly confined to scholars. It was precisely these sympathies that the Hellenic system of proxeny institutionalized.[9]

Claims have sometimes been made that the Greeks developed the first forms of international organizations. The bases of these claims are that the Olympic Games, and other similar festivals, during which a generally agreed truce occurred, represented a period of deliberately controlled international relations during which co-operative arrangements could be made; that the wide respect for and use made of oracles, perhaps particularly that of Delphi, amounted to a kind of international mechanism; and that the Amphictyonic leagues had similar characteristics.[10] These leagues were made up of a number of communities living in the area of a famous shrine. The league was responsible for the maintenance of the temple and for the care of the worship within it, and thus had to agree upon shared arrangements and responsibilities. Such leagues came sometimes to exercise political as well as religious influence and they were used for negotiating oaths of non-aggression and mutual defence or offence. Such oaths were regularly violated and any grand claims for their interstate significance seem too large. They represented the recognition, as did Greek shared legal principles, that the Greek city-states were part of the same religious and cultural environment and in that sense were prepared to share some institutions and practices. If they were sometimes the agency for making peace, they did not alter the truth of Plato's remark: '*Peace* as the term is commonly employed is nothing more than a name, the truth being that every state is by law of nature engaged perpetually in an informal war with every other state'.[11] These were not international organizations as they would be understood in the late twentieth century, and as far as the Olympic Games were concerned, there was an entirely familiar tendency to use them for immediate political ends to an extent which makes twentieth-century moralizing on the subject of the non-political nature of sport look weakly naive.

THE ROMAN EMPIRE

Remarkable as was its extent and its longevity, the Roman Empire contributed little to the development of diplomacy; and what did emerge was primarily legal in importance, and has none of the intrinsic interest which Greek dealings generated. It may be that this impression is unduly strong because of uncertainties about how the administration of the Roman Empire worked at the centre, and still more, the lack of archive materials – either because they did not exist or because they failed to survive. It is, however, of at least as much and probably more significance that the Roman Empire exhibited marked ambiguities about what was internal and what was external, as it also possessed dual functions in the conduct of affairs derived from the emergence of the Empire from the Republic and the continued existence of parallel institutions.[12] In the early days of the Roman Republic it is clear that procedures similar to those developed in Greece operated, and were used to keep the original federation together. As Rome came to dominate, the Senate took over – and never formally thereafter surrendered – the right of choosing and instructing ambassadors, and of receiving incoming embassies. After the establishment of the Empire, some of the formalities continued to be arranged through the surviving institutions of the Republic, but it is clear that even from Augustus' time, those from within or without the Empire who wished to influence decisions did so by sending embassies to the Emperor, wherever he might be – sometimes finding him was a difficult problem for visiting embassies. This fact illustrates an administrative difficulty about dealing with Rome on which no advance was made during the life of the Empire. Despite the continued ceremonial importance of the Senate, there were no central institutions at Rome for the conduct of foreign policy or the maintenance of records. Policy was where the Emperor was, and while he undoubtedly had staff whose duty was to write letters in both Latin and Greek, it seems likely that he composed most, perhaps all of them, himself. During the third century AD, the Emperor's involvement in the defence of the Empire against the Sassanid Persians, frequently led him to negotiate in person, and the question of how ambassadors were selected and what they actually did, still to some degree unresolved, became less relevant.

All these uncertainties of management were paralleled in uncertainties about the internal organization and limits of the Roman Empire. Like preceding great empires, the Romans allowed highly porous borders. It would have been very difficult for a traveller in the second or third centuries to be entirely clear when he was entering or leaving the Roman Empire. And even when he was certain that he must be within it, he would have found a wide variety of local relationships with Rome which were determined by the circumstances in which the area in question had been joined to the Roman Empire. There could be areas of unsubdued tribes, there could be varieties of client kingdoms, there could be provinces which were under senatorial rather than imperial jurisdiction; and on the peripheries, there were kingdoms and tribes which owed a greater or lesser degree of allegiance to Rome, in which there could even be grants of Roman citizenship. In a speech to the Senate in 48, the Emperor Claudius attributed some Greek problems to failure to assimilate those they conquered. 'Was there any cause for the ruin of the Lacedaemonians and the Athenians, though they were flourishing in arms, but the fact that they rejected the vanquished as aliens?'[13]

From the correspondence which was preserved by cities anxious to have their rights publicly remembered and who therefore inscribed the relevant letters on walls, it seems that there was probably little distinction drawn between the method of communicating with entities of some independence within the Empire and authorities beyond it. Rome was prepared to write in both Latin and Greek, and its neighbours in the East evidently reckoned to use Greek. Letter writers for both languages were maintained by the Emperor, and there are references to translators when face-to-face negotiations took place, increasingly with the Emperor in person from the second century, or when visiting embassies met the Senate, as they had in earlier times.

For all the evidence of a complex correspondence and long-travelled embassies, Rome did not yield the procedures and complications of diplomacy conducted between equals. Most of what was transacted was in response to requests of one sort or another from within, from the peripheries or from beyond. Immediate problems with neighbours were usually dealt with on the spot, often by military authorities, and this became more common when the great crisis developed in the East with the expanding Sassanid Empire in Persia. No records appear to have been kept, and thus no notion at all developed of a continuing diplomatic relationship with any other entity. Rome did not use diplomacy, as Byzantium was to do, as a means of maintaining its supremacy, but as a means of transacting often very humdrum business, and this may be why it was the methods of managing long-distance legal or commercial business principally within the Empire which were to constitute its more important legacy. The notion that the exchanges of ordinary life should occur in a stable and regulated environment was a consequence of the Roman system. It was this system that gave rise to the legal principles written into the Code of Justinian which became the first basis of a simple diplomatic law. Similarly, the Romans wanted to be very clear about the legality of warfare, and maintained an antiquated but symbolically significant set of procedures for marking war and peace. Observing these rituals was regarded as safeguarding good faith between nations – the *prisca fides* on which the Romans particularly prided themselves – by providing a legal distinction between just and pious war and brigandage. The only permanent body that Rome evolved with some role in international relations, the college of *Fetiales*, was responsible for making the correct responses. If war was to be declared, the *Fetiales* informed the enemy of the grievances of Rome, and if nothing happened after a fixed period to prevent war from being declared, certain formulas had to be recited on the border of the enemy's territory and a cornel wood spear cast into his land. If, as must almost always have been the case, distance prevented this, the ceremony was performed by the column of war in Rome. Peace was marked by the sacrifice of a pig as confirming the oath sworn at the time, and a curse was laid upon Rome should she be the first to break it. None of this conferred upon the twenty members of the college of *Fetiales* any rights or duties in the formulation or management of policy.

BYZANTIUM

In the later Roman Empire, as in the early days of the Republic, it was not possible to maintain a monolithic, non-international, attitude because of the force of external pressures; and the steady sharpening of this development brought about a revolution in the diplomatic stance and methods of the Eastern Empire at Byzantium (*c.* 330–1453). The Byzantine response to its circumstances came to give great importance, sometimes primary importance, to diplomatic activity. The expansion of its techniques, its immensely long range and its persistence made it a forerunner of the modern system to a degree which its predecessors could not have been, and the close relationship between Byzantium and Venice provided a channel of transmission to the Western world.

The external problems faced by the rulers of Byzantium arose out of the threat of invasion from virtually all quarters. The least of them was the rise of new authorities in the West in succession to Rome, owing allegiance to the Western Church. More serious were the series of nomadic incursions from central Asia into the northern and Black Sea areas. At intervals from the sixth century, the Germanic peoples, the Slavs, the Hungarians, the even more feared Pechenegs, the Russians, the Abasgians and the Khazars emerged from the Steppes in waves. To the east appeared the Persians, the Turks, Seljuk and then Ottoman; to the south, the Arabs, driven by the new religion of Islam, swept out of the Arabian peninsula. For the Byzantines, faced with this array of enemies, there was another problem: the internal resources of the Empire could not sustain a permanently successful military response, indeed, it often found any military victory elusive. The longevity of the Eastern Empire, against all the odds, suggested that whatever alternative means of survival lay to hand, other than indigenous weaknesses in the enemy, were of unusual effectiveness. Those means had to be diplomatic.

The background against which the Byzantine diplomatic hand was played was of great importance. The conversion of the Empire to Christianity gave to the Emperor a conjunction of powers, divine and secular. The traditional universal authority of Rome was joined by a new and sacred role as representative of God; and gave to both Empire and Emperor a limitless scope. The Byzantine Empire was co-extensive with the *oikoumene*, the whole civilized world. All other rulers were held to stand in a natural relationship of inferiority to the ruler at the centre of the world, located in the city of Constantinople, the capital of the Byzantine Empire, which was itself a symbol of overwhelming influence as the junction point of both Christianity and the idea of Rome. Constantine VII put this into theoretical form when 'he compared the Emperor's power, in its rhythm and order, to the harmonious movement given to the Universe by its Creator'.[14] Many expressions of this view, and the consequent invincibility of the Empire exist. A good example was the response which the Emperor Romanus I Lecapenus gave to the Tsar Symeon of Bulgaria when he dared to assume the ultimate title, *basileus* of the Romans: he told him that a title assumed by force is not permanent. 'This is not possible, it is not possible even though you long and strive to beautify yourself like a jackdaw with borrowed plumes, which will fall away from you and reveal the name which your race fits you for.' Symeon was also warned by the Patriarch Nicholas Mysticus, who was otherwise highly accommodating, that those who attack the empire must expect the wrath of God because it was 'superior to every authority on earth, the only one on earth which the Emperor of All has established'.[15]

In addition to seizing every opportunity of emphasizing both the longevity of the Empire – a serious point, given the ephemeral nature of the 'barbarian' political organizations – and the contrasting fates of their enemies, the Byzantines were happy to hint at their possession of what might now be called 'non-conventional' weapons. They were also careful to keep all the physical signs of their unique superiority in evidence. These included the evidently outstanding beauty of the ceremonial singing of the Offices in St Sophia, itself an architectural wonder. In the late tenth century, during the visit of envoys of Prince Vladimir of Russia, they 'seemed to behold amid wreaths of incense and the radiance of candles young men, wonderfully arrayed, floating in the air above the heads of the priests and singing in triumph, "Holy, Holy, Holy is the Eternal".' And on asking the meaning of this marvellous apparition they were answered, "If you were not ignorant of the Christian mysteries, you would know that the angels themselves descend from heaven to celebrate the Office with our priests."[16] It is comparatively easy to understand what an irresistible effect this would be likely to have, and did have, on visiting dignitaries, and how it was achieved. It is less easy to see quite how other, seemingly more childish, manifestations also had a profound effect. The throne room in the palace was equipped with numerous mechanical devices designed to emphasize the all commanding nature of the imperial office. Audience might be delayed for some time in any case, and when it came, the envoy or ruler was conducted through crowds of officials and dignitaries to a room, panelled in purple, which was stated to be of unimaginable age, and contained apparently intensely venerable regalia. It also contained mechanical lions which roared and thrashed their tails, golden birds which sang in trees, and a mobile throne, which while the visitors were making a compulsory, deep and lengthy bow of obeisance, ascended rapidly, so that the Emperor was revealed in a superior position when they arose. No conversation was permitted with the Emperor, who was dressed in incredible finery and remained in a personally immobile dignity during the whole occasion.[17]

The treatment of ambassadors throughout a visit was designed to impress, without allowing them to associate in any way with other than official persons or to see anything which it was not decided that they should see. Their physical circumstances were usually well arranged, but could be dramatically downgraded if things went unsatisfactorily, or if, as happened with an envoy from the Pope, when he presented letters of credence which referred only to the Emperor of the Greeks, there was any suggestion that the Byzantine world picture was not being acknowledged. In this case, the envoy was thrown into prison.

The position of the Empire at the centre of the universe was elaborated into a carefully worked out plan, which gave many opportunities for giving honorary cousinage to neighbouring or distant rulers, or offices of grand title to others. These were usually meaningless but gratifying, but might carry some obligation of service to Constantinople for the luckless recipient. The terminology of treaties makes the position clear. Impositions upon the other party were gifts from the Emperor, services to be rendered and disadvantages accepted were privileges awarded. It is quite surprising to the modern eye to see how widely the Byzantine view of its own superior position was accepted and to what degree medieval rulers, both Christian and non-Christian, for both practical and sentimental reasons wished to be incorporated within the Byzantine hierarchy of states.

Byzantine diplomatic methods in one respect at least made use of the religious basis of the Empire. It was much easier to make good the claim to general hegemony with Christian neighbours than with Muslim rulers. It is noticeable that warfare, particularly the rarely seen Byzantine-induced warfare, occurred more frequently in the East than in the West, because the Muslim world was less liable to be manoeuvred into ideological submission; though it should be remembered that when Constantinople finally fell,

16

Mehmet II obviously felt himself the heir to some of the city's mythical status. From and beyond its other borders, however, the Empire conducted a major missionary operation. Byzantine priests, like Byzantine merchants, could be found spreading the faith, sometimes in the wake of conquest, but more often in front of military authority, and as they did so, they consciously spread not just religious doctrine, but a whole world picture of ideas, sentiments and customs, all of which started from the assumption that the Empire was the source of all religious and political authority. Conversion was a formidable weapon indeed.

The consequences of these characteristics of the Byzantine Empire were that its diplomacy could be patient, because it thought in the longest possible terms and it could use flattery by granting of offices and positions related to the Empire to people who had been generally persuaded to accept the central and special position it had awarded itself. It was also unmoved by accusations – frequently and justly made – of duplicity in foreign relations, since its special role meant that the end always justified the means. The Emperor Anastasios wrote in 515: 'There is a law that orders the Emperor to lie and to violate his oath if it is necessary for the well being of the empire'.[18]

Most of what the Byzantines did, however, and how they did it, was based on the desire to avoid war, for which, over the centuries, the Empire became increasingly poorly equipped. There was no doubt what the principal weapon was: bribery. Every ruler and tribe was held to have its price in either money or flattery, and for so long as the treasury at Constantinople remained full, chiefly as the result of being at the centre of the financial world, huge sums were expended in the knowledge that however huge, they would almost certainly be less than the cost of mounting and then quite likely losing a war. As Steven Runciman put it, the Calif or the Tsar might call it tribute if they wished, but to the Emperor, it was merely a wise investment.[19] These payments might be made in a way which the recipient thought of as tribute from Byzantium, or carried as part of the stock in trade of an embassy. These were immensely carefully prepared, grandly and richly equipped. The show was undoubtedly on the road and it was certainly intended to overawe, to bribe and sometimes to pay its own way in part by the sale of goods.

If bribery and flattery failed to work, other methods lay to hand. One of them, the marriages of Byzantine princesses to foreign potentates, which was a weapon sparingly but effectively used during the period of the Porphyrogenitoi (tenth and eleventh centuries), came later on, when funds sank low, to be a diminishing return as the device was overused by the Comneni. Rulers in Russia, in Abasgia (Georgia), in Bulgaria, Doges of Venice, Lombard princes, western Emperors married relatives of the ruling house at Constantinople, and their connections were further solidified by generous dowries and wedding presents of relics – Theophano went to become western Empress accompanied by the entire body of St Pantaleon of Nicomedia. In addition Constantinople liked to have a resident store of disappointed claimants, defeated rebels and dispossessed rulers, ever ready to be used as negotiating material or inserted physically as circumstances suggested. They were comfortably accommodated in the city and often married off to well-connected ladies.

The other principal method employed by Byzantine diplomacy was to divide enemies and embroil them with each other, and thus induce them to undertake the fighting which the Empire wished to avoid. Treaty obligations might be scrupulously observed, but, as Sir Steven Runciman has written:

> the Byzantines saw nothing wrong in inciting some foreign tribe against a neighbour with whom they were at peace. Leo VI, who was too pious to fight himself against his fellow-Christians, the Bulgarians did not hesitate to subsidise the heathen Hungarians to attack them in the rear; and similarly Nicephorus Phocas incited the Russians against the Bulgarians, though he was at peace with the latter. It was a basic rule in Byzantine foreign politics to induce some other nation to oppose the enemy, and so to cut down the expenses and risks of a war. Thus it was the Frankish troops of the Western Emperor Louis II rather than Byzantine troops that drove the Saracens from Southern Italy and recaptured Bari in 871. The Byzantines managed to be there in time to take the fruits of victory and to manoeuvre the Franks out of the reconquered province.[20]

These tactics were also to the fore out on the Steppes, whence so many invasions had come. But after the seventh century none settled south of the Danube, having been either stopped on the edge of the Steppe or diverted, like the Hungarians, northward into central Europe. The design for achieving these results was set out in a famous treatise of Constantine VII (913–59), the *De Administrando Imperio*: against the Kazars, for example, the Pechenegs, or Black Bulgarians could be incited; against the Pechenegs, the Hungarians or Russians should be employed.

For this purpose, the gathering of information about the internal politics and external relationships of neighbouring societies was crucial and it was always the chief purpose of embassies and any other exchanges that the Empire might have. So much was this so, and so deeply engrained an expectation that it must be any visitor's intention, that it explains the care with which foreigners were watched, confined and guarded in Constantinople itself. The duty of obtaining and sending back intelligence was not confined to embassies and their staffs. Merchants, missionaries and the military were no less involved. Nor was it only an activity undertaken by Byzantines who were abroad. Much intelligence gathering was achieved by imperial officers, particularly the *strategoi* commanding frontier fortresses at the edges of the Empire. Intelligence was carefully collected at Constantinople, and then supplied to embassies, so that they should know where best to place their bribes, and to the Emperor, so that he should embroil his enemies to the maximum degree. It was such information that led Justinian to write to a Hun prince:

> I directed my presents to the most powerful of your chieftains, intending them for you. Another has seized them, declaring himself the foremost among you all. Show him that you excel the rest; take back what has been filched from you, and be revenged. If you do not, it will be clear that he is the true leader; we shall then bestow our favour on him and you will lose those benefits formerly received by you at our hands.[21]

Part of the purpose of Byzantine diplomacy was to gain time. It was not a mere claim that the Empire was eternal; its staying power by contemporary standards made it seem relatively endless. The internal political arrangements and the consequences of the generally nomadic lifestyle of the Empire's northern neighbours led to inherent instability and short-lived political authorities. This in itself could give formidable advantages to the ever present Constantinople and its accumulated memory. More purely practically, delays could devastate an attacker, whether by the onset of plague, or by the nomadic necessity to move from pasture to pasture and to find water: to stay too long produced hunger and fatal depletion of horses and stock. Well-placed expenditure to achieve this effect by essentially diplomatic means was cheap at the price.[22]

Although the Byzantine Empire used diplomacy more continuously, employed more of its devices and generally used it to play a more central role in imperial policies than had occurred in any preceding society, there was no parallel for these developments in institutional terms. No forerunner of the resident ambassador appeared, perhaps because the Empire relied so much on information-gathering and diplomatic initiatives undertaken by its frontier officers. This practice evidently led to the emergence of a kind of foreign bureau for co-ordinating policy in the Steppes which was handled by the Strategos of Cherson in the Crimea – always the Empire's listening post for central Asia. At some periods the evidence suggests that the same people were used for embassies in particular directions – e.g. to the Arabs – on several occasions, suggesting that linguistic competence had become a factor in the choice of ambassadors.[23] Certainly a large staff of interpreters and translators existed at the court at Constantinople and was available to be sent on embassies. This staff was attached to the only part of the chancellery which had some of the characteristics of a foreign ministry, the *drome* (post office), one part of which was called the *Scrinium Barbarorum*, the Office of the Barbarians. The official in charge was the *logothete* of the *drome*, who was a bureaucrat, neither a minister nor an ambassador, who arranged that the Emperor's policy should be carried out after frequent, often daily, interviews with him. As defined during the ninth and tenth centuries, the *logothete* was responsible for the imperial post, the supervision of imperial diplomatic officers within the Empire, the reception of foreign envoys and their formal introduction to the Emperor and his court, and the internal security of the Empire. This aspect meant also maintaining a constant surveillance of visiting envoys, most easily accomplished by confining them to the special residence – the *Xenodochium Romanorum* – maintained for them and accompanying them on highly structured excursions. The responsibility for escorting visitors outside the city lay with the *drome* and not with the *Scrinium Barbarorum*. Probably the most important activities of the *logothete's* offices concerned the collection and organization of information. They knew the weaknesses and strengths of the imperial neighbours, their internal political landscapes, the likes and dislikes of influential families, what and whose interests might most effectively be cultivated in the process of making the subtle combinations which might save the Empire from the expenses of war. From time to time, they issued general statements on the conduct of foreign policy, like that set out in Constantine VII's *De Administrando Imperio*.

Byzantine developments were certainly striking, and they seem the more so when seen against the far less sophisticated diplomatic system which emerged in post-Roman northern and western Europe. Not until the fourteenth century did anything comparable develop, and when it did, it was a response, as will be seen in the next chapter, to more complicated international conditions. Later developments were the consequence of the diffusion of much more advanced methods from Italy, which were themselves partly derived from the way the Venetian Republic systematized what it had learnt from the Byzantine Empire. The other source of power which had developed the need for a response to the outside world simultaneously with both Byzantium and medieval Europe was Arab, Islamic and deeply different.

THE ARAB WORLD

In theory, diplomacy for the Islamic world, rather as the Bolsheviks were later to expect, was a temporary necessity. It was required because progress towards global peace and order conferred by Islam – the Abode of Islam or *dar al-Islam* – was slower than expected and eventually indefinitely postponed. The world was thus divided into the area which was Islamic or acknowledged Islamic sovereignty and that which did not – the Abode of War or *dar al-Harb*. Between the two there was always a state of war of some kind. It might be latent, temporarily postponed, it might be in full flood in the form of Holy War or *jihad*, or it might be suspended for long periods. During periods of suspension, there was no equivalent of the more modern notion of recognition. The situation was not stable; it was merely that war was, for reasons of convenience, called off for the time being. In all these possible conditions, however, some form of communication was required, particularly if actual warfare was in view or reaching its end; and means had to be found for allowing safe passage through Islamic lands at unofficial levels.

For accredited diplomats, provided that they turned out to be what they said they were, and they were not caught spying or buying up war materials, no special passes were issued. Islam had acknowledged the immunity of emissaries from the beginning and had done so on the same ground as other rulers: its reciprocal usefulness, even necessity. In the earliest days, this kind of diplomacy was at the most basic level, and approximated more to the functions of a herald. The announcement of battle, the exchange of prisoners and the arrangement of truces were all part of diplomacy's contribution to what was incessant warfare. Only after the establishment of the Abbasid dynasty at Baghdad (AD 750–1258) was sufficient equilibrium achieved to require the exchange of missions for more complex purposes. Even when this occurred, Islamic diplomacy did not develop in the direction of establishing any semi-permanent relationships in the hands of resident representatives. Special missions were sent and received with the object of achieving short-term objectives. Visiting envoys were treated with great grandeur in Baghdad, but as in Byzantium, they were isolated from ordinary civilians and carefully watched, it being understood that gathering information was likely to be as much their concern as giving it. Emissaries leaving *dar al-Islam* were chosen for their skills, so broad a range of qualities being required that missions were usually made up of at least three envoys, often a soldier, a scholar and a scribe, who acted as secretary. Written accreditation was provided, but the important messages were delivered verbally by the senior representative. If a mission to Baghdad had succeeded, the ceremonies at departure might be as lavish as those on arrival, and rich gifts would be exchanged. If unsuccessful, a cool dismissal followed; and if war broke out before the ambassadors had left, they might be held captive or even executed.

The important device in Islamic diplomacy at levels lower than missions from or to foreign rulers was the *aman*, or safe-conduct. This entitled the holder to enter Islamic lands and to obtain the protection of the authorities for his person, his household and his property. It could be obtained both officially and unofficially. The official *aman* could be granted by the imam to a group of persons, to the population of a territory or to the inhabitants of a city whose ruler had signed a peace treaty with Islamic authorities. Such an *aman* would always be granted on a reciprocal basis. Unofficially, an *aman* could be obtained from any adult, verbally or by any other sign, and it was possible for the giver to be punished if the receiver behaved badly in some way while within the Islamic world. The same vagueness affected the discussion about what should happen to a non-Muslim who entered *dar al-Islam* without an *aman*: his fate might range from execution to being conducted in safety to the frontiers after a four-month stay. Like all other contacts between the Islamic and the non-Islamic world, the working of the *aman* was affected by the permanent, if largely suppressed, state of war between *dar al-Islam* and *dar al-Harb* and by the contrasting but evident need for goods, merchants and diplomats to pass between the two with reasonable ease. Certainly significant exchanges took place in the areas of science, medicine and literature and these could be quite deliberate. Islamic ambassadors were often asked to bring back examples of the skills and culture of the societies they had visited.[24]

THE MEDIEVAL WORLD

A *nuncius* is he who takes the place of a letter: and he is just like a magpie, and an organ, and the voice of the principal sending him, and he recites the words of the principal.

(Azo, *Summa*, Venice, 1594, 4: 50)

The diplomatic relations of the West for several centuries after the fall of Rome were, except for the communications of the Church, relatively infrequent, inevitably slow and subject to little, if any, organic development. In this quantitative sense it is possible to make a comparative remark about medieval diplomacy, but it is very difficult to do so in most other ways. The chief difficulty arises from the undeveloped nature of sovereignty in the period, and the consequentially vague notion that contemporaries had of the difference between private and public activity and and therefore of the representation of its source. Confusion arising from this is liable to be compounded by the wish of contemporary legal commentators to make clear distinctions where none existed and by the efforts of subsequent historians, particularly perhaps Maulde la Clavière who wrote in the late nineteenth century,[25] to create order out of what was naturally chaotic, but in the image of their own time. It is therefore wise to remember that it is not until the sixteenth century, and not completely even then, that a clearly defined sovereign state can be discerned, having an accepted diplomatic practice and nomenclature more or less confined to its like. This partly arose from a primitive state of administration, the limited powers of rulers, very poor communications and the likelihood that the most advanced entities would not abut directly upon each other, but be cushioned by areas of as yet unresolved geographical and political space.

It also arose, however, from the fact that as late as 1400, the Western world still thought of itself as one society. There were wars, doctrinal disputes, the Great Schism, the division between Pope and Emperor, eruptions of class war, but through it all, there continued to be 'a belief in the actual unity of

Christendom, however variously felt and expressed' which 'was a fundamental condition of all medieval political thought and activity'.[26] This
concept came to have a name – the *respublica christiana* – but it never
acquired any political expression. There did arise, nonetheless, a body of
generally accepted law formed by the intermingling of Roman law, feudal
law and canon law: two of them had universalist traditions or applications,
which gave them a role in regulating diplomatic relations, and the third,
feudal law, through its concern with rules for the chivalrous treatment of
heralds, prisoners and noncombatants as well as the proper arrangements
for observing truces and treaties had a clear element of 'international' law
about it.

Roman law – civil law – was increasingly used from the beginning of the
fifteenth century, and it offered both a general framework derived from its
Imperial past and practical responses to a political world more and more
filled with secular authorities and relatively large-scale pecuniary interests.
It was, however, the first aspect which filled the need to provide for a
common body of law for the *respublica christiana*, and gave to the civil law
the character of a kind of international law until the seventeenth century.
All contemporary advice to diplomats from the fourteenth to the late
seventeenth centuries stressed the importance of knowing civil law. Canon
law, even if it was inevitably to become less significant with the decline in
the authority of the Church, and ultimately to be overwhelmed by the
Reformation, was most obviously important in diplomatic relations. The
Church was coextensive with the *respublica christiana* and canon law was
administered by its own system of courts throughout Christendom. These
courts claimed jurisdiction, not without opposition, over a very wide range
of matters involving laity as well as clergy, and to regulate therefore on a
broad basis many legal relationships. More than this, canonists had come
to consider questions which today would fall to international lawyers: the
definition of sovereignty, the sanctity of treaties, the preservation of peace,
the rights of neutrals and noncombatants and the rules of war. The
determination of just and unjust wars and the identification of unjust
breakers of the peace also came under review by the canonists. In a more
purely practical way, canon law had come to frame rules about diplomatic
agents as the Church became a major user of diplomacy during the struggle
with the Holy Roman Emperors in the thirteenth century. The diplomatic
system of the Church was always recognized to be different, evident
sometimes in nomenclature,[27] and these rules were not simply transferred
to secular use as appropriate, but they were, nonetheless, adapted.[28]

One of the effects of such an unfamiliar international environment, at
least to the late-twentieth-century eye, was that the act of representation was
not and could not be confined to individual states, because they did not yet
exist. Despite retrospective attempts to bring a descriptive order to diplomacy, it is apparent that there was no clear *droit d'ambassade* until the end

of the sixteenth century. In addition to rulers, all sorts of authorities – commercial, ecclesiastical, provincial and personal – sent and received representatives. The right to do so was made effective by those who wielded sufficient power. What was also very different until the fifteenth century was the infrequency of diplomatic exchanges. Another difference was that the ceremonial aspect of a mission could be at least as important as the message it was carrying, for claims and counter claims about the relative significance of the parties were indirectly expressed via the apparently endless and infinitely tedious ceremonial procedures.[29] There has always been an element of this in diplomacy but it became of much less significance during the early eighteenth century and played its greatest role during the later Middle Ages.

Until the rise of the resident ambassador during the fifteenth century began a major revolution, two phases can be seen in the development of medieval diplomacy. The earliest was dominated by the use of the *nuncius*[30] – *nuntius* in classical Latin – and coincided with the least complex international society of the period and thus the least frequency of diplomatic exchange. It was most often principals – whoever or whatever they might be – who needed to prepare the ground before arranging a personal meeting. They wished to communicate with each other by message, but in a way that was as near a personal exchange as possible. It was this which led the *nuncius* to be described as a 'living letter' and strictly limited his powers unless they were quite expressly increased or altered in some way for a particular purpose. It was, for example, possible for a *nuncius* to agree to a clearly stated and previously defined variation to his message: Venetian *nuncii* to the Emperor Andronicus in 1283 were allowed to make a truce for between seven to ten years depending upon what they could obtain, though only if agreement was reached within two months.[31] This was not very common, however, and the letter of credence carried by a *nuncius* often made the tightly closed relationship with the principal quite clear: 'certain other things concerning our business touching the King of France we place in the mouth of our aforesaid *nuncii* for the purpose of explaining to you', wrote Henry III of England to the Emperor Frederick II in 1236.[32] Dealing with a *nuncius* was, for legal and practical purposes, the same as dealing with the principal. The *nuncius* had no power to negotiate or to conclude an agreement unless such an agreement, for example, a marriage, had already been drafted, in which case a *nuncius* might be sent with agreement to the final terms.[33] How complete the identification was between *nuncius* and principal can be further gauged from the fact that a *nuncius* could receive and make oaths that ought to be performed in the presence of the principal.[34] It was also clear that the status of the *nuncius* was reflected in the immunity from harm which he was expected to be given. All diplomatic messengers from the earliest times had been accorded some kind of security for their persons, usually on religious grounds, and the special status of ambassadors was clearly understood. In the case of *nuncii*, there was a special sense that harming a *nuncius* was the same as harming his principal, as there was that a *nuncius* should be received with the ceremony that would be due to his principal.

The extreme difficulty, slowness and danger of medieval journeying combined with the limited powers of the *nuncius* sometimes made him useful to more than one employer. Since there was no particular sense of nationality or of pursuing strictly national interests about the office of *nuncius*, he could and did pick up extra messages along his route. There was a greater possibility of such extra messages becoming garbled on the way, and they tended to be preparatory rather than definitive, or to be non-political. The fact that Stephen Voivode of Moldavia used a Venetian *nuncius* both to send an extra message to the Pope, and to request that a doctor be sent to treat an ulcer on his leg, gives an instructive glimpse of this kind of role.

If it was so clear that the *nuncius* was no more than a living letter, why was the office used at all? Part of the answer lies in the essentially blurred nature of most medieval arrangements. As has already been seen, it was possible by slightly varying the duties of a *nuncius* to use him more flexibly than the stern definitions offered by the authorities – from Durandus to Bernard du Rosier – would suggest,[35] and there was an argument for using a human messenger arising from the insecurities of medieval travel. There was also, however, the perhaps small but nonetheless significant flexibility which the use of a human being offered. The extra courtesies that the ceremonial rules injected were part of this, but the main considerations were set out by the Venetians when appointing an envoy to Genoa in 1306 when it was said that a person could convey meanings beyond the written word by the intonation of his words, his attitude, his actual wording – if that was left to him – and his response to questions.[36]

The *nuncius* was certainly the most widely used diplomatic agent of the first phase of the Middle Ages, his limited role being matched accurately with the limited requirements of the age. The relative simplicity of the office also rendered it useful over a very wide range of functions: arranging alliances, keeping allies up to the mark, arriving at truces, declaring war, making protests, settling details of military support, settling financial transactions (usually loans), and the recovery of debts, involving the physical transport of actual money and the multifarious dealings which *nuncii* undertook for private persons or commercial bodies. This list is not exhaustive, nor would it be profitable to consider every minor variant in the messages sent or the manner of their delivery. The main lines are quite clear:

> [the *nuncius*] conveyed the will of his principal and could not act upon his own will so as to commit his principal. He could negotiate

25

conventions in the form of a draft, but these could not be made obligatory upon the principal without their referral to him and an expression of his will to be bound. Whatever a *nuncius* could do was conceived to be done directly by the principal.[37]

The use of the *nuncius* was intended to lead either, and most likely, to a meeting of the principals, or to a final meeting of their minds through a last exchange of *nuncii*. 'Summit meetings' were more usual in an age where most diplomatic relationships were with neighbours, and they were occasions so fraught with anxiety about both the physical safety of the rulers concerned and the exact rectitude of the ceremonial involved,[38] that specially constructed meeting places were often arranged, if possible precisely on a border – a bridge, or on a barge on a river – and surrounded with protective devices such as wooden lattice work in order to remove the risk of physical violence or abduction.[39]

The growing complexity of European societies in the later Middle Ages produced a corresponding thickening in the web of diplomatic relationships and the need to have diplomatic relationships with more distant powers. The result was not the supercession of the *nuncius*, whose existence and duties did not change from Merovingian times until the fifteenth century,[40] but the development of a new official, the *procurator* from which came the English terms 'proctor' and 'proxy'. The procurator was not a new office in the early Middle Ages, but its significance was legal rather than diplomatic. In the later eleventh century, papal officials were issued with procurations and it is clear that other principals were sending procurators for the purpose of entering into private contracts. A hundred years later, at the Peace of Constance (1175), the powers given by Frederick Barbarossa to his representatives used the language of procuration to give them the authority to negotiate and conclude peace. The Emperor agreed to adopt and promulgate without question what they concluded in his name.[41] It is clear that the use of full powers – *plena potestas* – of this kind had occurred patchily before, attached to the letters of credence of *nuncii*, but pressure for rulers to give procurators full powers regularly arose at the turn of the twelfth and the thirteenth centuries. It was chiefly the consequence of the need to have dealings with other rulers located much further away and therefore subject to great delays and potential failure if *nuncii* were used, though greater complication of business was also involved. In 1201 an example occurred which though probably not typical nonetheless showed what had become possible. Geoffroi de Villehardouin and his embassy were given full powers to negotiate on behalf of the leaders of the Fourth Crusade. They exercised those powers to the extent of deciding that it was Venice with whom they should negotiate, concluded an agreement with Enrico Dandolo, involving the receipt by Venice of a share of the conquests, and 'borrowed money to carry it out. The principals had no knowledge of what their envoys were doing until their return, nor did they expect any – an early and spectacular example of the conclusive nature of *plena potestas*.'[42]

Anything done by a procurator, acting either for a private or a public principal, provided he was equipped with proper powers, had the same legal force as if it had been done by the principal himself, but, unlike the *nuncius*, the procurator was acting in his own name and on his own responsibility. He was not a magpie. His principal diplomatic use was therefore for negotiation. Other diplomatic exchanges, or messages, could be and were still conveyed by the *nuncius*. There thus arose a question as to how far the procurator possessed a representative function, and the frequent medieval practice of appointing someone to be both *nuncius* and procurator – and often several other titles as well – cast doubt on the difference between the two roles, even in the minds of contemporaries.[43] There was, however, a clear pattern in which certain activities did not occur unless the title of procurator was included: delivery and receipt of official documents, the actual payment or collection of debts, the conclusion of truces or treaties,[44] searching for allies,[45] contracting marriages – even to the point of standing in for the bride or groom[46] – and performing or receiving homage. This last had a particular advantage for rulers who wished to obtain the benefits of acquiring or retaining territory in vassalage to another ruler, but did not wish to suffer the inconveniences of actually acknowledging the fact personally. The procurator provided the perfect answer to this problem.[47]

Clearly the procurator did have a representative function, because while he spoke in his own person, it was on behalf of his principal. He had flexibility and discretion, but these were limited, precisely because the office was potentially so committing, by the mandate he received from his principal. It is noticeable that as the pace of diplomacy quickened in the fourteenth century, procurators were necessarily away from their principals for much longer periods and correspondingly could only be reached or report after long delays. In consequence, their mandates became much more restrictive, and although rulers generally did not repudiate the actions of procurators who had exceeded their mandates – the obvious ultimate disadvantages were too great – they were certainly prepared to do so in extreme cases.[48] They were also prepared to withdraw mandates, after which no procurator could reach a legally binding conclusion.

All in all, the variations, occasional confusions, the multiplication of nomenclature all bear witness to the extreme difficulty of conducting diplomacy during the Middle Ages, particularly when its range and purposes began to expand. The uncertainties of domestic administration, the weak sense of sovereignty, but above all the almost unimaginably poor means of communication, with its appalling delays, rendered the management of external dealings a highly chancy business. Because of this, its multifarious

27

practices cannot be easily or neatly parcelled into watertight categories. The next phase of development, however, the rise of the resident ambassador, was destined eventually to become the basis of a much more orderly diplomatic system.

2

THE DIPLOMACY OF THE RENAISSANCE AND THE RESIDENT AMBASSADOR

> The first duty of an ambassador is exactly the same as that of any other
> servant of a government, that is, to do, say, advise and think whatever
> may best serve the preservation and aggrandisement of his own state.
> (Ermolao Barbaro (*c.* 1490) in V. E. Hrabar, ed., *De Legatis et
> legationibus tractatus varii*, Dorpat, 1906, p. 66)

This kind of observation, of which this is perhaps a somewhat extreme
example, was part of a large-scale discussion which opened up at the end
of the fifteenth century and lasted until the early eighteenth century. The
most desirable characteristics, the most suitable training, the most correct
behaviour of ambassadors were all minutely, even tediously, examined; so
also was the moral dimension inherent in the job. To whom or what did the
first loyalty of an ambassador lie? How significant was the moral duty of
honesty in reporting, in exchanging information with other ambassadors
or officials, where advantage might be gained by not doing so? How far
should envoys intervene in the domestic affairs of the rulers to whom they
were accredited? To what extent could espionage, or even assassination be
resorted to? All these matters were endlessly discussed, often in tracts
replete with weighty – and obscure – references to biblical and classical
sources in order to support arguments both complex and tenuous. The
better examples can be found frequently cited: Bernard du Rosier, Philippe
de Commynes, Maulde la Clavière.[1] The fact of such an explosion of debate
was more significant than its content – which tended to conclude that
ambassadors ought to be well connected, well educated, particularly in
languages, elegant orators, good entertainers, skilful at gathering news and
effective – and frequent – in reporting home; and that the moral problem
was best solved by seeking the greatest advantage for one's ruler via
generally common-sense means. When it came to advice about negotiation,
du Rosier and many others offered entirely familiar ideas, albeit wrapped
in the flowery clichés of the period. Mattingly summarized him thus:

> One must be as clear as possible in exposition, but one need not say
> everything one has in mind at once before feeling out the opposite

point of view. One must listen attentively, and look especially for points of possible agreement; these it is usually desirable to settle first. One must adjust one's methods to circumstances, and be prepared to make all concessions consistent with the dignity and real interests of one's principal and the clear tenor of one's instructions. One must press steadily and persistently but patiently towards an agreement, remembering that the more quickly a just solution is arrived at, the more valuable it will be, since time is always an element in politics, and undue delay may in itself be a kind of failure. But one must always be polite and considerate of one's colleagues, not prod them or irritate them unnecessarily, not make a fuss over trifles, not allow oneself to be carried away by the vain desire to triumph in an argument or to score off an antagonist. Above all, one must not lose one's temper. One must remember that the diplomat's hope is in man's reason and goodwill.[2]

The cause of all this formalized agitation was a large increase in the quantity of diplomatic exchange and a significant addition to the machinery of diplomacy which began in northern Italy during the fifteenth century and spread to the rest of northern and western Europe in the following hundred years. This development was itself the consequence of political and structural changes which led to the gradual growth of the sovereign state in place of the medieval order, and thus greatly increased the number of entities which needed to relate to each other diplomatically. This process was emphasized by the collapse of the universal Western Church during the Reformation and the consequential secularization of state government and administration in Europe. King Henry VIII of England asserted this kind of sovereignty when in 1533 he passed an act through Parliament terminating papal jurisdiction on the grounds that 'this realm of England is an Empire', i.e., a fully sovereign state.[3]

The presence of some of these general developments, though not the consequences of the Reformation, which was still in the future, in fifteenth-century northern Italy helps to explain the expansion of diplomatic activity there. There were also powerful additional factors. Northern Italy enjoyed the first flowering of the Renaissance in Europe without coming under the influence or power of an external empire. The Venetian Republic was not chiefly a territorial power, Byzantium had declined, Muslim power stopped short in the Balkans and the eastern Mediterranean, the Holy Roman Empire was becoming a Habsburg and central European presence and the development of the great states of northern Europe was yet to come. As it turned out, the evolution of the small city-states of northern Italy produced a multipolar international system in miniature where each state had expanded to fill the geographical and political space available but in which hegemony could be acheived by none. Moreover, the small size of the actors made any prolonged military activity impossible without mercenaries, and therefore unsatisfactory as well as likely to be inconclusive. A further effect of the small size of the Italian city-states was that they were able, unlike the sprawling monarchies across the Alps, to organize the first efficient governmental systems of the modern world. Mattingly said of this situation:

> In external relations scale had a double effect. The comparative efficiency of the new Italian states ... enabled them to pursue the objectives of their foreign policy with greater agility and continuity than Europe could show elsewhere. At the same time, the presence within the limited space of upper Italy of armed neighbours, equally efficient, agile and predatory, made continuous vigilance in foreign affairs a prime necessity.[4]

By the mid-fifteenth century, the Peace of Lodi (1454) marked the logical consequence of this situation. The rough equality in the system had first led to persistent warfare, the results of which attested the reliability of the underlying equality, and thereafter competitive behaviour resorted to methods which largely stopped short of persistent or prolonged military conflict. Among these, diplomacy became the most significant, acting as the most effective substitute for warfare. Other conditions, too, contributed to this effect. The relatively short distances between the centres of power and the shared language and historical background made inter-communication both essential and unusually easy. The pattern which had been present much earlier in classical Greece was *mutatis mutandis* repeated in Renaissance Italy: an absence of outside threat, an equality of power among the states within the local system, sufficient proximity both to enable and compel communication, and a shared linguistic and cultural infrastructure which made such communication effective.

The consequences for the development of the diplomatic machine were dramatic. To begin with, as in the previous period, the expansion of diplomatic activity was not confined to the representatives of states. It was only to become quite clear in the next century that sovereign rulers alone had the right to send envoys. Representation could be arranged within apparently sovereign states, for example, Venice.[5] Sometimes, as with Burgundy or Brittany within France, representation abroad continued to take place, as a deliberate demonstration of their continuing rights in the face of the unification process, though it was forbidden with enemies of the King of France.[6] It was very common for commercial groups to arrange representation, usually on an *ad hoc* basis, wherever it appeared necessary or advantageous.[7]

There is no doubt, however, that it was in the representation of rulers to each other that the greatest expansion occurred; nor can there be any doubt that it was in the emergence of the permanent resident ambassador that the most significant change developed. It was natural that such a revolutionary

31

change should be initially patchy in its emergence. There were in any case two severely conflicting pressures: the urgent need to know as much as could be known about the internal politics of neighbouring states suggested the use of residents; but the equally urgent need to prevent others from knowing what they wished to know and to limit the opportunities for subversive activities by residents made them extremely unpopular with rulers. King Henry VII of England was known to be on the verge of expelling all ambassadors from London at the time of his death,[8] while in 1481 the Venetians forbade their ambassadors to discuss politics with any unofficial foreigner and their own citizens could be fined heavily for talking to foreign ambassadors.[9] Philippe de Commynes, that most professional of amateur diplomats, expressed the dilemma accurately enough in his memoirs:

> It is not very safe to have ambassadors coming and going so much because they often discuss evil things. But it is necessary to send and receive them . . . My advice is that it is both politer and safer that they be well treated. . . and (that) wise and trusty servants . . . attend them. For by this means it is possible to find out who goes to see them and to prevent malcontents from taking them news – for at no court are all content. . . For every messenger or ambassador sent to me, I would send two in return, and if the princes become bored with them and say that no more should be sent I would still send them whenever I had the chance or the means. For no better or safer way is known of sending a spy who has the opportunity to observe and find things out. And if you send two or three people it is impossible to remain on guard so constantly that one or the other cannot have a few words, either secretly or otherwise with someone.[10]

It can be seen from this how the introduction of the resident ambassador flowed from a new need on the part of rulers. Whereas the main thrust of diplomatic technique had hitherto been to send messages from one ruler to another, and also indirect messages about their relative power, the conditions of the fifteenth century demanded that rulers should have information about their neighbours as much as, if not more than, the ability to convey messages to them. For the latter purpose they continued to use special *ad hoc* embassies, surrounded with all the traditional ceremony. For the purpose of gathering information, they needed informed, involved representatives on the spot, with reasonably secure lines of communication. It was a long time, therefore, before the resident acquired the status, or was expected to come from as high a social station, as the ambassador *extraordinary*. It was also not until the sixteenth century that the title of ambassador came into general use – except for the representatives of the Pope, who continued to be called nuncios. The same functionary had been given a wide range of titles – orator, from the classical past, procurator, *nuncius, deputatus, consiliarius, legatus,* as well as the spreading use of *ambaxiator* or *ambasciatore*.[11] In the early sixteenth century, occasional complaints could be heard about the quality, even the odour, of resident envoys;[12] although it is clear that in Italy by 1500 the resident ambassador was likely to come from the *haute bourgeoisie* and that doctors of law were particularly common.[13] By the end of the century, the situation had changed throughout Europe, and it was clear that the relative balance of importance, and therefore status, had shifted towards the resident.

The principal duty of the resident was to convey news to increasingly efficient chanceries at home. Rulers had an insatiable appetite for accounts of the daily politics of other states, as has already been seen. The reports that they received were very detailed, seemingly filled with political trivia and endless verbatim accounts of conversations that the resident had held.[14] This practice must have been deliberately encouraged so that the sifting of many such reports by the clerks in the chancery could reveal important connections not comprehended by the man on the spot. The workload for such clerks was frightening. The assiduous ambassador might write home every day and one Venetian ambassador at Rome piled up 472 dispatches in one year,[15] and he is unlikely to have been exceptional. If the workload at home was heavy, it became clear during the fifteenth century that the resident, too, was in need of help. It became the general practice in Italy to give the resident an official salaried and accredited secretary, similar to those usually appointed to *ad hoc* embassies; and as the prestige of the resident grew, young men of good family sought early versions of the post of attaché by joining them. In 1498, the Signory of Florence formally regulated this practice.

This passion for constant news was a reflection of the purpose which the new residents principally served. The tension, almost hysteria, which characterized relations between the Italian city-states in part arose from the potential instability of their governments, who thought themselves, and to some degree were, particularly vulnerable to subversion – subversion which might easily be pursued by diplomatic agents plotting with opposition groups. It was particularly this aspect which led Harold Nicolson to refer to the 'wolf-like habits' of Italian diplomacy.[16] It arose also from the belief, so evident from the work of both Macchiavelli and Guicciardini, that clever, if necessarily unscrupulous, conduct of diplomacy might be able to achieve the great coup, or victorious alliance combination which would at last break the power deadlock in the system that warfare had not been able to shift. The achievement of this elusive *combinazione* was pursued as Nicolson remarked 'as a game of hazard for high immediate stakes; it was conducted in an atmosphere of excitement, and with that combination of cunning, recklessness and ruthlessness which was lauded as *virtu'*.[17] For this, constant communication was essential, since timing and secrecy might be all; for this, too, speed was important and the efficient assessment of news, which led to the development of embryo foreign ministries in the chanceries of Italian rulers.

Where was the origin of the resident ambassador? There have been various candidates: the Venetian *baiulo*, effectively a consul, at Constantinople had certainly been a kind of permanent representative, and this raises the question as to whether the origin of resident ambassadors, at least in the Venetian service, is not to be found in the expansion of consular representation from the twelfth century. The position of consuls was, however, very different in origin and function from the resident of the future, particularly outside the special case of Venice. Consuls were usually elected by expatriate communities of merchants to arbitrate in their disputes and to represent them to the local authorities. Their position was not legitimized on diplomatic grounds, but by direct and specific treaties made with the local ruler. They were not diplomats. Nonetheless, home governments certainly took an interest in the appointment of consuls, and used them from time to time both to gain information and to deliver messages. They behaved in a similar way with the representatives of banks residing abroad – usually for the purpose of supervising loans to foreign rulers or communities. Plainly the access that such figures had both to information and to highly placed officials gave them a potentially diplomatic use. However, when the need for permanent residents arrived, they did not evolve from the consuls, nor did they supplant them in anything but their occasional political as opposed to commercial function.[18] The habit of provinces under the Roman Empire of sending *legati* to Rome was suggested as the basis of permanent representation, but there is no evidence of continuity of this sort, though the procurators who represented rulers at the Papal *Curia* at Rome were closer to the new style of resident. But these procurators, as others appointed in different circumstances by and to different rulers, were empowered on essentially legal business, and dealt as a convenience with diplomatic business. In relations with the Pope, procurators had a mixed character reflecting the dual functions inherent in the position of the Church, exercising as it did some universal jurisdictions as well as acting as an international entity existing among a society of others.

It seems clear that while examples of quite lengthy representation of different kinds can be found, none supplies a convincing direct origin for the permanent representative as it developed in Renaissance Italy.[19] It was plainly a gradual development in response to particular circumstances, demonstrating, once begun, a continuously increasing importance, until it became what Martin Wight called 'the master-institution of the modern Western states-system'.[20] So much was this an organic growth that it is now hard to determine who was, or which ruler appointed the first permanent ambassador – although commentators have been happy to regard Nicodemus of Pontremoli, who represented Milan at Florence for twenty years with one short break, as at least one of the first.[21] It is also clear that Milan was the first state to build up a network of representation within Italy, as it was the first state to exchange permanent representatives outside Italy: from 1425 to 1432, Filippo Maria Visconti was continuously represented at the court of Sigismund, King of Hungary and Holy Roman Emperor elect, and for most of that time Sigismund maintained a reciprocal resident orator at Milan.[22] In the 1430s and 40s, the network thickened, and by the 1450s, the habit of permanent representation had spread not only across northern Italy, with the participation of Venice and Florence, but further south, as the Papacy and the Aragonese kingdom in Naples joined in.

Thus an institution which first emerged as an adjunct to the foreign and defence policies of the Italian city-states, came to be deemed essential as their relative positions were established by warfare during the first half of the fifteenth century. By the time diplomacy succeeded war as the principal buttress of security after 1454, it was firmly in place. The title of ambassador came to be generally used to describe the resident, his accreditation became definite and his instructions carefully composed. None of this yet disturbed the existing patterns of behaviour associated with the *ad hoc* embassies developed earlier, which continued to exist side by side with the new resident, performing different and well-established functions.

THE EMERGENCE OF THE RESIDENT IN NORTHERN AND WESTERN EUROPE

By the early seventeenth century, it was possible for a practising diplomat in northern Europe to complain:

> It goes against the grain for a man of honour to lie and cheat . . . like a low-born and low-hearted rogue. . . but one must conceal the follies of the *patrie* as one would those of a foolish mother . . . sometimes in the service of the king there is no choice.[23]

Lying, cheating and concealment had not been part of the technique of the ambassador, be he *nuncius*, procurator or legate, when engaged in the ordinary pre-sixteenth century mission outside Italy: all three would have been counter-productive. That it became possible, a century later, for Hotman to complain about the need to behave occasionally like a 'low-hearted rogue' was an indication that the office of resident ambassador had spread. As the practices of fifteenth-century Italy gradually diffused to the rest of Europe, transitions took place unevenly, so that it is not possible to speak of a complete European diplomatic system based upon the resident ambassador until well into the seventeenth century.

The most important transition was the exportation of the resident ambassador. From 1494 when the French invaded northern Italy, it was no longer possible, even with all the accumulated skills and experience of Italian diplomats and rulers, for the small states lying between Rome and the Alps to remain free from external interference, however much some of them supposed that their superior skills would protect them from the consequences of inviting the intervention of overwhelmingly larger states. Italy became the cockpit in which greater powers, specifically the Habsburgs in Austria and Spain, and the French ruling family, the Valois, fought for supremacy. In the early phases of this struggle, it was more necessary for the Italian states to be represented outside their own peninsula than it was for the new powers to reciprocate. Ludovico Sforza of Milan sent a resident to Spain in 1490 and accredited a Genoese merchant resident in London as his ambassador to Henry VII in the same year. In 1492 and 1493 respectively Milanese residents appeared at both the Habsburg court and at Paris. Naples sent residents to Spain, England and Germany in 1493, aware of the threat from the French and between 1495 and 1496 Venice converted most of its representation into residencies – a particularly significant move on the part of a republic which had always prided itself on maintaining highly complicated systems for electing and controlling ambassadors on specific missions. Florence followed suit, but less extensively, and by 1496 had residents with Charles VIII of France and in Spain. As the Italian states fell to invaders in the earliest years of the sixteenth century, even the Papacy succumbed to the pressure to appoint resident nuncios and by 1513 'the resident papal nuncios at the courts of the great European powers were as watchful and absorbed in power politics as ever their secular predecessors had been'.[24]

It took time for the host rulers to reciprocate. The Spaniards responded first. The determination of Ferdinand of Aragon to eject the French from Italy led to the creation of the Most Holy League at Venice in 1495. In pursuit of this arrangement and in its subsequent, unsuccessful, maintenance, a network of Spanish, largely Castilian, resident ambassadors emerged. Rome and Venice were the two Italian posts. London became a permanent embassy after 1495, and there were Spanish residents with Maximilian, the Holy Roman Emperor, and in the Netherlands from the same date. In doing this, it is clear that Ferdinand was following the tradition of being represented with allies or potential allies; it is equally true, however, that he tried to have ambassadors in France, but that periods of Franco-Spanish peace were so short as to prevent any sense of permanence developing about these missions. Compared with Italian practice of the fifteenth century, the new residents of northern Europe were plainly intended to play a more limited role, and this can be seen from the slow pace at which other powers caught up with Spanish practice. Maximilian of Austria began to appoint residents at two distinct points during his reign, after the French invasion of Italy and when he became interested in pressing his daughter-in-law's claim to Castile. None of his arrangements lasted, however. If he understood how much his position depended on the application of skilful policy rather than his unreliable sources of real power, he nonetheless failed to provide adequate, or quite frequently any, financial backing for his embassies. They regularly failed, as bankrupt and disillusioned ambassadors crept home 'their credit and their patience exhausted'.[25]

The French did not yet feel the need to use resident ambassadors on any scale. Charles VIII was represented at Rome and in Venice, but despite the opportunities offered by the presence of other residents at the French court, or the suggestions of Henry VIII of England, it was not until the struggle with the Habsburgs made the French value allies rather than dependents, that a network of French residents spread. Meanwhile, they relied on the much more expensive practice of paying pensions both to sitting princes and to exiles in France. Francis I initiated the change when he established a permanent mission in Switzerland after the establishment of the Franco-Swiss agreement in 1521. The ambassador, Boisrigaut, sent in 1522, remained for twenty-one years. After 1525 a resident embassy was also maintained with the cantons of the Grisons at Chur. The exigencies of France after the battle of Pavia (1525) at which Francis I was defeated, captured by the Habsburgs and taken to Madrid, where he was compelled to sign a humiliating treaty, speeded up the creation of a broader French diplomatic system. The French now needed allies, with whom to reverse the treaty of Madrid, even if those allies were infidels or heretics. Although the English were not yet heretics, the crisis with the Emperor and the Papacy caused by the King's need to divorce Catherine of Aragon gave good ground for preparing an Anglo-French alliance. Although Passano, who was sent by the French in 1526 to London, was not intended to be a resident, his mission lasted for two years, and it is clear from Venetian reports that there was a French resident in England from then on. French interest in other European extremities grew. A resident was sent to Lisbon shortly after Pavia and as the Lutheran revolution spread in Scandinavia during the 1530s, creating a potential anti-Habsburg league, the French came to be continuously, though peripatetically, represented there from 1541.[26]

At the eastern extremity, there lay the Ottoman Empire, probably the most important and effective centre of power of the age. Suleyman the Magnificent was anxious to play a role in Europe, yet the Turks were so convinced of their natural superiority to the rest of the world, certainly the Christian world, that they remained for another two centuries unwilling to adopt the European notion of the resident ambassador or venture much beyond the temporary application of military force as the basis of policy. Nonetheless, when Francis I of France, captive at Madrid, appealed for aid to Suleyman an answer came. 'Be not dismayed in your captivity', the Sultan wrote, 'Your appeal has been heard at the steps of our throne. . . night and day our horse is saddled and our sabre girt'. Shortly afterwards there followed perhaps the greatest of all Turkish victories over the Holy Roman Emperor at the battle of Mohacs in Hungary in 1526.[27] It took another ten years for the logical Franco-Turkish arrangement to be formalized, but after the treaty of 1536, the first French resident – Jean de la Forest

– arrived at Constantinople. The particular fear and distaste which the Turks aroused in Europe partly accounted for this delay. If the break up of the old *respublica christiana* into more or less sovereign states implied the collapse of crusading attitudes, that implication took some time to become an actual fact, and the continuing militancy of the Turks was paralleled by a continuing suspicion in the minds of European rulers and statesmen. The justification for a resident at Constantinople was thus likely to be different and to rest on equivalence with the long established Venetian *baiulo*, whose role was principally commercial, concerned with the affairs of Venetians working within the Empire and their relationships with the Ottomans. Clearly, however, French residents at Constantinople were actually acting as the managers of an intermittent military alliance, even if the Franco-Turkish treaty of 1536 also laid the foundations of French commercial and cultural predominance in the Levant which was to last in one form or another until the 1940s.

Thus, while the French were gradually appointing their first residents, the Spanish were enjoying the results of already possessing them and the Austrian Habsburgs were failing to maintain a network of their own. The English, meanwhile, under the relatively rich and very cautious Henry VII, were beginning to operate more widely in the diplomatic field. To begin with, England was represented only at Rome; then, in 1505, John Stile was told to extend a special mission to Spain so that he became a resident, matching the presence in London since 1496 of de Puebla, the resident of Spain. Most ambassadors used by the early Tudors were Italians, one of whom, Thomas Spinelly, was kept by Henry VII in the Netherlands as an unofficial agent. With Henry VIII's accession, the mounting difficulties over the royal divorce and the more efficient organization of Cardinal Wolsey led to an increase in the number of English residents: Spinelly was officially accredited in the Netherlands, Wingfield was sent to the Emperor's court and the arrival of Bainbridge, Archbishop of York, in great splendour at Rome raised the profile of English representation there quite sharply. By the early 1520s, there were residents also at Venice and in France.

By the 1550s, it was clear that in some parts of western and northern Europe, the expansion of what had been a basically north Italian diplomatic system was well under way. There were, however, several aspects in which it remained noticeably incomplete. Although the peripheries were becoming drawn into the highly tense international relations caused by the Habsburg–Valois struggle for European hegemony, diplomatic practice often lagged behind that of the centre. There was less willingness to appoint residents – in the case of the Turks an absolute refusal to do so – and thus a greater reliance on older-style special missions, which tended, in a traditional way, to have quite large numbers. Poland, for example, sent over ninety special embassies during a fourteen-year period at the turn of the fifteenth century, mainly to Hungary. Negotiations between the Archduke Ferdinand and the

King of Hungary in 1526 involved collective embassies of six on one side and seven on the other, and there continued to be a tendency to accredit missions to more than one principal in the receiving country.[28] There also continued to be a sense that the larger an embassy was, the more respect was being accorded to the host and that any reduction in an embassy's size or the dispatch of a small one, sent the opposite message. For highly ceremonial embassies within the more developed diplomatic systems, size remained significant. Embassies of congratulation, particularly to the Pope, of condolence or of obedience might fall into this category, as might proposals of marriage. The French attempt of 1581 to arrange a marriage between Elizabeth I and the Duke of Anjou led to the arrival of an embassy containing about 700 people in all, headed by thirteen ambassadors, including a member of the French royal family.[29]

The interests of Russia as she emerged from the post-Mongol period were as much Asiatic as European and, within the European sphere, largely confined to the almost self-contained world of the Baltic. An early and important example of this was the Russo-Danish treaty of 1562. Although there were occasional hopes that Russia might be induced to assist in the struggle with the Turks, it was not until 1586 that a French ambassador reached Moscow and not until 1615 that Russia reciprocated. On a commercial level, the English made the most effective connections with Muscovy with the arrival in 1555, via the White Sea, of the Chancellor expedition, followed by the appearance in London of a Russian envoy in 1559. English ambassadors went as necessary to Russia, thereafter, not as residents even though they stayed for quite long periods, and discussed political questions only in relation to promoting the success of Muscovy Company merchants.

Thus the spread of both resident ambassadors and a complete network from Italy to the rest of Europe was uncertain and patchy during the first half of the sixteenth century. This was partly due to the generally larger and less organized state structures with which early modern Europe was populated, partly due to the greater distances involved and partly to the wide variation of power and interests which those entities exhibited. It was also due to a factor of an entirely different kind: the consequences of the Reformation. In so far as there was a tendency for the diplomatic system to become ever more firmly tied to the representation of sovereign states and rulers to each other, it was reflecting a change in the nature of rulership which flowed from the secularization of government and administration – a process much accelerated by the Reformation. The removal of the jurisdiction of the Pope from the substantial areas of Protestant Europe and its notable reduction even in Catholic states and the increasing adoption of the principle that the ruler determined the religion of his territory,[30] led to the emergence of the fully sovereign state. It also inaugurated a long period of bitter civil and international warfare, ideological in its justification, which temporarily curtailed the role an ambassador could play, and sometimes rendered the very presence of resident ambassadors professing a different form of Christianity unacceptable to rulers. The reasons for this were quite clear. Resident ambassadors in Italy had been initially unpopular and subsequently carefully watched because of the implications of their presence for external state security. They were, it was felt, no more than licensed spies and Philippe de Commynes had suggested ways of reducing the inherent dangers.[31] This factor returned with interest when intense, religiously defined, conflict grew during the second half of the sixteenth century and came to dominate the relationships between rulers. In the first half of the seventeenth century the intensity faded, not to return until the cold war developed after 1947 and again reduced the function of diplomacy in the relationships between the protagonists and severely curtailed the activities of diplomats. From the 1550s, the problem expressed itself in two chief ways. First, a resident ambassador representing a ruler who espoused an opposed religion might be expected to spy on the military strength, preparedness and installations of his host and, second, his residence could and did become the focal point for disaffected groups within the host state, possibly sanctuaries for them, where they could attend religious services otherwise banned and develop plots for the future, perhaps aided and abetted by the forces of the resident's principal.[32]

It was not surprising, therefore, that it took until the mid-sixteenth century for resident ambassadors to achieve the role in the diplomatic system among the major powers of Europe that they had done in the mid-fifteenth century among the major powers of northern Italy.[33] It also helps to explain why special missions continued to be used for ceremonial purposes. It took longer than logic or convenience would have suggested for the resident ambassador to take over fully these roles and add them to his specific tasks of managing military alliances where they existed and gathering information to be sent regularly and frequently to his principal. When he did so, however, the nature and extent of his immunities became ever more important.

IMMUNITIES

The sources of diplomatic immunities in the later Middle Ages and the early modern world were threefold: religious, legal and practical. Some religious justification had been known since the most ancient times. The large-scale diplomatic activities of the medieval Church and the frequent use of clerics as envoys reinforced it. What also had an important effect was the unclear dividing line between ecclesiastical and secular sovereignties and the role of envoys as serving the broadly based but politically formless entity known as the *respublica christiana*. This role led to the frequent statement of what now appear to be impossibly idealistic statements about the nature of

40

envoys, just about comprehensible if made for form's sake alone. But if the universal assumptions about the essential unity of Christian Europe are allowed for, the idea that envoys served a larger purpose than merely transmitting messages or negotiating for their immediate principals seems less naive. Bernard du Rosier was repeating both himself and many other authorities when he said, 'The business of an ambassador is peace . . . an ambassador labours for the public good . . . .The speedy completion of an ambassador's business is in the interests of all . . . an ambassador is sacred because he acts for the general welfare'. The jurists were all agreed that 'an ambassador is a public official', and by 'public' they did not mean a state, but the society of Christian Europe as a whole.[34]

Legal sanction for diplomatic immunity was clear in Roman law, as was the proper punishment for those who transgressed, usually deemed to be that the guilty party should be handed over to the legate's principal. Canon law extended the range of immunity, for example to residences, and expressed the idea that harming a mission injured all those who might be affected by its failure, and that the agent of such harm might be excommunicated. Durandus made the point that the envoys of enemies were deemed to be sacred, and Baldus declared that the murder of an ambassador was *laesa majestas* and that ambassadors were not subject to the law of reprisals.[35]

The practical consequences of not having a system of immunities for ambassadors were particularly clear. The length and physical dangers of medieval and early modern journeys, the consequentially poor and slow communications, meant that reciprocity in respect of the safety of envoys while travelling and their friendly reception on arrival was quite simply essential. This was clearly put when, in 1339, the Venetians accepted a foreign ambassador's case for receiving immunity from judicial proceedings on the grounds that Venetian 'ambassadors, who go continually throughout the world, could continually encounter obstacles in this case, if an obstacle be placed in the way of others by us'.[36] In this period, as in all others, it is difficult to doubt that reciprocity represented the fundamental justification, for which religion and the laws provided both contemporarily acceptable explanations and sanctions against transgressors.

The generally accepted immunities began with safe conducts for journeys, particularly for enemy representatives. Occasionally they might be refused on the grounds that an ambassador was always safe, and they suffered from the disadvantage that they might not be accepted by the authorities of territories *en route*; they also lapsed on the death of the giver. On arrival, ambassadors, their retinues and their goods continued to enjoy physical inviolability. Despite a number of clear statements in medieval times that these conditions had no exceptions, by the time Grotius codified practice it was not clear that an ambassador's household was included, unless specifically agreed by the state concerned. Ambassadors were not subject to indictment for civil or criminal offences of their own, and they were permitted the practice of their own religion in private. This applied to Muslims also, though with greater certainty where Muslim lands, for example in Spain, abutted directly on the *respublica christiana*: in this instance, of course, reciprocity was more than usually necessary. Bernard du Rosier, here summarized by Mattingly, was quite clear what the position was, and he was supported by many other authorities whose work added to rather than subtracted from what du Rosier said.

> Ambassadors are immune for the period of their embassy, in their persons and in their property, both from actions in courts of law and from all other forms of interference. Among all peoples, in all kingdoms and lands, they are guaranteed complete freedom in access, transit and egress, and perfect safety from any hindrance and violence. These privileges are enshrined in the civil and canon law, sanctioned by universal custom and enforced by the authorities of states. Those who injure ambassadors, or imprison them, or rob them, who impede their passage, or even abet or approve such acts are properly regarded as enemies of mankind, worthy of universal execration. For whoever interferes with ambassadors in their public function injures the peace and tranquillity of all.

The lawyers added that an ambassador could not be subject to reprisals, or be liable for any debt contracted before his embassy began and that he was exempt from all local taxes, tolls or customs duties. All these things applied from the moment a mission began until it ended.[37]

Much of this sounds familiar and comprehensible. In practice, however, the complex relationships between universal and particular authorities meant that the immunities of ambassadors were much less straightforward than they appeared. These immunities were certainly intended to secure the safety of the mission, but only provided it was held to be pursuing its proper functions and serving society as a whole. The protection against pursuit at law was principally meant to secure an ambassador from any consequences of past actions affecting his ability to conduct a mission, and were not meant to allow him freedom from prosecution for crimes committed while at his post. It was understood that as the immunities of an ambassador were conferred by civil law, which stood by itself above states and rulers, so he himself was subject to it. This meant that if he were detected in political crimes – espionage, conspiracy, subversion – he could be arraigned, tried and sentenced by the ruler to whom he was accredited, because he was not fulfilling the purpose of an embassy even if he was attempting to further the interests of his principal.

> The law was intended to give the ambassador every privilege and immunity necessary for the performance of his office. It was not

intended to protect him in the abuse of those privileges and immunities for other ends, any more than it protected the tax collector who
practised blackmail.[38]

The appearance of truly sovereign states, and even more, their emergence
as the only plausible international actors, was the cause of the change in
this position which began to emerge in the fifteenth century in Italy and
gradually became general after 1648.

The first sign of stress came with the early-sixteenth-century tendency to
violate the rule that ambassadors in transit were free from molestation.
Rulers never did so without producing elaborate excuses; but the possibilities of gaining advantage from interfering with the diplomatic arrangements of a rival were both irresistible and proof of the rising significance of
diplomacy in the international system. The principle that an ambassador
had only to notify the local ruler of an intention to cross his territory to
obtain a safe conduct could be bent; for example, in cases where war broke
out while the transit was taking place, where the ambassador's credentials
might not, perhaps temporarily, be recognized, and where it could be
claimed that the ambassador had not accurately followed correct practice
or had concealed the nature of his mission. The most celebrated case of
this kind occurred in 1541 and involved the assassination of two ambassadors, Antonio Rincon, French envoy to the Sultan of Turkey, and Cesare
Fregoso, who was to be the French envoy at Venice, by the Emperor's troops
while crossing imperial territory near Pavia. Both were for different reasons
personae non gratae to the Emperor and had not, therefore, given notice of
their journey and had concealed their identities and thus provided the
excuse for their murders. But the French made it a cause of war, and the
lawyers discussed it minutely over the next hundred years. The real ground
was that the two ambassadors were engaged in an attempt to draw the Sultan
into an alliance against the Emperor.

Earlier, it might have been argued that such an intention could not serve
the general peace and thus caused immunity to be withdrawn; later, no one
would have supposed that the political purposes of a ruler could affect the
immunities of his ambassadors under any excuse: in the early sixteenth
century, practice was changing faster than customary immunities.

The problem which began to agitate both practitioners and lawyers
during the sixteenth century, however, arose from the spread of the resident
embassy. Immunities which were suitable for brief special missions broke
down under the strains caused by the permanent presence of resident
ambassadors, and particularly the presence of residents who were often
underpaid and thus heavily in debt, at a time when the practice of providing
for ambassadors from the resources of the receiving court was dying out. If
the ambassador was to remain and perform the function which both sender
and host regarded as necessary, he might have to be protected from his

creditors; and the difficulties of arranging this on any regular basis, which rulers tended to resist as a principle, but operated in some individual cases, led to great confusion and occasional scenes of physical violence.

Grotius resolved the conundrum by arguing that, since ambassadors had to have security of goods as well as person, the only legal remedy open to creditors who had tried all the usual forms of recovery either directly or via the ambassador's principal was to behave as if the ambassador was a debtor living abroad. In other words, he adopted a form of the doctrine of extraterritoriality. In practice, this resolution was not effective, and late into the seventeenth century, incidents occurred, though accompanied by an ever-increasing insistence by diplomats on their immunity from pursuit for debt. One famous example was that of the distinguished Russian ambassador, A.A. Matveyev, who was briefly arrested in London in 1708 on the complaint of his creditors. When he was released all the heads of mission in London returned with him to his residence to show support, and a special mission was subsequently sent to Moscow to apologize to Peter the Great for the embarrassment which Matveyev had been caused.[39] As late as 1772, however, a contrary example occurred, when the French foreign minister refused passports to the minister of Hesse-Cassel, Baron de Wrech, so that he should not return home without paying his debts. The diplomatic corps in Paris protested to both the minister and the King on behalf of the Baron, but to no avail. He had to await the arrival of a guarantee from the Landgrave of Hesse-Cassel before being allowed to leave. The ground given, in a lengthy and published memorandum from the Foreign Ministry, was that the issue did not affect the rights and privileges of the other ministers-resident and that his evident intention to escape his creditors authorized 'taking against him the same measures that would be taken if he had in effect left the kingdom, after having laid aside his character by presenting his letters of recall'. A contemporary commentator remarked with probably greater accuracy that this rule was not consistently followed and that variations occurred according to the mood of the minister for foreign affairs and the status of the indebted minister.[40]

However fraught or doubtful the position about civil immunities for ambassadors remained in principle, from the mid-eighteenth century they were honoured in practice almost universally. A greater difficulty arose as the spread of the resident ambassador created uncertainty about his immunity from criminal prosecution. The older rules were quite clear that an ambassador did not have immunity in respect of crimes such as murder, robbery or rape – nor did they very often occur. When they were committed by an ambassador's servants or other staff, it was usual for the accused to be handed over to the local authorities. Political offences would have been both incompatible with an ambassador's generally accepted role and inconsistent with any likely instruction. Immunity did not arise, since an ambassador caught behaving unacceptably lost his diplomatic status automatically. In the early years of residencies, rulers or ministers could and did achieve some successes at the expense of rivals by treating what were essentially resident envoys under the rules developed for a different situation. The case of the imperial resident in England, de Praet, who was arrested by Cardinal Wolsey in 1524 was an example. De Praet was brought before the King's Council, accused on the basis of dispatches stolen from his courier of slandering Henry VIII and thus declared to have lost his diplomatic status. His actual offence had been to warn his principal of a forthcoming change in English policy, which only a short time later would have been regarded as the plain duty of a resident.[41] When two internationally known authorities – Hotman and Gentili – were consulted about the notorious case of Bernardino de Mendoza, Spanish ambassador to Elizabeth I of England and deeply involved in the Throckmorton Plot, they concluded that he should certainly be punished. However, they also thought that he should be sent home to be dealt with by his own prince.[42] This device proved to be the line along which immunity developed, despite the obvious improbability that the source of their instructions would take any action against them. Nonetheless their unacceptability to their host was thus established and the inconvenience to their principal in an age of very slow communication was real.

By the 1620s Grotius was arguing that the security of ambassadors was necessary to the system, whatever the law might suggest, and that security was unobtainable unless ambassadors were accountable only to their sovereigns. The matter continued to be argued over, and events suggested that much depended on particular rulers and particular circumstances. But seventeenth-century practice, particularly once it was accepted that embassy chapels might follow the religion of their principals, conformed more and more to the principle of extraterritoriality.[43] This naturally led to disputes about both the numbers of embassy staff who might claim immunity, since most of the domestic staff were likely to be of the host state's nationality and were thus quite likely to abuse the privilege, and about the physical area the embassy was claimed to occupy.[44] Fighting in the streets and heavy defences applied to embassy buildings resulted, so that decisions tended to be made on a local basis. It was noticeable in Madrid, for example, that the ability of the monarch to control the rising demand for ever-extending diplomatic privileges declined in proportion to the decline of Spanish power. The last serious cases of ambassadors being arrested on grounds of conspiracy of one sort or another seem to have occurred in the early eighteenth century: the Swedish diplomats Gyllenborg and Gortz, and of the prince of Cellamare.

Cellamare was the Spanish ambassador at Paris from 1715, and in 1718 was discovered plotting to have the regency of France transferred to the King of Spain, the plot being discovered through the mistress of the Abbé Dubois, secretary of state in the foreign ministry. The offending papers and the ambassador were first confined to the Spanish embassy by the French authorities, the papers being subsequently removed to the Louvre to await collection by agents of the King of Spain. The ambassador was then incarcerated in the chateau at Blois until the French ambassador at Madrid should have returned safely to France. The latter only did so by exchanging identities with his servants at the frontier which he and his wife crossed on mules, while his servants were hauled back to Madrid in the coach, apparently the ambassadorial victims of a triumph by the Spanish authorities. War then followed, but came to little, and the ambassador's papers were eventually returned to the Spanish government.[45] It is clear that, later in the century, these events would have been most unlikely to occur. The contrast with the past was by then marked. Non-observance of immunities had occasionally been dramatic: the Byzantine, Manuel Comnenus imprisoned ambassadors of Roger II of Sicily for seeking a status for their principal equal with that of the Emperor – a particularly sensitive point for the Byzantines (see Chapter 1).[46] Barbarossa resorted to a scorched earth policy while on crusade in order to force Isaac II to release legates whom he had incarcerated, naked, and compensate them. More spectacularly, in 1241 Frederick II captured 100 representatives of the Lombard towns including archbishops, bishops, *nuncii* and procurators, but was forced by general complaint, including that of St Louis, to release them. Some of these examples have a very familiar ring. After a Venetian ambassador to Milan was murdered during the fifteenth century, Venice offered to anyone who was prepared to kill the murderer '20,000 pounds, recall from exile (if he should be exiled for anything except rebellion), the opportunity to recall anyone else from exile if he should not himself be an exile, and the command of a force of lances or of infantry for life'. Clearly the offer was designed to tempt a fairly hardened operator. There is an echo here of the *fatwa* declared in Iran in respect of the late-twentieth-century author, Salman Rushdie.

The post-1960s tendency to launch symbolic attacks upon embassy compounds can also be paralleled. In 1499, a band of about 800 well-connected Florentine youths walled up the entrance to the Milanese ambassador's residence with excrement, undisturbed by the local authorities. From about 1700 to the 1960s, the immunity of ambassadors, both civil and criminal, was widely accepted and widely observed.

As the practice of maintaining permanent resident embassies abroad spread across the whole of Europe during the sixteenth century, ideas about the immunities of ambassadors began to change. The protection which du Rosier had described was related to the needs of medieval diplomacy and specifically to the practice of sending special missions. Such missions were of their nature short and by custom paid for by the host ruler.

CEREMONY

If immunities were important, and thus caused such breaches to be strongly deplored, so was ceremonial. Ceremonial served a practical purpose. It gave a palpable demonstration of the relative power and influence of both sender and receiver of missions.[47] The lavishness or otherwise of a mission and the social or political seniority of its head said something both about the wealth and power of the sender and about the sender's rating of the importance of the recipient. The quality of reception offered,[48] the scale of the banqueting, the nature of the celebrations, the value of proffered gifts and the grandeur of accommodation said something about both the standing and the policy of the recipient. Moreover, the significance of ceremonial also operated sideways, as between different embassies, and, particularly after the arrival of the resident ambassador, led to the much commented upon intensity with which apparently insignificant minutiae of protocol and precedence were observed and disputed. Not to insist upon the highest placing that the host ruler could be induced to give was to weaken the position of the envoy's principal *vis à vis* others and was at least worth endless negotiation, and sometimes worth a duel or even murder.[49]

There were no absolute rules either for procedure or precedence. Nonetheless a picture can be drawn of how an embassy proceeded ceremonially.[50] The departure of important embassies – and of all legates *a latere* from Rome – was an occasion of great pomp. Du Rosier said that this was partly to cause word to be sent ahead to its destination that an embassy was coming, there often being no other way that the recipient could know that he was due to make the necessary elaborate preparations to receive it. At the final audience, the ambassadors received their documents – letters of credence, appointment as procurator, or whatever other powers that had been decided upon, any letters for the recipient ruler, and their instructions, which at this period might or might not be written down, though as time went on they increasingly were. Since for political reasons, instructions might be ambiguous, contemporary advice suggested that departing ambassadors ought to obtain an oral elucidation of their instructions, since the failure of a mission was often due to this kind of ambiguity.

Having set off, and departure might be long delayed for financial reasons, the embassy would proceed without undue haste to its destination, possibly also delivering messages *en route*. In medieval conditions, the journey might take months, certainly weeks. On arrival, an embassy would expect to be met by the host court some way from where the formal reception was to take place. The scale of this first encounter varied according to the nature of the embassy and the grandeur of its sender. If it was of a deeply ceremonial kind – to attend a wedding for example, or to congratulate a new ruler – it was likely that a large party, headed perhaps by a royal prince, dressed, as would be the embassy, in the finest clothing, would ride out to

47

meet it.[51] As the later Middle Ages shaded into the Renaissance, solemnity and a strongly religious tone, which caused the embassy usually to be led directly to the cathedral for a special service, gave way to something more akin to a carnival with chivalric overtones. A public procession, perhaps through decorated streets, where the fountains ran with wine, the ringing of peals from the churches, allegorical pageants by the local citizenry, trumpet fanfares and other music, often provided by orchestras from both sides, since the larger embassies might travel with their own troupes of entertainers and musicians, were eventually followed by a grand banquet.[52] Before then, however, came the formal reception, usually at the palace.[53] This was a reverse of the departing audience. The ambassador was conducted into the presence of the head of state by the senior welcoming dignitary, to hand over his credentials and, if appropriate, his powers. Credentials were by the fourteenth century expressed in a standard form and most chancelleries had a set description of the full names and titles – real or assumed – with which to address the rulers to whom they most frequently sent envoys. There then followed an oration in which the ambassador explained why he had come. Originally relatively straight-forward, the Renaissance preoccupation with classical rhetoric turned this part of the proceedings into what was supposed to be a literary *tour de force*.[54] So important did it become, that all contemporary lists of desirable qualities in an ambassador included the ability to turn an elegant Latin phrase and construct orations of considerable length, either dealing with or concealing business, but in any case paying compliments by means of elaborate references to classical and biblical sources, part of the common culture of both host and guest. The significance of this development can be understood from a short list of some of the poets and authors employed on diplomatic missions: Dante, Petrarch, Boccaccio, Latini, Machiavelli, Tasso, de Commynes – almost a professional – Ronsard, du Bellay, Chaucer, Sir Thomas Wyatt, Sir Philip Sidney and Sir David Lyndesay.[55] As well as the significance attaching to the etiquette of diplomacy as reflecting the power and influence of the principals, there seems also to have been a sense that the elaborate ceremonial gave some insulation from the barbarities and dangers of contemporary life and travel.

The numbers of people involved in these embassies steadily grew, and the Venetians were already by the 1370s trying to limit their size. Maulde la Clavière thought that by the late fifteenth century, a major embassy would have to include about 150 horses, though it is clear that powerful city-states such as Milan and Venice accepted much smaller groups – 80 horses or 55 horse and 25 footmen – as adequate. English evidence of the fourteenth century shows smaller numbers: an embassy headed by a great man might have between 32 and 107 men and from 22 to 83 horses; one headed by a clerk or notary might have one to four people and up to five horses. Earlier still, in the thirteenth century, an important Venetian embassy to Constantinople numbered only 17 men after the ambassadors.[56]

ROUTINE

After these events, all or part of which might be repeated on departure, when the embassy would also be presented with rich gifts,[57] the real business began, if the embassy was not purely ceremonial. Here, too, a pattern had developed by the later Middle Ages. If, as was likely, the ruler himself did not personally handle the ensuing discussions, the incoming ambassador's credentials were passed to a senior official at the initial reception and the two met a few days later, at which the ambassador explained unrhetorically what was the purpose of his visit and some at least of what he might be able to offer in return. At a subsequent meeting, he would be able to expect some response from his host, most probably in the form of searching questions about the extent of his powers, if he had come equipped with any. It was obviously crucial to discover what discretion was available to an ambassador and, more than that, whether his powers were properly executed. To discover after a negotiation had been concluded that the result could be rejected by a ruler because of some technical fault in the expression of his envoy's powers was both frustrating and, particularly in the sixteenth and seventeenth centuries, not uncommon. The result was very lengthy, and to the modern eye obsessively minute, examination of all powers, and the taking of legally attested copies. The powers most usually given to an envoy were limited to securing the signature, unaltered, of the documents he had brought with him. It was also possible for limited discretion to be given, and, much more rarely after the fourteenth century, for complete discretion to negotiate and sign an agreement.[58] In general, the greater the matter under discussion and the earlier the phase of negotiation, the less discretion would be given. For lesser matters where procuratorial powers would suffice, a broader brief would be allowed.

In addition to questions about the nature of the ambassador's powers, there were likely to be some sharp enquiries as to what was in his instructions.[59] This was naturally awkward, as the instructions would be likely to contain not only the object to be achieved but also the maximum concession that might be made and thus not to be revealed. This did not stop the habit of asking to see an ambassador's instructions from developing, despite their status, unlike credentials, as private documents. The response to this was either to reveal only a part of what had been issued or, increasingly common, to have two sets of instructions, one for handing over, after a display of suitable reluctance and only in exchange for a receipt, and one containing the real instructions, to remain unrevealed. The length of substantive discussions might be greatly extended by the need to refer home for additional or modified instructions, which appears to have been done far more often than the appalling state of contemporary communications would have suggested was effective. Du Rosier was quite clear that this was preferable to failure or the conclusion of an agreement which might not ultimately be authorized.[60]

Whether the subsequent ratification of agreements was required was dependent on the nature of the powers given to particular envoys. Until the fifteenth century, it is clear that even if ratification did subsequently follow, treaties nevertheless came into force on signature and could be both published and acted upon. As the complications of later fourteenth- and fifteenth-century diplomacy grew, particularly in Italy, there grew up a tendency to restrict the powers of envoys and this led to the general expectation that ambassadors would arrive at a draft requiring the ratification of the principals. Even at this stage, this practice owed more to the wish to emphasize the principals' intention to honour the agreement than to legal necessity. As such it was part of a number of measures that could be taken to ensure compliance. An oath upon the soul of the principal was usual, registration with the Pope was a further possibility, not always effective, as may be seen from the practice of swearing additionally not to ask the Pope to release principals from their obligations under a treaty.[61] Swearing on a holy relic was also common, though again not always effective. Vladimir, Prince of Galitch, on being upbraided for not honouring a promise made on the cross of St Stephen, retorted that it had only been a very small cross, to which the complainant's envoy replied that it was nonetheless miraculous and that the Prince should be fearful for his life![62] It is not surprising, therefore, that ratification used for this purpose was given much publicity. At the publication of a Franco-Venetian alliance in 1499, ambassadors and other dignitaries assembled formally in St Mark's Square, before a solemn mass in the cathedral, followed by a procession accompanied by bell-ringing and other music. In 1475, the Kings of England and France met to ratify a treaty between them while leading their respective forces, which were drawn up in full battle array.[63]

It was not always easy to persuade suitable candidates to take on embassies; and this may have reinforced the possibility, always open because of the very plastic sense of national identity that characterized the Middle Ages, that rulers would choose envoys from outside their own territory: the diplomat represented a principal and not necessarily a nation.[64] The difficulty about recruitment seems to have been particularly true of Venice, where failure to accept a mission was punishable. The reason for this was fundamentally financial, though the dangers of travel and the inevitably long absences were also used as reasons for declining or attempting to decline the office of ambassador. In theory, the ambassador was supposed to be reimbursed for his expenditure by his principal, and probably also paid a *per diem* allowance. Many contemporary commentators, however, recommended in the strongest terms that no ambassador should set out until he had hammered out watertight financial arrangements with his principal, and even then, it is quite clear that rulers frequently did not honour their obligations. This may have been because the expense of mounting a large embassy, likely to last for many months, actually passed beyond the financial resources of many rulers, once the full paraphernalia of representative ceremonial, clothing, staffing accommodation and gift giving got under way in the fifteenth century.[65] Certainly potential ambassadors were prone to regard the prospect of a long embassy, however powerful and distinguished it might be, as an invitation to personal ruin. Complaints that their principals denied them the tools of their trade in terms of competitive entertainment by starving them of resources were very common. The bulk of surviving records about Venetian diplomatic activity from the thirteenth to the fifteenth centuries concerns their accounts which were usually disputed and which were certainly carefully kept, often by a specially appointed bursar.[66] The arrangements, or collapse of them, about expenses seem to have been endlessly argued over and hopelessly chaotic to the modern eye; although it is also true that diplomats of all periods have seldom felt other than poorly treated by their principals.

There were other disadvantages. Wives were not expected to go on embassies, and by the Venetians not permitted to do so. Wives might gossip, but cooks were regarded as an essential part of a mission partly to minimize the risk of ambassadors being poisoned. Venetian ambassadors were not allowed to keep the gifts they were given, or to participate in any form of commerce on the side, in contrast to the Byzantines at an earlier period who expected to fund their embassies in part from such operations. Moreover, as the resident ambassador became more common, and the habit of regarding ambassadors as licensed spies grew, severe limitations were placed on the social activities that ambassadors might pursue at their post, and many governments attempted to limit the contact between their own citizens and foreign ambassadors.

Despite the disadvantages, ambassadors were found,[67] albeit with difficulty, or perforce; and they often took a very long time actually to set out, no doubt extended by their initial reluctance to serve. These delays were widely commented on, widely deplored, and in many states declared illegal. The ill effects were compounded not only by the slow pace of medieval travel, but also by the peripatetic nature of medieval courts. Having arrived in the intended territory, an ambassador then had to locate its ruler.

As the pace of diplomacy quickened during the late fourteenth century, embassies of all sorts occurred in increasing numbers. The social status of their active, rather than ceremonial, members tended increasingly to be professional and middle class. Guicciardini complained that the success of the Florentine nobility in evading self-bankrupting embassies was causing a much greater use of men of lower social station to lead embassies.[68] It was thought essential to include at least one lawyer, preferably more so as to include both a canonist and a Romanist. A secretary was usually appointed to draft dispatches and replies to the host court, although the ambassador signed them, and in the case of the death or incapacity of the ambassador, the secretary acted in his stead. A chaplain was often included, and given the need for aggressive recovery of expenses, a bursar was required. In the fifteenth century, the practice of appointing sub-ambassadors began with the object of providing both additional educated assistance, but also as a form of training for ambassadors-to-be.[69] Translators were generally not required because of the universality of Latin, although occasional exceptions occurred within Christian Europe,[70] but they were naturally essential when dealing with the Muslim world or beyond.[71] Security of communications was sometimes improved by providing an embassy with its own couriers, and all embassies had their own, sometimes very large, retinue of servants.

SECURITY

An ambassador, as has been seen, went on his mission already equipped with various forms of communication: his letters of credence; his powers – to whatever extent they might have been granted; his instructions, possibly in two versions; a safe conduct and until the fourteenth century, he might also carry officially accredited blank documents to use to complete the business if the mission succeeded. During an extended embassy, and particularly from the fourteenth century, it became necessary to communicate home, both to give information and often to obtain fresh instructions. Governments became extremely hungry for information of all kinds during the fifteenth century[72] and were often heavily critical of ambassadors for not writing enough. Sometimes this defect was more apparent than real, since the slow pace of communication could make the information given dangerously out of date by the time it was received, and in any case letters tended to arrive in large packages containing reports over a considerable period. Venice, for example, received all its information about Spain for the period 12 January to 8 April, 1497, in one delivery on 5 May.

There was in addition the risk that dispatches would be lost, stolen or damaged on the way. Principals used their own couriers less than might have been expected, no doubt because of the expense, and the security of communications was constantly at risk from the varied and sometimes unreliable means of transport. Venetian complaints of 1477 about paying the bill for couriers revealed incidentally that their ambassador was using his host's courier to send reports back to Venice.[73] Increasing tension, particularly in Italy, put a premium on secrecy from the later fourteenth century, and crude codes and ciphers began to be employed. They would not have delayed a serious investigator long; but they did serve to prevent the opportunistic thief from reading the contents quickly and returning the document undiscovered. Communication from the ambassador's principal generally took the form of further or revised instructions, when it was not demands for more news, but in the case of Venice, particularly, regular *avvisi*, or newsletters, were sent which kept an ambassador informed of domestic affairs and helped to answer a perennial and general ambassadorial complaint. Some, perhaps most, news of the kind for which such a hunger had developed was only to be obtained confidentially on the diplomatic circuit, and only then on the basis of barter or bribery. If an ambassador had no snippets of information to offer, he could obtain none in return. Mauroceno, Venetian ambassador to France in 1505, complained that he was not being sent the kind of gossip that would enable him to keep the Signory informed.[74] The situation was often worse for others who had no system of *avvisi* to help them.

The most celebrated form of ambassadorial reporting occurred at the end of a Venetian mission.[75] Because it was unique to Venice, and the Venetian records are particularly complete, it is possible that the practice of delivering a *relazione*, regarded by 1499 as 'ancient and laudable', has been given an undue importance by historians. It is understandable that this might be so, for it was the intention of a *relazione* that it should do much more than report the results of a particular mission, as was done in other states, for example, Florence, where the almost equally good records reveal final reports, but strictly related to the contents and results of the embassy. The Venetian *relazione* gave a full picture of the geography, politics and society of the territory from which the ambassador had returned, as well as the nature and relative success of Venetian policy in relation to it. The initial purpose when *relazioni* were instituted in 1268 was to give the senior statesmen of Venice an extended verbal report of a mission, but after the 1530s when *relazioni* began to be written and retained in the chancellery, they were available for the instruction of future ambassadors to the same places, and, as it turned out, became a mine of useful evidence for their future political and social, as well as diplomatic, historians. For those who want to chart the development of diplomacy itself, the *relazioni* are not as helpful as ordinary dispatches, however, nor are the Venetian records, though large in size, the most informative.[76]

The most significant changes in the style and type of communication to and from ambassadors up to the fifteenth century followed changes in their purpose. While the pace remained slow and the quantity of exchange was relatively small, when something important was occurring, principals gave their envoys very broad powers and communication with home was largely unnecessary. As the pace quickened and the discretion allowed to envoys was reduced, reference back, with all its concomitant delays, increased, and with it, ciphers and couriers. As diplomatic relations became more drawn out, and the influence of domestic politics on their outcome became more significant, so the emphasis switched from the almost purely technical to the more general and highly persistent demand for endless quantities of news, most likely to be provided in the form of gossip obtained by sheer persistence, or exchange or bribery. This development was fuelled by the same considerations which led to the emergence of the first resident embassies, and a consequential expansion in the scope of diplomatic activity, not to be equalled until the invention of the machinery of the peacetime conference in the early nineteenth century.

3

THE EMERGENCE OF THE 'OLD DIPLOMACY'

An ambassador ought to remember that he represents his Prince, when the question is about any function of his employment; and he ought to be firm in asserting all the rights and privileges belonging to it. But setting that aside, he should forget his rank, in order to live in a free and easy manner with his friends, and he may be civil and sociable with everybody. If he acts otherwise, and if he pretends always to be like a Herald King at Arms, upon the days of ceremony, he shows himself very unfit for his employment.

(François de Callières, *The Art of Diplomacy*, ed. by H. M. A. Keens-Soper and Karl W. Schweizer, New York, 1983, p. 153)

As the practices of fifteenth-century Italy gradually spread to the rest of Europe, the transitions took place patchily both in space and time, but by the early eighteenth century, most of the machinery of modern diplomacy was in place. The emergence of the resident ambassador to become the principal operator in the system has been discussed. Developments in five other areas also deserve attention: payment and recruitment, precedence and procedure, the evolution of diplomatic theory, the first appearance of foreign ministries and the emergence of the peacetime conference.

PAYMENT AND RECRUITMENT

In fifteenth-century Italy there had developed fairly clear practices about the payment and accommodation of ambassadors. The single culture, short distances and the high degree of reciprocation made this easier than it was later to be in Europe as a whole during the following two centuries. Resident ambassadors were reasonably well and regularly paid, and it was not expected that the host would either grant them an allowance or provide accommodation for them or their staff.[1] As the appointment of resident ambassadors increased during the sixteenth century there was, as has already been seen, a period during which only the Spaniards arranged a wide spread of ambassadors. Until greater reciprocation followed, traditional methods continued to exist, only gradually being supplanted by the Italian model. Thus special missions expected to be accommodated, usually in some state, by their host, and even in the second half of the sixteenth century, Spain and the Holy Roman Empire might make a gesture of special respect by meeting the entire expenses of an extraordinary embassy. At the peripheries, the obligations of the host continued almost unchanged and in the Ottoman Empire, which sent no residents of its own, ambassadors were completely provided for by the Sultan. This was partly to be able to control what they did – a practice highly reminiscent of their Byzantine predecessors – and partly because the Turks remained resistant to European changes and developments in diplomacy as in other fields until awareness of their growing relative weakness in the eighteenth century gave rise to half-hearted measures of reform. The patchy nature of change in respect of residents may be seen by comparing the refusal of some sixteenth-century rulers to accept any responsibilities for Spanish residents who, being inadequately paid, or often not paid at all by their principal, could find themselves destitute. The Dutch, by contrast, continued to provide free accommodation for residents in the Netherlands until 1649.[2]

Apart from the fragility of accepted practice, there were other purely practical reasons why resident ambassadors were so often in financial difficulties. The sheer length of time that it took to send money,[3] the problems of exchange, the ever present danger of theft *en route*,[4] were all significant. There was also a tendency on the part of rulers to pay allowances only if they were themselves reasonably in funds, or sometimes only when the social position of the ambassador concerned was significant enough, or even, as with Ferdinand of Aragon, when an ambassador's dispatch had actually found him at his peripatetic court and caused him to remember the country concerned, his ambassador there and his intentions towards it.[5]

The consequences of the consistent poverty of ambassadors could be serious. The most frequent complaint, apart from the cries of anguish as personal resources drained away in keeping body and soul together,[6] was that no news or gossip could be obtained without either paying for it or providing some in return. Lack of money militated against the first and lack of dispatches from home, by delay or neglect, against the second. The second unhappy result was that an embassy might not be able to keep up the scale of entertainment which the standing, or claimed standing, of its principal would suggest. Third, if an ambassador committed himself to loans in the service of his state, he might never escape his creditors. The French ambassador in Scotland in the late 1550s who commanded French forces there, also paid them and was owed 129,000 livres when he departed.[7] Perhaps the saddest example of ambassadorial financial disaster arose out of the Emperor Maximilian's notorious unreliability. His ambassador to Spain crossed with his opposite number coming to Germany, and they agreed to draw each other's stipend and thus avoid the chancy business of transmission and exchange. Ferdinand of Spain did pay Maximilian's envoy something, though not what had been agreed; Maximilian paid nothing to the Spaniard and 'the whole affair ended in ill-feeling and inconvenience'.[8]

For all the complaints and genuine difficulties, the practice of paying resident ambassadors from home became widespread by the end of the sixteenth century, and by 1700 it had become standard practice, except for the Ottoman Empire, which continued to pay an allowance to foreign ambassadors during the eighteenth century. The resident, whatever doubts there were about the desirability or morality of his position (see p. 29) , had come to be a necessity, and this increasingly set a limit to the neglect and caprice with which rulers treated him. The regularity of payment and the level of salary both improved, though the significance of the latter was partly offset both by inflation and by the increased activities of the resident. By 1510, England and Spain were paying about the same as Venice, by mid-century the rate had doubled, and by 1610 it had doubled again. Relativities between services altered – the Venetians paid less as the sixteenth century advanced – and within services different posts were paid at different rates, in relation to their perceived importance. Despite some systematization which began to appear around the turn of the seventeenth century,[9] these factors make comparative judgements across time hard to make; but it has been computed that an ambassador's salary – if paid – was

> not the income of a wealthy bishop or a great nobleman, but it was quite that of a prosperous merchant or a well-to-do country gentle-man. It would run to a household of twenty or so, a certain amount of entertaining, and a good appearance at court, though without lavish ostentation.[10]

There exists one example of an ambassador, Chapuys, the Savoyard envoy of the Emperor Charles V in London, who actually did well out of being a diplomat, and he represents one of the other ways in which diplomats were sometimes rewarded. His salary was lower than the average, but, towards the end of a successful career and in debt, he was rewarded with a rich sinecure, invested the proceeds with extreme shrewdness, and ended by founding two colleges, at Antwerp and Annecy, out of his own resources. If the grant of a sinecure was a way for the principal to supply the deficiencies of low or unpaid salaries, the giving of rich gifts was a way by which the host ruler could achieve the same object. Gold chains were a common gift, as was expensive clothing. Silver, horses, jewels, even sometimes cash, were also given. All these items could be tailored by weight or quantity to the message intended to be sent either about the sender or about the ambassador himself. The value could on occasion be staggering: an English ambassador to the Emperor Charles V received a gold chain valued at 2,000 ducats in 1529, at a time when an ambassador might expect about 25 or 30 ducats a month as salary. Many other examples show that gifts on departure represented an important part of an ambassador's remuneration; it was no doubt fortunate for him that they also formed part of the elaborate system of ceremonial by which more than financial or personal messages were sent.

The presentation of such gifts did not begin to decline until the later seventeenth century; in the 1620s a very complete account of an important French embassy to England revealed that James I gave the ambassador, Marshal de Bassompierre, some formidably valuable jewellery at the end of his mission. This must have come as something of a relief to the Marshal, as his journey illustrated some of the many physical dangers that continued to plague seventeenth-century travel. Very rough seas in the English Channel on the return journey to Paris involved throwing carriages overboard with the luggage they contained and the loss of 29 horses, who died of thirst during the five-day voyage.[11] By the 1670s, Russian expectations, whether in respect of gifts or maintenance, were beginning to excite unfavourable comment in England, though this was no doubt as much a comment on the anachronistic practices involved as it was evidence of the increasing reluctance of states and rulers to meet the expenses of resident ambassadors or to continue making presentations. By the reign of Peter the Great, Russia had conformed to the European standard,[12] and it was clear that the patterns of financial responsibility had settled completely into the hands of the sending authority. This did not mean an end to the constant complaints of ambassadors about the level of their pay, its tendency to arrive late or to be expressed in a form costly to exchange. Refusal to serve was frequent and usually justified on the grounds that a potential ambassador stood to lose a large part of his personal fortune in the service of his mission: this was still as true in the eighteenth century as it had been for the French ambassador to Scotland in the mid-sixteenth century mentioned earlier.[13]

Thus financial difficulties, even if they had lessened a little by the eighteenth century, taken together with the dangers of travelling[14] and, during much of the seventeenth century, the physical risks of residence at a court espousing an opposing religion, make it surprising that there were men willing to undertake resident embassies. Moreover, whereas in Italy shorter distances and a familiar language and culture made relatively short embassies practical and thus spread the load across the available candidates, over Europe more widely it took more time to arrive and return, and more time to acclimatize to what might be a very different society and language. This led rulers to leave ambassadors abroad for quite long periods on average and in some particular cases for what now seem like extraordinarily long missions: de Puebla served Spain in London, for example, for a total of eighteen years.[15] Although there were some examples which cut across this general point,[16] long absences from the domestic centre of political power did not make ambassadorships an effective route to subsequent influence and wealth. This was also rendered less likely by the lengthy period – not completely over even by the eighteenth century – which elapsed before ambassadors were necessarily of the same nationality as the sending principal. They were usually so by the seventeenth century, particularly in neighbouring countries; but they still might be Italians or Swiss, and the ethnic diversity of the Holy Roman Empire was certainly exemplified in its external representation.

So the puzzle remains as to why such generally effective, cultured and capable men were willing to serve as ambassadors. For there was no doubt that by the early seventeenth century, there had emerged across Europe a group of experienced, almost professional diplomats, and this particular transition led to a new discussion around 1600 about how the duties of the ambassador should best be performed and what qualities were required in the holders of the office (see p. 68). As to the puzzle, Garrett Mattingly commented,

> In spite of its doubtful rewards and in spite of the haphazard manner in which its members were selected, a diplomatic career seems to have had a peculiar attraction for alert and inquiring minds. It can only have been the fascination of the game of high politics for its own sake which led men of talent and principle to accept and even seek posts as resident ambassadors.[17]

While this may have been true in the early seventeenth century, difficulties of recruitment were quite visible by the eighteenth and could lead to posts being unfilled, or being left to secretaries for long periods. Despite the plethora of literature about what the intellectual and moral equipment of ambassadors ought to be, it was often found necessary to appoint unsuitable or inexperienced people to posts simply because they were available.[18]

ADMINISTRATION AND HIERARCHY

The functioning of diplomacy underwent little change in respect of embassies of ceremony or other special missions during the sixteenth and early seventeenth centuries. Resident ambassadors, and their staff, however, developed their roles until by the early seventeenth-century those of the greater powers at least had come to operate in a way which resembled, less efficiently, the practice of fifteenth-century Italy. Nonetheless, there were two clear differences. The emergence of the newly sovereign state had provoked changes in its government which placed great strains on its ruler and destroyed what was left of the medieval political and economic relationships in society. The result was an elevation of the power and importance of the monarch and an insupportable burden of executive authority. For a time, a common way of relieving the problem was to delegate powerful activities into the hands not of constitutionally appointed and circumscribed ministers, but of temporary favourites. The effect was to blur the lines of responsibility in diplomacy and foreign policy as much as in any other area of government, and to expose ambassadors to great difficulties, and frequent humiliations, as the power struggle, or sometimes power vacuum, at home produced conflicting policies derived from several sources. In such circumstances the effect of whim or fantasy could be crucial.

> In the decade after 1610, French, Spanish and English diplomats abroad had one thing in common. None of them could be certain that their objectives harmonized with those of their fellows at other courts or with the real views of their government, or whether, if this were so today, it would remain so tomorrow.[19]

The transition to an orderly control of foreign policy and management of diplomacy had not yet been completed.

This was also made clear in the sixteenth-century failure to develop any competent domestic administration of foreign policy. The Italian city-states in their record keeping and more or less continuous control of their foreign relations, had evolved embryo foreign ministries in their chancelleries; across the rest of Europe, this evolution was much slower. The principal problem arose out of the uncertainties surrounding the position of royal secretaries. Sometimes they were really foreign ministers – and many other things besides – sometimes they were merely clerks and cipher writers. Their responsibilities were often bizarrely arranged, particularly, as in France for much of the sixteenth century, if there were several of them. Philip II of Spain sought to control his secretaries by duplicating them and often operated independently, as he also, though decreasingly, spied on his ambassadors while they were abroad. Depending on court circumstances, royal secretaries and advisers might wield almost any conceivable degree of power at any given moment, and this situation did not encourage the establishment of organized or effective foreign offices. It also forced ambassadors to communicate with their governments by private contacts and the use of personal influence, which, if it was caused by the absence of prestige and power associated with holding a state office as opposed to social rank, or some other cause of influence, also contributed to the slow development of organized departments.

Another difficulty arose out of a casual attitude to the ownership and storage of state papers. In 1528, for example, the papers relating to the King of Spain's daughter's English marriage could not be found for months, and the texts of treaties were often lost. This was because when the volume of papers became too great for peripatetic courts to carry any further, they were just abandoned in their crates. Secretaries, ambassadors and ministers generally did not have a reliable sense of the distinction between state and private papers, and might simply remove them on leaving office or changing post. This was made more likely in the case of ambassadors since they did not generally leave their files for their successors to use – different ciphers might have made that impossible anyway – and since ambassadors employed their own secretaries who were not, as in Italy, state servants, the tendency for whole archives to disappear was quite marked. Some progress was certainly made towards greater domestic organization of papers relating to foreign affairs towards the end of the sixteenth century, particularly by the Spanish, whose growingly ponderous bureaucracy established the justly famous archive at Simancas; but it was noticeable that the effect on Spanish diplomacy was further to delay its already tortoise-like pace.[20]

Out in the resident embassy, the preoccupation was, as it had always been, with the acquisition of information. From the 1550s onward, this pursuit took on ever greater significance as the separateness of states increased and their hostilities grew, either beause of bids for European hegemony, or because of religious warfare, or both. The rising tension understandably emphasized the duty of the resident to supply to his principal more and better information than his rivals could do. To do this, he needed official and unofficial help. Official help came in the form of a confidential secretary, employed by the ambassador personally, as were the other staff, whose assistance took the form of making the embassy as frequented a centre of entertainment, and thus of gossip, as the ambassador's resources – usually stretched – would permit. There might also be young men seeking experience attached to embassies, who could spread the net more widely. Unofficial help came in the form of information obtained from the court, even from secretaries, whose internal quarrels and greed could be manipulated so as to produce it. Increasingly, the best sources for this were likely to be co-religionists of the ambassador's principal, if the host ruler was of an opposite persuasion. Good contacts with the merchant community and with bankers were usually also effective. Well-placed bribery – not always for money, special favours might also work – was supplemented by straightforward espionage. Breaking and entering, the use of undercover agents and the manipulation of political malcontents were all possible and in some cases common.[21]

Resident ambassadors were apt to complain of this aspect of their role, which the contemporary passion for information had certainly made into their primary duty. The sense of high persons engaged in high business, which still surrounded the special mission, was quite absent from the resident embassy. Whether it was in the complaint of Jean Hotman that 'there is no choice' about a resident having 'to lie and cheat', or in the famous or infamous Gondomar – Spanish ambassador to King James I – also complaining that 'it's a nasty job being an ambassador since one has to be mixed up in business like this', or in the dry pun of Sir Henry Wotton's 1604 remark that an 'ambassador is a good man sent to lie abroad for the sake of his country', it was quite clear that resident ambassadors were fully aware of the ill repute attached to their office.[22]

Having obtained all this information, sifted and evaluated it, the next duty of the ambassador and his secretary was to convey their very frequent reports safely home, untapped by others. The early-seventeenth-century embassy had learnt to go to much trouble about security without notable success; though it is worth remembering that matters have not much improved over time. The terms of the supposedly secret alliances of pre-1914 were pretty well known, if sometimes in a dangerously garbled form, and Anthony Eden while British foreign secretary during the Second World War, when asked to confirm an account of a conversation in Moscow, enquired if his questioner had been under the table. The loose habits with papers of early modern Europe did not help. Ambassadors sometimes removed their papers to insecure places, or occasionally simply left them in empty quarters on departure – waiting for the attentions of the local secret agents. In the early part of the sixteenth century, older notions of ambassadorial duty to the wider society and to peace in general enabled domestic authorities to argue that no immunity from the seizure and opening of an envoy's correspondence applied if there was suspicion that he was up to something nefarious.[23] As immunities came at least in practice more into line with the reality of the resident ambassador's existence and role dispatches were more often simply stolen *en route*, copied and returned, if possible, unobserved. Probably the most useful device in these circumstances was, as most residents did, to assume that correspondence would be read and to write accordingly, taking particular care with a communication that really mattered. For this purpose, there were two main protections: the use of reliable couriers, and the adoption of ciphers. There was a noticeable increase in the care with which couriers were provided and used between 1500 and the 1640s, though the expense of it made rulers reluctant to arrange a really secure system for their embassies. Merchants and other bona fide travellers continued sometimes to be preferred for the really significant message, perhaps with the text actually sewn into their clothing.

The use of codes and ciphers had begun quite early in the sixteenth century, earlier in Italy, and techniques became much more sophisticated by the early seventeenth century and passed from the realm of magic and cabbalism to become a branch of mathematical science. Nonetheless, there was a carelessness about the use of codes and ciphers. The same codes were used for too long, often for years after they had been broken. They were often quite easy to break, and frequently too hastily and inaccurately composed by embassy secretaries. Furthermore, the frequent habit of putting only sensitive parts of dispatches into code made decipherment even easier than it might otherwise have been. Nonetheless, if ambassadors and rulers knew that they could not rely on encoded dispatches for protection if stolen by another state's agents for any length of time, they did gain protection from instant perusal by burglars, embassy spies, frontier officers or even ministers at the court who might be passed a partly encoded dispatch to look over, in the knowledge that there would not be time for them to decipher the important parts.[24]

Unpopular though the resident remained, even dangerous, as the civil and international warfare of the Reformation period could make him, he could not be dispensed with. Since he was there, and had acquired some rights of residence and a small staff, it was not surprising that he began to be used for more tasks than just the acquisition of information. By the early seventeenth century, particularly during the period from the 1590s until the outbreak of renewed warfare after 1618, when the diplomatic system expanded again after the religious asperities and the gaps in representation of the 1570s and 80s,[25] the resident ambassador came to acquire some of the representative character that had formerly belonged only to the orators of the traditional special mission. The resident was also coming to expect that the affairs of his countrymen came under his general purview in his capacity as the representative of the crown under whose protection they came. The continuous presence and local knowledge of the resident was bringing a more important development still in its wake. Rulers were finding it convenient to use residents to negotiate minor agreements instead of dispatching specially empowered special missions, and, while they still expected to send an extraordinary embassy to conclude major agreements or peace treaties, they were using the man on the spot to prepare the ground by prior negotiation. Thus negotiation, as much as newsgathering, was becoming a principal occupation of the resident. This in turn greatly contributed towards a change of attitude, in the air in any case because of the contemporary change in the character of the state, in which diplomatic relations with other states were regarded as a continuous affair, not just something which opened up and closed down as each individual matter arose and was dealt with piecemeal. Much of the business of the resident', Mattingly said of the early seventeenth century,

> was of a sort not pointed towards any individual treaty, and not con-templated at all in the older theory of diplomacy. He was the man counted upon to influence the policies, or perhaps simply the attitudes, of the government to which he was sent in a sense favourable to his own; to minimise frictions, to win concessions, to achieve co-operation (or, what was sometimes just as valuable, the appearance of co-operation), and, if the worst came to the worst, to sound the first warning that things were getting out of hand, and that other pressures were required.[26]

As the seventeenth century progressed, these considerations steadily turned the resident into the standard form of diplomatic representative. He was both cheaper and more effective than any the more traditional forms of representation. Ceremonial embassies might still occur, though very infrequently by the mid-eighteenth century, and special, one-purpose missions to make peace remained common; but the ongoing business of international relations was conducted through resident embassies, and, significantly, there was a growing tendency by 1700 to grade diplomatic officials by their status within the diplomatic service rather than making some estimate of the status of their principal. Equally significantly, the title of *ambassador extraordinary* came to be generally applied to resident ambassadors, when it had formerly designated precisely the opposite personage, the leader of a special mission. The same was true of the use of the phrase *ambassador plenipotentiary*.[27] By 1789, the nomenclature and the internal hierarchy of diplomacy had arrived at a perceptibly modern form, and the process of transition was effectively over.

PRECEDENCE

The representative character of the resident led to the development of a new aspect of diplomatic life, which was to last for over a century and became notorious: an apparently obsessive preoccupation with precedence. The special embassies of the Middle Ages and the Renaissance had been preoccupied with ceremonial because of the quite precise messages it could send about the relationship of the two parties involved as well as indicating the seriousness of the matters involved and the act of representation itself. Only rarely, or at Rome, were rules of precedence required, and it was a pope, Julius II, who first issued a list of the relative order of rulers. It was not meant to apply for more than one occasion, but it was an indication that problems over precedence were arising. It was not until the emergence of the resident produced several embassies permanently established at one court that difficulties began to arise about how the relationships between them should be expressed. The increasing emphasis on the representative character of the resident ambassador determined that each ambassador would struggle for the highest position relative to others on all occasions, but never more so than at formal, court functions.

The result was bitter, often unedifying, sometimes comic battles over precedence. So important did it become that wars could be started, or fail to end because of it, improvements in position were offered as bribes from greater to lesser rulers, and particularly obvious strains occurred when the relative power of states increased. The Dutch, whose position was in any case complicated by not being strictly a monarchy, spent the latter part of the seventeenth century struggling for and eventually obtaining royal honours for their representatives. The title of Emperor assumed by Peter the Great of Russia was unacknowledged for some time except by his immediate neighbours, and was particularly objectionable to the Habsburgs as Holy Roman Emperors, hitherto uniquely imperial in Europe. The rise to greater importance of the Duchy of Savoy led by the late seventeenth century to the treatment of the dukes as effectively royal, a development which was quite clear in the reception given in London and Paris to ambassadors announcing the death of Charles Emmanuel II in 1675.[28]

The matter of titles was very sensitive. The Russians were particularly noted for their insistence on receiving an exact rendering of what they believed to be their due, sometimes valuing it beyond concessions which they were simultaneously making. They were a good example of Rousset de Missy's classic observation that 'Princes will cede towns, even provinces, but all the ability of the most adroit negotiators cannot decide them to give up a rank which they believe to be their right'.[29] Descriptions of rank were important, but so were statements of ownership, however improbable. An early indication of this occurred in the making of a Russo-Polish treaty of 1582 when it was clear that the surrender of fortresses was less important to Tsar Ivan IV than that he should be addressed as Tsar of Astrakhan and Kazan. Earlier the same Tsar had withdrawn the use of the term 'brother' in his communications with the Kings of Denmark and Sweden, as a sign of the changed relationship between them.[30] A later and different indication of this can be gathered from decisions which began to be taken during the late seventeenth century to ignore such claims. During the Congress of Oliva in 1660, Charles X of Sweden had demanded recognition as King of the Vandals, but by the Congress of Nijmegen, 1676–79, it could be agreed that the claims of the Emperor to be Duke of Burgundy, the Duke of Lorraine to be Count of Provence, the King of Spain to be King of France should be ignored. The Congress declared that titles assumed or omitted by any ruler did not prejudice the rights of anyone.[31]

The Russians were equally renowned at least until the reign of Peter the Great for their insistence on the complete observance of all the other niceties by which status was recognized; but they were scarcely unusual. They, whose relationships were distant and uncertain, and the Venetians, who were liable to feel that they were being slighted because they were a republic, were particularly demanding out of a sense of potential or actual inferiority. Others were merely following a preoccupation with status as representing that of their principal, a preoccupation clearly to be seen in one of the most compendious diplomatic manuals of the seventeenth century by Abraham Wicquefort, *L'Ambassadeur et ses fonctions*, published in the Hague in 1680.

Until the early eighteenth century, diplomacy was full of endless crises caused by intended or unintended slights occurring between ambassadors or their retinues – usually the latter – and also resulting from attempts by ambassadors to gain a higher status in their treatment by the ruler to whom they were accredited, sometimes by seeking to perform highly personal services.[32] Sheer chaos might follow. Sir John Finett, Master of Ceremonies to James I of England, left an account of his experiences which includes a description of the King's birthday celebrations in 1619. Disputes over physical placing caused the French ambassador and his wife to absent themselves, as did the Savoyard, which made the refusal of the Dutch representative to attend on the grounds that he ought to be superior to the Savoyard an unnecessary act of self-deprivation, even if it was demanded by his instructions. In this case the French ambassador's behaviour was motivated by France's desire to gain a general diplomatic precedence over Spain, the first evidence of which had occurred rather earlier at the Council of Trent, where the Spanish had succeeded in gaining ascendancy over the French, traditionally second only to the Emperor. Thereafter for a time, France refused to be represented at the Emperor's court and a century of diplomatic rivalry was inaugurated. Later in the century, again in London, came a more serious episode. The arrival of a new Swedish ambassador in 1661 provoked an outburst of highly traditional Franco-Spanish rivalry as to precedence, but on a grand scale: fifty men were either killed or wounded in a running battle in the streets which had been plainly prepared for by the French, who had brought a posse of troops with them. The Spaniards, however, won on the day by cutting loose the horses pulling the French ambassador's coach. Nonetheless, they did not win the war. Louis XIV decided to take the incident extremely seriously and threatened an exhausted Spain with war. The Spaniards had to agree to apologize and recognize French claims to precedence, which they had resisted for at least fifty years, before the assembled diplomatic corps in Paris. On the other hand, the resources of protocol were in the end limited, and, as had happened in other cases, the Spanish avoided some of the consequences of this humiliation by refusing to appear with the French representative and by continuing to be given precedence wherever a Habsburg ruled. Physical violence over precedence could have practical motives as well. When the Congress of Utrecht was breaking down in January 1712, it was later reported that the Dutch and the French had used disputes between their servants as an excuse for insulting each other and thus for breaking off negotiations.[33]

Placing at table, whether to eat or to negotiate, presented other opportunities for point scoring, as did the order of entry into rooms and the order of signature on documents. The effects of disputes on such matters were sarcastically discussed by Rousseau, who had some diplomatic experience as unofficial secretary of legation in Venice in the 1740s. There were, he said, solemn meetings from time to time at which, among problems about the arrangement of business, there were also questions about whether the table should be round or square, how many doors the room should have, which, if any, of the delegates should face or have his back towards the window, how many steps should be taken on any one visit, and, he added, countless other questions of equal importance, uselessly discussed over three centuries.[34]

Resolution of these kinds of disputes came during the eighteenth century, as the diplomatic process became in highly tense times fundamentally practical and a steadily emerging clarity about the contemporary distribution of power made its role as a descriptive barometer of power relativities an increasingly irrelevant hindrance to its main function. It took about 100 years for an agreed arrangement about precedence and the order of signature, by then regarded as an outmoded nuisance, to be formalized, mainly at or just after the Congress of Vienna in 1815. But the process was under way before the end of the seventeenth century. To begin with, it took the form of devices which would prevent disputes from arising. Special rooms, or even, as at Carlowitz in 1699, temporary wooden buildings were arranged, so that the number of doors could equal the number of delegates. Entry could be at the sound of a trumpet, so that no one entered first. Treaties were either signed on individual copies so that each took home the copy he had signed first; or the document was written on a round sheet, so that no one appeared to have signed first, or last. The order of precedence, when seated, was solved, apparently at Nijmegen, by meeting at round tables, where no one was above anyone else. These devices, however, like all devices, worked when the parties wanted them to. As time went on, there grew up a clear tendency to solve protocol problems by agreeing to ignore them. Meetings were preceded by a prior agreement not to operate the customary forms, lest real business be delayed, and private negotiations, as they always had to some degree, prepared the ground for the public sessions. By the end of the eighteenth century, the thickets of custom, precedence and antiquated procedure had been cleared away. If, as Napoleon did in 1813 at Prague, they were revivified, it was deemed to be for purely political purposes, and the appropriate conclusions drawn. The Congress of Vienna was conducted in a world which would be quite recognizable today; the Congress of Utrecht, 100 years earlier, though change was evidently on the way, breathed a different and an older air: between 1712 and 1815, the change to the modern world had been effected.[35]

While the struggle lasted, however, there was no doubt that victories or defeats on the battlefield of precedence were both significant in themselves and could be signals of shifts in the balance of power between states. They were also representative of something of more general importance. The structure and behaviour of the diplomatic machine has always been a response to the needs of the players on the international stage. When the distribution of power has been in a steady state an appropriate machinery of diplomacy has emerged to serve its particular characteristics. During periods of change and uncertainty about the actual distribution of power, the diplomatic machine has been made to deliver not only the function of communication and negotiation, but also the function of distinguishing a pecking order of real power. In the seventeenth century this function was of real significance. It was a period when the emergence of fully sovereign states was definite but not complete in the sense that they were not the only conceivable possessors of international power. The Papacy retained some; the Holy Roman Empire retained some;[36] the idea of Christian Europe seen in contrast to the Turks still had a shadowy existence. Thus there was not only a question as to how power lay between the states of Europe, but also still a question as to the relative authority of the older universalist institutions and ideas. The complicated disputes about procedure and precedence, the density and the intensity of diplomatic exchange were both ways of trying to achieve a kind of order out of what was inherently transitional and disorderly, and cannot be fully understood or appreciated unless seen in this light.

THE EVOLUTION OF DIPLOMATIC THEORY

Transition also occurred in the way in which commentators wrote about diplomacy and diplomats. As Mattingly pointed out when discussing the earlier writings on diplomacy, when the large quantity was boiled down it amounted 'to the tritest platitudes'.[37] This was because the literature divided itself into two: that which concerned the qualities an ambassador should have or acquire, a subject of apparently endless interest and equally endless regurgitation from author to author; and that which concerned the legal questions surrounding his position, rights and privileges. The balance of quantity shifted from the second to the first during the late sixteenth century, and while the legal treatises were largely technical, it was the discussions of the desirable qualities and skills in an ambassador which earned Mattingly's stricture.[38] Towards the end of the seventeenth century and in the early eighteenth century, however, the tone changed. The establishment of diplomacy as a constant feature of international relations, based on the arrival of the resident embassy as its chief motive power, and the use that rulers had come to make of it in pursuit of entirely independent, fully sovereign, foreign policies, began, perhaps rather late in the day, to induce a discussion about the political function of diplomacy and diplomats.

The first sign of this change came in the writings of perhaps the most celebrated authority on diplomacy of the period: Abraham de Wicquefort.[39] He, like his predecessors, started from a formidable knowledge of the previous literature, and, also like most of his predecessors, he set out to produce a definitive work. He differed from them in that he based his descriptions and instructions less on what earlier authorities – or classical and biblical sources – had suggested, and more on the actual practice of states and rulers. He applied this principle to international law as well as to the mechanism of diplomacy, and against the background of Grotius and Pufendorf appeared more advanced in the field of law than he did in his discussion of the diplomatic mechanism.

Wicquefort distinguished the *droit des gens* from the law of nature and from civil law. His determination to derive 'international' law from the consent of states effectively establishes the autonomy of law between states. With Wicquefort the *jus gentium* has become the *ius inter gentes*, and for this alone he deserves mention in the history of international law.[40]

His discussion of diplomacy, however, did not cross the bridge, except by implication, into the field of its political function.

The appearance of *De la manière de négocier avec les souverains, de l'utilité des négotiations, du choix des ambassadeurs et des envoyez, et des qualitez nécessaires pour réussir dans ces employs,* by François de Callières in Paris in 1716 marked the moment of change. De Callières' book became the most celebrated manual on diplomacy ever to have been written. The later nineteenth century valued it less than earlier periods, but the stresses brought on by the aftermath of the First World War brought it again to the largely admiring attention of practitioners of international relations. In 1957, Harold Nicolson described it as a 'great book'.[41] It was a discussion in an entirely different mould from its predecessors, and perhaps deliberately different from Wicquefort. It was comparatively slim and did not attempt to build up storehouses of instances or to mine the examples contained in previous books.

History and literature were both important to de Callières, but the use of history was to enable an understanding of how the political relationship between states actually worked; and the knowledge of literature was to induce economy and elegance of expression – necessary qualities in a diplomat and perhaps more readily to be found in a member of the French Academy, as de Callières' title page proudly indicated that he was, in the early eighteenth century than at any other time. Since de Callières so deliberately asserted the distinct political activity that international relations represented, he logically presented diplomacy as the mechanism through which that activity was conducted. He did not comment on ideas just emerging in his time which suggested that the international system could and should be reformed so as to eliminate the conflicts caused by the differing interests of states.[42] He seemed to assume both their permanence and their inevitability, and to regard it as the principal function of diplomacy to moderate and manage the clash of conflicting interests as efficiently as possible. Thus it was important, as Wicquefort had also said, that diplomats should be honest and straightforward in their dealings. Their dealings needed also to be secret for the same reason. The maximum amount of trust needed to be generated between those who had to cope professionally with a permanently difficult situation, and between them and their principals. This, too, rather than legal principle, was why diplomatic immunity must be upheld: the interest of princes compelled it. Even ceremonial was explained by reference to the needs of the system: it induced order in an inevitably disorderly world.

The most recent commentators on de Callières have summarized his conclusions in this way:

> In brief, political intelligence, the constant and accurate updating of the profile of events, the assessment and relaying of this information about the government and country to which an envoy has been sent, is the *sine qua non* of the aim or end of diplomacy which is to reconcile states on the basis of a true estimate of their respective interests. The staple ingredient of diplomacy is this search for accommodation, and only when adequately informed about events can bargains once struck issue in stable relations. The diplomatist. . .is the agent and not the architect of policy but his intelligence (in several senses of that word) is indispensable both to the framing of policy and even more to the exacting business of seeking to persuade the representatives of other, independent and rival, governments to 'see matters' in this rather than that light. Callières spends much time in arguing that the art of persuasion – unlike the art of imposing one's will through force of arms – is an art of insinuation; of persuading one's opposite number that one has indeed understood his position and is seeking to find terms acceptable to both.[43]

Just over sixty years divided the publication of de Callières' *De la manière de négocier*, from the appearance of the most widely disseminated French translation of de Vera's *Le parfait ambassadeur* in 1642, and undoubtedly, until the publication of Wicquefort, the most respected diplomatic handbook. The difference between them clearly indicates what a revolution there had been in the practice of diplomacy. Some of what de Vera had to say amounted only to mildly fanciful and commonly repeated platitudes about the qualities of an ambassador; but his preoccupation with the moral problems of the job arose out of the emerging institution of the resident ambassador. He could not resolve the possibility of conflict between the 'honour of the ambassador and the good of the state, between the welfare of the state and the welfare of Christendom', as Mattingly put it,[44] because he was trying to reconcile contemporary practice with an older set of ideas; and from that older set of ideas, there was no way of explaining what the fundamental purpose of the resident ambassador was, short of agreeing that he was a 'licensed spy'. Only when de Callières gave as much importance to describing and understanding the international political system as to the depiction of the nature of the office of ambassador could the ambassador's role, even the full function of diplomacy itself, be satisfactorily rationalized. He was not completely understood by his contemporaries.

Another French diplomat, Antoine Pecquet, wrote a book under a similar title in 1737 which continued the traditional list of ambassadorial virtues and criticized de Callières for not doing so.[45] Pecquet did, however, make explicit what was certainly implicit in both Wicquefort and de Callières: the notion that the body of diplomats at any capital or court constituted a body – a *corps diplomatique*. This body, he said, had an independent existence, whose members were doing the same job and would treat each other in a civilized way even when their principals were at war. They shared the same privileges and would jointly defend any of their number whose rights had been infringed.[46] This kind of development served to confirm in a different way what de Callières had been saying about the larger stage. The international business of the world could not be conducted without effective diplomacy and diplomats. The need of the sovereign state for the resident ambassador had triumphed over the problems that his existence caused. The terms of his existence had been regulated and described and his world had matured into a distinct political activity. As de Callières had understood, he and the foreign ministries that had developed to instruct him, made the functioning of the international political system possible.

THE DEVELOPMENT OF FOREIGN MINISTRIES

In most respects the rising power of France during the seventeenth century induced earlier examples of new developments in the machinery of diplomacy than elsewhere. This was certainly true of efforts to introduce some elements of training for French diplomats, as it was in the great weight of information contained in French *Instructions* given to ambassadors embarking on a mission. It was also noticeable that Richelieu's control of French policy during the first half of the seventeenth century assumed both that the international system in Europe consisted of a community of sovereign states and that the relationships between them had become continuous. This assumption led both to a new objective in foreign policy and a new theory of diplomacy. As one French commentator on Richelieu's France explained: 'Richelieu, by secularising the exchanges between states, imposed the notion of a European equilibrium as the guiding principle of international relations'.[47] The resulting addition to diplomatic theory was the conception that continuous foreign relationships required continual negotiation. In his *Testament Politique*, written privately in 1638 for the guidance of Louis XIII, he explained that 'I strongly assert that it is vitally important to negotiate continuously, openly, everywhere, even if one will make no present gain or even anticipate one in the future'.[48] This represented a formal distillation of the tendency to make ever greater use of resident ambassadors and would not have been possible without them. He also took a clear view that the purposes of diplomacy being principally to establish and maintain confidence, it had to be ideologically neutral and to operate on the basis of strict honesty. 'Rulers ought to be very careful about the treaties that they make: but, having made them, they should most scrupulously observe them.'[49]

Richelieu did not abandon the notion that *ambassadors extraordinary*, who were now employed, except in more backward areas, more or less only for ceremonial functions, were more senior than ordinary ambassadors, but he did recognize the practical consequences of his conviction about the necessity for international relations to be conducted continuously. Both the quality of ambassadors and the control exercised over them by ministers had become matters of profound importance.

> It is very important to be careful in choosing ambassadors and other representatives, and one cannot be too severe in punishing those who exceed their powers, since by such errors the reputation of rulers and the interests of states are compromised.[50]

Negotiators should, he said, be 'persons who can weigh the meaning of words exactly and who are natural drafters'.[51] It was the need to ensure an undivided control of these continuous relationships and to communicate with the resident ambassadors who thus had become the means of expressing such continuity, which led him to institute the first foreign ministry in 1626.[52] Until this point, French foreign affairs had been divided among the secretaries of state, with responsibility delegated according to geographical area. From 1624–6, for example, d'Herbault had responsibility for Spain, Piedmont, Italy and Switzerland; d'Oquerre for Lorraine, Flanders, the Low Countries, Germany and the Empire; while La Ville-aux-Clercs acted for England, Scotland, Ireland, Denmark and the Levant.[53] This piecemeal approach plainly discouraged an overall view of the interests of France as a whole, and led to rivalry between the secretaries. Even greater problems arose between the departments involved with war and foreign affairs, where responsibility for correspondence between an army abroad and the central authority devolved upon different secretaries as the army travelled through different jurisdictions. The *Règlement* of 1626 was intended to rationalize this situation.[54] By abolishing external geographical distinctions, the handling of communications with ambassadors abroad was certainly streamlined, although foreign ministry staff continued to have some responsibilities for provinces within France. The keeping of records, however, was rapidly found by d'Herbault, who became the first secretary for foreign affairs, to be inadequate, and another *Règlement*, of 1628, attempted to improve the situation.[55] A further *Règlement* of 1633 cleared up some of the confusion about responsibility for communication during wartime.[56] These developments led to the emergence of a line of able French foreign ministers – Lionne, Pomponne, Colbert de Croissy, Torcy, again rather earlier than occurred at other European courts.

In an administrative sense, there had been many previous examples of small sub-departments of royal chanceries which attempted to collect and supply information, some of it of a legal and ceremonial kind. It had been an inevitable consequence of the highly fraught international politics of the Renaissance Italian city-states, as it had also been even earlier a consequence of the peculiar position of the Papacy as a source of international jurisdiction, that new administrative methods emerged.[57] The habit of combining both domestic and foreign policy administration in the same departments was common throughout the greater states until the early eighteenth century. It particularly took the form of giving to domestic departments the management of policy towards foreign states which lay on the edges of the provinces under their control. In France, for example, in the first half of the sixteenth century, the provinces and their neighbours were divided in this fashion among the four financial secretaries. In England a similar situation existed in respect of the two secretaries of state until the Foreign and Home Offices were formed in 1782 – very late by the standards of the rest of Europe – and the new Foreign Office remained inexpensive and small, having only an under-secretary and a few clerks.[58]

It is clear that these arrangements were only possible for as long as foreign policy was not seen as a separate branch of government, but as the object of intermittent attention from monarchs or their ministers or favourites. As has been seen already in the evolution of diplomatic theory, the shift towards separating foreign affairs came patchily but steadily during the later seventeenth century; and one of the consequences showed itself in the emergence of foreign ministries whose responsibilities were increasingly political as much as administrative.

In France, the measures that Richelieu had taken survived the opening of Louis XIV's personal rule after 1661, although the occasional outburst of separate and secret activity by the King gave examples of the general contemporary tendency for monarchs to muddy the waters of foreign policy management by private interference. This was to become a clear and highly damaging feature of Louis XV's policy-making, particularly in respect of Poland. However, Louis XIV's normal practice was to ask for and follow foreign ministry briefs in his dealings with foreign visitors, and divided authority was much less of a characteristic than elsewhere. His foreign secretary was a permanent member of the *Conseil d'État*, and was generally an able and experienced man. The memoirs of Brienne give a picture of the French foreign ministry in 1661. When it was summoned to Vincennes as a body, 'Brienne the elder went there in a sedan chair; Brienne the younger went in a carriage accompanied by the two senior clerks or *commis*; the two junior clerks went on horseback, carrying with them ink and paper in case of need'.[59] Thus there were plainly five officials.

It is clear that the French near-hegemony of the later seventeenth century brought expansion to the foreign ministry based on a generally clear division of duties.[60] There was a political department, divided into two sections dealing with different groups of foreign states with an apparently effective system for answering and registering correspondence. A codes and ciphers department attempted to protect French correspondence and break into the communications of other states. A financial department, which also dealt with diplomatic privilege and watched the activities of foreigners in France, controlled the budget of the department. Legal advice was available from the 1720s, as was translation from the 1760s. Perhaps the most remarkable and complete development of the eighteenth century was the establishment of the cartographic department, which was stated to have about 10,000 maps by the 1780s.

> By 1784, the ministry had four main divisions: two *bureaux pour l'expédition des dépêches* which handled between them the correspondence with all French representatives abroad; a *bureau des fonds*, which controlled its finances; and a *bureau du dépôt* which supervised its archives, then lodged in a specially constructed fire proof building at Versailles.[61]

The past glories of Louis XIV's reign and the successes of French diplomacy during the eighteenth century gave the French foreign ministry great prestige, and if not everything worked as well as was intended, the ministry had reached a stage of development by 1789 which others were only to achieve in the nineteenth century.

The French arrangements were certainly the most advanced in Europe, and were widely imitated. The answer to a Russian enquiry of 1784 about the organization of the French foreign ministry provides both information about French practice and indicates the degree of Russian interest. This last was not surprising in view of the strenuous efforts that Peter the Great made to introduce a modernized system at St Petersburg. There had been a department of embassies in the Russian administration since the mid-sixteenth century, but it carried no political weight and in any case possessed other domestic responsibilities. By the end of the seventeenth century it had grown, particularly in numbers of translators and had been divided into geographical departments; but its real development was to come in the 1720s when a new college of foreign affairs was established, and unlike some of Tsar Peter's reforms survived a period of near chaos after his death and grew to have 261 members at the accession of Catherine the Great in 1762. The college had a president, vice-president and two chancery councillors at its establishment, and during the eighteenth century steadily lost its responsibilities for internal provincial (also Central Asian) administration, ecclesiastical administration, for tax gathering and for the postal system, which was separated in 1782.[62]

If France and Russia showed the most development during the eighteenth century, other states, too, reformed in various ways their conduct of foreign affairs. In Spain, where heavyweight bureaucracy and highly organized record keeping – at Simancas – made an early appearance, a more political and less purely administrative approach grew from the creation of a secretariat of state for foreign affairs in 1714. In the Habsburg Empire, the long service of Kaunitz as Chancellor gave continuity, and the particular problems caused by the dual role of the Emperor as both ruler of the Habsburg lands and Holy Roman Emperor were resolved in 1790. The two chancelleries concerned – the *Reichskanzlei*, for the Empire, and the *Hofkanzlei*, for the Habsburg lands – ended two centuries of bickering with a complicated agreement giving two sets of credentials to Habsburg diplomats and asking them to receive instructions from and report to whichever chancellery was appropriate in each individual negotiation.[63] By 1800, too, persistent difficulties in apportioning financial responsibility for the foreign ministry in Vienna were resolved, partly as a result of the conquest by Napoleon of areas whose tax revenue had hitherto been tapped for the purpose.[64] Even in Turkey, some concentration of foreign affairs in the hands of the *Reis Effendi*, the head of the Grand Vizier's chancery emerged after the Carlowitz peace conference in 1699, though the effect was often uncertain, and the Ottoman Empire remained, as in so many matters, partly a world of its own and partly simply anachronistic in its management of affairs.[65]

SECRECY

The effects of applying tighter political controls to the making of foreign policy and the political requirements of states and rulers were mutually reinforcing. One of the consequences, for example, of the highly nervous international relations of the eighteenth century was an intensification of concern about gathering and protecting information. The instructions given to Sir William Trumbull on his departure as ambassador to Paris in 1685 are an early and clear example:

> You shall constantly correspond with our ministers in other foreign courts, for our better service, and your mutual information and assistance in your respective negotiations; and you shall also maintain a good correspondence and intercourse with all the other ambassadors, envoys and ministers of princes and states in amity with us, and as far as you can penetrate into the designs of their respective superiors, and of what you can discover of this nature you shall give us a constant account by one of our principal Secretaries of State.[66]

Gaining information was principally achieved by the barter of carefully laundered news from home and other sources, and ambassadors regularly complained if they were left unfurnished with suitable items, or indeed, as they frequently were, allowed insufficient cash to buy intelligence, if that was necessary.

For foreign ministries, acquiring information was principally achieved by opening letters and dispatches and by breaking codes and ciphers where possible. In the Habsburg dominions, there existed a very effective network of secret chancellery offices, which was said in the single year 1780–1 to have broken fifteen foreign ciphers. Earlier on, the English were admired for their skill in this respect, and the post office developed a special department for opening and copying letters, derived from a Cromwellian initiative of 1653. In 1730, the Duke of Newcastle, then Prime Minister, ordered the Postmaster-General to copy correspondence addressed to a list of 112 people, mostly the sovereigns and leading statesmen of Europe.[67] After 1765, when all diplomatic correspondence was subjected to scrutiny, the department expanded so that it employed ten staff. It was later to be said that the termination of this practice in the very different moral climate of the 1840s deprived Lord Palmerston in his second term of office as foreign secretary of the precise information which had made remarkably perfect timing such a feature of his first. In France, the activities of the *Cabinet noir* became well known during the eighteenth century, not because it was particularly new, but because it did not confine its activities to foreign correspondence, and read domestic exchanges as well.

Protecting information was principally achieved by using the codes and ciphers least likely to be broken, and great efforts were made by cryptographers to create an unbreakable system. Both protection and acquisition were attempted in all states to a greater or lesser extent, and the greater efficiency which the tensions of the eighteenth century brought to the activity were both largely self-cancelling and in any case not always effective. The celebrated case of J. A. von Thugut, Habsburg representative at Constantinople, 1769–75, was a classic example of a breach occurring abroad: he was paid by the French to communicate confidential information to the Comte de Saint-Priest, French ambassador to the Porte. Such activity cannot have been regarded as treasonable, since the episode was well known, but Thugut became foreign minister at Vienna in 1793 and remained so until 1800. Internally, too, breaches occurred and could have serious consequences. The outbreak of the Seven Years War in 1756 was occasioned by Frederick the Great's invasion of Saxony, itself 'in part provoked by the contents of documents which a Saxon government clerk had been bribed to betray to the Prussians'.[68]

TRAINING

At much the same time as foreign ministries began to emerge outside France, attempts were made to improve the training of potential diplomats. There was no lack of advice about what skills and qualities diplomats should have, but there had as yet been little effort to inculcate them deliberately. Some training on the job had arisen out of the practice of allowing ambassadors to appoint attachés to assist them, though they were seldom given diplomatic credentials and were generally expected to be remunerated, if at all, by the ambassador who had recruited them. As the importance of having secretaries in embassies grew with the importance of the resident embassy itself and the general acceptance of Richelieu's notion of continuous diplomacy, their position became more regulated, though in a patchy way. The advantages of having well-informed and experienced secretaries who did not depart with their ambassador led some diplomatic services to appoint and pay secretaries during the later seventeenth century. But others continued to operate on the older model, and often both occurred simultaneously. The British, who did not respond to this development until the later eighteenth century, then began to provide all ambassadors and some ministers-resident with secretaries, and occasionally gave them diplomatic credentials.[69]

The expansion of diplomatic services in this way was no longer thought to provide opportunities for training, though it did offer one experience which was universally agreed to be desirable and could still be dealt with via attachments to embassies abroad: the experience of travel and residence in foreign places. Such experience was also thought to be the most effective way of learning languages. This was in itself a problem of declining significance except in relation to non-European languages, where most effort was expended on gaining knowledge of Turkish, because of the primacy that French had acquired by the eighteenth century. Commentators tended to agree that Latin was still the universal and essential language, but it was plainly in decline, as was that of Italian, compared with its use in the eastern Mediterranean since the fifteenth century. Nonetheless, considerable efforts were made, particularly in Russia, to broaden the translating capacities of diplomatic services and foreign ministries.[70]

In the Habsburg Empire, the effort to provide enough speakers of Turkish – essential for a country with so long a common frontier with the Ottoman Empire – which began in the mid-seventeenth century, developed into a much more broadly based training scheme in the early nineteenth century. Originally, Turkish language instruction took place in Constantinople at the *Sprachknaben Institut*, under the authority of the Austrian envoy. At that time other students from France, Russia and Venice were also to be found learning Turkish, attached to their own embassies in the city. In 1753, however, it was decided to move the institute to Vienna where it became the *K. K. Akademie der Orientalischen Sprachen*. It was run from the Jesuit College of Vienna University and was partly financed by the Order, but when the Jesuits were suppressed by Pope Clement XIV in 1773, it was thought sufficiently important to be funded entirely by the state. It continued to concentrate on languages – Turkish, Persian, Arabic and French – but also offered a general training for public service. In 1812, it was further extended to provide a grounding in Italian and modern Greek, history, geography, domestic and international law, the law of the sea and commercial law. The course of study lasted for five years and was particularly directed at those who intended to serve in the East.

Other additions to the good education which was assumed to be a prior but insufficient requirement might be supplied through, or closely related to, foreign ministries.[71] This was particularly so because of the contemporary belief that the study of treaties and histories of negotiations was important, and could be arranged through the increasingly efficient archives now being built up in foreign ministries. Schemes of this kind, as well as attachments to missions abroad specifically for training, made their appearance in Russia, France – typically the most elaborate programme, arranged while de Torcy was foreign minister – and Prussia between 1712 and 1747.[72] These efforts were short lived and though they were illustrative of the way in which the diplomatic machine was evolving, they were also likely to be ineffective. Most senior diplomatic figures were so because of their success in some other field, in domestic politics or in war, for example. Such men might have been willing to gain some diplomatic experience in youth by serving abroad as an attaché to a relative for a period, but they were unlikely to have been willing to undergo a formal training, which must have had tones of drudgery about it, for which neither their rank nor their intended occupations suited them. Diplomacy had become professional in many ways, and was becoming ever more so, but it had not yet become a profession – as in the United States – at the top of the tree; it still has not done so near the end of the twentieth century.

THE DEVELOPMENT OF THE PEACETIME CONFERENCE

By the late eighteenth century, the machinery of diplomacy, in particular after the evolution of the resident embassy with all its associated privileges and immunities, had achieved a form readily familiar to the late-twentieth-century eye, except in one important respect. Everything that the mechanism was asked to do had been derived from the need to represent one sovereign authority to another. The fading away of older, universalist, claims to jurisdiction, whether imperial or ecclesiastical, together with the declining threat from the great Muslim empire at Constantinople, had removed even the vestiges of the idea of a single Christian Europe and left the sovereign state triumphant. The medieval notion that an ambassador, under whatever title, was as much serving the interest of general harmony as that of his principal, had entirely given way to the almost tediously repeated dictum that his sole duty was to pursue the best interests of his prince. The only question that arose surrounded the morality of the methods he might employ, and even then the discussion of it might only lead to a debate as to whether particularly sharp practice was not self-defeating and therefore incompatible with the ambassador's primary purpose.[73]

The standardization of diplomatic privileges and immunities which also occurred during the eighteenth century only served to emphasize the ambassador's role as representing one sovereignty to another and there could be few more powerful demonstrations of this idea than the principle that an embassy building and compound might actually be an island of a foreign jurisdiction physically situated in the host prince or state's capital. So long as the objectives of states continued to be framed in similar terms, the mechanism remained a complete means of expressing the policies and ambitions that they generated. This was likely to continue for so long as they perceived the international system as a constant struggle for hegemony by one power or another. That perception, though deep seated and only reluctantly abandoned, could not survive the shift in the distribution of power which began in the very early eighteenth century and led to the emergence of a European states system based on the rough equality of five greater states – Austria, Prussia, Russia, France and Britain. Its emergence was accompanied by sharp bouts of warfare from the latter part of the seventeenth century until the end of the Seven Years War in 1763. But the impossibility of any hegemony being established led first to an uneasy truce in which diplomacy, much aided by espionage, became the principal motor of international relations. Thereafter, the entirely different but nonetheless universalist challenge mounted by the French Revolution and subsequently by the Napoleonic *imperium*, eventually succumbed to the resistance put up by powers, sometimes fitfully but ultimately quite definitely, who were determined not to tolerate any system that refused to recognize the plain facts about the contemporary distribution of power.

When that process was completed, the dominant objective of the great powers in the new system was not to attempt to seize advantages in respect of each other, but to defend the position in which they now jointly found themselves. What threatened that position was no longer the possible ambitions of any one power, but the possible consequences of any renewed spread of revolutionary ideology which seemed so clearly to have been the cause of the preceding struggle. Against this possibility what was wanted was a mechanism through which to organize a co-operative management of the international system, and for that purpose, the existing machinery of diplomacy was inadequate. It was simply not equipped to express a common objective or a shared international authority, and unless a suitable modification or extension of its functions could be developed, the powers would remain frustrated in their general intentions.

The diplomatic innovation which was to supply the deficiency emerged in the form of the peacetime conference. It was partly a modification of past practice about peace congresses, and partly the product of experience gained during the last stages of the war against Napoleon. There were two problems about the traditional peace congress which needed to be solved before it could be adapted to serve new purposes: the stultifying arguments about precedence and procedure on which seventeenth-century diplomacy had thrived, and the restriction of business to matters concerned with the termination of an existing, or imminently threatened conflict.

The first problem was largely dealt with during the eighteenth century, mainly because the more advanced style of diplomacy and the more precise management of policy through foreign ministries created an international system which was less and less prepared to tolerate the interminable delays which wrangling over procedure involved. The Peace of Westphalia of 1648, which had brought the Thirty Years War to an end, had taken seven years to conclude and had involved two separate congresses, at Münster and Osnabrück, partly in order to circumvent some of the arguments about procedure which would have followed from having the French and the Swedish at the same meeting.[74] Another potent source of delay arose out of the use of a mediator, to whom written submissions had to be made, whether in Latin or French being another rich cause of argument. By 1660, at the Congress of Oliva, the mediator achieved agreement that verbal discussion might be allowed, but the decision as to which method to employ continued to raise disputes for many years.[75] At the Congress of Ryswyck in 1697, where the neutral round table was first used, it was decided to hold formal discussions of written submissions on Wednesdays and Saturdays, while Mondays and Thursdays were set aside for verbal discussions, informally held at the Hague.[76] Ryswyck was also an example of the efficacy of parallel but private negotiations. As one French commentator observed:

> The meetings at Ryswick were only the ghost of a congress, where the plenipotentiaries were largely free of negotiations, since the conditions of peace with the King of England were discussed and settled at the four meetings which were held at Hall near Brussels between Lord Bentinck and Marshal Boufflers from July 8 to August 2, 1697.[77]

Two years later at the Congress of Carlowitz, at which an important stage in the relative decline of the Ottoman Empire *vis à vis* Russia and Austria was formalized, not only were extraordinary physical measures taken to reduce the possibility of procedural disputes arising, but it was decided after the first formal session to abandon strict diplomatic ceremony, and the proceedings remained informal until the treaties were actually signed in January 1700.[78] At the Congress of Utrecht, 1712–13, no formal session took place at all for the signature of the treaties, and no mediator was appointed and no discussion of the validity of the full powers – hitherto a most fruitful source of argument – occurred, the documents simply being handed to the, Dutch, congress secretary. The congress did collapse as a result of another faithful irritant: the question of whether written or verbal submissions should be made.[79] As the eighteenth century proceeded, despite these reductions in the size of the potential battlefield of procedure, there was a growing tendency for congresses to break down, or to meet in so sketchy a way as not to be congresses at all. The Congress of Aix-la-Chapelle of 1748 was an example of this, where the techniques of ordinary diplomacy were employed, and the single French delegate brought with him from Paris a foreign ministry official whose speciality was drafting.[80] By 1779, when the Congress of Teschen was bringing the war of the Bavarian Succession to an end, its role was restricted, at the suggestion of Catherine the Great of Russia, purely to the ratification of previously negotiated terms, all formalities and etiquette being specifically abandoned.

By the end of the eighteenth century, it was clear that the congress in its old form had been relegated to the sidelines of a diplomatic system which had become much more complete and sophisticated. It was still thought to be the usual way of marking, and to some degree enabling, the termination of warfare; but it was no longer providing the moving parts for a mechanism which would otherwise lack them; nor was it acting as a barometer of relative power and influence. It was significant that the last attempt to use procedural differences for political gain occurred very close to the birth of the new style of conference and was accurately estimated for what it was, and dismissed as anachronistic. The Congress of Prague in 1813 might have marked an important moment on the road to a settlement with Napoleon, as fortune turned against him after his return from Russia. But he wished to fight on to the end, believing that his position in France depended on doing so, and he prevented any serious discussion of terms at Prague by allowing a deadlock to develop on the old question of whether to proceed by discussions leading to agreed minutes, or to communicate entirely in writing through a mediator.[81] Thus, by the time he was finally or almost finally defeated, there was little left of the traditional congress except the notion that there would have to be some kind of congress to ratify the treaty that would bring the Napoleonic Wars to an end. Exactly what kind of congress it would be was determined by the immediate experience that the great powers had accumulated during the period of the last coalition against Napoleon, an experience that had effectively begun with the arrival of Robert Stewart, Lord Castlereagh, British foreign secretary, at Basel in January 1814, where he joined other ministers representing the combined great powers.

The reason for this hitherto unimaginable journey was to be found in Napoleon's declining fortunes. After the Battle of the Nations at Leipzig in 1813, it was generally thought likely that Napoleon would seek some kind of settlement with his enemies. Indeed, it seemed clear that the sooner he did so, the more favourable a settlement he would be likely to obtain. Since an approach from him therefore seemed more or less immediately probable, the British Cabinet spent part of the Christmas holiday of 1813 discussing how to avoid being unavoidably absent from such discussions when they began and what their position ought to be. It was decided to send the foreign secretary himself on a mission to Europe, equipped with instructions, and to give him eight weeks' leave for the purpose. Napoleon did not behave as anticipated, and put on a display of generalship under pressure that has been the admiration of strategists ever since. The war continued, the stresses on the coalition both political and military continued, and the assembled group of ministers followed the ebb and flow of the front line during one of the worst winters in European history in circumstances of extreme discomfort.

Because it was the inevitable strains on the coalition that dominated the situation rather than any attempt of Napoleon to sue for peace, the efforts of the allied ministers were much devoted to anticipating or repairing breaches in the alliance, and they became a kind of mobile conference, constantly in session. Castlereagh himself had foreseen the necessity for such a 'cabinet' of the great powers. While travelling to Basel in January, 1814, he had said to a companion, that:

> One of the great difficulties which he expected to encounter in the approaching negotiations would arise from the want of an habitual confidential and free intercourse between the Ministers of the Great Powers *as a body*; and that many of the pretensions might be modified, asperities removed, and the causes of irritation anticipated and met, by bringing the respective parties into unrestricted communications common to them all, and embracing in confidential and united discussions all the great points in which they were severally interested.[82]

Metternich, despite his suspicions both of Prussia and Tsar Alexander of Russia, whose eccentricities were yet to reach their height, soon sensed that Castlereagh's arrival had created a new situation. He wrote that the mission was without precedent and that Basel had become a world centre.[83] At the end of January just such a crisis within the coalition as Castlereagh had predicted duly occurred, caused partly by slow communication between the allies and the British ambassador at Vienna, Lord Aberdeen. Castlereagh described in a circular to his colleagues how it was resolved:

> It is impossible to have resided at allied headquarters even for the short period I have myself passed at them without perceiving how much the interests of the confederacy are exposed to prejudice and disunion from the want of some central council of deliberation, where the authorised ministers of the respective powers may discuss face to face the measures in progress, and prepare a result for the consideration of their respective sovereigns. You must all be aware how deep was the distrust and alarm which existed some days ago as to supposed divergencies of opinion, which it was feared were irreconcilable in themselves, and how soon these differences disappeared when the allied ministers were ordered officially to enter upon their discussion.

To such a degree did this happen, that every individual question which they were called upon to deliberate has been decided, not only unanimously, but with cordial concurrence.[84]

The next crisis occurred at Châtillon, where the allies had become involved in some rather desultory discussions with the French which had been terminated when the Tsar decided that Paris would shortly fall, when the French people could be asked what domestic political future they wanted. Castlereagh and Metternich went at once to the military headquarters to rescue what unity they could following this headstrong divergence. The procedure was evidently becoming familiar as well as successful, for Stadion reported to Metternich after Castlereagh's departure that he 'appeared decided . . . to treat of the objects which cause his return *only* in conferences of the four ministers'.[85] What had been desirable in January had become compulsory by March.

The end for Napoleon had arrived, and the problems of the allies became the problems of peacemaking: what to do with France, how to rearrange the map of Europe, particularly in Germany and Italy, how to revive Poland but, above all, how to achieve a lasting security. Over all these matters the allies were clear about only one thing: they were to be resolved by a continuation of the process that had held the alliance together since January. There would be a congress to confirm the treaties of peace, but it would be given an agenda agreed by the great powers and it was not intended that it should meet until they had also agreed what the results should be. They made peace with France and installed a restored regime, but left all substantive matters for later discussion. They held off attempts by both France and Sweden to protect the position of the smaller powers.

In October 1814, Metternich, for whom all these unfamiliar waters required a chart, published a newspaper article in which he gave the most interesting contemporary definition of what was happening:

> It does not require any great political insight to see that this Congress could not model itself on any predecessor. Previous meetings which have been called Congresses have confined themselves to making treaties of peace between parties which either were at war or ready to go to war. This time the treaty of peace is already made, and the parties are meeting as friends, not necessarily having the same interests, who wish to work together to complete and affirm the existing treaty. The matters to be negotiated are a multifarious list of questions, in some cases partly settled by previous discussions, in other cases, as yet untouched. The powers which made the Treaty of Paris will determine the meaning which they wish to attach to the word Congress, and will also decide the form which would seem most appropriate for reaching the goals they have set themselves. They will use this right of determination equally to the advantage of the interested parties, and thus

to the good of Europe as a whole, and the plenipotentiaries at Vienna will deal with matters in the most efficient, prompt and confidential way. Thus the Congress is brought into being of itself, without having received any formal authority, there being no source which could have given any.[86]

The Congress of Vienna was thus the point at which the older tradition, which expected peace to be made by a congress, was joined to the newer experience, which had rejected the rigid procedures of the past and exchanged them for a more flexible conception of the role of a meeting of the great powers.

What did not, however, become clear until after the battle of Waterloo and the need to make a second peace treaty with France in November 1815, was that the newly designed conference was to become the master institution of classical diplomacy in the concert of Europe. This development occurred more or less by default. To begin with it had been assumed that the protection of the international arrangements agreed at Vienna and with them protection from any resumption of the threat posed by revolution and particularly revolution in France, would be ensured by a special Treaty of General Guarantee. Such a treaty, though drafted many times, was never signed. This was not so much because of the obvious frailties of such a mechanism, but more because the Tsar had had a highly eccentric notion of his own, or more likely of his current mistress, which he preferred. This notion became the Holy Alliance.[87] This alliance was in fact a very short treaty of breathtaking naivety, signed amidst a good deal of covert giggling, stating that the signatories being Christian rulers would behave as such in their dealings with each other, and in particular therefore would support each other. Later, this treaty was to be regarded as the engine of autocracy and conservatism in foreign policy on the part of the Russian and Austrian Empires and Prussia; but that was not its intention in 1815, when it was to provide a better substitute for the Treaty of General Guarantee. Even if this had not been so, Castlereagh was becoming clear that the more time passed since the defeat of Napoleon, the less the British Parliament was likely to accept an obligation to intervene militarily in Europe to defend the Vienna settlement.

Like the US Congress in 1920, the House of Commons tended to regard the fruits of victory as bringing freedom from the need to fight in Europe for the general good and a return to the peaceful propagation of national commercial interests. The result was that the powers had decided that they wished to defend the settlement they had put together and to do so for the forseeable future, but that they had not found a way of expressing how they were going to do it.

In the emergency of the moment, when renewing the alliance in case of any further French adventurism as an accompaniment to the second Treaty of Paris of 20 November, 1815, they inserted a clause which represented a distillation of their recent experience of the effectiveness of great power conferences, and intended it to fill the gap between wish and fulfilment.[88] In doing so, they added to the permanent armoury of diplomatic method, a new weapon which for the first time gave it the ability to express the wish of rulers and governments to share international authority and provided the opportunity for a continuous management of the international system. It was a highly significant institutional change and it implied another of equal but highly political importance: those who had the greater power now accepted greater obligations. Machiavelli would have supposed that the reverse was true.

It was not to be expected, however, that such an innovation would function smoothly from the outset. It was for example, unlikely that the swiftly changing pr...   would permit the great powers to remain united,   highly conservative position, based on a particu...   'oly Alliance, brought about a division after 182(...   ...itable stress that fell on any arrangement mad...   ...r war purposes, when it was projected into a pe...   ...owers stick to their intentions without the incent...   ...and claims of Napoleon, or, once time had bro...   warfare, even the threat of revolution? Perhap...   ...on was not so much whether these factors woul...   ...ener that effect would be to destroy or to modify what had been added to the mechanism of diplomacy. The first phase of the post-1815 diplomatic system, the 'old diplomacy', was to yield the answer.

PART II

FROM 1815 TO THE PRESENT

4

THE 'OLD DIPLOMACY'

Transactions are nowadays delayed by hindrances of which previously
we were free. Yesterday it was only a question of material interests, of
an increase in territory or commerce; now one deals with moral
interests; the principles of social order figure in dispatches . . .

(Vicomte de Chateaubriand)[1]

We diplomats of the old days who were trained by Bismarck lived by
the maxim that the relation of courts to one another was of decisive
importance . . . Nowadays it is different.

(Count Anton von Monts)[2]

Diplomacy never was quite what it used to be. Ambassadorial memoirs
almost invariably relate the profound changes that their authors claim to
have witnessed in its methods, style and content. Allowance has to be made
for altered perspectives. The world perceived by a diplomat at the end of
his career is bound to seem a very different place from that which he knew,
or thought he knew, when as an attaché or junior clerk he transcribed and
translated the correspondence of his elders. Elements of continuity, both
in the manner and substance of negotiation, are in consequence sometimes
too easily overlooked. Nevertheless, it is probably fair to say that during the
100 years which followed the Napoleonic Wars there evolved in Europe a
system of international intercourse which was unique in the history of
diplomacy. Already by the end of the eighteenth century most European
states possessed specialized departments and ministries for the management of foreign policy. The Congress of Vienna of 1814–15 provided an
opportunity for the revision and regulation of established diplomatic
practices. And from then until the outbreak of the First World War five or
six great powers dominated the affairs of the continent. The result was an
orderliness in the conduct of international politics which was more than
superficial, and which in a later age, when so much appeared so new, was
designated the 'old diplomacy'.

During the years between the world wars ex-ambassadors were inclined
to look back nostalgically upon what seemed like the golden age of the

career diplomat. The nineteenth century did indeed witness the gradual professionalization of diplomacy. The emergence of the modern state with its centralized and complex bureaucratic structures led to the creation of foreign services with regular career patterns and rules governing such matters as recruitment, education, promotion, retirement, pay and pensions. The distinction between those who determined and those who executed foreign policy was often blurred, and the duties of home-based officials were more usually clerical than advisory. But the standards set by governments for admission to the profession, and its aristocratic ethos, ensured that diplomacy retained at least the aura of a socially exclusive occupation. In the great capitals of Europe, and especially in those with a flourishing court life, the *corps diplomatiques* formed an important component of society. Impressive buildings were acquired to house embassies and legations, and foreign ministries were provided with new and extended offices to enable them to cope with expanding workloads. The old diplomacy had also to adjust to technological advances and changes in economic, political and social circumstances. Railways, steamships and electric telegraphy revolutionized communications; the commercial and financial problems of industrializing societies helped define policy objectives; and relations amongst the powers were increasingly affected by developments in Africa and Asia. Diplomacy remained, however, a function of the states system it served, and during the post-Napoleonic era its form and procedures were in part determined by the readiness of statesmen to subscribe to the notion of a concert of Europe.

THE EUROPEAN CONCERT: USING CONFERENCES IN PEACETIME

The term 'concert' was derived from the Italian 'concerto', and since the sixteenth century had, when applied to diplomacy, embraced the idea of states acting in accord or harmony. But during the struggle against the hegemony of imperial France the word acquired a new connotation. Napoleon's opponents began to associate it with the prospect of a continuing allied coalition, not just for the achievement of victory, but for the containment of revolution, the maintenance of peace and the re-establishment of what was referred to as a 'general system of public law in Europe'. As has been seen in the previous chapter, the peacetime conference subsequently emerged as its clearest manifestation. In the past, international congresses had only assembled to terminate hostilities and had suffered from stultifying arguments over precedents and procedures. But with Napoleon's defeat in prospect, coalition leaders sought to assure their unity of purpose, and the presence at allied headquarters of the crowned heads of Austria, Prussia and Russia and their chief ministers constituted what amounted to a mobile summit conference. This in itself was a break with tradition for, although Napoleon had negotiated with Tsar Alexander at Tilsit, such meetings between reigning monarchs had previously been rare. It nevertheless facilitated the early resolution of questions which might otherwise have divided the coalition. Lord Castlereagh, the British foreign secretary, who joined the Allied ministers at Basle in January 1814, welcomed the opportunity for direct personal contact at this level. The Prince von Metternich, his Austrian counterpart, was similarly impressed. And when in March Austria, Great Britain, Prussia and Russia concluded a quadruple alliance treaty at Chaumont they agreed to guarantee the eventual peace settlement and 'to concert together on the conclusion of a peace with France, as to the means best adapted' to secure this end.[3] They thereby effectively arrogated to themselves the right to concert together in the name of Europe.

On 30 May 1814 the same four powers and their *sous-alliés* Portugal, Spain and Sweden, signed the first Treaty of Paris with a defeated France. The treaty, besides reducing France to her frontiers of 1792, made provision for the congress which assembled at Vienna in the following autumn. This too was a diplomatic innovation for, as Metternich explained, its purpose, unlike that of previous congresses, was not simply to make peace, but to affirm and complete an existing treaty. Yet of much more significance for the conduct of international politics were the procedural decisions of the allies, and in particular the distinction which they began to make between the greater and lesser powers. A secret article attached to the Paris Treaty obliged the French to accept that the disposal of the lands they had surrendered and the 'relations from whence a system of real and permanent Balance of Power in Europe [was] to be derived' should be regulated according to principles determined by the four major allies.[4] Then in September informal consultations amongst Castlereagh, Metternich, von Hardenberg, the Prussian chancellor, and Nesselrode, the Russian state secretary, resulted in an agreement that the directing cabinet of the congress should be composed of the six 'Powers of the first order'.[5] These included the four Chaumont Allies, France, and, as a matter of courtesy, Spain. Talleyrand, who was once more France's foreign minister, was less than enamoured with arrangements which still reserved to the allies the right to have the last word on territorial issues, and after his arrival in Vienna he insisted that all eight signatories of the Paris Treaty should participate in a committee to co-ordinate the workings of the congress. Nevertheless, the net result of his diplomatic manoeuvering was not to undermine the great power concert at Vienna, but to ensure that France was a party to it. In January 1815, after a quarrel over Poland had brought the allies to the verge of war, France was admitted to their counsels in what became the Committee of Five.

The five powers were to meet on forty-one occasions and, in the words of Professor Webster, 'represented the force that governed Europe'.[6] Indeed, despite the presence in Vienna of the heads of 221 royal and princely houses, the main business of the congress remained firmly in the grasp of a great power oligarchy which reflected an actual, rather than a theoretical, distribution of strength and resources. Prolonged squabbling over ancient rights of precedence, such as had inhibited negotiations amongst principals in the past, was thus averted. Even in the special committees which handled much of the detailed work of the congress it was the plenipotentiaries of the great powers who predominated. It was they who were primarily responsible for redrawing the map of Europe. Only in the German Committee, which was concerned with the constitutional framework of the proposed Germanic Confederation or Bund, were smaller states in the majority. But the German Committee was organized independently, and its connection with the Committee of Five was limited to the incorporation of eleven of the articles it drafted in the congress's final act: a process which in effect set the seal of the great powers on the new order in central Europe.

The final act, which was signed on 9 June, 1815, was not, as Castlereagh had once hoped, linked with a great power guarantee of the new status quo. Nevertheless, Napoleon's escape from his exile on Elba raised again the spectre of a Europe threatened by war and revolution, and in the aftermath of Waterloo the victors re-examined the means for upholding their hard-won peace. It was in these circumstances that in September 1815 the Tsar induced the bemused and embarrassed rulers of Austria and Prussia to accede to his Holy Alliance treaty. By it the three monarchs, guided by 'the precepts of Justice, Christian Charity and Peace', agreed to remain united by 'the bonds of a true and indissoluble fraternity, and considering each other as fellow countrymen, . . . [to] lend each other aid and assistance'.[7] The declaration, which Castlereagh dismissed as a 'piece of sublime mysticism and nonsense',[8] seemed both to echo the aspirations of a long-lost Christendom and to herald the specious rhetoric of future ideological alignments. Other Christian princes were eventually persuaded to subscribe to its terms. But of more immediate importance for great power co-operation was the conclusion on 20 November of a second peace treaty with France and the renewal and revision of the quadruple alliance. Article VI of the latter provided for meetings at fixed periods of the four allied sovereigns or their ministers

> for the purpose of consulting upon their common interests, and for the consideration of the measures which at each of these periods shall be considered the most salutary for the repose and prosperity of Nations, and for the maintenance of the Peace of Europe.[9]

A new weapon was thereby added to the permanent armoury of diplomatic method and a formal basis established for subsequent great power congresses at Aix-la-Chapelle (1818), Troppau (1820), Laibach (1821) and Verona (1822).

During the next seven years these gatherings were the most visible aspect of the newly emergent concert. But they hardly constituted a 'congress system'. They did not meet at regular intervals, participation in them was not restricted to the sovereigns and ministers of the great powers, and their assembly usually followed long and arduous diplomatic preparations, which in the case of the Congress of Verona involved a prior conference at Vienna. There was, in any event, no commonly accepted understanding of the implications of their remit. The Congress of Aix-la-Chapelle, the only one attended by a British foreign secretary, allowed the allies to wind up their military occupation of France, and led to her re-admission to their conclaves. Anglo-Russian rivalry and differences amongst the allies over the way in which they should react to insurrections in the Balkans, the Italian states and Spain, were, however, to impede further co-operation. Castlereagh rejected the Russian view that the corporate responsibility of the great powers for the territorial status quo extended to the protection of the restored political and social order, and Britain and France sent only observers to the meetings at Troppau and Laibach, which considered the risings in Italy. Moreover, the decision reached at Troppau to send an Austrian army to Naples on behalf of the Holy Alliance simply confused the issue as to whence the congresses derived their mandate. The Congress of Verona, which assembled in the autumn of 1822, did little to resolve these problems. Whilst it was a glittering assembly of European royalty, its sanctioning, against British wishes, of a French military intervention in Spain demonstrated the absence of that allied unity which the congresses had once been intended to proclaim.

Congress diplomacy, like the conference diplomacy of the early 1920s, had its origins in a wartime coalition, and came to depend very largely upon the individuals involved and their relations with each other. It was a method which particularly suited Metternich, an experienced and gifted diplomat, who was usually able to utilize his friendships with foreign sovereigns and statesmen to Austria's advantage. In discussions between ministers, Metternich remarked, the 'tongue becomes looser, the heart opens, and the need to make oneself understood sometimes outweighs the dictates of a cold hard calculation'.[10] But the congresses failed to provide a satisfactory mechanism for reconciling the conflicting interests of the great powers, and although Metternich remained a devotee of personal diplomacy, after 1822 he displayed less enthusiasm for continuing the process. He was certainly in no mood to accept the proposal made by the Tsar in 1823 for a congress at St Petersburg to discuss the revolt of the Greeks against their Turkish overlords. Without a preliminary accord amongst the powers he doubted if much could be achieved by such a gathering. George Canning, Castlereagh's successor as British foreign secretary, was even more averse to becoming embroiled in further congresses. Nevertheless, despite the gulf which seemed sometimes to separate the conservative autocracies of Austria, Prussia and Russia, from the constitutional, and after 1830 increasingly liberal, monarchies of Britain and France, the great powers continued to adhere to the notion of a European concert. Ambassadorial conferences, rather than ministerial congresses, became the means by which they sought both to regulate the affairs of their smaller and weaker neighbours and to meet the challenges which national revolutions posed to the territorial status quo.

Already in 1816 a standing conference of the ambassadors of the victorious allies had been established at Paris to oversee the application of the peace treaty to France. The French military intervention in Spain led to ambassadorial gatherings at Paris and Madrid, and in June 1824 Russian efforts to promote the idea of a congress on the Near East ended in what was in effect an ambassadors' conference at St Petersburg. Three years later Britain, France and Russia attempted mediation in the Greco-Turkish conflict, with the result that in August 1827 a conference of ambassadors began to meet intermittently in London, and in the following summer the ambassadors of the three powers to Turkey conferred on the Aegean island of Poros. London was also to become the venue for a conference when in 1830 the Belgic provinces of the Netherlands revolted and demanded an end to their fifteen-year union with the Dutch. Under the chairmanship of the British foreign secretary, Lord Palmerston, and composed of the permanent representatives at London of Austria, France, Prussia and Russia, the conference had the tedious task of deciding the fate and frontiers of Belgium. For long periods during the next two years it met several times a week, before going into a lingering suspension until its proposals won general acceptance in 1839. Its exact powers and purposes were in the first instance uncertain. But the conference assumed the right to revise the Vienna settlement, and it endorsed the coercion of the King of the Netherlands when he attempted to resist its rulings. In time its members acquired an *esprit de corps* of their own, and they displayed a remarkable flexibility in helping to preserve the unity of the great powers whilst effecting dynastic and territorial changes.

Other conferences were to follow. For the most part they dealt with specific issues which required urgent attention. Thus in 1852 and 1864 ambassadorial conferences at London wrestled with the intricacies of the Schleswig-Holstein question. In 1853 at Vienna, in 1876 at Constantinople, and in 1912–13 at London, the great powers tried through their ambassadors to achieve some kind of accord on the seemingly intractable problems of the Near East. Indeed, between 1822 and 1914 there were some twenty-six conferences at which all the great powers were represented. At others only three or four of them participated, and when the interests of smaller powers were involved they too were usually represented. There were also two congresses: one at Paris, which followed the ending of the Crimean War in 1856, and another at Berlin, after the Russo-Turkish conflict of

1877–8. Both of these, like previous congresses, differed from mere conferences in as much as they were attended by senior statesmen from three or more of the major powers. Amongst those at Paris were the Austrian, British and French foreign ministers, and the Congress of Berlin included the British prime minister and the chancellors of Germany and Russia. These two gatherings were, however, more akin to the Congress of Vienna than to the congresses of 1818–22. Their prime purpose was the making, rather than the management, of post-war peace settlements. Nevertheless, in the 1850s and 1860s congress diplomacy found a new advocate in the person of the French emperor, Napoleon III. He was attracted by the grandeur and prestige that such assemblies could confer upon the host nation and saw in them an instrument for revising the Vienna Settlement in accordance with French aspirations and the principle of nationality. In November 1863, in the wake of a revolt by Poles against their Russian rulers, and then in May 1866, on the eve of the Austro-Prussian War, he proposed congresses to resolve the chief issues of the day.

Neither of these French initiatives was welcomed by other governments. The trouble was that the successful functioning of the concert of Europe required a degree of consensus amongst the great powers which was rarely present in the years between the outbreak of the Crimean War in 1854 and the conclusion of the Franco-Prussian War in 1871. Within the space of seventeen years Britain and France fought and defeated Russia, and first France, and then Prussia, waged war against Austria before fighting each other. A new kingdom of Italy emerged under the leadership of Piedmont-Sardinia, a new German Empire was founded in which Prussia was the dominant force, and Austria, excluded from both Germany and Italy, transformed itself into the dual monarchy of Austria-Hungary. Moreover, most of this was accomplished without any reference to a real, or supposed, European concert. The assumption that territorial changes required the assent of the great powers was suspended, and only revived again when the reconstruction of Europe was practically complete. Thus in March 1871, by the London protocol the six great powers Austria-Hungary, France, Germany, Great Britain, Italy and Russia re-affirmed that treaties could only be changed with the consent of all their signatories. Henceforth, however, peace in Europe seemed to depend more upon armed might than upon co-operation amongst the great powers, and diplomats were increasingly engaged in building alliances to deter potential enemies and to ensure military superiority in the event of war.

The new nationalisms in Europe bred new imperialisms in Africa and Asia, and this was reflected in the subject matter of diplomacy. Conferences at Madrid in 1880 and Algeçiras in 1906 dealt with questions pertaining to Morocco, and at Berlin in 1884–5 the representatives of the powers considered the future of west Africa and the Congo basin. Moreover, participation in these conferences was not restricted to European states. In

1823 Metternich had rejected the idea of inviting the United States to join in a congress to consider the revolutions against Spanish rule in Latin America. He insisted that while the purpose of the congresses was the preservation of peace, the legitimate order, and 'the material and spiritual well-being of the great European family',[11] the interests of the United States were those of commerce and political aggrandizement. But by 1880 relations amongst the European powers were being conducted upon a world stage, and it would hardly take a Marxist historian to demonstrate that commercial interests counted for more than dynastic legitimacy in Africa's partition. The Madrid Conference was in any case concerned with the 'protection' granted by foreign consuls and diplomats to subjects of the Sultan of Morocco, and all powers with representatives at Tangier, including the United States and Brazil, were therefore invited to take part. Later at Berlin and Algeciras the United States was again able to make its own peculiar contribution to the diplomacy of imperialism. The world had grown smaller, and neither the states system nor its values could any longer be confined to the 'great European family'.

Apart from the question of who were to be the participants, two other issues had to be settled before a conference or congress could assemble: first, what it was to discuss; and second, where it was to be held. The choice of one city rather than another could have political and symbolic implications. Custom required that conferences should be chaired by the chief delegate of the host country, and, in so far as a chairman could influence procedure, this could be of obvious advantage. Metternich was certainly fortunate in being able to ensure that the Congresses of Vienna, Troppau, Laibach and Verona, all took place on what was then Austrian soil. Moreover, just as the convening of a congress at Paris in 1856 seemed to demonstrate that France had regained a position of strength in Europe, so the summoning of a congress at Berlin in 1878 was indicative of the transformation which Prussia's victories had wrought in the continental balance of power. Vienna, Paris and Berlin were each in their turn to be briefly the diplomatic and social capitals of Europe. On the other hand, conferences in small provincial towns afforded delegates ample opportunity to come to know each other better. Troppau, the capital of Austrian Silesia, had few distractions to offer its guests in the icy autumn of 1820, and long tea-drinking sessions with Tsar Alexander allowed Metternich to make good use of his persuasive talents. Likewise, Algeciras, the Andalusian port just opposite Gibraltar, could provide its diplomatic visitors with no more amusement than the slaughtering of a few wretched bulls at a corrida, and a cinema performance which so scandalized the Moorish delegates as to leave them 'more than ever perplexed regarding the merits of European civilization'.[12] But the sheer monotony of the meals served at the Hôtel Reina Cristina, where most of the delegates were lodged, did at least provide its participants with a common grievance. And, despite the widely held view that a good cook was an asset in negotiation, at Algeçiras it was apparent that even a poor one could achieve unity of spirit.

A conference's success was, however, more than likely to depend upon its agenda. This was particularly the case when the interests of the great powers were directly involved. 'Conferences and Congresses are no good', observed the British foreign secretary in 1895, 'unless everyone agrees in advance what they are to accomplish'.[13] There was, after all, little to be said for holding a conference if there were no prospect of agreement, and few diplomats or statesman were prepared to run the risk of isolation and public humiliation. Yet it could take months of negotiation before an understanding was reached on the subjects with which a conference should, or should not, attempt to deal. In the spring of 1878 both Britain and Russia were prepared to accept a congress on the Near East, but the two countries were to come close to war before finally settling on an agenda. And by the time the Berlin Congress assembled in June, accords had already been reached on most of the contentious issues. Then in 1905 the Germans only succeeded in overcoming French opposition to an international conference on Morocco by first accepting France's special interest in the country. Indeed, there was perhaps in this instance an element of truth in the argument employed by one French diplomat that a conference would be dangerous if there were no previous understanding, and pointless if there already were one. Gatherings like that at Algeçiras could all too easily publicize and dramatize issues that might otherwise have been settled through the quiet and patient processes of bilateral negotiation.

When the great powers were disposed to co-operate, conference diplomacy could of course alleviate local tensions. This was also a function of the one permanent diplomatic assembly to result from the Vienna settlement of 1815, namely the diet of the Germanic Confederation (*Deutscher Bund*). Defined by its members as 'a collective Power', the confederation's purpose was the maintenance of the external and internal security of a politically fragmented Germany. Since, however, it was composed of over thirty sovereign states and free towns, including the German, Czech and Slovene lands of Austria, all but the most easterly provinces of Prussia, and such tiny polities as Schaumburg-Lippe and Schwarzburg-Sonderhausen, it might equally well be regarded as what in modern parlance is termed a regional organization. The Diet, over which Austria presided, had its seat at Frankfurt-am-Main, and was made up of an ordinary assembly of seventeen plenipotentiaries (the smaller states being grouped in six *curiae* for voting purposes) and a general assembly or plenum. But the functions of the latter, in which votes were distributed roughly in proportion to the population size of its members, were restricted to deciding, rather than deliberating, on constitutional issues and questions of war and peace, and it met on only sixteen occasions in the entire life of the *Bund*.

In this form the Diet responded more to the particularist tendencies of the sovereigns of the new and restored kingdoms and principalities of Germany than to the aspirations of those who hankered after national unity. Its members, whose number initially included the British, Danish and Dutch kings in their capacity as German rulers, while maintaining representatives in each other's capitals and in some instances abroad, sent their envoys to Frankfurt to participate in what was essentially an ambassadorial congress. Ministers of other European powers were likewise accredited to the Diet. But although it acted as an arbitrator in intra-German disputes, legislated against freedom of expression, and sanctioned armed intervention in states threatened by revolution, its record in other respects was hardly impressive. The Diet's attempt to create a federal army was near farcical; it failed to promote either a uniform system of law or freer trade in Germany; and it was a prey to an Austro-Prussian rivalry which ultimately ended in war and the *Bund's* dissolution in 1866. Scorned by liberals and nationalists, who saw it as an instrument of reaction, it nevertheless provided an early example of diplomats engaged in a quasigovernmental role. It was also as Prussian envoy to the Diet that the future German chancellor, Otto von Bismarck, earned his diplomatic spurs.

BUREAUCRACIES AND DIPLOMATS

Bismarck's appointment to Frankfurt in 1851 was by Prussian standards an unusual one. Although he possessed parliamentary skills, which he used to great effect in his verbal duelling with the Austrian delegate, Bismarck was at the time of his nomination wholly without diplomatic experience. Indeed, during his first two months at Frankfurt the legation was formally headed by the Prussian minister at St Petersburg, whose job it was to show the newcomer the ropes. Yet, Prussia set great store by the professional expertise of its officials. Napoleon's triumphs in Germany had been followed by an era of civil and administrative rejuvenation in Berlin, one result of which was the creation of an autonomous foreign ministry. By 1819, when the ministry was moved to Wilhelmstrasse 76, an address which was to become synonymous with the makers of Prussian, and later German, foreign policy, its political and commercial divisions had been established. And with the addition of a legal division it acquired an administrative form which was to last for more than a century. Admission to a diplomatic career was normally by examination. According to regulations laid down in 1827 and amplified in 1842, candidates had (1) to have completed three years at university; (2) to have passed the two first examinations required by the state civil service; and (3) to have served for eighteen months in provincial government. If then selected by the minister, they had to work for a year as unpaid attachés before sitting further examinations in modern political history, commerce and law, and oral and written tests in French, failure in which could mean exclusion from the service.

Other countries were similarly engaged in the professionalization of their diplomacy and the institutionalization of its management. In France the revolution had transformed the *ancien régime*'s secretariat of state for foreign affairs into a ministry for external relations, and, despite the administrative turmoil of these years, the department's authority was confirmed and expanded. Executive orders issued by the Directory and Napoleon gave it sole jurisdiction over official foreign correspondence, and the consular service was brought under its auspices. By the end of the First Empire the ministry occupied two substantial buildings and employed about seventy officials. Plans had even been made for the construction of a new and more grandiose foreign ministry on the left bank of the Seine. But it was not until September 1853, by which time Napoleon's nephew, Napoleon III, had assumed the imperial title, that the department moved to its present purpose-built quarters on the Quai d'Orsay. The renamed ministry of foreign affairs had by then undergone several changes in its organizational structure. In 1814 the restored monarchy had inherited a ministry made up of functional and geopolitical divisions. Political affairs were, as under Louis XVI, still the responsibility of divisions for northern and southern Europe (*Nord* and *Midi*), whilst other divisions dealt with accounts, archives, commerce and ciphers. Eleven years later a simpler and more functionally orientated structure was adopted in which the Nord and Midi survived as sections of a single political division.

It was during the restoration period that the office of *directeur politique*, which had first been created in 1792, emerged as a key position within the French foreign ministry. The *directeur* was responsible for supervising the political work of the department and, after the revolution of 1830, he was, in the absence of an under-secretary, to become one of the government's chief advisers on foreign policy. In the meantime, another product of the reforms of 1825, the *cabinet du ministre*, became increasingly important. It served as a sort of personal secretariat of the foreign minister, and since its membership was not restricted to agents and functionaries of the department, it allowed him to seek assistance from elsewhere. A number of technical offices were gradually attached to the cabinet, including those relating to ciphers, the press and personnel, and during the Third Republic it came also to function as an intermediary between ministers, their fellow parliamentarians and their constituents. Indeed, by the end of the century the minister's *chef de cabinet* was often regarded as a rival to the *directeur politique*, and appointment to the cabinet could permit a young diplomat, or even a complete outsider, to rise quickly to a senior position in France's foreign service. Philippe Berthelot, who in 1920 became the secretary-general of the Quai d'Orsay, might never have gained admission to the service had not his father, who was briefly foreign minister during 1895–6, attached him to his cabinet.

Berthelot's success was all the more ironic since, although he possessed impeccable republican credentials, he had failed in his first attempt to secure a diplomatic appointment by examination. Yet set in the context of nineteenth-century French diplomacy his career was hardly extraordinary. Prior to 1877, entrance to the French foreign service had tended to depend more upon patronage than upon academic achievement. At the time of the restoration there seems to have been no generally accepted rule concerning the selection of young diplomats or foreign ministry officials. Good hand-writing was usually specified as an important qualification, but all else appeared to depend on nepotism. Moreover, since most would-be diplomats were chosen by their heads of mission, and not only had to serve long apprenticeships as unpaid attaches, but also had to possess incomes of 6,000 francs per annum, diplomacy remained a noble calling. The revolution of 1830 and the deposition of Charles X, France's last Bourbon king, led some aristocrats to resign their diplomatic posts, but there was little change in methods of recruitment. In fact the Orleanist monarchy took a retrogressive step when it abolished a school for young diplomats, which since the days of the consulate had been attached to the department of archives, and which offered an alternative route to a diplomatic career. It was not until the proclamation of a republic in February 1848 that any fresh attempt was made to transform diplomacy into a profession open to talent. But the establishment of a national school of administration proved to be no more than a temporary experiment, and the foreign ministers of the Second Empire (1852–70) reverted to older practices. Édouard Thouvenel, who was minister in the early 1860s, explicitly rejected the idea of an entrance examination on the grounds that in France 'who says examination says competition'.[14] He nevertheless implemented a measure, first introduced in 1844, which required applicants to have a law degree, and a ministerial report of 1860 proposed that in some circumstances candidates without degrees might be permitted to sit an examination in international law, political history and foreign languages.

Once admitted to the service an unpaid attaché or supernumerary might be appointed either to the ministry in Paris or to a mission in a foreign capital. But above the rank of attaché and below that of *directeur* there was under the Second Empire very little interchange between officials within the central administration and diplomats abroad. Moreover, some 60 per cent of the latter were still drawn from the aristocracy. Their ancient, and not so ancient, titles added lustre to imperial representation and ensured social acceptance in the great courts of Europe. Their family fortunes also provided the private means upon which attachés often had to depend for several years. Until 1858 grades were attached to posts, rather than to persons, and since according to one contemporary witness there were about one hundred unpaid attachés for every vacant salaried position, with promotion slow and frequently haphazard. Only in February 1877 did the then foreign minister, Louis Decazes, yield to republican pressure for a more democratic system and introduce measures aimed both at a more thorough integrating of the functionaries of the Quai d'Orsay with diplomatic and consular agents, and at ensuring that all entrants had to sit an examination. This, however, was a qualifying test. Another three years had to pass before open competition became the norm, and until 1905 it was still necessary for a young entrant to serve for three years in an unpaid capacity. Nevertheless, the republic had triumphed, and despite the persistence of diplomatic dynasties in France, by the early years of the twentieth century a diploma from the *École libre des sciences politiques* counted for more than a noble lineage when it came to the selection of diplomats.

Amongst the several requirements of the Quai d'Orsay was that its agents should be French nationals. This may seem to have been an obvious condition of service. By the 1860s even the multi-national empire of the Habsburgs insisted that its diplomats possess Austrian citizenship. But during the first half of the nineteenth century some governments continued with the earlier custom of seeking out diplomatic skills wherever they could be found. In Prussia, for instance, there was a reversion to this practice, and in the 1830s the known prejudice of the foreign minister, Friedrich von Ancillon, against the local nobility discouraged Bismarck from seeking direct admission to the foreign service. A lack of native talent had likewise led Tsar Alexander I to recruit non-Russian diplomats. At the time of the Congress of Vienna he had in his employ Nesselrode, the son of a Westphalian landowner; Count Pozzo di Borgo, a Corsican refugee; Prince Adam Czartoryski, the head of a great Polish family; and John Capodistrias, a Corfiote who was subsequently to head a Greek republic. Another tsar, Alexander II, was later to offer Bismarck the prospect of a high position in the Russian diplomatic service, and although a chauvinistic backlash eventually curbed the employment of outsiders, the names of Baltic Germans, like Benckendorff and Lamsdorff, were to continue to figure large in tsarist diplomacy.

After 1859 aspiring Russian diplomats had to pass an examination in modern languages, 'diplomatic science' (i.e., international law, economics and statistics), and précis writing. The regulations governing the eligibility of candidates for the Russian civil and foreign services were, however, almost oriental in their inspiration. Nobles were thus admitted 'in personal right' – a provision which may help explain how diplomatic careers seemed sometimes to pass from one generation of a family to another. Also eligible were 'young choristers discharged from the court choir after loss of voice', and the sons of 'men of science or art'. Emancipated peasants, 'persons belonging to the classes liable to taxation' and 'Jews, excepting those who may have degrees in medicine', were on the other hand judged unsuitable for the profession.[15] Such restrictions seem not to have impeded the bureaucratization of Russia's foreign relations. In an attempt to streamline the management of diplomacy an imperial ministry of foreign affairs was founded in 1802. But it was another thirty years before it supplanted Peter the Great's collegiate system. Over 250 officials were in the meanwhile employed in the ministry, and the needs of an expanding empire were met by the creation of provincial branch offices in such cities as Warsaw and Odessa. The result was a large and cumbersome administrative machine which contrasted sharply with the leaner and meaner establishment that served British foreign secretaries.

Business generated by the Revolutionary and Napoleonic Wars had led to a doubling in the number of clerks employed in the British Foreign Office. But in 1822 Canning's department still had a staff of no more than thirty-one, including two under-secretaries (one of whom was effectively permanent), two office keepers, a door porter, and a printer. Moreover, despite an ever-increasing workload, the office grew slowly in size. Even in 1861, when it finally vacated its cramped and labyrinthine premises in Downing Street to await the construction of Gilbert Scott's Italianate edifice in Whitehall, it had in all only fifty-two employees. Most of them had very little, if any, say in the framing of policy. They were there to provide the foreign secretary with clerical assistance in the handling of his correspondence with diplomats and other departments of state. As permanent under-secretary between 1854 and 1873 Edmond Hammond began to fulfil an advisory role, and pressure of work in the 1890s left the assistant under-secretaries with more opportunities for volunteering their opinions on matters political. The junior staff of the office was, nevertheless, very largely engaged in the administrative drudgery of copying, ciphering, distributing, docketing and registering papers. Indeed, the employment of talented young men in essentially mechanical tasks was by the end of the century a persistent cause of complaint. The Foreign Office claimed that its work was so confidential that it could only be done by completely trustworthy staff who were known by, or recommended to, the foreign secretary. It therefore strenuously resisted attempts by the Treasury to introduce copy clerks into its political departments, and not until 1906 were the office's more menial chores delegated to a general registry. This permitted a greater devolution of diplomatic work, and allowed the more precocious junior clerks a greater chance to exercise their intellects.

The modernization of the Foreign Office was accompanied by a reform in its methods of recruitment. In 1855 when the Northcote–Trevelyan report had proposed admission to the civil service by competitive examination, Lord Clarendon, the foreign secretary, had insisted on the Foreign Office's having its own examination. Moreover, he succeeded in retaining the right to nominate candidates (in practice three competing for each vacancy), and the diplomatic service, with its separate and evolving career structure, set different and initially tougher papers. When these two examinations were amalgamated in the early 1890s aspiring attachés were still assessed separately from would-be junior clerks, and it was only in 1905 that the foreign service examination was assimilated with that for the home civil service. Even then, the Foreign Office continued with the practice of nominating candidates. These procedures helped to ensure a homogeneity of the educational, and to a lesser extent social, backgrounds of the newcomers to the service. By the turn of the century the vast majority of entrants came from the major public schools, with Eton predominating, and it was customary for intending applicants to spend some time abroad perfecting their modern languages before attending a cramming establishment to acquire the skills and knowledge to pass the service's examination. A university degree was not a necessity, and between 1871 and 1907 only 38 per cent of foreign service recruits were graduates. Academic standards were, however, raised as a result of the changes of 1905, and during the seven years that preceded the outbreak of war in 1914 all but four of the successful candidates had been to university. Nevertheless, until 1919 budding diplomats were required to have a private income of £400 per annum, and their professional survival depended more upon their family fortunes than the public purse.

This property qualification, the patronage implicit in the system of nominating candidates, and the courtly mannerisms and protocol associated with diplomacy, all helped substantiate the claims of later left-wing critics of the British foreign service that it was an effete and aristocratic body which had imposed its will on popularly elected governments. As with many such generalizations this one contained an element of truth. Between 1815 and 1860 60 per cent of the attachés appointed to British missions were drawn from the aristocracy, and of the twenty-three diplomats made ambassadors in these years only three were commoners. Moreover, although in the following fifty-four years the proportion of aristocrats in the diplomatic service dropped to less than 40 per cent, nineteen of the thirty-one career diplomats who attained ambassadorial rank were of aristocratic origin. Diplomats of noble birth were more acceptable in the courts of Europe, and the great political families of England were usually capable of persuading foreign secretaries to nominate their offspring. Yet, as R.A. Jones has demonstrated, the early Victorian diplomatic service was no more, nor no less, aristocratic than the traditional British political élite as measured by membership of the House of Commons. And even in the period 1860–1914 the seniors of the home civil service were, according to Jones's findings, more aristocratic than those of the diplomatic service. Of greater significance was the fact that at a time when Britain was becoming more democratic and more industrial the diplomatic service failed to attract a greater number of recruits from the new industrial power bases.[16]

This was equally apparent in the foreign services of some of Britain's continental neighbours. Thus, despite the growing industrial might of Imperial Germany and the rigorous examination procedures maintained by the Wilhelmstrasse, German diplomacy in Europe remained firmly in the grasp of the aristocracy. As in other European countries, the requirement that recruits first act as unpaid attachés made financial independence a prerequisite for admission to the service. But in selecting their ambassadors Bismarck and his successors were in any case inclined to place the social graces associated with the nobility above the skills derived from book-learning. After all, in an age when the aristocratic salon could still be a valuable source of information and a locus for political initiatives, it was important that diplomats should be both *salonfähig* (presentable in society) and sufficiently wealthy to wine and dine their peers. The Count von Mensdorff-Pouilly-Dietrichstein, the Austro-Hungarian ambassador in London in the decade before 1914, entertained some 850 persons at his table during 1905 alone. He was also a cousin of King George V. Indeed, such ties of friendship, blood and marriage as linked the noble houses of Europe helped reinforce that sense shared by many diplomats of belonging to a single cosmopolitan fraternity. Nowhere, however, was diplomacy wholly insulated from the influence of the emerging middle classes. Even in 1847 some 27 per cent of the leading positions in the Austrian diplomatic service were occupied by commoners, and by 1918 this figure had risen to 44 per cent. Viennese society was undoubtedly snobbish and its court protocol amongst the most obscure in Europe. Nevertheless, in the last years of the Habsburg monarchy some two-thirds of the staff of the foreign ministry in Vienna's Ballhausplatz were of non-noble origin.

The expansion of diplomacy in terms of both geography and subject matter contributed to a dilution of its aristocratic practitioners. Germany's new missions in the Americas and Asia were, for instance, regarded by the Prussian nobility with disdain, and since the social niceties of Europe counted for little in these remote postings, they were deemed more suitable for the Wilhelmstrasse's bourgeois recruits. Successful middle-class applicants were similarly appointed to vacancies in the office's less illustrious commercial, legal and newly founded colonial divisions. But the composition of Europe's diplomatic services tended in the end to reflect the political structure of the societies they represented. Thus while over 80 per cent of the envoys of the German Empire were of noble descent, in France, where governments were actively engaged in republicanizing national institutions, the incidence of aristocratic appointments fell in period 1903–14 to less than 8 per cent. Diplomatic assignments were given to officials from other public services, journalists and politicians. The brothers Paul and Jules Cambon, who in 1914 were respectively French ambassadors at London and Berlin, had begun their careers in departmental prefectures, and Camille Barrère, who from 1897 to 1924 was France's ambassador at Rome, had once been war correspondent of *The Times*. On the eve of the First World War all of France's ambassadors in Europe were drawn from the *haute bourgeoisie*. Only at the Quai d'Orsay, where Pierre de

Margerie was both *chef de cabinet* and *directeur politique*, did the old order retain a position of authority and distinction.

MISSIONS, RANK AND LANGUAGE

The aristocratic ethos of nineteenth-century diplomacy was in large part derived from the social origins and aspirations of its European practitioners. But their place in the wider international hierarchy was fixed by rules established at the Congress of Vienna. Prior to 1815 there had been no general agreement on diplomatic precedence, and in an attempt to overcome the discord to which this had given rise the congress formed a committee to examine the issues involved. After two months' deliberation it recommended that states should be divided into three classes, and that these should determine the relative positions of their agents. Since, however, such a classification seemed likely to lead to further wrangling, it was eventually decided that precedence amongst diplomats of the same rank should depend upon the seniority of their residence in a particular capital. The *règlement de Vienne* at the same time recognized three categories of diplomats: (1) ambassadors, nuncios and legates; (2) envoys, ministers or other agents accredited to a sovereign; and (3) chargés d'affaires accredited to ministers of foreign affairs. To these was added another category in 1818, i.e., that of ministers-resident, which ranked after envoys and ministers plenipotentiary. And except in those capitals where the papal nuncio was automatically dean or doyen of the *corps diplomatique*, this position was henceforth held by the longest serving ambassador or minister. It was likewise agreed to suppress the *alternat*: the system whereby several different copies of a treaty were prepared so that the signatures of each of the plenipotentiaries appeared at the top of one document. Instead, it was agreed at Vienna that the appending of signatures would be decided by a drawing of lots. Then three years later at the Congress of Aix-la-Chapelle this course was abandoned in favour of a system whereby representatives signed according to the alphabetical order of the French spelling of their country's name.

This was a minor but not insignificant triumph for the use of French in diplomacy. Another had been its employment throughout the Congress of Vienna and then in the drafting of the final act. True, the same act stipulated that this was not intended to set a precedent, and that the powers reserved to themselves the right to adopt in future negotiations and conventions the languages they had previously used. But similar provisions had also appeared in the Treaties of Aix-la-Chapelle (1748), Paris (1763) and Versailles (1783). Moreover, despite the insistence of British foreign secretaries, including Canning and Lords Granville and Palmerston, on the use of English in official correspondence with foreign diplomats and governments, French continued throughout the nineteenth century to occupy a special position in international intercourse. There was in Metternich's opinion a good reason for this: diplomacy required a lingua franca which French quite obviously provided. When in 1817 the British attempted to persuade the Ballhausplatz to accept notes in English, Metternich threatened to reply in German. Several years later he explained that without a generally accepted diplomatic language confusion would prevail, and the whole purpose of the modern practice of establishing permanent missions would be contradicted. 'It would', he observed, 'mean a return to the Constantinople system in which negotiation is carried on only in Turkish and through the agency of a dragoman because the Turks can speak no other language'.[17] The same point was made by other diplomats, and Bismarck was later to recall how his refusal to receive notes in Russian from the Tsar's representative in Berlin led to a mutual understanding that in future their written communications would be in French.

The French naturally regarded the use of their language as more than just an administrative convenience. In the eyes of some it was a measure of their cultural superiority. That indeed was the implication of Jules Cambon's claim that French had become the language of diplomacy on account of the intellectual hegemony that France had exercised over Europe in the seventeenth and eighteenth centuries. More than 100 years after the Congress of Vienna he contended that French possessed an orderliness and a clarity of expression which made it particularly suitable as a vehicle for international relations.[18] The British diplomat, Harold Nicolson, agreed. 'It is impossible', he asserted in 1939, 'to use French correctly without being obliged to place one's ideas in proper order, to develop them in logical sequence, and to use words of almost geometrical accuracy'.[19] Anyone familiar with the impossibility of rendering the subtle but once important distinction between 'British' and 'Britannic' in French, and with the peculiar but useful inexactitude of such expressions as '*en principe*' and '*entente cordiale*', may have good cause to contest this last assertion. But the argument against delivering diplomatic messages in French was probably most forcefully put by Palmerston. In 1851 he informed Britain's minister at Frankfurt that the British government considered that every government was entitled to use its own language in official communications on the grounds that in that way it was certain of giving true expression to its views. He also objected to the practice of providing foreign governments with English and French versions of British notes, since it seemed likely that the French translation would then be treated as the original.

French was not, however, easily toppled from its diplomatic perch. Oral communications between states were usually made in the tongue best understood by the statesmen or diplomats concerned, and as the century wore on the vernacular was increasingly employed in both written communications and bilateral accords. But the custom of drafting multilateral engagements in French persisted. Thus French was the language of the

Paris Congress of 1856 and the treaty that followed from it. Moreover, the Quai d'Orsay staunchly resisted what it regarded as the desire of the Anglo-Saxon powers to achieve for English an at least equal status with French. Britain's commercial and imperial position in the world and the growing involvement of the United States in the affairs of the old continent certainly seemed by the end of the nineteenth century to mark out English as the language of an emerging global states system. The Americans showed little respect for the ceremonial and linguistic traditions of European diplomacy, and in the summer of 1902 French diplomats mounted a concerted effort to prevent the newly assembled machinery for international arbitration at the Hague from adopting English as its official language. Fearful lest this should result from the first case to come before a Hague tribunal, a dispute between Mexico and the United States, France's minister to the Netherlands fought hard and successfully to ensure that the hearings were in French.

Outside Christian Europe and the Americas the question of whether or not to use French was of little relevance to the agents of the great powers. They had in their dealings with the Ottoman, Moorish and Persian courts, and later with those of Abyssinia and east and south-east Asia, to practise Metternich's 'Constantinople system'. In other words, diplomats, if they were not themselves oriental scholars, had to communicate and negotiate through interpreters or dragomans, as they were usually known in the Islamic world. Ever since the seventeenth century French governments had taken in hand the training of linguists for their Levantine missions and consulates, and by 1815 there were schools for *les jeunes de langues* at Paris and Constantinople. By contrast, the British had continued to rely upon locally recruited dragomans. When in 1825 the Foreign Office took charge of the British embassy at Constantinople from the Levant Company, it had an establishment of ten interpreters, four of whom belonged to the hereditary dragoman family of Pisani. The disclosure of secret information was, however, to bring the system into disrepute, and in the 1840s a scheme was introduced which aimed at eventually replacing the native dragomans with British university graduates. It was not a success. The new oriental attachés were, after having learnt Turkish, simply absorbed into the ordinary diplomatic work of the mission, whilst pressure of business necessitated the retention of the Levantine dragomans.

This experiment with professional specialists coincided with the decline of the family embassy. During the first half of the nineteenth century the permanent missions which the powers maintained abroad continued to operate more or less as extended families. Once selected, ambassadors or ministers were paid salaries and certain specific allowances out of which they were expected to meet the living costs of an entire household. And at a time when governments rarely owned embassy or legation buildings, this usually meant renting and furnishing a house, transporting, feeding and lodging staff, and fulfilling such representational duties as the entertainment of foreign statesmen and other dignatories. The size of missions varied according to their importance. British ambassadors, who until the 1860s were still regarded as political appointees and therefore liable to recall with a change of government, were normally provided with at least a secretary, whose primary function was to act as chargé d'affaires when the ambassador was absent, and a paid attaché. During the Restoration period French embassies tended to be a little larger and less informal in their organization. But they too relied upon the services of unpaid attachés. The latter, who were often the workhorses of the chancery and engaged in copying and other clerical chores, were for the most part young men seeking a career in diplomacy. Others simply availed themselves of the opportunity to make headway in society and gain some acquaintance with public service. The experience could be rewarding in more ways than one. Those who served the Vicomte de Chateaubriand during his embassy in London were, for instance, able to sample the cuisine of Montmirel, the most celebrated cook of his era and the inventor of such culinary delights as *filet de boeuf à la Chateaubriand* and *le pudding diplomate*.

Not all French diplomats could afford such hospitality. The revolution had drastically reduced the wealth of the nobility, and in the 1820s ambassadors like the Marquis de Caraman at Vienna were hard pushed to maintain their expensive missions. There was, none the less, no apparent shortage of unpaid attachés. They, like their British counterparts, were still ready to enter a service in which there was no clearly delineated career structure, and in which duties and promotion often seemed to depend upon chance, patronage and ambassadorial whim. Indeed, in an age of administrative and bureaucratic reform and at a time when workload of foreign missions was steadily expanding, the treatment of junior diplomats seemed distinctly anachronistic. Yet it was not until 1858 that France's foreign minister, the Comte de Walewski, insisted upon grading embassy and legation staff. Henceforth, France's diplomatic service had three classes of secretary with a corresponding salary scale and order of promotion, and no one could become a third secretary without having first served for three years as an unpaid attaché or supernumerary at the foreign ministry. Three years later, after a decade of debate and two parliamentary reports relating to pay and conditions in the service, the British adopted a similar grading system. This, along with the introduction of entrance examinations and the depoliticization of senior appointments, went a long way towards completing the professionalization of the British diplomatic service. It also undermined the notion of the embassy as an extended family. The junior staff of British missions were, however, like their equivalents in the Foreign Office, still burdened with a great deal of rudimentary and mechanical work, and it was only after 1904 that funds were made available for archivists and clerical assistance.

The staffing of diplomatic missions was in part determined by their classification, and that in turn reflected the importance which countries attached to specific relationships. After 1876 all the great powers were represented in each other's capitals by ambassadors, and the reciprocal elevation of legations to embassies was associated with the political status of the countries involved. This had not, however, invariably been the case. Prussia, for example, had not a single embassy in 1860. And ten years before the British government had for reasons of economy reduced its tally of embassies to those in Constantinople and Paris, which, as it happened, were the first two cities where it owned embassy buildings, the one having been constructed on land presented by the Ottoman Sultan, and the other having been purchased by the Duke of Wellington. France, on the other hand, still had in 1825 embassies in the capitals of such minor powers as Piedmont, Portugal, Switzerland and the Two Sicilies and, until 1905 it, in common with other Roman Catholic powers, accredited an ambassador to the Holy See at Rome. But it was not until after the conclusion of a commercial treaty with the Prussian-dominated German customs union (*Zollverein*) in 1862 that France consistently maintained an embassy at Berlin. Some missions were, of course, hardly worthy of their titles. Even in 1831 the French foreign ministry classified its embassies at Berne and Naples as second-class missions, and some of the legations and residences which the great powers appointed to the lesser German courts were barely more than glorified consulates. They could nevertheless be useful listening-posts at a time of great political and social upheaval in central Europe.

The diplomatic machinery of some of the smallest of the German states also deserves more attention since it is not without relevance to the micro-state diplomacy of the late twentieth century. The Hanse towns of Bremen, Hamburg and Lübeck thus provide an excellent example of three tiny republics pooling their resources to support a rudimentary diplomatic service. Their external interests were primarily commercial, and although they did not possess, either singularly or collectively, a foreign department, they maintained at their joint expense ministers-resident at Berlin, Copenhagen, London and Paris. Moreover, while Bremen had a minister of its own at Washington, Hamburg likewise had one at Vienna, and all three towns were represented through their *curia* in the Diet at Frankfurt. After the foundation of the new Reich the surviving, but no longer sovereign, German kingdoms and principalities continued to maintain representatives with diplomatic titles at each other's capitals, and the great powers retained resident missions at Munich as well as Berlin and multiply accredited these to the remaining German courts. This, however, was a kind of honorific courtesy diplomacy, useful as a means of gathering information on, and sometimes influencing, public opinion in provincial Germany, but of little other value in relations amongst independent states. The tale of how on one May morning in the late 1900s the British ambassador at Berlin finally discovered the foreign ministry of Oldenburg in a building which his private secretary thought to resemble a 'model cowshed' might be well worth re-telling.[20] Sadly, however, Oldenburg, like the two Mecklenburgs and the Saxon duchies, no longer mattered in an age of *Macht-* and *Weltpolitik.*

THE EXPANSION OF DIPLOMACY

The unification of Germany and Italy simplified the diplomatic map of Europe. But the emergence of new states in the Balkans and Latin America, and the institution of formal and regular contacts between the European governments and some of the ancient monarchies of Africa and Asia, meant that the international network of diplomatic relations continued to expand throughout the nineteenth century. Great Britain had in 1815 nineteen resident diplomatic missions, only two of which, her embassy at Constantinople and her legation at Washington, were in non-European countries. By 1914 there were forty-one British missions abroad, and nineteen of these were outside of Europe. Other major powers experienced a similar increase in their overseas representation. The establishment of diplomatic relations did not, however, always lead to an exchange of ministers or chargés d'affaires. The British consulates in Greece, Serbia, Romania and Bulgaria thus effectively served as diplomatic agencies whilst these lands remained under Ottoman suzerainty. Moreover, although between 1827 and 1842 France appointed legations to Brazil, Mexico, Colombia and Argentina, in their relations with other former Spanish colonies the French simply utilized their existing consulates-general as diplomatic missions, in some instances adding chargé d'affaires to consular titles. Gradually, however, the majority of the latter were upgraded, and by 1905 France had in Latin America twelve ministers-plenipotentiary, two ministers-resident and two permanent chargés d'affaires, with one single legation at Guatemala City covering all five Central American republics.

The new states of the Americas were all countries in which European culture predominated, and such difficulties as arose in the establishment with them of diplomatic relations mainly concerned the legitimacy their governments and the political instability of the region. But in Asia, and to a lesser extent in Africa, the European powers had to deal both with local potentates who were reluctant to open their countries to alien influences, and with political structures and values which could not easily be reconciled with a system based upon the equality of sovereign states and clearly defined territorial frontiers. Thus in the Far East, where Confucian principles required universal acknowledgement of China's superior civilization, the Europeans had to employ their superior military might to secure permanent representation at Peking. And their relations with the rulers of Korea and some of the south-east Asian lands were complicated by the continued existence of a pyramidical political order whose theoretical overlord was the

Manchu Emperor. Such diplomatic contacts as the British had with the Chinese were, in any event, until 1833 in the hands of the East India Company and its Chief Superintendent of Trade. Early attempts by Britain in 1793–4 and 1816–17 to establish diplomatic relations with China on the European model had ended in failure. British envoys were treated as though they were the representatives of a vassal kingdom, and it took two wars before in 1860 the Chinese accepted a resident British mission in Peking and dropped their demand that European diplomats kowtow before the imperial throne.

The French, whose forces fought alongside those of Britain in 1856–8 and 1860, also opened up a legation at Peking, and, as other European powers and the United States followed their example, a diplomatic quarter complete with palatial residences and armed guards developed there. The compound of the British legation alone occupied a full three acres. In the meanwhile the arrival in 1853 of Commodore Matthew Perry and a small squadron of American warships in Yedo bay sufficed to persuade the Japanese to abandon 200 years of relative seclusion and to accept the presence of Western consuls on their soil. A failure on the part of Asian or African rulers to meet the standards set by Europeans in the conduct of international relations sometimes resulted in the exaction of terrible retribution. In 1860 the British responded to the murder of Christian missionaries in China by burning the Emperor's summer palace. Three years later, after the murder of a British merchant in Japan, the Royal Navy opened fire on the provincial capital of Kagoshima, and in 1907 the French took redress for the loss of European lives by bombarding the Moroccan port of Casablanca. But even with gunboats the 'diplomacy of imperialism' could be a precarious business. In Morocco a Spanish consular agent was summarily executed in 1844, and latent hostility towards foreign intruders in Japan led in 1861 to a nocturnal attack upon the newly established British legation at Yedo and the wounding of two of its staff. Then in 1900 occurred one of the best-known assaults upon European notions of diplomatic practice, the fifty-five-day-long siege of the foreign legations at Peking. The culmination of a series of incidents associated with the growth of the anti-Western Boxer movement, the siege, which was conducted with the complicity of the Chinese court, followed the shooting of the German minister to China. It was only lifted after the armed intervention of an international force.

The clash of cultures which was usually associated with the establishment of formal relations between Western and non-Western governments was not invariably accompanied by a clash of arms. Nevertheless, outside of Europe and the Americas those countries which succeeded in retaining their political independence were very often those which most readily adopted European diplomatic methods. Despite the injunctions of the Sharia against dealings with the infidel, Islamic lands such as the Ottoman Empire, Persia and the Barbary states (Morocco and the regencies of Algiers, Tunis and Tripoli) had long had diplomatic relations of a kind with European rulers. There had been permanent foreign missions at Constantinople since the sixteenth century, and in the 1790s the reforming sultan, Selim III, appointed resident embassies at London, Paris, Vienna and Berlin. This experiment with reciprocal diplomacy was admittedly short-lived. Opposition to change, a failure to co-ordinate the work of the embassies, a lack of experienced personnel and a consequent reliance upon the services of Ottoman Greeks, led to its abandonment after the outbreak of the Hellenic struggle for independence. Only in the 1830s when the Empire was again threatened by revolt from within and intervention from without did the Sublime Porte move to establish embassies and legations in the principal capitals of Europe. And the appointment in 1849 of an Ottoman embassy to Tehran constituted part of what was probably the first exchange of permanent diplomatic missions between Muslim states. A rudimentary foreign ministry in the meanwhile emerged from the antiquated Ottoman chancery, and in 1836 the *Reis Effendi*, or chief scribe, was designated foreign minister. The efforts of the Porte to remedy the Empire's ills likewise led to the progressive Westernization of its diplomacy with the increased use of French terminology and modern communications, and in 1856 the Treaty of Paris formally admitted Turkey to the concert of Europe.

The Persians, who received a British resident mission in 1809, relied for far longer than the Turks upon the use of *ad hoc* special missions. It was not until 1862–3, by which time France and Russia had appointed legations to Tehran, that Persia established a permanent mission in London. Even this move was far in advance of anything attempted by the sultans of Morocco. Engaged in seemingly endless conflict with the rebel tribes of the interior, they preferred to communicate with the outside world through their agents at Tangier and the foreign diplomats who resided there. European diplomats occasionally ventured to the sultan's court, but apart from a consul at Gibraltar and the religious head of the Moorish community at Cairo, the only representatives whom the sultans dispatched abroad were special and mainly ceremonial missions, intended more as a weapon of obstruction than a means of enlightenment. Such methods were not, however, to save Morocco from partition in 1912. By contrast the Ottoman Empire, which one Moorish sultan reckoned to have been ruined by the cultivation of relations with foreign powers, persisted until 1922, and Turkey's subsequent survival as an independent nation was in no small measure due to the skilful application of diplomacy.

The reluctance of Morocco's Prince of All Believers to do business with the infidel was matched by the disdain displayed towards the barbarians by the servants of China's Son of Heaven. Envoys of tributary and foreign states had in the past been catered for at Peking, the Chinese court of colonial affairs had handled relations with an ever-expanding Russia, and treaties had customarily been negotiated by provincial governors and generals at imperial outposts. But the notion of solving the barbarian problem by diplomacy was unpopular in China. The presence at Peking of the permanent missions of powers claiming equality of status was a negation of the Emperor's heavenly mandate, and their establishment was quickly followed by fresh demands for indemnities and the opening of ports to foreign trade.

It was to deal with these matters and the wider problem of China's modernization that in 1861 the *Tsungli Yamen* was set up as a temporary body to manage foreign policy. Fourteen years later the murder of a British consular official and pressure from Britain for a formal apology led to the appointment to London of China's first resident mission abroad. The *Tsungli Yamen* was not, however, to become an effective instrument for the centralized administration of foreign relations. Its functions were too diverse, and it was characteristic of the prevailing geographical confusion in Peking that the Chinese minister at Washington should also have been accredited concurrently to Lima and Madrid. In addition, conservative forces worked to make the legations at Peking redundant by restoring diplomatic authority to provincial governors, and after 1870 Li Hung-chang, the powerful Commissioner for the Northern Ocean at Tientsin, virtually usurped the role of the *Tsungli Yamen* in negotiating with other powers. There were also occasions when, as in the settlement of the war with France in 1885, foreign employees were used to represent China in international bargaining. Only in the wake of the Boxer Rebellion, and then at the behest of the occupying powers, did the Chinese replace the *Tsungli Yamen* with a regular foreign ministry.

Amongst the powers which compelled the Chinese to make their diplomacy conform to European standards was their Asian neighbour, Japan. Prior to 1853 its limited contacts with the Dutch and the courts of China and Korea had not necessitated the institution of any separate body concerned exclusively with external affairs. But after the Meiji Restoration of 1867 the island empire moved rapidly towards the creation of a foreign service, and by 1873 Japan had nine overseas legations. Hindered by a shortage of experienced staff, its rulers welcomed the advice of outsiders, such as the American, Henry Willard Denison, who assisted both with the drafting of documents and in negotiation, and in the 1890s they began the work of revising the 'unequal treaties' which the Western states had initially imposed upon them. Moreover, after the Japanese defeat of Russia in the war of 1904–5, Japan's missions in the West and those of the principal Western powers in Tokyo were progressively upgraded to the rank of embassies – a move which immensely enhanced Japan's prestige and in effect meant the international recognition of its new status as a quasi-great power.

In 1894, barely eleven years before the appointment of Japan's first ambassador to Britain, the United States had similarly elevated its legations in London, Paris, Berlin and Rome to the status of embassies. Yet the United States had been ably represented abroad since the earliest days of the Republic. The Continental Congress (1774–89) had sent secret agents to Europe during the War of Independence, and in 1778 Benjamin Franklin, a former colonial agent in London, had been appointed minister-plenipotentiary to France. Foreign relations were in the first place overseen by the Congress's Committee of Secret Correspondence, and then in 1789 the Department of State was formally constituted under the stewardship of Thomas Jefferson. Nevertheless, despite the considerable achievements of United States representatives abroad in winning allies, negotiating trade treaties, and eventually in securing the purchase of Louisiana, diplomacy was widely perceived by Americans as being of little relevance to a nation of free men separated by 3,000 miles of ocean from the political cockpit of Europe. The future Democratic president, Woodrow Wilson, wrote of it in 1905: 'There is little of serious importance to do; the activities are those of society rather than those of business; the unimportant things are always at the front'.[21] And although the United States designated its missions according to the Vienna *règlement*, it was reluctant to have any truck with the titles and trappings of the old world. A State Department circular of 1853 urged envoys to shun the ceremonial garb of European diplomats, and, if possible, to appear at court in the 'simple dress of an American citizen'.[22] Until the 1890s the rank of ambassador was likewise considered too exalted for the representatives of a democracy.

The State Department grew only slowly in size, and in 1820 still had a staff of no more than fifteen. Nevertheless, by 1854 the United States had twenty-eight diplomatic missions abroad headed by ten ministers-plenipotentiary, two ministers-resident, fourteen chargés d'affaires and two commissioners. Elsewhere in the Americas a similar pattern of diplomatic growth was observable. Brazil, for example, had by 1860 a diplomatic network of twenty-two missions, including four legations in European cities. It had also established the rudiments of a career structure with no one being admitted to the service except as an attaché, and then only after having graduated from university or passed a special examination. But some of Brazil's neighbours were not averse to employing foreign adventurers and irregulars as diplomats. Alfred Marbais du Graty, who was appointed in 1864 to represent Paraguay in Berlin, had once been a Belgian attaché at Rio de Janeiro, and then, after running up heavy debts, had become a colonel in the Argentinian artillery and subsequently an under-secretary in the foreign ministry at Buenos Aires. Du Graty had, however, at least had some experience of diplomacy. By contrast, the foreign representation of the United States remained throughout the nineteenth century very largely in the hands of non-professionals. The prevalence of the 'spoils system', much favoured by Andrew Jackson, meant that American diplomatic appointments were usually given as rewards for political services and that they lasted only so long as the current administration. Representation was also conducted with a minimum of subordinate assistance. Even in 1881 only twelve out of thirty American legations were allowed secretaries at the public expense, and very few of the unpaid attachés, upon whom most ministers had to rely for assistance, were to make a career of diplomacy. Henry Vignaud, who during the Civil War joined a Confederate mission to Paris and went on to serve for thirty-four years as second and then first secretary of the United States legation there, was a rare exception to the rule.

American heads of mission were not only for the most part inexperienced. They were also poorly remunerated. Congress continued to regard diplomacy as ephemeral to the national well-being and was niggardly in its appropriation of funds. The modest stipends paid to ministers had usually to be supplemented from private means, and in consequence personal wealth was a prerequisite of the acceptance of a post. Moreover, since the United States did not possess any mission buildings abroad, newly appointed envoys had to seek out and rent suitable accommodation. David Jayne Hill, who took up his appointment as ambassador at Berlin in June 1908, had at first to make do with cramped offices above a bookstore in Unter den Linden, and not until December 1910 did he find a residence large enough both to house his family and to serve as a chancery. Yet by then pressure was already mounting for the reform and greater professionalization of American diplomacy. The emergence of the United States as a major industrial power and its increased involvement in world politics and trade led to an enhanced public awareness of the potential value of diplomacy. Executive orders of 1905 and 1909 required entrants to the service below the level of head of mission to pass examinations, and sixteen years of Republican administrations between 1896 and 1912 contributed to a degree of continuity in diplomatic appointments. But in 1913 Woodrow Wilson, the new Democratic president, was anxious to encourage a new 'moral' diplomacy, and, distrustful of Republican professionals, he resorted to the appointment of his own political nominees. The result was in some instances quite ludicrous. By 1914 the United States was represented at Bucharest by a former Bohemian brewer, at Lisbon by a minister who could not distinguish between an embassy and a legation, and at Athens by an envoy who took leave to assist in the Albanian struggle for independence. Such amateurs were neither capable of inspiring confidence abroad, nor of enlightening policy-makers at home.

CONSULS, COMMERCE AND FINANCE

One argument often deployed in favour of professionalizing American diplomacy was that it would be good for business. Indeed, the assistance given by consuls in the promotion and protection of American commerce enabled bureaucrats and politicians to win Congressional support for the creation of a career consular service. Official backing for concession-seekers in China and the rhetoric of this 'dollar diplomacy' likewise served the cause of proponents of diplomatic reform. Trade and finance were, however, both subjects and instruments of diplomacy throughout the nineteenth century. The younger Pitt had declared 'British Policy is British Trade',[23] and during the 1820s and 1830s Prussia enhanced its influence in Germany through the construction of a customs union, or *Zollverein*, from which Austria was excluded. This in turn meant Prussia's greater reliance upon the fiscal expertise of its largely middle-class state functionaries, and it is worth recalling that Bismarck was advised that if he wanted a career in diplomacy he should first enter the *Zollverein* administration. Industrial revolutions in Europe and North America, the development of modern banking systems, and the consequent competition for markets, raw materials and investment opportunities, were in any event to place economic issues firmly upon the diplomatic agenda. The point was put plainly by the Belgian foreign minister in a dispatch of December 1841. 'At a time when our industry is searching arduously for markets', he observed, 'our agents abroad must above all endeavour to trace the way for our commerce'.[24] Economic expansion overseas was increasingly regarded as an aspect of national grandeur. Through the commercial and financial penetration of Africa and Asia, European powers affirmed their political pretensions and staked out spheres of interest, and in the last quarter of the century governments readily utilized their influence over capital markets and movements for diplomatic ends.

The response of foreign ministries and diplomats to the needs of business and the methods by which they sought to apply their economic resources varied from country to country. Ministries of commerce and other domestic departments usually had a hand in negotiating tariff and trade agreements, and in some instances, such as the conclusion of the Anglo-French 'Cobden treaty' of 1860, private citizens had a vital part to play. But the primary functions of gathering economic intelligence and aiding merchants were those of the consuls and consular agents which governments nominated in the trading centres of the world. Their duties had steadily expanded since they were first brought under state patronage in the seventeenth century. At the seaports, where the majority of them resided, they were mainly concerned with such maritime matters as the regulation of ships' charters, the certification of their cargoes, and the welfare of their crews. They were sometimes, especially when appointed to provincial capitals like Budapest and Warsaw, sources of political and military information, and where, as in China and the Ottoman Empire, foreign nationals enjoyed extraterritorial rights (capitulations), consuls were responsible for administering justice. Others, such as those appointed to the Balkans, the Barbary coast and Latin America, also had a diplomatic

116

role in so far as they dealt directly with local rulers. There were even occasions when some consuls felt obliged to bear arms in defence of their national interests. Thus in 1805 the former United States consul in Tunis led an invasion of Libya against the troublesome pasha of Tripoli, and in 1840 the French consul-general at Lima considered that France's honour and pecuniary claims warranted his challenging the Peruvian finance minister to an equestrian duel with lance and sabre.

Aptly described as the stepchildren of diplomacy, nineteenth-century consuls were often ill-rewarded and were in general held in low esteem by home-based officials and their more illustrious colleagues in the embassies and legations. American consuls were particularly hard done by. Until 1856 they were, with the exception of those in London, Paris and the Barbary states, unsalaried. Fees charged for consular services could provide an income. In many cases, however, the title of consul was sought by American traders who hoped to gain advantage from their official status. British governments were equally prepared to exploit the Victorian craving for a respectable position, and although from 1825 onwards all but honorary consuls, who might well be foreigners, were remunerated, there was no systematic grading of posts, or provision for promotion and transfer. Like those of the United States, British consular appointments were subject to patronage (in this instance that of the foreign secretary), and despite the introduction after 1855 of a qualifying examination, recruits to the 'general service' were given no special training beyond a spell of three months in the Foreign Office. Prior to 1903 when recruitment was reformed only candidates for the Far Eastern and Levant services, in which legal and linguistic skills were obviously important, had to reckon with anything resembling an open competition. The selection of French consular officials was, by contrast, more tightly regulated than that for diplomats. Ordinances of 1815 and 1816 required prospective vice-consuls to have completed university courses and to know either English, German or Spanish. Then in 1825 a system of appointing consular pupils (*élèves*) was instituted, and from 1833 French consuls were graded with ranks attached to persons rather than posts. Nevertheless, as preference in recruitment was given to the sons and grandsons of consuls, consular dynasties were to become as much a feature of the French foreign service as were diplomatic ones.

Throughout the nineteenth century the consular and diplomatic services of most European countries remained quite distinct. This is not to say that there was no interchange of personnel. Consuls with a specialist knowledge of a region which was either remote, or whose languages were judged particularly difficult, were occasionally rewarded with diplomatic ranking. In Germany, Bismarck, who liked to be kept abreast of economic developments abroad, favoured the exposure of his officials to consular duties. Indeed, about a third of the German Empire's foreign office staff and a quarter of it diplomats were at one time or another in such employ. The

Baron von Richthofen, who in 1900 became state secretary, the senior functionary of the Wilhelmstrasse, had started his career as a dragoman. And amongst other examples of high-ranking diplomats who had had consular beginnings are Vincent Benedetti, France's ambassador at Berlin from 1864 until 1870, and Sir William White, who in 1885 became British ambassador at Constantinople. Moreover, despite the distaste with which some aristocratic diplomats regarded commercial work, by the late 1870s they could hardly ignore the way in which trade and finance were impinging on foreign policy. Bismarck was thus to engage himself in a protracted diplomatic defence of the interests of German shareholders in Romania's railways, and Germany's investment and tariff policies contributed to a steady deterioration in Russo-German relations. Britain's military occupation of Egypt in 1882, which was to become one of the key issues of European diplomacy, also had its roots in the political problems connected with Egyptian insolvency.

As British foreign secretary in 1879 Lord Salisbury was disturbed by the way in which Egypt's creditors seemed able to influence the diplomatic actions of the continental powers. This, he complained, 'was a new feature in diplomacy'.[25] Governments in London, wedded to the *laissez-faire* doctrines of the mid-Victorian era, had assumed that while diplomats should seek the best possible terms for trade and enterprise in general, it was no part of their function to tout for orders and concessions. The Foreign Office had, however, increasingly to reckon with the determination of other governments to encourage and assist their bankers and entrepreneurs abroad. Foreign quotations on the Paris bourse required the French government's sanction, and the Quai d'Orsay made ample use of France's financial resources to achieve its diplomatic objectives. Russian borrowing on the Paris money market was a vital element in the emergence and evolution of the Franco-Russian alliance. Sergei Witte, the Russian finance minister, maintained his own agent in Paris, and since each of the loans contracted by the Russian government with French financial institutions between 1888 and 1912 was preceded by diplomatic negotiations, the Quai d'Orsay was able to attach political conditions. France's diplomats were equally active in promoting investment in the Ottoman Empire, where the exorbitant interest rates pressed upon the Porte by the French ambassador, Ernest Constans, earned him the nickname of 'Monsieur Douze pour cent'. And if British suspicions were correct, some French envoys were not averse to a little financial speculation of their own. 'French policy in most foreign countries', noted one British official in 1908, 'is very largely influenced by the the prospects of direct pecuniary benefit to be derived by officials and ministers.'[26]

It was not, of course, unknown for British consuls and diplomats to act on behalf of bondholders, either as agents, or simply as channels of communication with foreign governments. But the general practice of the

Foreign Office and its representatives was only to engage in concession-mongering when broader economic, political and strategic issues were at stake. Thus when in 1898 China's integrity and the continued access of British traders to potentially lucrative markets was threatened by a frantic competition for concessions, Sir Claude MacDonald, the British minister at Peking, joined in the scramble. The Foreign Office was similarly alarmed by the politico-strategic implications of German investment and enterprise in Turkey, and between 1906 and 1909 tried to create an 'industrial entente' with France with a view to containing the growth of Germany's economic influence in the region. As a result British and French diplomats at London, Paris and Constantinople attempted to encourage a consortium of businessmen and bankers for the purpose of seeking out and exploiting industrial contracts in the Ottoman dominions. It was an exercise in economic diplomacy which, though ultimately unsuccessful, made nonsense of later claims that diplomats of the pre-1914 era had no grasp of economics.

The involvement of diplomats in the promotion of capital ventures abroad was rarely matched by an equivalent effort on behalf of traders and merchants. Perturbed by the extent to which French finance was being used to purchase German goods, the Quai d'Orsay tried to link foreign loan flotations in Paris with orders for French manufacturers, and in 1913 an official of the ministry of public works was appointed to advise the department on how this might be done. But the commercial role of foreign ministries was more usually limited to the provision of information on overseas markets and produce, and to the negotiation of tariff accords. After all, had not Richard Cobden claimed that free trade was 'God's diplomacy',[27] and could mere mortals be expected to do more than further and safeguard its application? The British Foreign Office did not acquire a department specifically charged with commercial affairs until 1865, and even then the utilization of commercial reports from consulates and missions was in practice left to the Board of Trade. Nevertheless, the need for a more general representation of British commercial interests abroad was recognized, and in 1880 a commercial attaché was nominated to the British embassy at Paris. Freed from routine consular work, it was hoped that he would gather intelligence on economic developments in France as a whole. In this respect the experiment was considered a success, and similar appointments were subsequently made to Berlin, Constantinople, Peking and Yokohama. Both France and Germany followed the British example, and in 1906 the French government formally constituted a corps of commercial attachés which was assimilated to the grade of first class consuls. The subordinate staff of missions was thus expanded by a new breed of specialists, though prior to 1914 the true value of this brand of commercial diplomacy remained in doubt.

SERVICE ATTACHÉS

The appointment of commercial attachés coincided with a period of increased economic rivalry amongst the great industrial and industrializing nations, a shift towards protectionism in continental Europe, and a growing awareness on the part of governments of the extent to which power in international relations was dependent upon a state's manufacturing capacity. At the same time modern technology was also transforming the art of war and making it all the more important that those responsible for national defence should have the fullest possible information on the armaments and armed forces of likely friends and foes. It was in order to meet this requirement that first military, and then naval, attachés became permanent members of embassy and legation staffs. This, however, was a gradual development. Machiavelli had written of ambassadors being accompanied by military experts in the guise of valets, and during the coalition wars of the seventeenth and eighteenth centuries military observers had acted as liaison officers between allied commanders. In 1806 Napoleon had made an army captain second secretary of the French embassy at Vienna in order to keep watch on the strength of the Austrian army, and in 1809 the Austrians had reciprocated by sending a military aide to their embassy at Paris. Prussia too recognized the value of including officers in diplomatic missions. Like other German states, it was represented on the federal military commission at Frankfurt, and in 1830 it appointed a military expert to its Paris legation. Three years later the French made provision for the employment of general staff officers by the foreign ministry with a view to their being attached to embassies and other missions. But it was not until the 1860s that the practice of accrediting military attachés became widespread in Europe, and even then there was no general agreement on their nomenclature.

The decisive factors in bringing about this extension of the attaché system was the failure of the European concert to maintain peace amongst the great powers, and the advances made in mechanized warfare in the second half of the nineteenth century. In order to facilitate allied co-operation during the Crimean War the British government appointed army officers as commissioners to Paris, Turin and Constantinople. After the peace settlement of 1856 those at Paris and Turin were retained, and from 1857 Lieutenant Colonel Claremont at Paris was designated military attaché. Then, in the wake of the Austro-Prusso-Danish War of 1864, further such appointments were made to Berlin, Frankfurt, St Petersburg and Vienna. Meanwhile the Austrians and the Prussians had exchanged military plenipotentiaries, and in 1860 the French war ministry, which already had an officer in Berlin, formally appointed military attachés to the other principal European capitals, along with a naval attaché to London. Spurred on by their military defeat of 1870–1, the French rapidly expanded their attaché service, so that by 1914 they had in all twenty-six service attachés. Even the United States, which did not possess any service attachés before 1889, followed the European example, and by 1914 shared pride of place with Russia in having more military and naval appointees upon the staff of their overseas missions than any other country.

The true value of service attachés lay in their ability as technical experts to keep their governments abreast of military and strategic developments abroad. They could also liaise between admiralties, war ministries and general staffs when in times of crisis and war friendly and allied powers wished to co-ordinate their military preparations. Yet service attachés could also pose a persistent threat to the authority of the ambassadors to whom they were theoretically subordinated. They were, after all, selected on the recommendation of their respective ministries, and although provision was usually made for the transmission of their official reports through existing diplomatic channels, with heads of mission sometimes having a right to append comments of their own, this did not prevent attachés from corresponding privately with their military and naval superiors. Moreover, their preoccupation with defence issues meant that their assessment of the intentions of potentially hostile neighbours could seem peculiarly pessimistic when compared with the more broadly based evaluations of their civilian colleagues. This was evident in the attitude of the Russian embassy at Constantinople to the reorganization of the Ottoman armed forces after the Young Turk revolution of 1908. Whilst the ambassador, Charykov, welcomed the reforms in the hope that they would lead to greater stability in the Balkans, his military attaché feared that a revived Turkey might menace Russian interests in the Near East.

The difficulties inherent in such dual reporting were all the more apparent in countries like Germany where the military establishment occupied a prominent political and social position, and in which admirals and generals were prepared to use information from, and contacts established by, service attachés to promote policies contrary to those favoured by other elements in the governing élite. Personal and bureaucratic rivalries, a penchant for intrigue amongst service appointees and their resentment of civilian control, all strained ambassador–attaché relations. During the 1890s Alfred von Waldersee, the chief of the general staff, relied upon his 'truly Prussian' attachés to assist him in impressing his Russophobic views upon successive chancellors. And later at London Germany's ambassador, Paul von Metternich, was unable to control a naval attaché whose enthusiasm for *Flottenpolitik* negated his own conciliatory counsels. Yet even without attachés, some of Germany's most important missions would still have contained sizeable military contingents. The Wilhelmstrasse deliberately sought out potential diplomats within the officer corps. Over a fifth of the diplomatic positions of the Prusso-German state were thus filled by military personnel in the period 1867–95, and ambassadors appointed to

St Petersburg and Vienna were almost without exception generals. From 1819 until the 1890s the Prussian and Russian sovereigns also consecrated the traditionally close relationship between their courts by exchanging military plenipotentiaries, who were nominated quite independently of established diplomatic missions. This system, to which the German emperor, William II, reverted in 1904, allowed the two sovereigns to communicate on military matters without what the Kaiser called 'the lumbering and indiscreet apparatus of chancelleries, embassies, etc.'.[28]

An active and ambitious service attaché could cast doubt upon the value of his ambassador's advice. He could also compromise the position of the embassy if he were found to be exploiting its immunities and privileges in order to engage in clandestine operations. A distinction was usually made between the overt gathering of information and such covert intelligence work as might include the bribing of foreign nationals. Moreover, the use of diplomatic missions for espionage was officially frowned upon by most European governments. Imperial directives of 1878, 1890 and 1900 warned Germany's representatives against seeking information from ignoble sources, and it is probably true to say that most German attachés preferred to rely for their intelligence upon such social contacts as they could cultivate. Nevertheless, when at the time of the Dreyfus affair in France the German ambassador at Paris complained of his military attaché's engagement in espionage, William II curtly annotated his dispatch: 'Damn it! What are my attachés for then?'[29] The Russians seem to have had even fewer qualms about such work. Prior to the outbreak of the First World War their military attaché at Copenhagen controlled an extensive network of agents in Germany, and in 1914 his colleague at Berlin was declared *persona non grata* because of his spying activities.

SECRET SERVICES

Most European ambassadors disapproved of the involvement of their service attachés in espionage. Yet long before the appointment of the first military attachés civilian diplomats had been embroiled in all sorts of bribery and deception. During the eighteenth century it had been quite common for foreign envoys to distribute funds in order to secure information, sympathy and support. Metternich possessed one of the best-organized secret police forces in Europe, and at the Congress of Vienna the reports of his agents, the venality of couriers and embassy servants, and whatever could be gleaned from diplomatic wastepaper baskets, provided him with ample political intelligence. He also had the assistance of a team of cryptographers in his secret cipher chancellery (or *cabinet noir*, as such institutions were generally known), whose purpose was to open and decipher the coded correspondence of foreign governments and envoys. Moreover, in subsequent years Metternich capitalized upon the geographical extent of the Habsburg dominions and tried to impress upon other powers the advantages in terms of cost and time of using Austria's postal network. With the exception of Piedmont-Sardinia all the Italian states eventually entrusted their mails to the Austrians, and after 1817 Austrian couriers also handled the bulk of French postal communications with Italy. Metternich thus acquired access to the official correspondence of several governments, and with the assistance of his *cabinet noir*, which by the 1840s had broken eighty-five diplomatic codes, including the particularly stubborn Russian one, he was able to boast that he had become 'chief minister of police in Europe'.[30]

Other countries had their own *cabinets noirs*. A Deciphering Branch was established in London in 1703, and the British occupation of the Ionian islands from 1809 until 1864 gave them a 'listening post' and espionage centre in the eastern Mediterranean. Foreign mail which passed through the islands was thus detained and routinely inspected under British-applied quarantine regulations. But the value of this kind of interception declined as governments developed their own courier services with correspondence confided to sealed diplomatic bags. In addition, liberal opinion reacted strongly against the purloining of public and private mails. There were furious protests in the British House of Commons when in 1854 it was discovered that the correspondence of the Italian nationalist exile, Giuseppe Mazzini, had been tampered with, and as a result the Deciphering Branch was formally abolished. Likewise, in the aftermath of the 1848 revolutions the operations of the Austrian and French *cabinets noirs* were temporarily suspended. The invention of electric telegraphy and its widespread adoption for diplomatic communications was, however, soon followed by a revival of officially sponsored decoding. Although no attempt was made in Britain to reconstitute the Deciphering Branch, republican France responded eagerly to the challenge. Telegrams sent by foreign governments and officials via French cables were monitored and relayed to the the Quai d'Orsay where enthusiastic cryptographers sought to reveal their secrets. At the same time a *cabinet noir* within the French interior ministry was also engaged in cracking foreign codes.

French cryptographers enjoyed some considerable successes in the twenty years that preceded the First World War. German and Italian diplomatic codes were broken and during the Russo-Japanese War Japanese telegrams were deciphered in Paris. Foreknowledge of the intentions of friends, foes and rivals was of obvious advantage in negotiation. But other foreign ministries were aware that their neighbours might have access to their telegraphic communications, and they took appropriate precautions. Number codes were in some instances regularly changed, paraphrased messages were sent in the hope of confusing cryptographers, and it seems likely that redundant ciphers were deliberately used with the object of deception. Intercepted messages were in any case not always accurately deciphered and excessive reliance upon them could weaken, rather than strengthen, a power's negotiating stance. Moreover, the existence of separate *cabinets noirs* fuelled inter-ministerial rivalry, and in 1905 and 1911 intercepted German diplomatic telegrams led to domestic political crises in France when they revealed that the Quai d'Orsay was being bypassed by prime ministers anxious for understandings with Germany.

Older forms of diplomatic espionage also persisted. Embassy wastepaper baskets remained a fruitful source of intelligence, as did valets and embassy servants. And in 1914 the Wilhelmstrasse had in the person of Bernt von Siebert, a Baltic German on the staff of the Russian embassy at London, a spy who readily supplied Berlin with copies of his ambassador's correspondence. It was he who in the spring of 1914 warned the Wilhelmstrasse that the British and Russian Navies were contemplating joint contingency planning – news which the German government deliberately leaked to the press in an attempt to influence public opinion in Britain against the Anglo-Russian alignment.

PUBLICITY AND PROPAGANDA

During the early part of the nineteenth century the interception and opening of mails was probably undertaken as much for the purpose of monitoring domestic opinion as for extracting information about foreign powers. The restored and reconstituted monarchies of Europe may not have needed the consent of the governed, but they required their acquiescence, and rulers who had witnessed the effects of the Revolution in France and the upsurge of liberal and national sentiment elsewhere could hardly ignore the opinions of their subjects. 'Public opinion', noted Metternich in June 1808, 'is the most powerful medium of all. Like religion it penetrates into the darkest corners'.[31] In the words of Louis XVIII's envoy at Hanover, it had 'become one of the motivating forces of general policy'.[32] Yet what Metternich had in mind cannot easily be equated with the public opinion whose shifts and trends are measured by modern methods of polling and statistical analysis. The term is perhaps better understood as embracing all those non-governmental opinions which were given public expression. This would include views aired in the press and pamphlets, national and provincial assemblies, the universities and other centres of learning, and the great houses, salons and societies of intellectual and political élites. The impact of such opinions upon foreign policy naturally varied according to the political and social institutions of different countries. But even in autocratic Russia the Tsar's ministers had to take account of a Slavophile intelligentsia when it came to handling relations with Ottoman Turkey. Moreover, the growth of literacy, the emergence of mass circulation newspapers, and the establishment of popularly elected parliaments led to the greater involvement of chancelleries, ministries and diplomats in attempting to defend their actions at home, and in seeking to influence governments abroad, by the manipulation of the press and other means of public communication.

Metternich was fully aware of the advantages to be had from mobilizing public sentiment in favour of particular policies. During the Congress of Vienna, when Talleyrand was suspected of trying to stir up public strife in Germany over the fate of Saxony, Metternich sought to counter his influence through the *Oesterreichische Beobachter*. And in London, where parliamentary debates were keenly followed by foreign observers, both the Austrian and Bavarian envoys inserted articles and letters in the British press. Prince Lieven, the Russian ambassador, was similarly employed. He was instructed that if he could not win over Castlereagh's opponents in the cabinet, he should endeavour to work with the parliamentary opposition and journalists. Whether such efforts seriously affected decisions taken at Vienna is doubtful. But in later years foreign ministers and ministries continued to use the press to influence opinion abroad. Metternich helped to finance the *Journal de Francfort*, a newspaper which was published in French, and which, besides enjoying a wide circulation, syndicated material to other papers. He also inspired pieces in the Paris *Journal des débats* and the London *Morning Chronicle*. Palmerston was equally conscious of the utility of the press: as British foreign secretary he made sure that his important speeches had a wide distribution, and he encouraged his agents to supply articles to foreign journals. In March 1840, at a time when Britain and France were at odds over developments in the Near East, he urged the British minister at Stuttgart to use the *Allgemeine Zeitung* with a view 'to keeping Germany right'.[33] The support of British newspapers for his policies and their abuse of foreign statesmen was in the meanwhile secured through a supply of government advertisements and advance information.

Nevertheless, contact between the British Foreign Office, its representatives and the press remained informal and sporadic. Much depended upon personal relationships established by foreign secretaries and officials with individual journalists. By the end of the century editors of serious newspapers, such as *The Times*, were usually afforded an entrée to the department, and their correspondents were, despite a reluctance on the part of ambassadors to grant personal interviews for publication, valued guests at British missions. On occasions *The Times* was also used to reinforce diplomatic initiatives and to warn vacillating foreign governments of 'public disquiet' over matters in dispute. Yet such methods were amateurish when compared with the mechanisms evolved by continental powers for dealing with the press. After all, by 1870 both the Ballhausplatz and the Quai d'Orsay had their own press services. Acutely conscious of the fact that the legitimacy of his régime rested upon public sentiment, Napoleon III endeavoured through inspired articles and pamphlets to manipulate opinion in France and abroad. Such behaviour could be embarrassing to French diplomats, especially when, as in September 1866, a circular appeared in *Le Moniteur* before it reached the embassies for which it was intended. The politicians of the Third Republic were no less aware of the value of a sympathetic press. In 1879 a *Bureau de Presse* was created in the foreign ministry, and when in 1907 the structure of the Quai d'Orsay was reorganized on lines proposed by Philippe Berthelot, a *Bureau des Communications* was specifically entrusted with the responsiblity for purchasing and analysing publications and for supervising relations with the press and public.

A section of the Paris press had in the meanwhile responded gratefully to offers of Russian subventions. In 1884 a regular officer of the Tsar's secret police had been attached to Russia's embassy at Paris with the object of surveying and combating the activities and influence of revolutionary fugitives there. His work was to become all the more important when, with a view to ensuring successful loan flotations on the Paris bourse, the imperial government tried to create a favourable climate of opinion in France. Later, after the outbreak of the Italo-Turkish War in 1911, his colleague, Tommaso Tittoni, Italy's ambassador at Paris, seems to have followed the Russian example in bribing newspapers to take a sympathetic attitude towards Italy's ambitions. More traditionally minded Italian diplomats had once regarded journalists as 'dangerous and compromising elements, to be avoided at all costs'.[34] But after the establishment in 1901 of a press bureau within the Consulta (the Italian foreign ministry), and more especially after its enlargement and reform in 1908, newspaper articles were regularly reviewed and summarized for the foreign minister, and, as elsewhere in Europe, the press was increasingly regarded as a means of diplomatic action. Indeed, according to a report drafted by one senior official of the Consulta in September 1913, the advent of democracy had made public opinion an 'indispensable basis for any foreign policy'.[35]

Mounting public criticism of Germany's lacklustre diplomacy in the years immediately preceding the First World War also in part explains the Wilhelmstrasse's decision to charge Otto Hammann, a former journalist, with the task of keeping in close touch with public opinion and guiding it whenever necessary. Embarrassed by its mishandling of the foreign press and outclassed by the propagandists of the imperial navy office, the Wilhelmstrasse was attacked in the Reichstag for its aristocratic recruitment and its failure to comprehend the requirements of trade and industry. Similar accusations were levelled at the British Foreign Office. In the aftermath of the Agadir crisis of 1911, which had seemed to bring Britain to the verge of war with Germany, Sir Edward Grey, the Liberal foreign secretary, had both to fend off the claims of radicals inside and outside of parliament that his policy was being determined by a narrow aristocratic élite, and to face demands for a more open and democratically controlled diplomacy. Such criticisms were not new. Nor were they wholly misplaced. Most diplomacy was conducted in secret, and it was only in the autumn of

1911 that all the provisions of the Anglo-French accords of 1904 were made known to British parliamentarians. Yet in one very important respect, the Foreign Office had, despite its lack of a press department, been far more open in the provision of information than any of its continental counterparts. This was in the publication of selections of its diplomatic correspondence in the form of parliamentary papers or Blue Books.

Already in the wake of the Seven Years' War the British government had released documents relating to the negotiation of the Peace of Paris of 1763. But it was in the 1820s and 1830s, when Canning and Palmerston were at the Foreign Office, that the supply of Blue Books on a variety of international issues was taken up in earnest. They were intended to inform and influence parliamentarians at home and opinion abroad, and documents were often selected for frankly propagandistic ends. Foreign secretaries thus attempted to justify their conduct and to win support against domestic opponents and foreign rivals. Other countries followed Britain's example. After the British re-occupation of the Falkland islands in 1833 the government in Buenos Aires published diplomatic correspondence dating from the crisis over the islands of 1770–1, and over fifty years later Anglo-German friction over colonial claims led Bismarck to lay the first of his White Books before the Reichstag. By then Napoleon III had sanctioned the annual publication of a selection of Quai d'Orsay papers, and in 1861 the State Department launched a similar but more enduring series of volumes in the form of *The Foreign Relations of the United States*. Unfortunately for historians the French experiment did not survive the Franco-Prussian War. Nevertheless, the Quai d'Orsay continued to publish Yellow Books, which, like the British Blue Books, dealt with specific negotiations and external developments.

Documents thus published were sometimes emasculated and occasionally falsified. There were also instances when dispatches were deliberately drafted with publication in mind. But this does not detract from the fact that long before the 'old diplomacy' supposedly gave way to the 'new', foreign ministries and diplomats had realized the advantage of appealing to audiences outside the cabinets and chancelleries of Europe. This too was implicit in what later generations would call 'cultural diplomacy', i.e., government backing for the protection and projection of national culture abroad. In an age of nationalism in Europe and imperial rivalry in Africa and Asia, it was perhaps natural that states should have sought to extend their influence through assisting and sponsoring schools and colleges in foreign lands. It was undoubtedly true of France, a country which had been deprived by military defeat of its ascendancy in Europe and which was actively engaged in the extension of its formal and informal empire overseas. Prior to 1870 French governments had aided the educational work of French religious missions, especially in the Near and Middle East, and it is worth remembering that the Crimean War had its ostensible origins in a dispute over the rights of French Catholics in the Holy Land. Moreover, despite the anti-clerical stance of some republican administrations, French diplomats and consuls continued to support religious as well as secular foundations whose teaching of the French language and literature seemed to enhance France's cultural, and ultimately economic and political, patrimony.

Private institutions in Germany and Italy also received state support and subsidies for their efforts to preserve the language and culture of German and Italian communities abroad. The *Allgemeine Deutsche Schulverein* (later the *Verein für das Deutschtum im Ausland* – VDA) was founded in 1881, and with aid from the Prussian state it provided funds for schools and language teaching in those areas of eastern Europe where there were substantial ethnic German minorities. It was, however, the French who made the vital administrative link between culture and diplomacy when in 1910 the *Bureau des écoles et des oeuvres françaises à l'étranger* (the office for French schools and foundations abroad) was situated in the Quai d'Orsay in order to co-ordinate state support for organizations working in this field. As Jules Cambon reminded his superiors in June 1914, ideas and sentiments were 'effective tools' and in diplomacy easily became 'useful instruments of propaganda'.[36]

PERSONAL AND PRIVATE DIPLOMACY

Another very public aspect of international politics which assumed a new significance in the 1890s and 1900s was the official visits made by crowned heads, presidents and lesser dignitaries to foreign capitals and ports. Often tiresome and tedious for resident diplomats, who had to settle problems of protocol and precedence and participate in time-consuming 'entertainments', their purpose was mainly symbolic. They were well-orchestrated displays of international goodwill, the diplomatic equivalent of military manoeuvres and parades, contrived to take advantage of the increasingly populistic politics of the age. New friendships were thereby affirmed, old ones re-affirmed, and changes of course in foreign policy proclaimed. The arrival of the Russian fleet at Toulon and the reception of its officers at Paris in 1893, the visits of Tsar Nicholas II to Paris in 1896 and 1901, and those of President Faure and Loubet to St Petersburg in 1891 and 1902, were all part of a process by which the French people were associated with, and other powers made aware of, the Franco-Russian alliance. Likewise, King Edward VII's journey to Paris in 1903 signalled a *détente* in Anglo-French relations, and the German Emperor's perambulations in Turkey in 1898 and his landing at Tangier in 1905 demonstrated Germany's determination to have a say in the future of the Ottoman and Shereefian Empires. But such royal visits, though largely ceremonial, also afforded opportunities for diplomatic discussion and negotiation. The meeting of the British and Spanish monarchs at Cartagena in 1907 allowed the accompanying ministers and diplomats to complete the drafting of an exchange of notes on the Mediterranean status quo, and the visit of King George V to Paris in 1914 permitted Grey to review the state of the entente cordiale with the French foreign minister.

Meetings amongst heads of state and government, their ministers and officials, were, however, hardly novel in themselves. The Emperor Joseph II had met with Frederick II of Prussia, and at the invitation of Catherine II of Russia had journeyed to St Petersburg, Kiev and the Crimea. Indeed, at irregular intervals throughout the nineteenth century the rulers of Austria, Prussia and Russia resorted to a personal dynastic diplomacy which reinforced their conservative alignment against domestic change and revolution. This was true of the confabulations between the Austrian and Russian Emperors at Münchengrätz in September 1833. It was equally true of the conversations amongst the Austrian, German and Russian sovereigns at Berlin in September 1872, and of the subsequent round of imperial visits to St Petersburg and Vienna, which resulted in the *Dreikaiserbund* or Three Emperors' League. These meetings obviously derived much of their importance from the presence at them of chief and foreign ministers. The same might also be said of the visit made by Queen Victoria to Louis-Philippe at the Château d'Eu in Normandy in 1843. The occasion, though historically interesting because it was the first time since 1520, when Henry VIII had met Francis I on the Field of the Cloth of Gold, that an English monarch had made a courtesy visit to a French king, was diplomatically significant because of the attendance of the British and French foreign ministers.

Most professional diplomats would probably have agreed with Philip zu Eulenburg, himself a former German ambassador in Vienna, 'that a discussion between two princes is propitious only when it confines itself to the weather'.[37] Yet so intertwined were the lineages of Europe's royals that during the latter half of the nineteenth century a family gathering at Copenhagen or Windsor could constitute a veritable monarchical summit. The construction and expansion of the European railway network also allowed crowned heads to travel further and more quickly, and their presence at the fashionable spas of central Europe and the more salubrious of the continental coastal resorts afforded plenty of time for the discussion of political as well as meteorological topics. However, whilst royal whims and prejudices could try the patience of chancellors and diplomats, constitutional constraints usually meant that wandering princes were kept in check. Denied the support of their political advisers, neither the German nor the Russian Emperors could implement the defensive alliance which they concluded during their Baltic cruises in July 1905. There were none the less instances when the imperial will prevailed. As Emperor of the French, Napoleon III had both the inclination and the power to dispatch his favourites on special missions, and to take diplomatic initiatives without consulting the Quai d'Orsay. Thus in 1858 two days elapsed before his foreign minister learned that during a conversation with the Sardinian prime minister at Plombières he had committed France to waging an aggressive war against Austria in the name of Italian unity.

Opportunities for foreign travel and vacations abroad also allowed Europe's political leaders to dabble in a kind of holiday and spa-time diplomacy. At Biarritz in 1865 Bismarck considered developments in Germany with Napoleon III, and at Dieppe in 1879 the French foreign minister examined African affairs with Lord Salisbury. Georges Clemenceau as French premier made full use of his visits to the Bohemian spas to discuss politics with cure-seeking foreign dignitaries, and after 1904 British ministers visiting the Mediterranean always risked being waylaid in Paris by Frenchmen anxious for reassurances about Britain's loyalty to the entente. Such informal conversations could lead to serious misunderstandings. Clemenceau was flabbergasted when in 1907 the British prime minister seemed to suggest that, despite the Anglo-French staff talks of the previous year, no British government could contemplate sending an army to the continent. But diplomatic experience was no guarantee of success. When in September 1908 the Austro-Hungarian and Russian foreign ministers, Lexa von Aehrenthal and Alexander Izvolsky, both of whom were career diplomats, met at Buchlau in Moravia to discuss the Balkans they failed to draft a joint statement on what they had agreed. As a result relations between their two countries were brought close to breaking point when shortly afterwards Aehrenthal acted according to his version of the accord.

A more consistent cause for concern amongst professional diplomats was, however, the growth of alternative channels of international dialogue. In a sense this too was an old problem. Special and secret emissaries had always posed a challenge to established missions. But with the expansion of the European economy politicians with a tendency towards intrigue and backstairs diplomacy readily availed themselves of the transnational links established amongst businessmen and financiers. Bismarck's banker, Gerson von Bleichröder, was, for instance, to act as the chancellor's unofficial ambassador at large. He supplied Bismarck with economic and political intelligence, and in 1884 was sent to Paris to promote greater Franco-German co-operation. The Moroccan crises of 1905 and 1911 were both also characterized by the way in which the French premiers of the day utilized their financial contacts to circumvent the foreign ministry. On another two occasions, in 1909 and 1911–12, Sir Ernest Cassell, a banker of German-Jewish extraction, and Albert Ballin, a Hamburg shipping magnate, served as intermediaries in the unsuccessful pursuit of an Anglo-German naval accord. Moreover, in addition to such unofficial agencies foreign ministries and diplomats had to reckon with the increased involvement in their work of other government departments. These included not just those responsible for colonies, commerce and the armed service, which were traditionally associated with foreign relations, but also ministries which had previously been almost wholly concerned with domestic affairs.

Improvements in transportation and communications and advances in science and technology all contributed to a broadening of the subject matter of international politics. Issues which had once been only of domestic interest acquired an international dimension. And as governments tried through bilateral and multilateral diplomacy to regulate the international postal system, the transmission of telegraphic messages, and rail, road and eventually air traffic in Europe, so foreign ministries required the aid of technical specialists. Typical examples of this new-style diplomacy were the International Automobile Conference of 1909, which, amongst other things, settled the shape and size of international identity plates, and the International Aerial Navigation Conference of 1910. To the latter, which met at Paris, the British government sent a delegation composed of army and naval officers and representatives of the Home Office. Initially the delegates even reported to the Home Office, and it was only when it became apparent that they were being out-manoeuvred by those of France and Germany and that decisions relating to civil aviation had strategic implications, that the Foreign Office effected a diplomatic coup. It demanded the adjournment of the conference, and Britain's ambassador at Paris was appointed to head its delegation. In effect the Foreign Office thereby came face to face with one of the key problems of twentieth-century diplomacy: that of deciding the respective roles of the diplomatic generalist and the departmental expert when essentially technical issues are the subject of negotiation.

THE COMMUNICATIONS REVOLUTION

The same technological achievements that expanded the agenda of diplomacy restricted the scope of its individual practitioners. Eighteenth-century ambassadors had departed for foreign courts replete with instructions which were intended to acquaint them with the objects of current policy and guide them with regard to what courses they should pursue. When all diplomatic correspondence travelled no faster than a good rider and a fleet horse, envoys had considerable scope for acting on their own initiative, especially when local crises demanded rapid responses. The greater their distance from home, the greater was likely to be their freedom of action. James Monroe, who in 1803 was sent to Paris to assist Robert Livingstone, the United States minister there, in negotiating the purchase of New Orleans and the adjacent territory, was authorized to spend 10 million dollars. But at a time when a dispatch could take almost two months to reach Washington from Europe, neither he nor Livingstone thought it necessary to request further instructions when the French offered the whole Louisiana territory for 5 million dollars more. Without a transatlantic cable an

American envoy in Europe was truly 'extraordinary and plenipotentiary'. So also were the agents of other powers. Pozzo di Borgo, Tsar Alexander's ambassador to restoration France, had ample opportunity to help shape, as well as execute, Russian policy at Paris, and Stratford Canning, the long-serving British ambassador at Constantinople, assumed an almost pro-consular status in Turkey.

Road communications were particularly poor in eastern and south-eastern Europe at the beginning of the nineteenth century. In winter a journey from London to St Petersburg could take a month, and it might be three, four weeks or more before a dispatch reached London from Constantinople. Letters between Paris and the French delegates at the Congresses of Troppau and Laibach took twenty days, and in 1822 the record time for an urgent dispatch from London to Vienna was a week. The pace of diplomatic communications within France was improved when from 1829 Claude Chappe's semaphore telegraph system was employed for the transmission of political intelligence. Moreover, the completion in 1838 of a similar chain of semaphore towers in Russia and the adoption of the system in Prussia meant that messages could be sent from St Petersburg to Berlin in just fifty hours. Foreign ministries also established regular courier services with messengers crisscrossing Europe to deliver and receive correspondence at set intervals. But only with the construction of railways and steamships in the 1840s and 1850s and the invention of electric telegraphy is it possible to speak of a true communications revolution. By 1853 telegraph cables linked London, Paris and Berlin, and within half a century the telegram had become the primary means of communication between foreign ministries, their embassies and legations. Ministers and diplomats continued to use dispatches, along with less formal and often more interesting private letters, for routine and non-urgent business and in order to provide more detailed information and advice. Yet, except in the case of distant posts, such as European missions in the Far East, for which the cost of telegraphy was prohibitively high, the dispatch had by 1914 lost its former pre-eminence in diplomatic correspondence.

All this had an obvious impact upon the nature of diplomatic representation. Once instructions could be relayed to an envoy in less than twenty-four hours his conduct could be supervised on a more or less daily basis. Stratford Canning was to argue that the very brevity of telegrams left a diplomat with more discretion in communicating with foreign governments. And there had indeed been cautious ambassadors in the past who in the absence of regular dispatches had been inhibited from acting. Nevertheless, even as early as 1861 economy-minded reformers in Britain concluded that the new technology had rendered the expensive embassy obsolescent. Their views seem to have been shared by Queen Victoria, for when in 1876 consideration was given to raising the British legation at Rome to the status of an embassy she strongly opposed it on the grounds 'that the time for

Ambassadors and their pretensions [was] past'.[38] In any event the development of telegraphy seemed to reinforce the trend towards centralized decision-making in foreign policy. Almost everywhere foreign ministries were of necessity becoming more efficient bureaucratic machines. Pressure of business, itself in part the result of a greater inflow of telegraphically transmitted information, and new working practices (including the use of the typewriter and the telephone) transformed officials from scribes into advisers. It is this which helps to explain the lament of one prominent Edwardian diplomat, Sir Francis Bertie: 'In Downing Street [i.e., the Foreign Office] one can at least pull the wires whereas an Ambassador is only a d–d marionette'.[39] Before his appointment in 1903 as British ambassador at Rome, Bertie had spent almost forty years in the Foreign Office, and during the previous two he had played a prominent part in the negotiations which led to the Anglo-Japanese alliance. By contrast, one of his principal achievements at Rome was the arranging of a royal visit to the Vatican.

Bertie was better able to utilize his past experience when in January 1905 he became British ambassador at Paris, a post he held for another thirteen years. But, despite the claim of one of his staff – a diplomat who later became permanent under-secretary – that he was 'the very last of the great ambassadors',[40] Bertie never enjoyed a fraction of the independence that diplomats of Stratford Canning's generation knew. His actions were effectively governed by telegraphic instructions, and his reputation rested upon his robust personality, his identification with the entente cordiale, and, above all, the readiness of the foreign secretary and his officials to heed his advice. Real power, the ablity to determine the form and timing of diplomatic initiatives, had shifted towards the Foreign Office. Nevertheless, where ministerial instability and administrative rivalries persisted, ambassadors could still exercise considerable influence. This was certainly the case in republican France, where Barrère at Rome, the Cambon brothers at Berlin and London, and other senior diplomats corresponded regularly with each other, and constituted what one historian has called 'a sort of aulic council' through which they guided successive foreign ministers.[41] Rail transport and the ability to reach Paris quickly facilitated their task, and during the summer and autumn of 1911 Jules Cambon with the aid of the premier, Joseph Caillaux, effectively countered the officials of the Quai d'Orsay in negotiating at Berlin a settlement of the Agadir crisis. In the meanwhile his brother, Paul, reminded the foreign minister: 'An ambassador is not a subaltern charged with executing instructions, he is a collaborator who must always, even at the risk of displeasing, explain himself freely on questions that are seen at Paris from only one viewpoint.'[42] The advance of democracy in France did not coincide with a decline in ambassadorial pretensions.

The conclusion of a Franco-German bargain on Morocco in 1911 was a triumph for secret diplomacy. Yet the negotiators had constantly to reckon with inflamed nationalistic passions on both sides of the Vosges. Indeed electric telegraphy had, as the French historian Albert Sorel, concluded, made diplomacy more vulnerable to such popular emotions. When dispatches took between five days and a month to reach their destination ambassadors could devote more time to drafting their reports, chancelleries had more time to reflect upon their replies, and in consequence passions had more time to cool.[43] The same point had been made by the British foreign secretary, Lord John Russell, when in October 1853 he learned by telegraph of Turkey's declaration of war on Russia. 'These telegraphic dispatches', he complained, 'are the very devil. Formerly Cabinets used to deliberate on a fact & a proposition from foreign Govts. Now we have only a fact.'[44] And Lord Lyons, the British minister at Washington during the Civil War, later claimed that had there been a transatlantic cable in 1861 the crisis that arose between Britain and the United States over the latter's seizure of Confederate agents aboard a British ship would have ended in war. As it happened, Lyons had time in which to make it clear to the Americans that they must surrender their prisoners or face war 'without making such threats as would render the humiliation too great to be borne'.[45] Moreover, the electric telegraph also permitted a decline in standards of international conduct. Thus the early departure of the Austro-Hungarian minister from Belgrade in July 1914 meant that Vienna's declaration of war on Serbia was sent by cable. The Serbian prime minister, who received the telegram on the afternoon of the 28th, at one stage suspected that he had been the victim of a practical joke. Only a few hours later when the bombardment of Belgrade began did he discover that diplomacy without diplomats was no joking matter.

DIPLOMACY IN TRANSITION

The outbreak of the First World War brought an end to forty-three years of peace amongst the great powers of Europe. They were years in which the European nations had become more aware of their interdependence, particularly in the economic, social and technological spheres. Neither governments nor diplomats had been slow to grasp the meaning of this development. 'The field of diplomacy', explained a Quai d'Orsay report of 1890, 'is truly unlimited. No human interest is foreign to it.'[46] And in May 1914 the British ambassador at Vienna recommended that his government should appoint attachés or secretaries whose 'special duty it would be to watch labour questions or social questions'.[47] The European peace had, however, been marred by periodic crises, by colonial wars and by conflict in the Balkans and the Far East, and had seemed increasingly to depend upon the maintenance of a precarious balance between competing military alliances, whose exact terms were a secret to the public at large. There were those too who urged that the states system and the methods by which governments dealt with each other needed reform. Participants in the socialist Second International advocated world revolution as a solution to the problem of world peace. But supporters of organizations such as the Interparliamentary Union and the Universal Peace Congress, both of which were founded in 1889, adopted essentially legalistic approaches to the resolution of conflict, and advocated the greater use of arbitration and mediation, along with arms limitation and disarmament.

Such ideas, which were also to inspire disciples of the 'new diplomacy', found expression in the Hague peace conferences of 1899 and 1907: international gatherings which assembled at the instigation of the Russian emperor, and amongst whose achievements was the creation of the Permanent Court of Arbitration. Nevertheless, neither arbitration nor the older mechanisms of the concert of Europe could prevent the great powers from resorting to war once they felt their survival and status to be at stake. Diplomacy had seemed to fail, and even those who did not hold it responsible for the catastrophe, felt that in its present form its prospects were distinctly dismal. Charles Lister, a promising young British diplomat, who resigned in September 1914 to seek a commission in the army, was clear on this point. 'Diplomacy', he declared, 'is dead'.[48] So within a year was Lister. He died from wounds received in the Dardanelles campaign. Diplomacy, reformed rather than resurrected, survived.

5

THE 'NEW DIPLOMACY'

The public is revolting against orthodox diplomacy, much as it did against orthodox divinity, and for the same reason – its failure to secure peace on earth to men of good will.

(George Young)[1]

Few events in modern history have attracted more instant academic attention than the outbreak of the First World War. Hardly had the first battles been fought before the task of analysing the preceding crisis began. Belligerent governments hastened to demonstrate the justice of their respective causes by publishing selections of their diplomatic correspondence, and patriotic historians were at hand to assist them in explaining the evil intentions of their foes. Yet, despite the political truces which prevailed in Berlin, London and Paris, and the readiness of socialists to join with other parties of the left in voting for military credits, there was no universal acceptance of the thesis that the war could be attributed solely to the ambitions of any one power or coalition. Liberal and radical critics of British foreign policy continued, for example, to emphasize the shortcomings of the European states system. These included the commercial and imperial rivalries of the recent past, the concomitant arms races, the pursuit of balance-of-power policies, the secret treaties and conventions which had underpinned and buttressed the pre-war alliances and ententes, and a territorial status quo which took insufficient account of the principle of national self-determination. And while individual diplomats were arraigned for their bellicosity and conspiratorial machinations, their profession was blamed for its failure to halt the drift towards war. George Young, who in 1914 was the first secretary in the British legation at Lisbon, was not alone in expressing his disillusionment with 'orthodox diplomacy'. Like many of his generation he was converted to the view that if war were to be avoided in the future there would have to be fundamental changes in the way in which nations dealt with each other. Old practices would have to be abandoned and be replaced by what in the aftermath of the war was popularly labelled the 'new diplomacy'.

THE IMPACT OF WAR

The term 'new diplomacy' was neither novel in its application, nor precise in its definition. Jules Cambon insisted in 1905 that faster communications, the press and democratic indiscretion had overthrown the 'old diplomacy', and that he and his brother, Paul, were representatives of a new school in ambassadorial behaviour.[2] A quarter of a century later he was to observe that to talk about new and old diplomacy was 'to make a distinction without a difference'.[3] The new diplomacy seems, indeed, to have been a peculiarly undiplomatic expression. The problem is that it was used by those who wished to end the prevailing 'international anarchy' to describe a multitude of virtues. Some of these, such as the notion of making the world safe for democracy, were more concerned with the objectives of foreign policy than with the activities of ambassadors and other diplomatic agents. Two themes can, however, be discerned in the writings of the would-be reformers which had a direct bearing upon the processes by which relations were conducted amongst states. These were, first, the demand that diplomacy should be more open to public scrutiny and control, and, second, the projected establishment of an international organization which would act both as a forum for the peaceful settlement of disputes and as a deterrent to the waging of aggressive war. Open diplomacy, it was assumed, would introduce greater honesty into international politics, and new legal constraints, backed by 'world public opinion' and the threat of collective sanctions, would impede the reckless use of force.

In the autumn of 1914 opponents of war both in Europe and North America hastened to proclaim the need for just such changes in the conduct of diplomacy. Thus the *Bund Neues Vaterland*, a newly formed and relatively small group of German pacifists, called for a radical break 'with the existing system, in which a certain very few men have the power to decide the fate of millions'.[4] But whilst the *Bund*'s activities were soon proscribed by the German military authorities, pre-war critics of British foreign policy remained free to renew their onslaught against the mandarins of Whitehall. Ramsay MacDonald, who resigned on 7 August 1914 from the leadership of the parliamentary Labour Party, was soon urging that socialists must co-operate 'to put an end to secret diplomacy and to the handing over of foreign policy to a handful of men drawn from the aristocratic and plutocratic classes'.[5] In this respect MacDonald's views were broadly in line with those of his associates in the Union of Democratic Control (UDC) – an organization which had been founded shortly after the commencement of the war by a number of prominent intellectuals and left-wing politicians. Amongst its members it included Norman Angell, Bertrand Russell, H.N. Brailsford, Charles Trevelyan and Arthur Ponsonby, who had himself once been in the diplomatic service. It was, however, E.D. Morel, the secretary of the UDC, who was to emerge as its moving spirit. Before the war he had distinguished himself by his campaigning against European misrule in the Congo. He had later begun to attack 'influences' within the Foreign Office which he believed to be dragging Britain into entangling commitments with France and Russia and towards a war with Germany. Yet, he had also been careful to explain that the democratizing of foreign policy, which he favoured, did not mean 'that diplomatists should carry on their conversations in public squares, any more. . .[than] the novelist invites his readers to follow the unravelling of the plot while he is engaged upon it'.[6] What Morel considered important was not that diplomats should cease to negotiate in private, but that the public should have a greater say over the substance of what they discussed, and that parliament should be kept fully informed of any agreements that might thereby be concluded.

Other advocates of reform placed more emphasis on the creation of new instruments for the regulation of international politics. Inherent in some of their less utopian projects was the notion of institutionalizing the old concert of Europe upon a permanent basis. They were, however, also inspired by the ideas of the nineteenth-century peace movement, such progress as had been made towards inter-governmental co-operation on humanitarian, social and technological issues, and the achievements of the two Hague peace conferences in promoting arbitration and mediation as means of peacefully resolving international disputes. Léon Bourgeois, a lawyer who had twice been foreign minister of France, had urged the second conference to establish a sovereign international tribunal, and in the following year, 1908, he had expanded upon this proposal in a book, prophetically entitled *La Société des Nations*. Indeed, arbitration, conciliation, disarmament and publicity were by 1914 already part of the standard fare of radical-liberal thinking about the maintenance of peace. But conservatives, evidently alarmed by the subversive impact of war, were ultimately to play as prominent a part as their radical rivals in elaborating schemes for an international organization whose member states would be pledged to the collective maintenance of peace. During the first twelve months of the war two British groups, one chaired by Lord Bryce, a jurist and former ambassador in Washington, and another, the League of Nations Society, took up this task. Grey and Lord Robert Cecil, his parliamentary under-secretary, were sympathetic to their cause, and in the United States ex-President Taft assisted in the foundation of the League to Enforce Peace, their American equivalent. Like the UDC, these pressure groups sought to educate public and official opinion on the malfunctioning of the international system, and their efforts were rewarded when the United States president, Woodrow Wilson, publicly embraced their collectivist aspirations. On 27 May 1916 in an address to the League to Enforce Peace, Wilson appealed for a 'universal association of the nations. . .to prevent any war begun either contrary to treaty covenants or without warning and full submission of the causes to the opinion of the world'.[7]

It was singularly appropriate that the new world should have provided the new diplomacy with its most powerful political exponent. Geography had so far permitted the United States to avoid embroilment in Europe's alliances and alignments, and Wilson, who had already sponsored a series of bilateral arbitration treaties, apparently felt able to adopt a strong moral stance in seeking to persuade the statesmen of the old world of the error of their ways. But long before his intervention, the hostilities in Europe had modified the form and content of great power diplomacy. There was almost everywhere an inclination on the part of professional diplomats to accept that the war, like the inter-allied contingency planning that had preceded it, was properly the business of admirals and generals. Foreign ministries and their agents seemed at first all too ready to accept that in wartime diplomacy must be subordinated to the requirements of grand strategy. 'In war', Grey later recalled, '. . . diplomacy is the handmaiden of the necessities of the War Office and the Admiralty'.[8] This was an attitude of mind which to some extent reflected the ignorance of most senior diplomats of the nature of modern warfare. Accustomed to a long period of peace, they perceived the war as a temporary, though perhaps necessary, aberration, and were ill-equipped to resist the increasing role assumed by military missions and their ancillary intelligence agencies in inter-allied relations. In time, however, representatives of departments and ministries concerned with commerce, finance, propaganda and supply also intruded into what had once been the privileged world of the ambassadors. Moreover, the need to take speedy decisions in wartime tempted political leaders to try their hand at personal diplomacy, and this and the evolution of new adminis-trative structures and machinery for allied co-operation, posed a fresh challenge to the authority of the professional diplomats. By 1918 some of the embassies of the chief belligerents, such as those of the British at Paris and at Washington, appeared, if not yet redundant, at any rate, obsolescent.

The war from its commencement confronted diplomats with its own peculiar kind of problems. Not the least of these was that of maintaining communications between missions and home governments. When, for instance, prompt action by the Royal Navy led to the severing of Germany's transatlantic cables, Count Bernstorff, the German ambassador at Washing-ton, had to rely for his instructions upon faint wireless messages relayed from a transmitter near Berlin. In the meanwhile his French colleague, Jules Jusserand, who had been holidaying in France, risked being stranded on the wrong side of the Atlantic, and it was only with the assistance of Myron T. Herrick, the American ambassador in Paris, that he was able to return quickly to Washington, travelling incognito aboard a British ship. Herrick, for his part, had like other diplomats to provide aid, comfort and advice to those of his vacationing compatriots who feared that they might be caught up in the fighting. But besides this, he, as the representative of a powerful neutral, took under his protection the embassy buildings of Germany and

Austria-Hungary, and when at the beginning of September 1914 the proximity of the German army to Paris led the French government and the greater part of the *corps diplomatique* to flee southwards to Bordeaux, he agreed to look after the interests and property of Britain, Russia and other states. Deluged with requests for help from his own and foreign nationals, Herrick soon found that his embassy had become 'a bank and a relief society and a railway exchange'.[9]

In other respects too the workload of diplomatic missions expanded considerably in the early stages of the conflict. Alliances had to be consolidated and allied policies co-ordinated, and the representatives of both the entente and the central powers sought to persuade non-belligerent states either to join their side, or to observe a benevolent neutrality. Cabinet diplomacy was conducted with the manners, but not the openness, of the market-place as allies endeavoured to reconcile their territorial ambitions, and vied with their friends and opponents in bidding for the services of predatory neutrals. And British attempts to impose a naval blockade upon Germany raised commercial and legal issues which soon became the source of protracted and onerous diplomatic wrangling over the rights and duties of neutrals.

During the first three years of the war diplomacy was practised with every bit as much secrecy and guile as it had been in the recent past. The entente powers negotiated in camera in preparing for the dismemberment and division of the Ottoman Empire, and, like their enemies, they held out the prospect of territorial gain to their potential allies. Yet it is an oversimplification to suggest, as Arno J. Mayer has done, that the secret wartime treaties represented 'the most vivid incarnation of the spirit, the techniques, and the objectives of the Old Diplomacy'.[10] It is certainly true that the majority of these arrangements were inspired more by a desire for military victory, territorial aggrandizement and post-war security, than by the high moral principles that some political leaders espoused. The Treaty of London of April 1915, which brought Italy into the war on the side of the entente powers, contained, for example, territorial provisions which were clearly irreconcilable with the notion of national self-determination. Nevertheless, the methods by which wartime agreements were achieved sometimes differed markedly from those of the pre-war era. Governments were more prepared to bypass conventional channels of diplomatic dialogue, and they displayed an increased willingness to resort to the use of propaganda and subversion – techniques which, in so far as they involved influencing peoples as well as their rulers, were not so much manifestations of the old diplomacy as precursors of the new. In south-eastern Europe traditional diplomacy gave way to all kinds of political subterfuge and intrigue as the belligerents competed for the assistance of the smaller Balkan powers. Moreover, since many of the wartime agreements envisaged territorial changes which had economic and strategic implications, departments other than foreign ministries obtained a greater say not only in the formulation of policy, but also in its implementation. Thus in Britain, the Admiralty, the War Office, and the India Office were all to become involved in the preparation for, and the monitoring of, negotiations with France on the future governance of the Arab Middle East. Sir Mark Sykes, a co-author of the resulting Sykes–Picot accord, was in no sense a professional diplomat. He had once been an honourary attaché in the British embassy at Constantinople, but in December 1915 when he began his negotiations with the Frenchman, Charles Georges-Picot, he was an Arabist in the employ of the War Office.

There was, of course, nothing particularly novel about using individuals with specialist knowledge in international negotiations. Moreover, in time of war there was scope for the greater involvement of semi-official and unofficial intermediaries in the conduct of foreign relations. Discretion was at a premium in such contacts as were made amongst enemy governments with a view to achieving an early, or separate, peace, and there was an obvious advantage in utilizing the services of emissaries whose actions could, if necessary, be disavowed. Amongst those, for instance, who became directly involved in the pursuit of a separate peace between Austria-Hungary and Britain and France were a British civil servant, a Danish merchant, a former Austrian ambassador in London, two Bourbon princes, an assortment of aristocratic ladies, an ex-prime minister of France, and a future prime minister of South Africa. Had their efforts succeeded the war might have been brought to a speedier conclusion, and at least some of the old order preserved in central Europe. But in seeking to weaken their opponents each of the major belligerents also encouraged, and sometimes assisted, revolutionaries of both a nationalist and a socialist persuasion. Ironically, it was the Russians who began this process when on 14 August 1914 the Grand Duke Nicholas issued a proclamation to the Slavs of Austria-Hungary. During the next four years Arab tribesmen, dissident Czechs and Poles, disgruntled Irishmen, Ukrainian separatists, Russian Bolsheviks and ambitious Zionists, were exploited, and very often amply rewarded, for purposes of subversion and propaganda. Strictly speaking, it is questionable whether such activities should properly be regarded as diplomacy. Nevertheless, diplomats were responsible for seeking out, and negotiating with, potential rebels. In March 1915 the German treasury provided the Wilhelmstrasse with 2 million gold marks for propaganda in Russia. Links were subsequently established between the authorities in Berlin and exiled Bolsheviks in Switzerland, and by January 1918 the Wilhelmstrasse had spent 41 million gold marks in helping to bring about a revolution which threatened to make diplomacy irrelevant.

Subversion in Russia assisted Germany in the achievement of her territorial ambitions in the east. But it was also a substitute for the failure of the German army to secure a decisive victory in the west. Propaganda likewise became an essential adjunct of German diplomacy in its effort to secure and maintain the goodwill of neutral powers in a war which it seemed increasingly difficult to win by force of arms alone. Under the direction of a former ambassador the *Zentralstelle für Auslandsdienst* was established in the Wilhelmstrasse to co-ordinate other government agencies involved in trying to influence opinion abroad. Its work consisted very largely of disbursing large sums of money to buy friendly journalists overseas, to print foreign language newspapers and books, and to support private patriotic groups. Moreover, a new *Nachrichtenabteilung* (news division) was created with a section devoted to *Kulturpropaganda*. Foreigners were to learn not only of the tragedy of Germany's encirclement, but also of the superiority of her culture. The Quai d'Orsay responded in a similar fashion. Thus in October 1915 Berthelot instituted the *Maison de la Presse*. Under the auspices of the foreign ministry, it utilized newspapers, books, pamphlets, films and works of art to explain France's good intentions to the world and to demonstrate the value of her civilization. The *Maison* was, however, subjected to constant criticism from diplomats, soldiers, and parliamentarians, who disliked its autonomy and denounced its disorderly conduct of business. And though it survived the war it did so with a much reduced staff and with the much longer, yet undoubtedly more accurate, title of the *Commissariat général à l'infomation et à la propagande*.

The increased involvement of foreign ministries and diplomats with propaganda reflected the enhanced significance of public opinion in international politics. The war required the mobilization of national resources, including manpower, on an unprecedented scale, and just as it was advantageous to undermine the enemy's morale and to win friends abroad, so it was vital to maintain the loyalty of the public at home. Recent diplomatic conduct had to be explained and justified to elements of society which in the past had rarely taken more than a transient interest in foreign policy. In an age of near total war governments thus found it expedient to pay lip-service to at least some of the tenets of open diplomacy. The British Foreign Office broke with tradition and at the commencement of the war moved quickly to set up a news department in order to place the dissemination of news about foreign affairs on a formal and systematic basis. Like its continental counterparts it also looked towards the universities and the press for assistance in its new work of public enlightenment. The War Propaganda Bureau, a body composed largely of academics and journalists, which was sponsored initially by the Home Office, was placed under the aegis of the Foreign Office at the beginning of 1916. Then two years later, after a thorough reorganization of the machinery of propaganda and the creation of a separate Ministry of Information under the press baron, Lord Beaverbrook, a number of distinguished scholars joined the Foreign Office in what became the Political Intelligence Department. Its duties consisted mainly of preparing and circulating up-to-date summaries of information on current issues. From the start, however, its assistant director, the historian, Professor James Headlam-Morley, was keen that his staff should be able to publish articles, books and pamphlets on international affairs, and he emerged as a powerful force in encouraging the Foreign Office to take the public more into its confidence, not simply through 'inspired guidance', but by providing it with the information upon which policy decisions were based.[11] He feared that unless the Foreign Office were prepared to undertake this task the public would continue to regard it as aloof, and that its authority and influence within the government would thereby be further diminished.

Headlam-Morley later became the Foreign Office's historical adviser and as such helped to pave the way for the publication of the British diplomatic correspondence of the pre-war era. But diplomatists and propagandists were not invariably the best of bedfellows. True, embassies and consulates did participate in the distribution of political and military information in the countries to which they were appointed. Individual diplomats also gave their backing to the work of private citizens such as the appropriately named Donna Bettina di Casanova, who, with the encouragement of the British ambassador at Rome, set out to woo Italy for the entente powers. It was, however, apparent that while many diplomats did not feel themselves suited to conducting propaganda, they resented the activities of those who were. This was natural enough. Successful propaganda meant appealing to, and influencing, a wide public audience, and in this sense it threatened to replace a system based upon restraint, discretion and private conversations, with one marred by widespread misunderstanding and the stimulation of uncontrollable mass emotions. Both Jusserand, the French ambassador at Washington, and Sir Cecil Spring Rice, his British colleague, conceived of their role as that of interpreting, rather than instructing, American public opinion, and in consequence they were criticized for their passivity and failure to grasp what could be achieved by the proper use of publicity. Yet it is not obvious that Spring Rice, who held regular interviews with representatives of the press, was mistaken in his assumption that the only propaganda that paid was 'proved facts' and that the American people disliked being 'preached at'.[12] The endeavours of the German embassy to advance its national cause by the establishment of an information service and the foundation, with the assistance of German immigrant societies and German-language newspapers, of a propaganda committee, did not prevent the United States from entering the war on the side of their opponents. In addition the engagement of the German military and naval attachés in this work, and their efforts to obstruct the sale of armaments to Britain and France, led to accusations that they and the Austro-Hungarian ambassador had supported industrial sabotage, and in 1915 all three were declared *personae non grata* by the State Department.

Shortly after the United States' declaration of war on Germany in April

1917 the French government dispatched André Tardieu, a former foreign editor of *Le Temps*, to New York with the title of high commissioner. Once in America he overrode Jusserand's reservations and proceeded to establish a vast propaganda and information service of his own. But Tardieu's appointment was symptomatic of another development in international politics which posed as great a challenge to the authority of professional diplomats as did propaganda to their methods. This was the direct involvement of departments other than foreign ministries in inter-governmental relations, the consequent multiplying of special missions, and the emergence of autonomous and semi-autonomous agencies alongside embassies and legations. The French war ministry, for example, sent a plethora of representatives abroad, especially to Britain and the United States, to oversee the procurement of armaments and other military equipment. Likewise, France's economic plight led to the appointment of Jean Monnet, a former cognac salesman, as the representative of the French ministry of commerce in London, and the sending of Octave Homberg to New York as the delegate of the ministry of finance.

It was the need for some kind of centralized control over these various missions, and the evident inability of the resident ambassadors to fulfil this function, that led the French government to establish high commissions in Britain and the United States. That of Marie Guernier in London lasted only a few months, but Tardieu's organization grew until it employed over 1,000 people and it even came to have its own representative in Britain. Moreover, just as military liaison amongst the entente powers was assisted by the creation at Paris of such bodies as the *Bureau Central Interallié*, whose primary responsibility was the pooling of intelligence, so also a variety of inter-allied institutions were formed to facilitate collaboration on matters relating to the blockade, shipping and the purchase and supply of food, munitions and raw materials. One of the first of these was the Wheat Executive, which was set up in the autumn of 1916, and whose purpose was to buy and redistribute wheat amongst Britain, France and Italy. A more interesting experiment, however, was the Allied Maritime Transport Executive (AMTE), which came into being in the spring of 1918. Originally conceived of by Monnet as a means of dealing with the perennial problem of a shortage of allied shipping, the AMTE was composed of civil servants, who met daily under the chairmanship of Sir Arthur Salter, and who attempted to ration tonnage amongst the allied powers. It, like other allied executive councils, had considerable decision-making powers delegated to it, and in so far as it was essentially a group of technocrats acting as a supranational authority, it represented a further shift away from traditional diplomatic practice. The state *dirigisme*, which was such a characteristic feature of the management of national economies in wartime, was thereby translated from the domestic to the international sphere.

Etienne Clémentel, France's far-sighted minister of commerce, had hoped that these new instruments of allied economic co-operation would survive the war and ease the transition to peace in Europe. But neither the United States, nor ultimately, Britain, favoured the continuation of the wartime controls that this implied, and the Supreme Economic Council which the allied and associated powers established in February 1919 had no executive powers of its own. In so far, however, as economic warfare necessitated not just greater inter-allied, but also increased inter-departmental, co-operation, it was to have a more enduring influence upon the scope and content of diplomacy. The administration of the blockade against the Central Powers forced the British Foreign Office to work more closely, though hardly more easily, with the Admiralty and the Board of Trade, and the process spawned numerous *ad hoc* committees and eventually a separate ministry responsible for the co-ordination of policy. Eyre Crowe, who was in charge of the British Foreign Office's contraband department, was quick to recognize that economic issues were likely to assume a new importance in the post-war world, and an internal committee which he chaired emphasized that the Office could no longer regard trade and finance as being outside the sphere of its normal work. This brought the Foreign Office into conflict with the Board of Trade, one result of which was a not particularly satisfactory compromise by which the two ministries agreed to establish and jointly surpervise the Department of Overseas Trade. The Quai d'Orsay was in this respect perhaps more successful than the Foreign Office. In any event, Jacques Seydoux, who in May 1919 took over the newly created *sous-direction des relations commerciales*, was able to play a far more important role in post-war debates on financial matters, such as war debts and reparations, than was any British diplomat. At the Paris Peace Conference it was the British Treasury, not the Foreign Office, which provided Britain's representatives on the reparation commission, and despite the immense significance of reparations for international relations, the Treasury was to continue to exert a pre-eminent influence on this aspect of foreign policy.

Of greater immediate significance for international politics was, however, the wartime evolution of what Maurice Hankey, the secretary of the British war cabinet, termed 'Diplomacy by Conference'. Hankey meant by this the conduct of inter-governmental relations by 'direct and frequent consultations between the principal Ministers concerned'. It was in many respects a perfectly natural development in wartime, when decisions had to be taken quickly by allied governments, and when, in Hankey's words, 'the problems presenting themselves to the Allies were too numerous, too varied, too technical and too urgent to be dealt with solely through the normal diplomatic channels'.[13] In so far as the entente powers were concerned, the process began with a conference at Calais on 6 July 1915 of the British and French prime ministers along with other members of their respective governments. The close geographical proximity of London and

Paris meant that, though such gatherings were sometimes put at risk when there were German submarines in the Channel, it was relatively easy to arrange further meetings between British and French ministers, and by January 1916 the ground rules had been laid down for the establishment of an allied committee consisting of the prime minister of any of the Allies and such members of the allied governments and their military and naval staffs as might be required. Quite apart from such missions as that of Gaston Doumergue, the French colonial minister, to Russia, and that of Balfour, the British foreign secretary, to the United States, there were during the first ten months of 1917 no fewer than eleven inter-allied ministerial conferences. And following the defeat of the Italian forces at Caporetto in the autumn, the British, French and Italian prime ministers sought to centralize and co-ordinate the allied command structure by the establishment of the Supreme War Council, a body made up of the allied political leaders, a permanent advisory general staff, and a secretariat. In practice this became a sort of cabinet of the principal Western Allies, deciding and directing the grand strategy of the war.

David Lloyd George, the British prime minister, was especially fond of the personal contact that conference diplomacy permitted him to have with his continental counterparts. It suited his own style of government in which effective political power was concentrated in a war cabinet of five members, and it allowed him to overcome what he regarded as the time-wasting of professional diplomats. He had, in any case, little respect for traditional institutions such as the Foreign Office, and he readily ignored its advice and sometimes even its existence. He preferred, instead, to listen to the counsels of members of his own secretariat in Downing Street and of the cabinet secretariat in Whitehall Gardens, and to utilize the services of such amateur diplomats as were anxious to display their talents. Much to the embarrassment of Spring Rice, he sent Lord Northcliffe, the proprietor of *The Times*, to Washington as the head of a British War Mission, and to the irritation of Bertie, who was still ambassador at Paris, he consorted with Lord Esher, who had endeavoured to establish himself as a sort of unofficial intermediary between the British and French governments. Indeed, in January 1918 Spring Rice was summarily removed from Washington, and three months later Bertie's ill-health provided Lloyd George with a pretext to replace him with Lord Derby, who, as secretary of state for war, had become a political inconvenience. Yet such changes cannot be explained simply in terms of the prime minister's penchant for intrigue and administrative innovation. They were also quite rational responses to situations in which veteran ambassadors had both ceased to be the main channel of communication between governments, and failed to exert their authority over an ever-growing number of non-diplomatic representatives of their country. Besides which, as Lloyd George explained to the war cabinet in April 1918, 'there was not very much diplomacy required in Paris'.[14] Anglo-

French relations were primarily inter-allied relations and were therefore subsumed in the discussions of the Supreme War Council. Derby, though he was appointed ambassador and head of the British war missions at Paris, was generally regarded as a decorative *grand seigneur,* providing accommodation and entertainment for visiting British ministers and officials.

Neither Georges Clemenceau, who became prime minister of France in November 1917, nor Woodrow Wilson held traditional diplomacy in any higher esteem than did Lloyd George, and both, like him, were confident of their own abilities as negotiators. And just as Clemenceau dominated his foreign minister, so Wilson treated his secretary of state as though he were an office clerk. While, however, Clemenceau was usually prepared to speak his mind to all comers, Wilson was rarely accessible, or for that matter comprehensible, to foreign diplomats. He preferred to work through unofficial agents and in particular his friend and confidant, the honorary Texan colonel, Edward House. The latter became Wilson's representative at large, travelling to Europe in 1915 and 1916 with a view to promoting the idea of a negotiated peace, and turning his Manhattan apartment into an alternative foreign ministry, where he received ambassadors, and from whence he issued unobtrusive guidance to the State Department. In such circumstances, Sir William Wiseman, a British intelligence officer in New York, was able to ingratiate himself with House and Wilson, and he eventually became a vital link between the British and American political hierarchies, providing advice and assistance to the Foreign Office and the cabinet in London. Paradiplomacy on this scale was frustrating for an ambassador of Spring Rice's calibre and temperament. Excluded from direct access to the president, he complained of Wilson's 'pronounced taste for the employment of secret foreign agents', and bemoaned his own inability to provide his government with useful information. 'He is', Spring Rice observed of Wilson, 'already a mysterious, a rather Olympian personage, and shrouded in darkness from which issue occasional thunderbolts'.[15]

One such thunderbolt was Wilson's address to the American Senate of 22 January 1917 in which, after having sounded the major belligerents on their war aims, he appealed for a 'peace without victory' negotiated amongst equals. Then, in language which echoed that of British radicals, he reaffirmed his support for the notion of replacing the balance of power with a 'community of power', and for an international organization in which states would strive for the common, rather than their separate, interests. This was all the more portentous since when, in the absence of any progress towards a negotiated peace, the United States entered the war as an associate of the entente powers, Wilson compounded his moral crusade against the values of the old international order with the economic might and military potential of a power which was capable of undermining its Eurocentric foundations. But Wilson aimed at reforming a diplomacy which was already being transformed by a long and all-embracing war. Moreover, revolution in Russia and the disintegration of the domestic political truces elsewhere in Europe constituted equally powerful catalysts in accelerating the process of change towards a more open, if not necessarily more democratic, diplomacy.

BOLSHEVIK DIPLOMACY

The collapse of the tsarist autocracy in Russia in March 1917 and the establishment there of a liberal provisional government under Prince Lvov did not in itself necessitate any substantial change in the practice of diplomacy. The republican régime could after all be more easily accommodated as a partner of the entente powers in what Wilson now labelled a 'war for democracy'. There remained, however, the possibility of a further leftwards shift of power in Russia, and the prospect of the new administration, under pressure from the social revolutionaries and Bolsheviks in the recently formed workers' and soldiers' councils (soviets), making a separate peace with Germany and its allies. To mitigate this danger the Western powers attempted to make their diplomatic representation in Russia accord more closely with the political climate there. The French sent Albert Thomas, their socialist minister of munitions, to Russia, and Lloyd George dispatched eastwards his Labour colleague, Arthur Henderson, to report, favourably it turned out, upon the work of Britain's resident ambassador in Petrograd (since 1914 the official name for St Petersburg). But events in Russia also encouraged political discontent elsewhere. During the spring and summer of 1917 there were signs of a growing war weariness throughout Europe. Industrial unrest, mutinies in the French army, a split in the ranks of the German social democrats, the passage through the Reichstag of a peace resolution, and the summoning of a conclave of the socialist Second International at Stockholm, all seemed to portend a social revolution which would transcend existing national frontiers. Faced with this spectre belligerent governments contemplated redefining their war aims on radical-populist lines. There was too a brief reversion to Renaissance diplomacy when on 1 August the Pope appealed to Christian universalism and urged governments to make peace on the basis of the pre-war territorial status quo. In so far as the papal message contained proposals for international arbitration and disarmament it evoked the spirit of the new diplomacy. Yet those who were soon to prove themselves amongst the most adept at translating the latest diplomatic theory into practice put their faith, not in Christian redemption, but in Marxist materialism.

The Bolshevik seizure of power in Petrograd on the night of 7/8 November 1917 was regarded by its chief initiators as more than a purely Russian affair. Both Lenin and Léon Trotsky saw themselves as participants in a global class struggle which, they anticipated, must spread rapidly to the more highly industrialized nations of western and central Europe. In the ensuing world revolution the state and the states system would presumably perish, and they, along with other manifestations of bourgeois society, would be replaced by a new socialist order. Whether diplomacy of any variety would have a function in the post-revolutionary world remained an open question to which Marxist theory provided no obvious answer. Bolsheviks might still have to resort to more or less traditional diplomatic practices in order to extricate Russia from the war and safeguard their revolution whilst they awaited the completion of the Marxist dialectic in the West. For Trotsky, who became the peoples commissar for foreign affairs, this was, however, no more than a temporary expedient. As Theodore von Laue has observed, Soviet diplomacy began with Trotsky, 'and Trotsky began by abolishing diplomacy'.[16] A revolutionary agitator, he accepted his new position because he thought that it would leave him time to deal with what he considered to be more important domestic and party issues. All he thought that would be necessary was for him to 'issue a few revolutionary proclamations to the peoples and then close up the joint'.[17] But prediction is a risky business even for prophets armed with scientific insights into the evolution of society, and more especially for those who grasp the reins of power in a land which is on the verge of losing a major war. There was to be no revolution elsewhere in Europe on the scale envisaged by the Bolsheviks, and faced with the demoralized state of Russia's fighting forces and the presence of a well-organized and ably commanded German army in the western provinces of the former empire, Trotsky and his comrades had firstly to conclude an armistice and then to set about the melancholy task of attempting to negotiate a peace treaty with the Central Powers. The Bolsheviks thus had diplomacy thrust upon them, and in later years were to find it an invaluable instrument in helping to accommodate Soviet Russia to a capitalist and largely hostile world.

Unlike the provisional government, the Bolsheviks had to start virtually from scratch in constituting a diplomatic service. The staff of the foreign ministry resisted the Bolshevik takeover and Trotsky, who distrusted and despised the servants of imperial Russia, kept on only a handful of their number. As a result *Narkomindel*, the Russian acronym by which the People's Commissariat for Foreign Affairs was usually known, came to rely on a cadre of Bolsheviks assigned to it by the Petrograd party committee. Outside of Russia only ten of the previous government's representatives were prepared to take instructions from Trotsky, and several Russian ambassadors worked actively against the Bolsheviks, turning their embassies into centres of opposition. Denied their expertise and experience, Trotsky and his swashbuckling deputy, Ivan Zalkind, tried instead to make use of Bolshevik exiles. Maxim Litvinov, who had for some years been resident in England, was thus appointed chargé d'affaires in London. But while the Foreign Office, which was anxious about the fate of its embassy and British nationals in Russia, accepted Litvinov as an agent of the new régime, it refused either to grant him official status or to evict the provisional government's representative from the Russian embassy in London.

Elsewhere the Bolsheviks were equally unsuccessful in their attempts to secure hold of Russia's foreign missions, and they had to suffer the indignity of having their emissaries, whose revolutionary credentials and pronouncements made them suspect in the West, arrested and deported. This made it all the more important, if the Soviet government were not to lapse into complete isolation, that Russia's allies should continue to be represented in Petrograd. As it happened the Western Powers were also keen to keep open some channels of communication with the Bolsheviks, and, whilst they prepared for a possible military intervention in Russia, they reluctantly adjusted to the requirements of what the British foreign secretary called 'this crazy system'.[18] Once more embassies were bypassed, and individuals such as Bruce Lockhart, the newly appointed British high commissioner in Petrograd, Captain Jacques Sadoul of the French military mission in Russia, and Raymond Robins of the American Red Cross, became their countries' chief intermediaries with the Bolsheviks. Not that Zalkind's chaotic administration of *Narkomindel*, where he installed machine guns in the corridors, inspired much confidence in foreign diplomats. But fortunately for those who may have been perturbed by the trigger-happy militiamen who guarded the commissariat, all really important decisions with regard to foreign policy were taken in the Smolny Institute, the headquarters of the Council of People's Commissars (*Sovnarkom*).

In the immediate aftermath of the Bolshevik coup Soviet foreign relations were conducted with an unprecedented degree of openness. The publication on 8 November 1917 of *Sovnarkom*'s decree on peace, which demanded the commencement of negotiations for a 'just and democratic peace without annexations or indemnities', was another landmark in the history of the new diplomacy. Devised as a means of reinforcing Bolshevism in Russia and of igniting revolution abroad, it addressed itself firstly to 'all belligerent peoples' and only secondly to 'their governments'. At the same time the Soviet government proclaimed the end of secret diplomacy, the abrogation of all international engagements which were designed to benefit Russian capitalists and landlords, and they promised to conduct all future negotiations 'absolutely openly before the entire people', and to publish the secret treaties in the Russian archives.[19] Thus, whilst they hoped that popular opinion would compel belligerent governments to enter into negotiations for a general peace, they threatened to break both with Russia's allies and with the mores of the old diplomacy.

The Bolsheviks also set precedent aside when in settling the terms of an armistice with the Central Powers and in subsequent peace negotiations they insisted that German and Russian troops be allowed to fraternize, and that the proceedings of the peace conference be conducted in public session. The result was a series of bizarre verbal exchanges in the fortress city of

Brest-Litovsk in which Richard von Kühlmann, the German state secretary, presented his demands for the Bolshevik abandonment of Russia's Baltic provinces, Poland and the Ukraine in the name of national self-determination, and Trotsky denounced the 'annexationist' ambitions of the Central Powers. Their raillery, like the accompanying appeals from *Narkomindel* to the workers and 'exploited' of the world, were calculated to win the sympathy of a wider public audience, and seemed to presage the debates in the assembly of the League of Nations. When finally on 10 February 1918 Trotsky rejected the latest German demands, reverted to his 'no war, no peace' formula, and informed an astonished Kühlmann that Russia would neither continue the war nor sign a peace treaty, he in effect renounced armed might and diplomacy as instruments of foreign policy. But the renewed advance of the German army towards Petrograd soon wrung from the Bolsheviks their acceptance of the draconian, though hardly 'unjust', terms of the Treaty of Brest-Litovsk. Without a repetition of their revolution in central Europe neither Lenin nor Trotsky could opt out of international politics.

The responsibility for re-integrating Russia in the European states system fell eventually upon the broad shoulders of Georgii Chicherin. A former archivist in the imperial foreign ministry, Chicherin, who succeeded Trotsky as commissar for foreign affairs in March 1918, had a good diplomatic pedigree. And though only a recent convert to Bolshevism, he had been secretary to the foreign bureau of the Russian Social Democratic Party, and was to prove a reliable exponent of Lenin's foreign policy. Under his guidance, *Narkomindel*, which, along with the rest of the Soviet administrative machine, was moved to Moscow on 25 March, gradually acquired a semblance of bureaucratic order. Nevertheless, diplomacy remained both a servant and a whipping boy of the revolution. Its élitist practices were regarded as anomalous in a revolutionary society, and its practitioners were held in low esteem. In a single egalitarian gesture *Sovnarkom* moved in June 1918 to abolish all diplomatic ranks, and henceforth *Narkomindel*'s envoys were to have the title of plenipotentiary representative or *polpred*. Likewise the Soviet authorities declined to recognize the traditional distinction between great and small powers. But when, after the opening of full diplomatic relations between Bolshevik Russia and the major European powers, it proved impossible to determine the exact position of a *polpred* in the diplomatic corps of foreign capitals, the Soviets gave obtuse recognition to the long-established diplomatic ranking of individuals and states. Bolshevik emphasis on the need for economy and simplicity of style was similarly set aside in order to satisfy the requirements of protocol. Indeed, early Soviet diplomats were in some instances left with considerable personal discretion. They had, in seeking to bridge the gap between the new and old orders in Europe, frequently to act on their own initiative, and in this respect the initial impact of the communist revolution on diplomacy might be said to have been the reverse of that of the communications revolution of the previous century.

Soviet diplomacy was, nevertheless, revolutionary in its form and content – a fact that was only too apparent in a capital such as Berlin where Russia's representatives had to rely on the assistance of local communists. Moreover, the outbreak of civil war in Russia and the intervention in it of some of Russia's former allies further diminished the opportunities for formal diplomatic contacts between the Bolsheviks and the outside world. The invasion of the British consulate at Petrograd by a riotous mob, the murder of the British naval attaché, the arrest of Lockhart in September 1918, and the expulsion of Litvinov from London on a charge of having used his diplomatic bag to import revolutionary material, led to a complete break in Anglo-Soviet relations. Even the Germans, who had endured the assassination of their ambassador to Russia, ended all official contacts with the Bolsheviks in the autumn of 1918. Russia's diplomatic representation was soon limited to a few Asian capitals, and the Bolsheviks had to depend increasingly upon public appeals to opinion in the West and unofficial channels of communication. All kinds of non-diplomatic personnel and bodies were utilized. Karl Radek, who was arrested by the Prussian authorities after having slipped into Germany to attend the All-German Congress of Workers' and Soldiers' Councils in December 1918, received industrialists and military men in his prison cell which became a virtual diplomatic mission. On other occasions bodies engaged in relief work and the care and repatriation of prisoners of war served a similar function.

Only after the victory of the Bolsheviks over their domestic opponents and the ending of the military conflict on Russia's western frontiers were more conventional links gradually established between Moscow and other European capitals. These were initially achieved through commercial and financial negotiations and responded to the desire of the industrial powers to re-open Russia to trade and to secure compensation for the debts of the Tsarist governments which the Bolsheviks had repudiated. Leonid Krassin, the head of the Soviet trade mission in London, was thus to become an ambassador in all but name, and contracts arranged between German industry and the Bolsheviks were to play a vital role in helping to bring about the German–Soviet Treaty of Rapallo of April 1922.

The emerging Soviet state meanwhile refined and formalized its techniques of subversion and propaganda. Assistance to non-Russian revolutionary movements, whether they were of a proletarian, national or anti-colonialist variety, became a recognized object of Soviet diplomacy. But subversion was also effectively institutionalized in Comintern, the Russian-sponsored communist international. Founded in March 1919, it co-ordinated and promoted revolutionary activities throughout the world. It had its own information service and intelligence gathering centre, and in so far as it was Soviet-dominated it provided the Politburo in Moscow with the opportunity to penetrate and influence the domestic politics of other states. Long after Soviet Russia had gained international recognition and exchanged ambassadors with the capitalist powers of the West, the Bolsheviks continued to conduct their foreign relations on two planes – a diplomatic and a revolutionary one. The ideological dimension had its advantages for the agents of *Narkomindel*. At a time when Russia was weak in almost every other respect the threat of subversion that Comintern posed to order in other countries meant that the socialist motherland could not simply be ignored. This was evident in the way that both the German and the British governments sought in negotiating with the Russians to limit communist propaganda. Comintern was, however, also quite capable of hampering and undermining the patient work of Soviet diplomats. It was, for instance, particularly difficult for *Narkomindel* to maintain friendly relations with a government which Comintern was working simultaneously to overthrow. Outwardly the Soviet authorities tried to maintain the fiction that Comintern was an international organization for which they had no responsibility. Yet Comintern agents regularly served in Soviet diplomatic missions and enjoyed the immunities and privileges which their positions conferred upon them. The presence alongside them of members of the security services, and the influence exercised by local party cells, frequently meant that Soviet embassies were hotbeds of conspiracy and intrigue. The Bolsheviks may have been amongst the first practitioners of the new diplomacy, but their methods often seemed to bear a closer resemblance to those recommended by Machiavelli than those demanded by E.D. Morel.

PUBLICITY AND PEACEMAKING

The Bolshevik experiment with open diplomacy in the autumn of 1917 failed either to provoke an early revolution in the West, or to promote negotiations for a general peace. It did, however, encourage the British government to reformulate and state publicly its war aims in terms which were calculated to appeal to its critics on the left. Confronted with the grim prospect of another winter campaign, Lloyd George sought, amongst other things, to maintain the support of organized labour for continuing the war and to dissuade the Russians from abandoning their allies. In an address to the British Trades Union Congress on 5 January 1918 he insisted that the future of European civilization could not be submitted to the 'arbitrary decisions of a few negotiators striving to secure by chicanery or persuasion the interests of this or that dynasty or nation', and he called for a territorial settlement based upon 'the right of self-determination or the consent of the governed'. He also added that the peacemakers would have 'to seek the creation of some international organisation to limit the burden of armaments and diminish the probability of war'.[20] Three days later Woodrow Wilson spoke in similar though more precise terms when in his speech to

Congress he set out his famous fourteen points. Anxious as ever to democratize society and diplomacy in the old world, he too advocated a peace founded upon the principle of national self-determination, and he reiterated his support for a 'general association of nations'. But equally significant for the history of diplomatic practice was his first point: 'Open covenants of peace, openly arrived at, after which there shall be no private international understandings of any kind but diplomacy shall proceed always frankly and in the public view.'[21] The UDC, from which Wilson evidently drew many of his ideas, had seemed to triumph. One of its most cherished ideals had been enshrined in both the American and Bolshevik programmes for peace. Moreover, the fact that the armistice concluded with Germany in November 1918 was tied to the qualified acceptance by its signatories of Wilson's fourteen points as the basis of the future peace, seemed to herald a new age of what Harold Nicolson later dubbed 'democratic diplomacy'.[22]

The Paris Peace Conference of 1919–20 was, however, hardly the open forum that many journalists had expected. It soon transpired that Wilson, like Morel, favoured submitting the results, rather than the process, of negotiation to public examination, and in January 1919 he agreed that, whilst the press should be admitted to the plenary sessions of the conference, it would be excluded from the deliberations of the Council of Ten (Wilson, his secretary of state, the two chief delegates of Japan, and the prime ministers and foreign ministers of Britain, France and Italy). Conscious of the differences that were likely to arise amongst them, the representatives of the great powers feared that premature revelations in the newspapers might inflame public opinion and limit the scope for compromise. As in the past the public learned of what was being decided in their name from press leaks and official communiqués. Yet in other respects the conference did constitute a break with the traditions of nineteenth-century diplomacy. Wilson's decision to attend the conference in person was itself an innovation. No previous American president had left the United States to negotiate an international treaty. Nor for that matter had any of his predecessors exercised so much influence upon politics in Europe. His presence at Paris was itself a reflection of the decline of the European states system. After all, by the time the conference began its work, two of the key elements of the pre-war concert had disappeared. The Russian Empire had collapsed into revolution and civil war, and Austria-Hungary had disinte-Grated into its component national parts. Old dynasties had departed and many of the aristocratic virtues and pretensions which had provided Europe with a veneer of unity had been discredited and discarded. Four years of war had also eroded Europe's economic and political pre-eminence in world affairs, and the decisive part played by the United States in the defeat of the Central Powers seemed like evidence of an impending transition from a European to a global system of international politics. At Paris Wilson was in a strong position to impose his methods upon the victors as well as the defeated.

One consequence of Wilson's participation in the conference was the abandonment of the usual European practice of proceeding rapidly from an armistice to the conclusion of peace preliminaries, and thence to the negotiation of a definitive peace treaty. There was instead a delay of two months between the armistice and the assembling of the delegations at Paris, and during the next four weeks the timetable of the conference was largely dictated by the president's preoccupation with the establishment of the League of Nations. Moreover, his presence alongside the heads of government of the principal European allies seemed to have the effect of transforming the conference into what one American scholar has seen as an early example of 'summit diplomacy' – a term which only entered the vocabulary of international politics in the early 1950s.[23] There were in all six plenary sessions of the conference between 18 January and the conclusion of the Treaty of Versailles with Germany. But these were for the most part mere formalities. As in 1814 so in 1919 the great victorious powers were determined that they should make the great decisions. This was all the more apparent when towards the end of March the lack of progress made towards the drafting of a peace treaty, and the unwieldy size of the Council of Ten, whose sessions could be attended by as many as fifty-three people when officials and secretaries were included, led Wilson to propose that he and the prime ministers of Britain, France and Italy should in future meet privately in his apartment. There was some irony in the fact that Wilson, the apostle of open diplomacy, should have made this proposal in response to a complaint from Lloyd George over the leaking of the details of conference discussions to the press. Nevertheless, the informal, and at first rather disorganized, meetings of the Council of Four accelerated the process of decision-making. Indeed, on the one occasion that Wilson was tempted to resort to open diplomacy the result was almost a disaster. When on 23 April he appealed to the Italian people against the territorial demands of their government the manoeuvre backfired, and the Italian leaders departed from the conference in high dudgeon. Only on 6 May did they return to Paris in order to witness the presentation on the next day of the draft treaty to the Germans.

Excluded from this process of negotiation, the Germans also fell back upon the techniques of open diplomacy. Ulrich von Brockdorff-Rantzau, the career diplomat whom the new republican government in Berlin chose as its foreign minister and chief delegate at Paris, never had the opportunity to become a Prussian Talleyrand. The terms of the draft treaty were hammered out by the Council of Four, and although the Germans were asked to submit their observations on the text and were able to secure some modifications favourable to themselves, the only real choice open to them was that of acceptance or rejection. The Versailles Treaty was in its essentials a dictated peace. In these circumstances the Germans, with no allies and few friends, forsook the finesse of the old diplomacy, and, like the Bolsheviks, appealed to a wider public audience. They hoped in vain that the allied governments would thus be pressurized into adopting a liberal interpretation of the fourteen points in their handling of Germany. Public opinion in Britain and France was even less inclined than Clemenceau and Lloyd George towards a peace of reconciliation. But the Germans quickly mastered the new diplomacy. The fact that the post-war territorial settlement was in many instances patently irreconcilable with the principle of national self-determination provided German politicians and diplomats with good grounds for claiming that Germany had been unjustly treated. In addition the inclusion in the reparations section of the treaty of the assertion that the war had been 'imposed' upon the allied and associated powers 'by the aggression of Germany and her allies' encouraged the Wilhelmstrasse to harness historians to its cause.[24]

A *Schuldreferat* (War Guilt Section) was established in the German foreign office for the express purpose of mobilizing all available means of convincing people that Germany had not been responsible for the war. If this battle could be won then the moral, and presumably the legal, basis for reparations would disappear. One result of the *Schuldreferat's* work was the publication of a massive selection of German and Russian diplomatic documents of the pre-war period, and eventually first the British and then the French government felt compelled to follow the German example by opening their archives to historians. In this fashion the war guilt question gave rise to an open diplomacy which was competitive and retrospective: a version of the new diplomacy which responded to the demands of more democratic societies and to the nationalistic passions released by the war. Its object was above all to influence governments through public opinion. And in a world in which the United States had assumed a new importance, especially where war debts and the financing of reparations were concerned, both the Foreign Office and the Wilhelmstrasse were aware of the advantages of making their respective interpretations of recent history prevail in North America. There were also good domestic reasons for this new openness. Brockdorff-Rantzau wished to secure popular support for his diplomacy at Paris, and he and his successors endeavoured to unite the German public behind their policies by rejecting the charge of war guilt. The British Foreign Office had in the meanwhile to defend itself against the accusations of its critics that it had fabricated or tampered with documentary evidence relating to the origins of the war. Indeed the wartime eclipse of the Foreign Office in the counsels of government helped generate the interest of British diplomats in enlightening the public with regard to the object of their work.

Officials within the Foreign Office had hoped that peace would bring with it a restoration of that power and influence of which the war and Lloyd

George had seemed to deprive them. But British diplomats were, like their French counterparts, to be disappointed and frustrated by the limited role allotted to them at the peace conference. Neither the elaborate plans of the Foreign Office, nor those of the Quai d'Orsay, for the organization of the conference were to be put into effect. Lloyd George continued to rely on the advice and assistance of figures such as Hankey and Philip Kerr, who had been close to him during the war, and he showed his contempt for professional diplomacy in choosing Hankey, rather than the permanent under-secretary at the Foreign Office, to head the secretariat of the British delegation. Clemenceau treated the Quai d'Orsay with similar disdain, and although Jules Cambon, its first secretary-general, was to be one of France's principal delegates, the prime minister appointed Paul Dutasta, a diplomatic nonentity, to the prestigious post of secretary-general of the conference. Dutasta remained a mediocrity. He was publicly humiliated by Clemenceau and excluded from the Council of Four, to whose gatherings only an interpreter and eventually Hankey were admitted on a permanent basis. The main contribution of professional diplomacy to the drafting of the Treaty of Versailles was not therefore made in the councils of the chief decision-makers, but in the various technical commissions and committees which were set up to make recommendations to the conference.

The determination of the allied and associated leaders to negotiate personally with each other did, however, have one advantage from the American and British points of view. This was the formal acceptance of English as a language of equal standing with French in international relations. The Quai d'Orsay had thus far succeeded in maintaining a special position for French in diplomatic exchanges. Even Lenin in his first meeting with the *corps diplomatique* at Petrograd had, more, it would seem, out of a sense of the ridiculous than out of any respect for tradition, insisted that its doyen, a monolingual American, address him in French, 'the language of diplomacy'.[25] But at Paris in 1919 Hankey fought hard to ensure an equal status for English in the proceedings of the conference. His task was made easier by the fact that while Clemenceau was fluent in English, neither Wilson nor Lloyd George were adept in the use of French. The odd man out was the Italian prime minister, Vittorio Orlando, who spoke French but knew no English. When his foreign minister pleaded that Italian be accorded equal status, he was reminded that, unlike English, his native tongue was hardly spoken outside of Europe. In the end Orlando sulked, the French gave way, and the Versailles Treaty made it plain that both the English and French texts were to be regarded as authentic. The change was regretted by those ambassadors who saw advantage in maintaining French as 'so to speak the private language of diplomacy' in an increasingly fragmented and multilingual states system. Yet for Stephen Gaselee, the Foreign Office librarian, the achievement of equal status for the English language was 'one of the few solid gains of the Paris Peace Conference'.[26]

It was all the more appropriate that it should have been achieved by men who were regarded as outsiders to diplomacy.

THE LEAGUE OF NATIONS

Many more amateur diplomats were destined to become involved in the process of international negotiation as the result of another achievement of the conference: the drafting of the covenant of the League of Nations which formed the first part of each of the five post-war treaties. Within governing circles in Britain the notion of establishing a league had gained considerable support from Lord Robert Cecil, who was appointed minister of blockade in February 1916, and the omnipresent Jan Smuts, who joined the war cabinet in the summer of 1917. Others, who were more sceptical about Britain involving itself in entangling international commitments, soon recognized the value of the project as a means of enticing Wilson's America into the entente camp. Yet it evoked little enthusiasm amongst professional diplomats. Even such modest proposals as those put forward by the Phillimore Committee (a body appointed by Lloyd George in January 1918), which recommended little more than the institutionalizing of the concert of Europe through *ad hoc* conferences of ministers and ambassadors with limited powers to impose sanctions upon lawbreaking states, were regarded with suspicion by senior functionaries in the Foreign Office. And the plan advocated by Kerr and Hankey for transforming the Supreme War Council into a league of nations, was anathema to diplomats who considered conference diplomacy a negation of their craft. Nevertheless, the determination of Wilson, Cecil and Smuts to have their way, the desire of the British to retain American goodwill, and the hopes of the French that such an organization would become an instrument for policing Germany and maintaining the security of France, ensured the triumph of the league idea. For the first time permanent political institutions were created to facilitate the peaceful settlement of disputes, new agencies of international co-operation were formed, and a new code of principles, rights and obligations was instituted to regulate international behaviour.

Where the maintenance of peace was concerned the theory of collective security, as represented by the League of Nations, was simple enough. Its member states were obliged to settle their disputes peacefully and not to go to war with each other until they had exhausted the procedures for arbitration and conciliation laid down in the covenant. Those who ignored or transgressed these rules and resorted to war would be 'deemed' to have committed an act of war against all the other member states, and they would be subjected automatically to economic sanctions and threatened by the preponderant military might of the remainder of the membership. In addition Article X of the covenant required members to 'respect and preserve as against external aggression' the territorial integrity and independence of other members, and an oblique recognition of the need for peaceful change was given in Article XIX which provided for the 'consideration' of 'international conditions whose continuance might endanger the peace of the world'.[27] Aggression might thus be deterred without resort to divisive alliances and costly and potentially dangerous arms races. But for the daily practice of diplomacy the novelty of the League lay not so much in these provisions, whose main effect was to broaden and universalize the sort of commitments that states had previously entered into through treaties of alliance and arbitration, as in the political and administrative machinery which were established in the form of the Council, the Assembly and the Secretariat. Of these the Council, which, as originally conceived, was to consist of the representatives of the five principal allied and associated powers plus those of four other powers, was the most consistent with the traditions of the European states system. It could, despite its broader and more egalitarian composition, be regarded as the heir to the old concert of European great powers. There was, however, no obvious precedent for either the Assembly in which all member states were to be represented with equal voting rights, or the Secretariat which was intended to serve the other two organs of the League. The former provided a new theatre for multilateral diplomacy, and the latter gave birth to a new actor, the international civil servant.

There were any number of professional diplomats in 1919 who wondered if the world really needed these new institutions at all. Paul Cambon, whose son, Henri, had recently been appointed to the French legation at Bucharest, viewed the League and Wilsonian diplomacy with a sense of deep foreboding. 'Every day', he lamented in April 1919, 'I regret having allowed my son to choose a dying career'.[28] In principle the League certainly stood in contradistinction to the secret diplomacy of which he was a past master. Its covenant required the registration and publication of treaties and other engagements amongst member states, and its Assembly was intended to be nothing less than what Wilson liked to call 'the organised opinion of mankind'. The Assembly's first meeting in 1920 was attended by some of the best-known statesmen of the period. The British government even sent along a member of its parliamentary opposition, and the Japanese delegation was so large that a ship had to be specially chartered to take it to Europe. In the Assembly's parliamentary-style debates success often depended upon oratorical display rather than upon the traditional skills of diplomatic bargaining. But the covenant also accepted that bilateral diplomacy still had its place in international intercourse. It thus stipulated that disputes should be referred to arbitration if they could not 'be satisfactorily settled by diplomacy'.[29]

The size of the Assembly and the very openness of its debates in any case disqualified it as an efficient instrument for either reconciling disputants or managing crises. The composition of the Council likewise hindered its development as a directorate of the great powers, and its authority was diminished by the American Senate's rejection of the Versailles Treaty and the covenant and the consequent non-participation of the United States. After Germany's admission to the League in 1926 the meetings of the Council and the annual sessions of the Assembly provided the British, French and German foreign ministers with the opportunity to meet regularly to examine, and sometimes settle, their unresolved mutual differences. Subsequent divisions amongst the great powers, and in particular the challenge posed by first Japan, then Germany and Italy, to the status quo, were, however, to deprive the Council of its unity of purpose and eventually much of its influence. Like the other organs of the League it ended by supplementing rather than supplanting the work of professional diplomacy.

The early pioneers of the League idea had envisaged an organization which would have a larger and more central role in international affairs. But Sir Eric Drummond, the League's first secretary-general, seems from the start to have conceived of his own and the League's actions as peripheral to the everyday business of diplomacy. A former private secretary to Sir Edward Grey, he recognized that a permanent organization such as the League might enable the powers to avoid a repetition of the war crisis of 1914 when all Grey's efforts to assemble the representatives of the great powers in concert had come to nought. At the same time Drummond, who in Ramsay MacDonald's words had been 'trained in the methods of discredited diplomacy',[30] sought to put his training and experience to good use, not by bold public pronouncements, but through private initiatives. He maintained close links with his former colleagues in the Foreign Office, who kept him supplied with copies of the confidential print, and his first deputy, Jean Monnet, was a valuable channel of communication with the Quai d'Orsay. This hardly matched Cecil's idealistic notion of the secretary-general as an international 'chancellor', who would be the very embodiment of the League, summoning up world opinion to keep delinquent powers in check. Drummond was, however, a peculiar example of the old diplomacy serving the purposes of the new.

It was perhaps typical of Drummond that he should have discouraged the establishment by member states of permanent delegations at Geneva, the seat of the League. He regarded the Secretariat as an executor of the decisions of the Council and the Assembly, and he preferred to deal directly with governments rather than through intermediaries. Besides which, the Swiss authorities, who readily granted diplomatic immunity to the internationally recruited Secretariat, were less enthusiastic about extending it to an increasing number of foreign representatives in what, after all, was only a provincial city. The resident delegations, nevertheless, grew steadily in size and by 1937 there were forty-six such missions, organized into a *corps diplomatique* with an elected *doyen*. They varied in their composition, nomenclature and powers. More than half of them were autonomous and accredited exclusively to the League. Others, though they might possess offices at Geneva, were included in, or dependent upon, their countries' missions elsewhere. In some instances they were no more than consulates performing the functions of permanent delegations. Initially their main purpose was advisory rather than representational. Most governments preferred to send political leaders or senior foreign ministry officials to participate in Assembly and Council debates, and on such occasions delegation members were often relegated to an auxiliary role. Only slowly did they begin to take on more responsibilities, such as representing their countries in the League's technical commissions and committees. Indeed, with the exception of Japan, none of the permanent members of the League Council maintained a resident delegation at Geneva. But this did not deter some important non-member states from creating *de facto* missions there. Thus in 1930 Prentiss Gilbert, a former State Department official, was appointed United States consul-general in Geneva in order to oversee relations between Washington and the League Secretariat. Even Japan, the first major power to leave the League, retained in Geneva an office for international conferences.

The permanent delegations were a measure of the prestige of the League. They were also symptomatic of its integration into the existing states system. And although they may have identified themselves with the so-called 'spirit of Geneva', they rarely forgot that they were there to promote their own distinctly national interests. In this respect it is interesting to note that few countries (perhaps twelve at most) responded positively to the Secretariat's proposal that members should establish special offices in their own capitals to receive, collate and circulate communications from the League. More often than not those states that began by creating such departments soon allowed them to merge with other divisions of their foreign ministries so that in time they lost their unique status. The British Foreign Office's League of Nations section was in fact only a sub-section of its western department, consisting by the end of the 1930s of three officials who regularly decamped from London to Geneva for sessions of the Assembly and Council. Only the Quai d'Orsay retained a completely separate League of Nations section throughout the inter-war years. It was responsible for liaison with Geneva and for the co-ordination of French policy towards the League. Yet within the twenty years of its existence it too shrank to half its original size.

Amongst the functions of the *Section française de la Société des Nations* were those of examining in conjunction with other interested ministries the line to be pursued by France, and the mode of her representation, in the several economic, social and technical agencies for which the League was responsible. Thus the League acted as a sort of umbrella organization for a variety of international humanitarian and social endeavours, some of which pre-dated its establishment. It set up commissions and committees to consider and report on particular issues as, for example the economic and financial reconstruction of Austria, and summoned conferences such as those which dealt with the world economy in 1927 and 1933, and that on disarmament in 1932–3. Under its auspices bodies were also created to foster international collaboration in the spheres of education, health and hygiene, and communications and transit. And alongside the League the International Labour Organization, itself the product of the peace treaties, brought together representatives of employers and employees in an effort to study and improve conditions of work. The effect of all this intense activity at Geneva was not simply to expand the subject matter of diplomacy. After all, European governments had in the past co-operated in an effort to set in order the finances of the Ottoman Empire, and they had tried through international agreements to tackle such diverse subjects as the status of Romanian Jews and trafficking in white slaves and Abyssinian eunuchs. The League and its agencies did, however, involve the employment of a much larger number of non-diplomatic specialists and experts in international politics than had previously been the case. In so far as it made more work for lawyers the same might also be said of the Permanent Court of International Justice which came into being in 1922. Composed in the first place of eleven jurisconsults, it was able to offer advisory opinions on matters relating to international law and to make judgements on such quarrels as were brought before it. It responded to the desire of peoples and governments for a more orderly conduct of international relations, and encouraged recourse to judicial, rather than strictly diplomatic, procedures in the handling of disputes.

CONFERENCE DIPLOMACY

Many of the more contentious issues of international politics in the early post-war years were subjected neither to investigation by the League, nor judgement by the Permanent Court. Instead, they were dealt with by two other organs of multilateral diplomacy which had their roots in the war and the subsequent peace negotiations. These were the standing conference of the ambassadors of the principal allied and associated powers at Paris, and the *ad hoc* gatherings of international leaders which were convened at irregular intervals during the first three years of peace. The former, which was better known simply as the ambassadors' conference, resulted from a decision taken by the allies in July 1919 to establish a permanent commission of their representatives for the interpretation of the peace treaties. It came formally into existence on 26 January 1920, met usually once a week, and supervised the work of the various commissions on frontier delimitation, plebiscites, arms control and reparations, for which the peace conference had provided. Under the chairmanship of Jules Cambon, the ambassadors' conference developed its own *esprit de corps* and soon became a general clearing house through which co-operation of a kind was maintained amongst the former allies by traditional diplomatic methods. Yet at a time when wars were still being fought in eastern Europe and western Anatolia, and when Bolshevism and revived Turkish nationalism threatened to overturn the new territorial status quo, there were questions upon which the ambassadors could not agree, and which required urgent consideration by governments. The ministerial conferences which sought to tackle these problems were, in so far as they involved the leaders of the wartime allies, heirs to the Supreme Council (as the Supreme War Council had become during the making of the peace). They differed considerably in their size and composition, varying from the three day meeting of the British and French prime ministers at Hythe in May 1920 to the six-week conference in which thirty-four states were represented at Genoa in the spring of 1922. Moreover, after the Spa conference of July 1920, which the Germans attended to discuss reparations, conference diplomacy increasingly involved representatives of the defeated powers, and at Genoa even the Bolsheviks were present.

In the first instance these inter-governmental reunions were, like the ambassadors' conference, mainly concerned with the application of the peace settlement. And, despite the fact that there could be few international problems which were unrelated to the post-war treaties, the League Council attempted to concentrate upon the more permanent issues of international relations. It therefore ignored an appeal from Germany in March 1921 when a quarrel over reparations led the Allies to extend their military occupation of the Rhineland to the Ruhr ports. But the victorious powers themselves readily discarded responsibility for those aspects of the peace treaties that threatened to divide them. The League was thus left with the thankless task of determining the German–Polish frontier in Upper Silesia when the plebiscite required by the Versailles Treaty failed to provide an obvious answer to the question of who should have sovereignty over the province. On the other hand the absence from the League of the United States, Soviet Russia and Germany made conference diplomacy a more convenient means of dealing with naval disarmament and the economic reconstruction of Europe. There was also a reluctance on the part of some great powers to take matters to the League, especially when their dignity and interests were involved. When in 1923 the murder of an Italian officer engaged in delimiting the Greco-Albanian frontier was followed by the Italian bombardment of Corfu, Benito Mussolini, who had come to power in the previous autumn, insisted that the affair be settled by the ambassadors' conference. There was indeed always an inclination on the part of the great powers to side-step the League if a more satisfactory procedure could be found.

The persistence of conference diplomacy not only limited the League's scope for action, it also obstructed the return to more conventional patterns of diplomatic dialogue amongst the European powers. Lloyd George, who continued to occupy a prominent position in world affairs until the collapse of his government in October 1922, still preferred to settle the 'great questions' of the day through discussions amongst principals rather than between diplomats. And although there were many aspects of British foreign policy with which the prime minister did not directly concern himself, his interventions could be distinctly disconcerting, especially when they were taken on his own initiative and without reference to Lord Curzon, the foreign secretary. He continued, as during the war, to rely on his private secretaries and the cabinet secretariat in order to communicate with foreign governments, and Hankey assumed powers of organization and co-ordination which seemed to deny the competence of the Foreign Office. In consequence morale remained low within the British foreign service. These developments cannot, however, be attributed solely to the prime minister's aversion to 'negotiation by Notes'.[31] Problems such as those concerned with disarmament and the assessment, collection and attri-bution of reparations required a knowledge of strategy and finance which traditional diplomacy was ill-equipped to supply, and lent themselves to multilateral rather than bilateral negotiations. The war had in any case accustomed Europe's statesmen to personal diplomacy, and in its aftermath there seemed to be great sense in their continuing to meet to examine and enforce the conditions of peace.

After Lloyd George's resignation there was a decline in the frequency of ministerial reunions in Europe. Raymond Poincaré, who in January 1922 once more became prime minister of France, was an avowed opponent of the practice, and neither of the next two British prime ministers were inclined to follow the example of their illustrious predecessor. But both of the major issues which dominated great power relations in Europe during 1923, the establishment of peace in the Near East, where Turkish national-ists succeeded in defying the victors of 1918, and the Franco-Belgian attempt to wring reparation payments out of Germany through a military occupation of the Ruhr, were eventually settled by conferences. Indeed the Lausanne conference, in which Curzon personally participated and which remade the peace settlement with Turkey, was one of the most enduring achievements of British diplomacy in the inter-war years; and the London conference of 1924, which adopted the recommendations of a committee of financial experts on German reparations payments, opened the way to a Franco-German *détente* and the treaties eventually concluded at the Locarno conference of October 1925. The central feature of the latter arrangements was the formal acceptance by Belgium, France and Germany of the status quo in the Rhineland, and its guarantee by Britain and Italy. Yet they also represented a movement towards a political reconciliation in western Europe through the furtherance of which the British, French and German governments hoped to achieve their own specific goals. For the French this meant above all security and the regular payment of reparations; and for the Germans it included the revision of the Versailles settlement in a sense favourable to themselves, and international recognition of their equality of rights and status. These ends were pursued through what were popularly known as the Geneva 'tea-parties' – the more or less regular meetings of Austen Chamberlain, Aristide Briand and Gustav Stresemann, the foreign ministers respectively of Britain, France and Germany, which, after Germany's admission to the League in September 1926, usually coincided with the quarterly sessions of the Council.

One of the prevailing assumptions of the protagonists of conference diplomacy was that international conflict was essentially the product of misunderstanding and of a failure in communications, and that these could be avoided if those ultimately responsible for the making of foreign policy could meet together to discuss matters without the complication of intermediaries. They would, it was presumed, be better able to appreciate each other's fears, hopes and aspirations, and if they were also answerable to elected assemblies, their conversations would ensure a greater degree of democratic control of policy. Experienced parliamentarians, as Briand, Chamberlain and Stresemann were, thus had the opportunity to apply skills learned in cabinet and party politics to their informal conclaves. In the privacy of hotel bedrooms they were able to co-ordinate their policies and arrange the affairs of Europe, while the role of their ambassadors was reduced to that of handling low-level and routine matters, preparing for future meetings, and putting ministerial decisions into effect. Their endeavours which coincided with a period of political stability and relative economic prosperity acquired an aura of success. Some progress was made towards modifying the Versailles Treaty as it related to the disarmament of Germany and the military occupation of the Rhineland, and as a confidence-building exercise the 'tea-parties' helped to remove some French doubts about Germany's intentions. Nevertheless, it remains a matter for speculation whether the French could ever have voluntarily accepted a stronger Germany, or whether the Germans could have reconciled themselves to continued restrictions on the exercise of their power. The gulf which separated the two nations was a wide one, and with the onset of the economic depression at the end of the 1920s and the lurch towards political extremism in Germany, the prospects for what Lloyd George had called the 'general appeasement' of Europe rapidly receded.

Well before the removal of Austen Chamberlain from office in the spring of 1929 and Stresemann's death in the following October it was plain to see that Locarno diplomacy had serious shortcomings. Conservative critics of the new diplomacy had all along held that the conduct of international relations was a professional and sophisticated business which required a grasp of special negotiating skills that few politicians possessed. Anxious for success and public acclaim, political leaders might be tempted either to make unnecessary concessions, or to take up too rigid a stance. And in the absence of formal written accords, their meetings could lead to confusion over what, if anything, had been settled, and end by generating almost as much international friction as they were originally intended to remove. Talks between Lloyd George and Clemenceau had been followed by French claims and British disclaimers of what one had promised to the other. Likewise, Briand and Stresemann disagreed over the terms of a verbal accord which had preceded Germany's signing of the Locarno Treaties, and in December 1928 an irate Stresemann returned from a League Council meeting under the mistaken impression that Chamberlain had accused the German army of extensive breaches of the Versailles Treaty. Professional diplomats were not, however, immune to such errors. They too were capable of biased and selective reporting. But ambassadors could be repudiated, and if their negotiations were kept secret their mistakes were less likely to lead to the sort of political embarrassments that resulted from the *faux pas* of leading statesmen.

The Locarnoites sought to avoid the dangers of adverse public criticism by conducting their conversations in the utmost secrecy. To League supporters this seemed like a reversion to pre-war methods, with the representatives of the great powers simply presenting their decisions to the Assembly and Council for comment. Robert Cecil accused Chamberlain of using the organization 'merely as a convenient lot of machinery for the old diplomacy'.[32] And, although the consequences were not so dire, there was a certain resemblance between Briand's meeting with Stresemann at Thoiry in September 1926 and that which had taken place some eighteen years before between Izvolsky and Aehrenthal at Buchlau. Both Briand and Stresemann, who had been at Geneva for Germany's formal entry into the League, deliberately took measures to avoid the press and travelled separately to the hamlet of Thoiry in the French Jura, where, over a luncheon which included four bottles of table wine and one of champagne, they explored the basis for a Franco-German bargain which would have modified the current reparations settlement and changed the status of the Rhineland. During the previous twelve months French diplomats had been putting out feelers for such a deal, but at Thoiry the two foreign ministers appear to have projected more enthusiasm and determination than they possessed. Briand had subsequently to reckon with considerable domestic opposition to any large concessions to Germany, and in defending himself against charges of having sacrificed France's security, he deliberately obscured the part played by the Quai d'Orsay in promoting the scheme. As so often happened during the Locarno era, expectations were raised that could not be realized, and this in turn led to frustration and disappointment. The methodology of Locarno diplomacy helped to create an illusion of reconciliation in Europe when in fact there is very little reason to suppose that

Franco-German relations were any more harmonious in the autumn of 1929 than they had been in the summer of 1925.

Notwithstanding the meagre results of the Geneva 'tea-parties', the practice of foreign ministers and other national leaders negotiating with their opposite numbers remained very much in vogue. In 1929 Ramsay MacDonald became the first British prime minister to visit the United States, and he and President Hoover were able to consider the prospects for a new Anglo-American agreement on naval arms limitation. Five years later the French foreign minister, Louis Barthou, took advantage of the presence of the Soviet commissar for foreign affairs at Geneva in order to suggest to him the idea of what became the Franco-Soviet alliance. Such successes were, however, rare, and the 1930s were littered with examples of ministerial diplomacy which ended in misunderstanding and discord. Both Mussolini's first meeting with Hitler at Venice in June 1934 and his conversations in January 1935 with Barthou's successor, Pierre Laval, led to confusion and the misinterpretation of the other party's intentions. Moreover, the perambulations of French foreign ministers in east and central Europe did little either to clarify or strengthen France's alliances and alignments there, and the endeavours of Barthou to reconcile two potential allies ended in disaster when both he and King Alexander of Yugoslavia were assassinated at Marseilles in October 1934. Even when professional diplomats had a hand in preparing the grounds for agreement, subsequent meetings between the relevant ministers could end in political turmoil. There was a public outcry in Britain when in December 1935 the press learned of talks between Samuel Hoare, the foreign secretary, and Laval on the settlement of the Italo-Abyssinian War. And despite the fact that the basis of the 'Hoare–Laval plan' had long been under consideration in the Foreign Office, Hoare was forced out of office for having dared envisage the dismemberment of a victim of Fascist aggression.

The statesman-diplomat had of course long been a feature of international politics. Yet there was during the inter-war years a quickening in the pace and tempo of ministerial diplomacy. Thus, although the Munich conference of September 1938, at which were present the heads of government of four major powers, bore a superficial resemblance to the Congress of Berlin of 1878, the hastily prepared flights of the British prime minister, Neville Chamberlain, to Berchtesgaden and Bad Godesberg, and the accompanying talks between British and French ministers in London, had no obvious nineteenth-century equivalent. None of this can be explained simply by reference to improved and faster methods of communication. During this period the telephone came into more general usage for diplomatic purposes, and by the mid-1930s the aeroplane had become a tolerably comfortable means of travel. But while the telephone may have facilitated speedier and closer contact between world leaders, it had little to do with their increased propensity for foreign travel, and the train and the steamship remained the commonest mode of transport. Of more significance was the still prevailing assumption that if a repetition of the cataclysmic events of 1914 were to be avoided, those responsible for making policy must deal directly with each other. And the inability of the League either to halt Japanese military action in Manchuria or Italy's aggression in Abyssinia, and the departure from it of Japan, Germany and Italy, seemed to make it all the more important that Western statesmen should be seen to be working for peace. The crisis-laden atmosphere of the late 1930s, and the resort by the totalitarian states to propaganda, subversion and flagrant bullying tactics, led British and French statesmen to take initiatives that might otherwise have been left to diplomatic agents, and to endeavour through high-level ministerial meetings to co-ordinate their policies.

Another feature of diplomacy in the 1930s was the use once more made by governments of unofficial and non-diplomatic intermediaries. Neville Chamberlain, who as chancellor of the exchequer had himself taken a hand in negotiating on reparations, sent the British government's chief industrial adviser, Horace Wilson, to Berlin in September 1938 to warn Hitler of Britain's intention to fight over Czechoslovakia, and during the following summer Wilson, Robert Hudson, the secretary of the Department of Overseas Trade, and two Swedish businessmen, all had their part to play in trying to find a solution to the Polish question. The French prime minister, Édouard Daladier, and his foreign minister, Georges Bonnet, likewise turned to Paul Baudouin, a banker, and Count Fernand de Brinon, a right-wing publicist, in their efforts to improve relations with the Axis Powers. Yet in truth this was hardly a recent innovation. Financiers, businessmen and publicists had because of their international contacts been used in the past to supplement and sometimes by-pass more formal channels of diplomatic communication, especially in periods of crisis. Their employment seemed, however, inevitably to raise the ire of career diplomats, who complained bitterly over the way in which their work had been usurped by ministers and their private agents.

After the Second World War professional diplomats also protested at the way in which their advice had been ignored by governments. Had their wise words been heeded ambitious programmes of territorial expansion would have been either abandoned or modified, rash promises would have been avoided, old friends would not have been deserted, potential allies would not have been alienated, and the demands of dangerous rivals would not have been conceded. The story as revealed in diplomatic recollections and repeated by some historians is a familiar one. The political leaders of the inter-war years too often confused the execution with the making of foreign policy, espoused the principles of the new diplomacy while adopting its techniques to pursue objectives worthy of the old, and through an excess of zeal and want of foresight plunged the world into a war which completed the destruction of the European states system. These are, however, generalizations which too easily overlook the extent to which ambassadorial advice coincided with ministerial designs, and the degree to which the experience of diplomats varied from one country to another. Thus while Ernst von Weizsäcker, the state secretary of the Wilhelmstrasse, maintained in his memoirs that during the Nazi era his department had been reduced to a 'mere technical apparatus',[33] a French parliamentary committee placed some of the blame for France's collapse in 1940 on the manner in which senior bureaucrats at the Quai d'Orsay had gained an almost exclusive control over foreign policy and come to constitute a barrier between the political leadership and French diplomats abroad. It is in any case difficult to assess the influence of individual diplomats upon decision-making – so much depends upon personal relationships and the access which a diplomat may or may not have to a minister. There is also reason to suppose that the growing complexity of international politics and the inability of ministers to cope effectively with all the issues with which they were confronted may have tended to expand, rather than diminish, the role of career diplomats in the framing of policy. The rank amateur may on occasions have appeared to reign supreme. But the new diplomacy made new demands upon foreign ministries and extended the work of overseas missions and consulates.

FOREIGN SERVICES: REFORM AND RETRENCHMENT

The inter-war years constituted for the foreign services of most of the major powers a new period of adaptation and reform. Governments, acting partly in response to public criticism, attempted to reorganize their foreign ministries, to broaden, and with varying degrees of success, democratize, the recruitment of diplomatic personnel, and to restructure career patterns so as to allow for greater flexibility and improved promotion prospects for individuals with special skills. In some instances this was no more than a continuation of a process of institutional modernization that had begun before the First World War. But almost everywhere changes were effected which took into account recent technological advances and which gave greater recognition to the enhanced significance of economic issues and public opinion for the conduct of international politics. The number of specialists on the staffs of diplomatic missions was thus increased. Military and naval attachés, who were initially forbidden to the defeated powers and with whom some disarming neutrals optimistically dispensed, were eventually joined by air attachés. There were also more commercial attachés, and the enlarged volume of international debt and the interest taken by governments in propaganda work led to the emergence of new breeds of financial and press attachés. Their appointment was not always welcomed by ambassadors who frequently resented the semi-autonomous status that they acquired. In addition the involvement of ministries of commerce, finance and, in some countries, propaganda, in their selection and designation highlighted once more the problem of defining the roles of departments other than foreign ministries in the making and execution of foreign policy.

In Germany where the Wilhelmstrasse's prestige had deteriorated rapidly during the war, the work of reform began in the last months of the empire. Its prime mover was Edmund Schüler, a former consular official, who in the autumn of 1918 became superintendent of the Wilhelmstrasse's personnel department. Pressure for change came, however, from outside, particularly from the trading communities of the north German ports, who accused the aristocratic élite in Berlin of having insufficient understanding of their problems, and from the newly established economics office, which threatened to take over the foreign office's commercial and consular work. Worried by this challenge to their competence, even some of the most conservative elements in the office supported Schüler's establishment of a large foreign trade department. Public expenditure cuts subsequently led to its replacement by a more modest enterprise. But Schüler's other reforms reflected his desire to co-ordinate the economic and political aspects of foreign policy. Thus functional divisions were replaced by geographical ones; the consular and diplomatic careers were fused; and the foreign service was opened to businessmen, politicians and journalists. The result was a veritable bourgeois revolution. Functionaries from the consular services were elevated to some of the highest positions in the office; outsiders were appointed to important missions; and the Weimar constitution provided Germany with a foreign minister responsible to the Reichstag.

The British Foreign Office likewise tried to rectify what its pre-war critics had pinpointed as its shortcomings in the economic sphere. But the replacement of its commercial attachés by commercial counsellors, under the auspices of the hybrid Department of Overseas Trade, tended ultimately to diminish, rather than enhance, the Office's role in the promotion and fostering of commerce. Moreover, further efforts by the Foreign Office to provide itself with the means of utilizing Britain's economic and financial resources for political objectives were frustrated by a suspicious Treasury. Not that Sir Warren Fisher, the permanent under-secretary at the Treasury, was averse to taking his own initiatives in that grey area where international trade and finance merge with foreign policy. At the Ottawa conference of 1932, which decided upon imperial tariff policy, a subject vital to Britain's relations with many other powers, the senior representative of the Foreign Office had no more than observer status. And three years later Fisher dispatched Sir Frederick Leith Ross, the government's chief economic adviser, to the Far East in the hope that he would bring about a Sino-Japanese *rapprochement.* The Foreign Office lacked the necessary expertise to defend itself against the Treasury's infringement of its administrative domain. It was also inhibited by the reluctance of Sir Robert Vansittart, its permanent under-secretary between 1930 and 1938, to make the kind of institutional concessions that might have permitted the greater co-ordination of policy at an inter-departmental level. By contrast with the Wilhelmstrasse, which, in combination with the German ministries of agriculture, economics and finance, mounted a successful economic and political offensive in east-central Europe in the early 1930s, British diplomacy often seemed tardy and too beset by departmental particularism.

The further reform of the British foreign service was a slow and indecisive process. The fusion of the career structures of the diplomatic service and the Foreign Office, which had been recommended by a Royal Commission (the MacDonnell Commission) in 1914, was thus only partially achieved in the aftermath of the war. Conservatives within the department argued that the two careers required different talents and different kinds of personality, and although in subsequent years the rate of interchange between representatives abroad and bureaucrats in London increased, the amalgamated foreign service was in the end limited to the adoption of a common system of diplomatic titles and a joint list of second and third secretaries. With public interest in the Foreign Office waning, the department was also better able to make a stand against Treasury pressure to bring its processes of recruitment, promotion and remuneration into line with those of the rest of the civil service. Aspiring diplomats were no longer required to have an annual income of £400, entrance procedures were liberalized, and although most of the new recruits continued to come from the older universities of Oxford and Cambridge, the number of Etonians entering the service in the 1920s fell to half its pre-war level. Nevertheless, the Foreign Office still emphasized the importance of an oral examination as a means of determining a candidate's suitability for a career in the diplomatic service. After all, as one senior official remarked, there would otherwise be no way of excluding 'Jews, coloured men and infidels, who ... [were] British subjects'.[34] Similar prejudices fuelled opposition to Britain following the example of its major commercial competitors in unifying the consular career with the rest of the foreign service. Those who questioned such a move were apprehensive lest men trained in consular work should not possess what a former British minister in China described as that 'personality, "address" and *savoir-faire*', which would permit them 'to fraternize with the governing class in no matter what country'.[35]

Even in the United States, where the public image of diplomacy probably accorded closely with Arthur Schlesinger's description of it as a 'refuge for effete and conventional men who adored countesses, pushed cookies and wore handkerchiefs in their sleeves', would-be reformers stressed the virtues of a profession which required above all '*une certaine habitude du monde*'.[36] But the essential features of foreign service reform in Washington were the adoption of the career principle and an attempt to extend to American diplomacy the bureaucratic organization of the more highly regarded and more specialized consular service. Undoubtedly, the war heightened awareness in the United States of the shortcomings of a system which left the country's overseas representation largely in the hands of inexperienced presidential nominees and rich young men who could survive without adequate remuneration or security of tenure. Some scholars even went so far as to suggest that if the United States had not been represented by amateurs in the summer of 1914, it might have been better able to exercise a pacifying influence upon the situation in Europe. Yet Woodrow Wilson had blatantly reverted to the spoils system, and during the war and the peace negotiations the State Department had been overshadowed by House and his advisers, whilst America's diplomats had been outflanked by the agents of the Treasury and War Departments. Only in the early 1920s as Congress grew increasingly conscious of the need to protect and foster the United States' new-found economic strength was the political climate to become favourable to radical changes in the structure of the foreign service. The National Civil Service Reform League urged Congress to legislate for a service based on merit and with improved prospects for pay and promotion, and diplomats joined consuls in proclaiming the advantages that American business would derive from the support of a properly established profession.

The Rogers Act of May 1924 (named after its sponsor, Congressman John Jacob Rogers) appeared to achieve most of the objectives of the reformers. It provided for the common classification of diplomats and consuls by grade, remuneration by rank, promotion by merit, substantial salary increases for diplomats and the payment of post allowances and pensions. And although the spoils system persisted, in so far as heads of mission were not included in the classified list, foreign service officers could henceforth be formally recommended as ministers. In theory wealth was no longer a prerequisite for entry into the service, and a young recruit could look forward to rising to the pinnacle of his profession. Nevertheless, the Act did not work wholly as anticipated. It had been assumed that in future consuls well-versed in commercial work might be employed in embassies and legations, and that diplomats might be sent to consulates in politically sensitive areas, such as British India, where no other kind of mission existed. But the same diplomats who, in the hope of winning Congressional support for their proposals, had seemed to acquiesce in the amalgamation with the consular service, subsequently resisted the transfer of socially inferior consuls to diplomatic work. They also opposed, though not with complete success, the admission of women and negroes to the service. Only in 1927, after public complaints over the way in which the act was functioning, was Wilbur Carr, the director of the consular service, made chairman of the department's personnel board, and the process of promoting a more active interchange between consular and diplomatic staff begun. America's foreign service officers none the less retained, as did their cousins in the old world, their élitist sentiments and values, and they bequeathed their strong sense of *esprit de corps* to a rising generation of diplomats. At the same time the State Department defeated the endeavours of the Departments of Agriculture and Commerce to establish their own attaché services.

The Quai d'Orsay did not have to reckon with the degree of institutional rivalry and squabbling that so often beset the Foreign Office and the State Department during the inter-war years. This may be attributed to two factors: first, the prestige which the Quai d'Orsay and its representatives continued to enjoy; and second, the fact that throughout most of the period 1920–33 the prime minister was concurrently foreign minister. Moreover, the Quai d'Orsay had already been substantially transformed by reforms introduced in the previous two decades. Since 1907 the geographical divisions of the ministry had been responsible for both commercial and political matters; and, although old prejudices persisted, the equivalent ranking of consular and diplomatic officials had gone some way towards achieving an integrated service. There was certainly little soul-searching amongst the diplomats of the Third Republic over the social complexion of their *carrière*. A prey to nepotism, the Quai d'Orsay continued to recruit from the '*bonne bourgeoisie*' and the nobility, and a decree of 1929 declared with Gallic brevity that women were excluded from diplomatic postings. Apart from the creation of the *Maison de la Presse*, the only major administrative innovation of the war years had been the establishment in October 1915 of the post of secretary-general. Its functions, as defined by a ministerial decree, were the superintendence of all the services of the ministry, and Berthelot, who became secretary-general in September 1920, and his successor, Alexis Saint-Léger Léger, helped to provide French foreign policy with a continuity, which in a period of ministerial instability it might otherwise have lacked. It was a continuity that some commentators felt France might have been better off without. Léger and his associates were subsequently blamed for having clung too long to political conceptions which, though suited to the era of Briand and Stresemann, were patently inadequate in the age of Adolf Hitler, and France's representatives abroad complained that their reports were insufficiently distributed. The short-comings of French foreign policy were, however, probably due less to the malfunctioning of the diplomatic machine itself than to the failure of the political leadership to supply the necessary mechanism for reconciling diplomacy with grand strategy.

Where the Quai d'Orsay did leave a lasting imprint upon diplomacy in these years was in the expansion of its news and cultural services. Alongside the Service de presse et d'information, the successor to the *Maison de la Presse*, there emerged in 1920 the *Service des oeuvres françaises à l'étranger*. The latter, which had its origins in the pre-war *Bureau des écoles*, was charged with the august task of fostering the 'intellectual expansion' of France abroad. This meant that, besides administering the budgets of French educational institutions overseas, the Quai d'Orsay became directly involved in the establishment of chairs of French literature in the universities of eastern and central Europe, the promotion of exhibitions of French art and the encouragement of foreign tourism in France. Its rationale was the belief that, through a greater appreciation of French culture and values, foreigners would become more susceptible to France's commercial and political advances. Other countries, however, embraced cultural diplomacy with less obvious enthusiasm. In Britain, for example, the principal agencies of wartime propaganda were dissolved, and the endeavours of the Foreign Office to retain a reconstituted news department were hampered by the miserly attitude of the Treasury to what was still widely regarded as rather distasteful work. The department was able to continue supplying books, newspapers and films to institutes and societies abroad, and the former British Bureau of Information in New York was for the sake of appearances transformed into a library. Nevertheless, the bulk of the news department's work in the 1920s consisted of the provision of factual information to the press, and its distribution overseas by cable and wireless. Not until the end of the decade did the attitude of the Treasury towards cultural diplomacy begin to mellow, and the Foreign Office had to wait until December 1934 before it was decided to establish under its auspices the British Council for the express purpose of national self-advertisement.

The interest of the Foreign Office in cultural diplomacy was stimulated not only by the French example, but also by the huge sums devoted by other foreign ministries to this work. Amongst these had to be numbered the Wilhelmstrasse. Quite apart from the time and energy which the Germans expended on the war guilt question, they also matched the French in propagating their culture abroad. As a result of the Schüler reforms much of this work was brought under the administration of a single cultural department of the foreign office. It, like its counterpart in Paris, sponsored lecture tours, artistic displays and athletic competitions. There was, however, an aspect of Germany's cultural diplomacy which had no clear parallel with that of the French. This was the concern of the Wilhelmstrasse with the defence of the German language and culture in those lands which had been separated from the Reich and Austria as a result of the post-war treaties. It was a laudable endeavour to protect the interests of ethnic Germans against the sometimes brutal intolerance of the successor states of east-central Europe. Yet it was also inspired by a desire to re-establish Germany's political and economic pre-eminence in the region, and with the accession of Hitler to power in Germany it acquired new and ideological connotations.

IDEOLOGIES AND DIPLOMACY

The attunement of diplomatic practice to the exigencies of ideology has been a recurrent theme of world politics in the twentieth century. In 1917 Trotsky had mistakenly assumed that Bolshevism would soon be able to dispense with conventional diplomacy and its aristocratic paraphernalia. The proclamation of 'socialism in one country', the emergence of the Soviet state and its entry in 1934 into the League of Nations, had, however, made the new Russia more, rather than less, dependent upon its diplomats. Both in its organization and in its structure the *Narkomindel* of Chicherin and his successor, Maxim Litvinov, came to resemble its Tsarist predecessor. Its functionaries and representatives, many of whom had been forced to live abroad before the revolution, were largely of middle-class origin, well-versed in foreign affairs and adept in the art of negotiation. Their dossiers were scrutinized by a secret police which distrusted their cosmopolitan culture and liberal sentiments, and they had always to live with the danger that in a world which was fearful of revolutionary subversion, they might fall victim, as some did, to anti-Bolshevik violence. In the meanwhile Comintern continued to complicate Soviet diplomatic initiatives, appealing for class warfare when Litvinov was calling for world peace and international disarmament. But with the decline of revolutionary activity abroad, the Third International lost much of its influence within the Soviet system, and, as was evident during the era of the popular fronts and the Spanish Civil War, became increasingly an instrument for rallying foreign trade unionists and movements of the left in support of Soviet policies. Moreover, despite their inflexibility and their tendency to couch their arguments in Marxist–Leninist terminology, Soviet diplomats employed negotiating techniques which were not wholly foreign to those of their Western colleagues.

Nor, for that matter, were many of the institutional problems encountered by *Narkomindel* unique to the Soviet Union. As with foreign ministries elsewhere the political muscle exercised by *Narkomindel* at home depended primarily upon the experience, expertise and information that it was able to provide, and so long as its officials remained within the policy guidelines set by the politburo they enjoyed considerable freedom of action. Stalin's personal secretariat had a foreign section, and there were occasions when the Soviet dictator circumvented *Narkomindel*. The feelers he put out for an understanding with Berlin, initially through the ministry of foreign trade, and which culminated in the Nazi–Soviet pact of August 1939, are an obvious example. But the greatest domestic challenge which *Narkomindel* had to face came from the onset of the purges of 1937–8. Ostensibly aimed at rooting out spies and anti-Soviet influences, they decimated the Commissariat. Its bureaucrats and diplomats were particularly suspect because of their foreign connections, and because an unusually high proportion of them were of Jewish or non-Great Russian descent. By the end of the purges *Narkomindel* had lost over one-third of its staff, and those who remained came under the sway of the new deputy commissar and former secret police agent, Vladimir Dekanozov. Several diplomats with well established international reputations, such as Ivan Maisky in London, kept their posts. Others defected. Some may have been kidnapped and forced to return to Russia. The net effect was to reduce drastically the influence of *Narkomindel* upon the formulation of policy, and to bring in and promote a new generation of diplomats, few of whom had any knowledge of foreign lands or languages. Yet, in a sense these changes were at one with the spirit of the age. The newcomers were for the most part Great Russians. Their formative years had been the 1920s and they did not belong to that international fraternity of revolutionaries from which many of the associates of Chicherin and Litvinov had drawn their inspiration. They represented a shift towards an essentially Russian foreign policy at a time when Mussolini in Italy and Hitler in Germany were trumpeting the virtues of their own peculiarly national brands of diplomacy.

There was, however, an obvious difference between Bolshevik dogma and Fascist rhetoric when applied to international politics. While the former predicted the decline and inevitable demise of the state as a manifestation of bourgeois capitalism, the latter was predicated upon its survival and ultimate triumph as an expression of national identity. But the invective of Mussolini and his lieutenants, and their social-Darwinian assumptions about international society, could not easily be reconciled with any definition of diplomacy which encompassed such notions as the patient negotiation of treaties, and the moderation of national ambitions for the sake of peaceful compromise. One senior Italian diplomat, Count Sforza, had no doubt that in practice Fascist foreign policy would be a 'mere summary of sentiments and resentments',[37] and after Mussolini's acquisition of power in October 1922 he promptly resigned his embassy at Paris. Other Italian diplomats regarded the Fascist régime as a victory for the forces of order. They anticipated that they would be able to curb its radical excesses and utilize its energy in order to secure the respect and influence which they felt Italy's former allies had denied her since the war. And despite Mussolini's personal ventures into conference diplomacy and the Corfu affair of 1923, their hopes were not disappointed. There were no great changes in the administration of the foreign ministry, apart from its removal from its old residence in the Consulta to the Palazzo Chigi. Nor during Fascism's first decade was there any major confrontation between the professionals and the party. A public slanging match between Mussolini and Stresemann over Italy's maltreatment of its newly-acquired German minority in the South Tyrol was followed early in 1926 by the resignations of the Italian ambassador in Berlin and the secretary-general of the foreign ministry. Dino Grandi, one of Mussolini's henchmen, who was appointed under-secretary in 1925, and who subsequently succeeded Mussolini as foreign minister, was none the less quite malleable in the hands of the career diplomats. They likewise succeeded in taming the *Ventottisti*, a group of party members who in 1928, without any special training in diplomacy, were drafted into the foreign service to provide it with a new Fascist spirit.

More worrying from the point of view of the careerists was Mussolini's penchant for conspiracy and intrigue abroad. He employed unofficial agents in international negotiations, and provided assistance to a variety of nationalist and dissident movements abroad. It was a practice from which he derived few tangible gains, and which contributed to the collapse of the Weimar and Austrian Republics, the destabilizing of the Balkans and a costly intervention in the Spanish Civil War. Moreover, Italy's relations with two hitherto friendly powers were damaged by his attempts to counter the activities of anti-Fascist *émigrés* in France, and the endeavours of the *Segretaria dei fasci all'estero* to transform Italian immigrant societies in the United States into branches of the Fascist movement. Mussolini's contempt for the League of Nations, his proposals made in 1933 for a new European concert in the form of a four-power pact, and his invasion of Abyssinia, were similarly distressing for those who still believed in the principles of the new diplomacy. Nevertheless, if Fascist Italy had any distinct contribution to make to the history of diplomacy it was one of style rather than content, and this was never more apparent than in the years that followed the appointment in 1936 of Galeazzo Ciano as foreign minister. The son-in-law of Mussolini and his former propaganda minister, Ciano filled his personal secretariat with young contemporaries from the party and out-manoeuvred Italy's veteran diplomats through confidants and secret missions. Under him greater emphasis was placed upon the *tona fascista*, on decisive action and the heroic gesture, and on direct dealings with foreign leaders. Negotiation was handicapped by a disrespect of conventional usages; ideology in the guise of opposition to communist internationalism was employed to forge new and ominous links with Italy's neighbours; and treaties were drafted in a slipshod fashion which, as in the case of the Pact of Steel with Germany (1939), left Italy with imprecise and dangerous commitments.

Adolf Hitler had long advocated an alliance between Germany and Italy. In *Mein Kampf,* the two volumes of which were published in 1925 and 1926, he foresaw alliances with Britain and Italy as a means of overcoming French resistance to the winning of 'living space' for Germany. This latter objective was presented as a derivative of his own deeply pessimistic view of world politics in which races, like species, were locked in a struggle for survival whose logical conclusion must be the achievement by one people, strengthened and purified by its participation in the conflict, of world domination. The relevance of this thesis to the foreign policy pursued by National Socialist Germany, the extent of Hitler's commitment to a programme of phased expansion, and the degree of pure opportunism in his conduct, are matters of historical controversy and speculation. But the conservative officials of the Wilhelmstrasse appear to have hoped that the Nazis could strengthen Germany in order to enable them to achieve the revision of the Versailles Treaty, the 'restoration' of German Austria to the Reich, and the eventual creation of a German sphere of influence in east-central Europe.

A sense of loyalty towards the state, a belief that they, like their counterparts in Italy, could temper the revolutionaries in the party, and a natural concern with their career prospects, also played a part in persuading them to remain at their desks. In any event the Nazi 'seizure of power' in January 1933 provoked the resignation of only one serving ambassador. Hitler kept as his foreign minister Constantin von Neurath, a career diplomat who had first entered the government in June 1932, and Bernhard Wilhelm von Bülow, a nephew of the former imperial chancellor, remained state secretary until his death in 1936. Moreover, the only substantial administrative changes in the Wilhelmstrasse before 1938 were of a very conservative character. Thus in 1936 the functional divisions of the pre-Schüler era were revived.

Hitler had little that was flattering to say about either the Wilhelmstrasse or its agents. The foreign office he called an 'intellectual garbage dump', and he despised its 'Santaclauses', who were only good for 'quiet times'. Yet Hitler soon found that old-fashioned diplomats could be an asset. There was no prominent figure within the National Socialist movement who had any experience of diplomacy, and neither the chancellor nor his cohorts could afford to ignore the expert intelligence which the Wilhelmstrasse could provide. And if Nazi Germany were ever to be able to proceed successfully with even a modest revision of Versailles, it would first have to convince other powers of the honesty of its intentions and continuity of its methods. Otherwise Germany, which was still militarily weak, would risk provoking a pre-emptive attack from one or a combination of its neighbours. In addition, whatever may have been the long-term aims of the National Socialist leadership, its short-term goals were bound to include the liberation of Germany from the restrictions which Versailles had placed upon her armaments and her defences in the west, and in this respect they coincided with those of the officials of the foreign office. There was then good reason for Hitler leaving the Wilhelmstrasse alone while National Socialists proceeded with the co-ordination and assimilation of other departments and ministries.

This is not to say that the National Socialists posed no threat to the authority of the Wilhelmstrasse. There were any number of would-be party experts on foreign policy, and the foreign office had to reckon constantly with competition from these and other power-seeking individuals. Thus in April 1933 Alfred Rosenberg, the party's 'chief ideologue' and the author of a book on the future of German foreign policy, was permitted by Hitler to establish a foreign policy office for the party (the *Aussenpolitischesamt* or APA). But although Rosenberg anticipated that he would have ultimate responsibility for co-ordinating foreign policy, Hitler never seems to have viewed the APA as anything more than a party agency for carrying out specific non-bureaucratic assignments. At best a muddle-headed racial theorist, Rosenberg was a poor envoy, and despite his title of 'personal representative of the Führer', his first venture into diplomacy, an ill-prepared visit to London in May 1933, ended in embarrassment and frustration when he was unable to gain access to anyone in power. A more serious rival to the Wilhelmstrasse was another party organ, the numerically strong *Auslandsorganisation* (AO). Under the protection of Hitler's deputy, Rudolf Hess, and the direction of Ernst Wilhelm Bohle, it sought to maintain links with Nazi party members and German citizens (*Reichsdeutsche*) overseas. This naturally created problems for professional diplomats in those countries whose governments objected to the AO's attempts to Nazify the local German community, and this was more especially so, when, as in the case of Poland, Bohle tried to broaden his mandate to cover relations with ethnic Germans (*Volksdeutsche*) who lived beyond the frontiers of the Reich. Moreover, Bohle inevitably clashed with the foreign office when he insisted that diplomats should come within the AO's administrative purview, and urged that party attachés should be appointed to German embassies. His endeavours were, nevertheless, rewarded when in July 1936 the AO became a channel of communication between General Franco and Hitler and allowed the Nazi leadership to circumvent Neurath and his staff, who were opposed to German intervention in the Spanish Civil War. Then in the following January Bohle was brought into the Wilhelmstrasse, and subsequently accorded the rank of state secretary, and party representatives abroad were given equivalent status to German diplomats. Henceforth the whole German foreign service was subordinated to the *Gauleitung Ausland.*

Neurath correctly assumed that Bohle could be assimilated into the structure of the Wilhelmstrasse. He also reckoned that he would be able to count upon Hess and Bohle as allies against their mutual enemy, Joachim von Ribbentrop. Perhaps too easily dismissed as a slavish sycophant of Hitler, Ribbentrop, a late convert to National Socialism, had travelled widely, was fluent in foreign languages, and liked to pose as a specialist on relations with Britain and France. He evidently impressed Hitler, to whose whims he pandered, and at the Führer's instigation he received the title of commissioner for disarmament questions, with the rank of ambassador. In the meanwhile, Ribbentrop established his own organization, the *Diensstelle Ribbentrop*, in a building opposite to the foreign office, and began sending his own agents on foreign missions. Much to the chagrin of Neurath, he succeeded in negotiating a naval arms limitation agreement with the British in June 1935 and, despite his appointment to London as ambassador in 1936, he achieved another triumph through the conclusion of the Anticomintern Pact with Japan. When finally Neurath's resignation and other radical changes in the political and military leadership in Germany opened the way to Ribbentrop's appointment as foreign minister in February 1938, he was able to proceed with the progressive Nazification of the Wilhelmstrasse and the co-ordination of the foreign service with the other institutions of Hitler's Reich.

Ribbentrop's rise to power and the para-diplomacy which he, Rosenberg, Bohle, and their emissaries practised were symptomatic of the authoritarian anarchy which pervaded Nazi Germany, and from which its foreign policy derived much of its peculiar dynamism. Within the Third Reich individuals and state and party agencies vied for power and influence, with Hitler frequently acting as a sort of final arbiter. Nazi leaders, such as Heinrich Himmler, the *Reichsführer* of the para-military *Schutzstaffel* (SS), Reinhard Heydrich, the chief of the Reich's security police, and Hermann Göring, the commander-in-chief of the air force and minister responsible for the four-year rearmament plan, devoted themselves to constructing bureaucratic empires in which offices and departments were submerged. Their activities soon spilled over into Germany's foreign relations and diplomacy. Thus, quite apart from such institutional competition as existed between Hjalmar Schacht's economics ministry, Josef Goebbels's propaganda ministry, and the Wilhelmstrasse, German diplomats had also to reckon with the desire of Göring to play his own part on the world stage, and eventually the involvement of Hess, Heydrich and Himmler with ethnic organizations like the VDA in Germany and the Sudeten German Party in neighbouring Czechoslovakia. And while the objectives of foreign policy may have been defined and determined by Hitler, and German minorities exploited to suit the long-term interests of the Reich, vital decisions had sometimes to be taken in response to initiatives pursued by rival Nazi and pseudo-Nazi groups abroad. Franz von Papen, himself no stranger to conspiratorial politics, had, as German ambassador in Vienna in the years preceding the *Anschluss*, to contend with an Austrian government which was reluctant to be pressurized into closer ties with Germany, and with factional conflict amongst the illegal Austrian Nazis, some of whom were anxious to provoke a German military intervention and had their own links with party dignitaries in the Reich. The days when Austro-German relations could be explained in terms of what passed between the Wilhelmstrasse and the Ballhausplatz were unfortunately long since past.

This dispersion of authority in the execution of foreign policy had parallels elsewhere. The demands of modern warfare, the expansion of the subject matter of diplomacy, and the institutionalization of revolutionary propaganda and subversion, had almost everywhere tended to diminish the prestige of diplomatic establishments. But Hitler in his own ruthless fashion struck a potentially devastating blow against what remained of the traditions and values of European diplomacy. Decisions relating to foreign policy were made without any prior reference to the Wilhelmstrasse, and whilst protesting his good intentions Hitler showed scant respect for international law and treaty obligations. Rarely accessible to foreign diplomats, in conversation with other national leaders he adopted a declamatory style which left little scope for either bargaining or compromise. He seemed more concerned with impressing a wider public audience and with the psychological impact of his demeanour. An atmosphere of crisis could be deliberately created and exploited. Thus at Berchtesgarten in February 1938 he so arranged matters as to convince his guest, the Austrian chancellor, that German forces were poised to overwhelm his country and that all depended on his initialling a new agreement with Germany. Thirteen months later President Hacha of Czechoslovakia signed away his country under the threat of an aerial bombardment of Prague. At the same time Hitler was quite prepared to dispose altogether with individual diplomats if it suited his purpose. Already in January 1938 Papen had discovered that local Nazis had been considering his murder as a way of inducing a German invasion of Austria, and in the following April Hitler contemplated arranging the assassination of Kurt Eisenlohr, the German minister in Prague, in order to provide a pretext for war with Czechoslovakia. Diplomacy, if not yet a dead profession, was well on its way to becoming a high-risk one.

DEVIANT DIPLOMACY

Hitler no doubt felt that the deaths of one or two ambassadors would be no great loss to Germany. He was in any case looking forward to a new generation of National Socialist diplomats – men fashioned in the image of Ribbentrop, 'the only diplomat to do the Third Reich proud overseas'. 'Diplomats', Hitler complained to a group of newspaper editors in November 1938, 'do not represent their countries, but an international Society clique'.[38] There were, indeed, German diplomats who regretted the passing of an age in which political power had been vested in a nobility which shared common values and a common perception of a European system. In his memoirs Papen noted how much easier it would have been to deal with international problems if effective power in each country had been exclusively in the hands of old-world aristocrats, 'each forming part of a world-wide family'.[39] It was a view of the past which was almost as distorted as Hitler's vision of the future. After all, the aristocratic diplomats of the pre-1914 era had been every bit as nationalistically minded as their fellow citizens, and the fraternity of Europe's kings had no more impeded the way to war than had the workers of the world. There was, however, a sense in which Papen was right. Successful diplomacy must ultimately depend upon the mutual acceptance by governments and their representatives of certain common standards of conduct and behaviour. If international agreements are to mean anything, those who negotiate them must have at least some degree of confidence in each other's honesty of purpose. Yet Hitler through his disregard of former promises, his twisting of the meaning of engagements solemnly entered into, and finally his resort to violence, eroded Germany's international credibility. His manipulation of mass sentiment and appeals to the right of national self-determination came to represent a gross perversion of the methods and principles of the new diplomacy.

Perplexed by the Nazi phenomenon, Western statesmen and diplomats, who had only recently accustomed themselves to the devious practices of the Bolsheviks, eventually decided that the idea of further negotiations with Germany was futile. As in 1914 so in 1939 diplomacy failed to 'secure peace on earth to men of goodwill'. But it was a distinctly unorthodox variant of the craft which did much to determine the timing and configuration of this second global struggle.

6

TOTAL DIPLOMACY

We are coming to realize that foreign operations in today's world call for a total diplomacy. . . . American ambassadors can no longer be content with wining and dining, reporting, analyzing and cautiously predicting.

(Chester B. Bowles)[1]

One of the salient features of the development of the modern state has been the steady expansion of the functions ascribed to government. Even in those societies which have clung the most tenaciously to the doctrine of free trade, governments have been expected to play an ever more active role in the management of the national economy. The process has, perhaps, been only a logical consequence of the industrialization and urbanization of much of the world in the past 100 years. Yet it has also been encouraged and facilitated by war. The two world wars involved the principal belligerents in the mobilization, not just of their manpower, but also of their economic and financial resources. Allied governments had likewise in their dealings with each other, with neutrals, and eventually with ex-enemy administrations, to concern themselves with matters of economic assistance and containment. The problems associated with the reconstruction of Europe after the Second World War thus tended to confirm the lesson of the interwar years that no clear distinction could be made between international politics and international economics. An ever-increasing number of industrial, social and technological matters were perceived as having an international, and therefore a diplomatic, dimension. Moreover, the onset of the cold war had the effect of reversing Clausewitz's celebrated maxim. Diplomacy remained closely wedded to grand strategy and often seemed as though it were no more than an extension of war by other means. And like warfare in the twentieth century, diplomacy became total in its objectives and subject matter.

Whilst the content of diplomacy was expanding, so too was its context being rapidly transformed. The fall of France, the defeat of the Axis, the decline of Britain, and the emergence in 1945 of the Soviet Union and the

United States as two victorious superpowers, completed the destruction of the old European states system. By 1949, when the Soviet Union exploded its first atomic bomb, a new and bipolar global balance of terror was well on its way to replacing the former continental balance of power. Meanwhile the European empires which had held sway over most of Africa and much of Asia began to disintegrate. The French were denied the opportunity to re-establish their authority in the Middle East, the British abandoned the lands of the Indian subcontinent in 1947, and two years later the Dutch granted independence to Indonesia.

The process of decolonization, which continued throughout the next decade, gathered pace in the 1960s, and within thirty years of the ending of the Second World War the number of sovereign states had almost trebled. Most of the new actors on the world political stage were relatively poor, and some of them, particularly in the Caribbean and the Pacific, were so small in population and territory as to bear comparison with the city-states of Renaissance Italy. Many of them could barely afford to maintain more than skeletal foreign services. Few of them were prepared to forego the formal trappings of independent statehood. Yet the birth of this Third World was also accompanied by the rise of atavistic and xenophobic nationalisms, which, like the Bolshevism of a previous generation, challenged the cultural and economic values of the West and the methods and mores of its diplomacy.

WARLORDS, WARRIORS AND DIPLOMATS

The European war which broke out in September 1939 was not in itself responsible for any radical innovation in the methods by which governments dealt with each other. As during the First World War, so during the Second, the representatives of the belligerent powers were primarily concerned with arranging with allies and neutrals the most favourable conditions for waging war. Once more commercial issues, and, especially in the case of Britain and France, those relating to the blockade of Germany, figured large in their diplomacy. Jean Monnet thus resumed his former role in the United States, but this time with supranational functions as the head of a joint Anglo-French commission for the purchase of provisions and supplies. The political leaders of the great powers meanwhile exhibited an even greater predilection for personal diplomacy than had their predecessors of twenty years before. After the defeat of Germany's continental enemies Hitler traversed France in October 1940 for conversations with General Franco at Hendaye on the Spanish frontier, and following subsequent discussions with Marshal Pétain, the leader of Vichy France, he went on to Italy to co-ordinate Axis policy with Mussolini. During the next three years Winston Churchill, who had succeeded Chamberlain as British prime minister, crossed the Atlantic to confer with Roosevelt on no less than five occasions. He journeyed to Moscow to see Stalin in August 1942, and in 1943 and 1945 he participated in tripartite negotiations with the American and Soviet leaders at Tehran, Yalta and Potsdam. And although Stalin appeared reluctant to stray far beyond the frontiers of the Soviet Union, Roosevelt made history when in January 1943 he flew to meet Churchill at Casablanca, thereby becoming both the first United States president to leave his country during wartime and the first to travel in an aeroplane.

This summitry was accompanied by frenzied activity on the part of foreign ministers. Ciano, Eden, Molotov and Ribbentrop scurried from capital to capital in their endeavours to settle the modalities of neutrality, belligerency and peace. In many respects this was no more than an extension of practices established in the pre-war years. But after the German invasion of the Soviet Union in June 1941 and the Japanese attack upon Pearl Harbor the following December such high-level diplomacy might not have continued to flourish without the availability of air transport. Geographical proximity had permitted British and French ministers to maintain frequent and direct personal contact with each other during the First World War. By contrast, the members of the Grand Alliance were separated by continents and oceans, and between Japan and her partners in the Axis lay 6,000 miles of the Eurasian landmass. In the spring of 1941 the Japanese foreign minister travelled by rail to Moscow and thence to Berlin and Rome, and nine months later his British counterpart was still able to make his way to Moscow via the Arctic Ocean and Murmansk. Yet within two years Ribbentrop had, in the absence of a safe air route, to abandon his tentative plans for a visit to Tokyo. It would, however, be glib to attribute the wartime conferences of Churchill, Roosevelt and Stalin to the advent of aviation. After all, Churchill's first meeting with Roosevelt in August 1941 took place on board a warship off the Newfoundland coast, and in May 1943 the prime minister crossed the Atlantic by ocean liner. The new technology aided, but it did not determine, the methods of wartime diplomacy.

Of more significance was probably the predisposition of the leaders of the Western democracies to arrange matters amongst themselves. Like Clemenceau and Lloyd George, Churchill and Roosevelt were confident of their own abilities as negotiators and they were jealous guardians of the considerable powers with which they had been entrusted. Moreover, when issues of strategy became entwined with those of diplomacy and planning for a future peace it seemed both sensible and efficient that those with ultimate political responsibility should try to settle them in conference. Conventional diplomacy was a time-consuming process, and politicians who were accustomed to having their own way at home soon grew impatient with the constraints which it imposed upon their conduct abroad. 'You should go through the experience of trying to get any changes in the thinking, policy and action of the career diplomats and then you'd know what a real problem was', Roosevelt once complained to Marriner Eccles of the Federal

Reserve Board. His words might equally well have been those of Lloyd George or Hitler.[2] For statesmen turned warlords diplomats often seemed superfluous to the management of inter-allied affairs. Even their foreign ministers were at times reduced to the level of errand boys. Anthony Eden, who replaced Halifax as British foreign secretary in December 1940, gave definition to Churchill's bold gestures, but he rarely had a free hand in the formulation of policy. The prime minister, who had begun to correspond privately with Roosevelt at the outset of the war, readily interfered in the business of the Foreign Office and by 1941 he was bypassing the department in his dealings with Stalin. Cordell Hull, the United States secretary of state, had, however, more cause for complaint than Eden. Information was withheld from him by Roosevelt, who deliberately created parallel lines of command and turned for assistance to Sumner Welles, Hull's under-secretary. Indeed, on Roosevelt's insistence, both Eden and Hull were excluded from the dialogue between the prime minister and the president at Casablanca.

There was once again ample opportunity for amateur diplomats to exercise their talents. One obvious example was Harry L. Hopkins, Roosevelt's confidant and former secretary of commerce. Thus in January 1941 Roosevelt, for whom personality usually counted more than rank, sent Hopkins as his 'personal representative on a special mission' to London.[3] Roosevelt wished to assist the British war effort against Nazi Germany, and Hopkins, who spent six weeks in Britain, was able to explore with Churchill the problems confronting Britain and the prospects for American aid. He defined his own task as that of trying 'to find a way to be a catalytic agent between two prima donnas',[4] and at a time when there was no resident American ambassador in London few could have doubted the value of his work. But after his return to Washington his continued involvement in diplomacy was assured by his appointment as administrator of the Lend–Lease programme – a mandate which covered the provision to Britain and eventually other powers of weapons, merchant shipping, vehicles, food, fuel, industrial equipment and numerous services. The programme became a vital element in relations between the United States and combatant and neutral governments, and several foreign missions in Washington were soon conducting business with Hopkins and his agents. Moreover, the appointment of W. Averell Harriman to London as 'Expediter' of Lend–Lease posed a further challenge to the authority of Hull and the State Department. In theory Harriman was on the staff of John Winant, the new American ambassador in London. Yet in practice he was able to act independently of his chief. He corresponded directly with Hopkins, and although the British Foreign Office continued to deal with Winant, Churchill, as minister of defence, maintained close personal relations with Harriman and through him with Hopkins and Roosevelt. Hopkins, who was to undertake several missions abroad, had, it seemed, become a new

Colonel House, and, like the latter, he was soon identified with the president's 'personal Foreign Office'.[5]

Roosevelt also encouraged men from the worlds of industry and commerce to undertake what were essentially diplomatic missions. Both William R. Davis, an American businessman with extensive German contacts, and James D. Mooney, an executive of General Motors, were utilized by the president in the early stages of the European conflict to explore the possibilities for a mediated peace. There was certainly no shortage of would-be intermediaries. In Germany, for example, Albrecht Haushofer, a prominent figure in ethnic politics, attempted during the winter of 1940–1 to establish links with the British establishment in the hope of arranging an Anglo-German settlement. His efforts were, however, ruined by the precipi-Tate action of Hitler's deputy, Rudolf Hess, who in May 1941 flew to Scotland with the object of meeting the Duke of Hamilton. It was an absurd venture which did nothing to shorten the war and which left Hess in prison for the remainder of his life – a martyr to misguided enthusiasm and private diplomacy. Yet governments felt compelled to seek the assistance of private citizens when there was no other obvious or satisfactory channel for communication in wartime. Thus after France's defeat in June 1940 and the effective severing of diplomatic relations between Britain and her former ally, Churchill's government was faced with the problem of how best to influence Pétain's administration at Vichy. Desultory negotiations proceeded between the ambassadors of the two countries at Madrid on colonial and other matters, and the British Treasury sent an official to Vichy to settle various outstanding financial questions. But unusual circumstances required unorthodox diplomacy, and the Foreign Office also made use of Professor Louis Rougier and Jacques Dupuy, a former Canadian diplomat, to explain its views to Vichy. Not that either proved to be a particularly reliable agent. In their endeavour to gain credit for their achievements, they, like many of the unofficial emissaries of the last war, soon forfeited the confidence of their political employers.

Amongst the other parallels that might be drawn between the two world wars was the readiness of governments to send on foreign missions individuals who, though inexperienced in diplomacy, seemed suited by their profession or political inclinations to particular posts. Already in March 1939 Marshal Pétain, the hero of Verdun, had been nominated French ambas-Sador to Franco's Spain, and less than two years later the same Pétain received Admiral William D. Leahy, one of Roosevelt's closest advisers, as the United States ambassador at Vichy. Stafford Cripps, a leading figure on the left wing of the British Labour Party, was meanwhile sent as Britain's ambassador to Moscow. There was also a crop of failed or otherwise disposable politicians who found their way into wartime diplomacy. In the spring of 1939 the smooth-tongued von Papen, one of the least impressive chancellors of the Weimar Republic and more recently Hitler's ambassador at Vienna, took charge of the German embassy at Ankara. Then in May 1940 Sir Samuel Hoare, a former British foreign secretary, was sent to represent Britain at Madrid, and seven months later Lord Halifax reluctantly left the Foreign Office to become ambassador at Washington. As with Lord Derby's appointment to Paris in 1918, Halifax's selection for Washington in 1940 was justified on the grounds that his post required a man who knew 'the whole policy of the Government'.[6] This, however, was a political pretext rather than a diplomatic expedient. Much of Halifax's work in fact consisted of helping to co-ordinate the activities of the several permanent and special British missions in the United States which handled matters of finance and supply.

Halifax eventually presided over an administrative machine which rivalled the Foreign Office in the scale and scope of its operations. The pattern was repeated elsewhere. Even in neutral Turkey the number of British diplomatic and associated personnel rose by leaps and bounds. In 1939 a mere nineteen attended the embassy's Christmas dinner at Ankara. Yet within five years the British military mission in Turkey had so expanded that in 1944 the ambassador, Sir Hugh Knatchbull-Hugessen, had to cater for some 360 guests at his Christmas celebrations. This large foreign presence was a reflection of the importance that Britain and other belligerents attached to maintaining the goodwill of the Turks. Indeed, the war's strong ideological overtones gave a new significance to the task of winning public sympathy and support in non-belligerent countries. Halifax recognized the value of getting out of Washington whenever possible in order to put across the British point of view. And Otto Abetz, who in November 1940 became German ambassador in Paris, was able to apply expertise acquired as an agent of the Dienststelle Ribbentrop in promoting Franco-German collaboration in building a 'New European order'. Professional diplomats also seem to have displayed a better understanding of the techniques of propaganda and popular enlightenment than their predecessors of the Great War. Sir David Kelly, the British minister in Berne during the first three years of the war, kept the Swiss public informed of the British interpretation of events through a legation bulletin which his press attaché prepared from the radio transmissions of the Ministry of Information. Then, after his appointment to Buenos Aires, in 1942 he cultivated the friendship of the proprietors of an influential daily, *La Prensa*, and in time it came to rely on British sources for its information and comment. As Kelly later recalled, this was an area in which an ambassador could still achieve results 'without any reference to his Government, or indeed their knowing anything about it'.[7]

INTELLIGENCE AND SECURITY

Modern warfare may have encouraged professional diplomats to develop new skills in the handling of the public and the press. But it has also been in part responsible for the progressive encroachment upon their terrain of practitioners of that most secret craft – the collection, collation and evaluation of intelligence. As purveyors of advice and information diplomats have by definition long been involved in intelligence-gathering of a kind. Wicquefort described the ambassador as an 'honourable spy', and the assessment of the military capabilities of potential friends and foes has always been one of the principal duties of the service attaché. A distinction is usually made, however, between knowledge derived honestly, though not necessarily openly, from publications and conversations with journalists, officials and politicians, and intelligence acquired by clandestine means, which might include bribery, cryptoanalysis, and the employment of secret agents and devices. While the provision of the former is generally regarded as a legitimate function of diplomacy, the supply of the latter is better understood as espionage.

Prior to 1914 few governments had been prepared to forgo the advantages of intelligence distilled from covert sources. And although Europe's aristocratic ambassadors may have frowned upon the 'indiscreet and reprehensible curiosity' of their military associates, the majority of them would probably have agreed with the complaint made in 1901 by the Marquis de Noailles that this had been 'at all times, more or less, the besetting sin of the attachés wearing the epaulettes'.[8] Since then most countries have acquired agencies concerned specifically with espionage, counter-espionage and the decoding of the signals and communications (cable, radio and satellite) of other powers. Almost everywhere such organizations have had a chequered and uncertain history, with foreign ministries, armed services and police forces often establishing their own separate and competing mechanisms for security, surveillance and analysis. The British Foreign Office had by the early 1920s assumed responsibility for both the Secret Intelligence Service (SIS or MI6), which emerged from the foreign department of the Secret Intelligence Bureau, and the Government Code and Cypher School (GC&CS), which was founded in 1918. Whilst the SIS dispatched agents abroad in the guise of passport control officers (PCOs) attached to British missions and consulates, the GC&CS continued with the codebreaking that the Admiralty had successfully revived during the First World War. But military and economic intelligence was also collected by the service ministries and the Industrial Intelligence Centre; and MI5, the British counter-intelligence department, functioned in the 1930s as a channel of communication between anti-Nazis in the German embassy in London and the Foreign Office. Moreover, Vansittart, as permanent under-secretary and then as the government's chief diplomatic adviser, operated his own 'private detective agency' with a network of contacts in central Europe, and he encouraged the formation by Claude Dansey, a former PCO, of the top secret Z organization.

In the aftermath of the First World War the GC&CS achieved some notable successes in cracking American, French and Soviet diplomatic codes. Likewise in the United States, the newly established Cypher Bureau (or Black Chamber) made its contribution to open diplomacy by deciphering Japanese cable traffic before and during the Washington conference of 1921–2, with the result that the State Department had foreknowledge of Tokyo's maximum and minimum requirements regarding the projected naval arms limitation treaty. But the work of British and United States cryptographers was seriously jeopardized by their political masters. The determination of Stanley Baldwin's government in Britain to demonstrate to the Soviet authorities that it knew of their subversive designs revealed to Moscow the fact that Russian telegrams were being read in London, and after his appointment in 1929 as secretary of state, Henry L. Stimson disbanded the Cypher Bureau on the grounds that 'gentlemen do not read each other's mail'.[9] Fortunately for both countries this was not the end of the story. During the Second World War their codebreakers exceeded all expectations, and through their efforts the conflict was probably shortened by several years. Thus, with the assistance of French and Polish cryptoanalysts the GC&CS gained access to the German 'Enigma' cipher machine, and by the late summer of 1940 American army and navy cryptographers had broken the Japanese diplomatic cipher. Indeed, one of the main problems confronting decision-makers in Britain and the United States was that of assessing and collating an excess of data. Their difficulties were in the first place exacerbated by rivalries amongst and within established and evolving bureaucratic structures.

The British Foreign Office had been distinctly unenthusiastic about sharing its responsibilities with other departments and agencies, and only under the threat and impact of war was the effective co-ordination of economic, military and political intelligence achieved in Britain. But almost everywhere diplomats were reluctant to relinquish their prerogatives in this sphere. Germany's ambassadors certainly regarded as a mixed blessing the lifting in December 1932 of the ban imposed by the Versailles Treaty on the appointment of German service attachés, and some of the new appointees met with a particularly chilly reception. The Wilhelmstrasse and the Reichswehr were initially able to reach an understanding that embassies would not be used for espionage. Nevertheless, the foreign ministry still had to compete with a bewildering array of party and state organizations for which the acquisition of intelligence was a vital element in their incessant struggle for power and influence in Hitler's Reich. Whilst the Wilhelmstrasse had its own cryptographic service, which by the end of the 1930s was decoding about half the cable traffic of foreign missions in Berlin, Göring had under his command the *Forschungsamt*, an office whose several functions included the tapping of those telephone and telegraph wires which crossed German soil. Germany's air force, army and navy also had their own separate communications–intelligence organizations, and under Admiral Canaris, the *Abwehr*, which was meant to serve all three forces, concentrated upon military espionage, counter-espionage and sabotage.

Ideological and social intelligence in Nazi Germany was originally the speciality of the SD and the SS, which, although they were mainly interested in internal security matters, had contacts and informants within German ethnic groups abroad. And, after its formation in 1939, the *Reichssicherheitshauptamt* (RSHA – the Reich Security Office) was permitted to maintain police attachés in diplomatic missions in return for providing the Wilhelmstrasse with information. When, however, these new attachés began to meddle in diplomacy and even to withhold intelligence, Ribbentrop responded by setting up his own espionage service within the foreign ministry. This was only one of a number of steps which Ribbentrop took towards broadening the activities of his department. He had already established the *Deutschlandabteilung* (Germany Division) under his protégé, Martin Luther, who, besides supervising the new espionage service, had responsibility for co-operation with the RSHA and for the surveillance of political opponents. In time Luther's division became the centre of what was in effect a new National Socialist Wilhelmstrasse which was concerned less with the diplomacy of great power relations than with the overall assessment of potential friends and enemies (i.e., with their domestic political conflicts and their economic, ideological and social development). This hardly qualified as total diplomacy. After all, by 1942 the Wilhelmstrasse had missions in only ten neutral states, and its representatives in allied and dependent countries were essentially executive assistants of the politics of observance and occupation. The ministry was none the less engaged in the collection and processing of total intelligence, and its success in this respect helped it to reassert its authority within the Reich.

Some of the most useful political intelligence with which Hitler was provided came from the wiretaps of the *Forschungsamt*. During the summer of 1938 it supplied the Führer with transcripts of telephone conversations between Czechoslovakia's president and his ministers in London and Paris, and these were subsequently used to discredit Czech diplomacy. The Germans were also aware from their cable intercepts of the extent of the territorial concessions which the British were likely to urge upon Prague. But some Axis successes were due to lamentable lapses in the security of British missions. One of the most notorious examples of this was the case of Secundo Constantini, a chancery servant of the British embassy at Rome, who regularly purloined documents from the ambassador's safe for photographing by the Italian intelligence services. Even after the theft in January 1937 of a diamond necklace which belonged to the ambassador's wife, and an investigation into the security of the embassy, Constantini kept his job, and after Italy's entry into the war in June 1940 he was transferred to the British legation at the Vatican. In another instance 'Cicero', the Albanian valet of Knatchbull-Hugessen, was paid by the German embassy at Ankara to steal from the ambassador's safe-boxes. German missions were, however, far from being leak-proof. Richard Sorge, the celebrated Soviet spy in the German embassy at Tokyo, supplied Moscow with invaluable information on the progress of Germany's efforts to transform the Anti-Comintern Pact into a tripartite alliance.

The Soviet intelligence and security services benefited enormously from the loyalty of foreign communists to the socialist fatherland. Aided by the German communist party they extended their network of informants in the Weimar Republic, and during the 1930s youthful idealism assisted their penetration of the British Foreign Office and the SIS through the so-called 'Cambridge Comintern'. Ideology lent direction and purpose to the new servants of the world revolution, and, like the SD and the SS in their relations with Nazified ethnic movements in central Europe, the Soviets mixed subversion with intelligence. In this respect the totalitarian states were not unique. Faced with the prospect of a major war, the intelligence agencies of the Western democracies also became engaged in propaganda work, psychological warfare, and eventually sabotage. And their representatives in embassies and legations assisted in illicit activities which went far beyond the bounds of either diplomacy or espionage. Few such schemes were as audacious as the suggestion made in 1938 by Colonel Mason-Macfarlane, the British military attaché at Berlin, that Hitler's birthday parade might provide an opportunity for shooting the Führer and that he 'could pick the bastard off as easy as winking'.[10] Nevertheless, in the wake of the *Anschluss* the SIS established a special section (Section D) to handle sabotage. Then, in 1940, with the object of disrupting Swedish iron ore exports to Germany, plastic explosives were sent by diplomatic bag to Stockholm, and there, without the knowledge of the British minister, were stored in the cellar of the legation. The distinctions between diplomacy and espionage, and between espionage and covert military operations, were thus steadily eroded in a new world of institutionalized and professionalized secrecy.

In Britain sabotage was administratively separated from intelligence work when in the summer of 1940 Section D was absorbed into the Special Operations Executive (SOE). But the Office of Strategic Services (OSS), which the American government formally created after the United States' entry into the war, combined both practices. Moreover, although its cold war successor, the Central Intelligence Agency (CIA), was initially intended to co-ordinate information collected by other departments and bureaux, it soon gave priority to covert operations against a perceived communist offensive. It became an instrument of executive power and a means of defending the status quo in those parts of the world in which American interests seemed menaced by national and communist revolutions. True, the CIA is only one component of an intelligence community which includes the National Security Agency, which is responsible for communications intelligence, the Defense Intelligence Agency of the Department of Defense, and the State Department's own Bureau of Intelligence and Research. There have, however, been occasions when the CIA has appeared to be conducting its own foreign policy, independently of, and sometimes in competition with, the State Department and its representatives. Edward Korry, the United States ambassador in Santiago, was not even informed when in the autumn of 1970 the agency used the diplomatic bag to supply submachine guns to the opponents of Chile's Marxist president. Meanwhile, co-operation amongst intelligence agencies at an international level has resulted in the forging of new and parallel links between allied and friendly powers. Wartime liaison between the OSS and the SIS complemented existing diplomatic communications between London and Washington, and, as has been remarked in one recent study of the subject, 'the most special part of the "special relationship". . .has been the intelligence relationship'.[11]

Anglo-American collaboration has probably been at its best in regard to communications and signals intelligence. And it is in this very area that modern technology, especially satellite surveillance, has most conspicuously diminished the value of the diplomatic mission and its service attachés as collectors of information on military strategy and weapons deployment and development. Not that this seems to have led to any dramatic reduction in the numbers actively employed in espionage. Human intelligence may still be invaluable when it comes to obtaining access to classified material and assessing the attitudes and intentions of military and political leaders. This is particularly the case when, as in Moscow during the 1940s and 1950s, foreign diplomats are segregated from the ordinary citizens of a country and denied all but very limited access to ministers and officials. Moreover, the nuclear stalemate which characterized much of the cold war made all the more important the acquisition of information on scientific advances in potential enemy countries. The Soviet Union thus maintained a 'vacuum cleaner' approach to intelligence-gathering on the assumption that all information, whether it concerned highly secret industrial and techno-logical achievements or material that might be obtained from public sources, was important simply because knowledge is power. In consequence the representatives of the state security committee (KGB) and the Soviet military intelligence service (GRU) constituted a high proportion of the resident staff of its diplomatic missions. One estimate put the figures at 40–5 per cent of embassy staff in some Western capitals and at 75 per cent in some developing countries. There were, indeed, instances when KGB diplomats were appointed to senior positions. This was true of S.M. Kudriavtsev, the former operator of an atomic spy ring in Ottawa, who in 1960 was appointed Soviet ambassador in Havana in order that he might assist in the consolidation of Fidel Castro's régime. Yet, for the most part, KGB and GRU representatives had third secretary or attaché ranking.

One of the duties of KGB officers in Soviet missions was that of monitoring the loyalty and performance of other members of staff. Since the disintegration of the Soviet Union it has been reported that some Soviet diplomats pretended to be employees of the KGB simply in order to keep their posts. But in any event few modern diplomats can afford to ignore security. They have to reckon with the possibility of their conversations being overheard and recorded by foreign intelligence services equipped with the most sophisticated forms of electronic bugging equipment. Security against the planting of such devices has become a major problem of the modern embassy, particularly at a time when new buildings and extensions are under construction.[12] Some large embassies now contain specially insulated areas so that confidential discussions can remain just that. Yet even in the capital of a friendly country an embassy may become the target of the host government's intelligence services. If the former British intelligence officer, Peter Wright, is to be believed, in the early 1960s MI5, in conjunction with the Post Office, mounted 'Operation Stockade' against the French embassy in London with the object of locating the cipher room and placing taps upon the relevant telephone and telex cables. Then, Wright alleges, with the assistance of the Government Communications Headquarters (GCHQ), the French diplomatic cipher was broken so that for three years during which the British government was negotiating for entry into the European Economic Community (EEC) the Foreign Office had full access to communications between the French embassy and the Quai d'Orsay. Nevertheless, as Wright has noted, 'Stockade' simply affirmed the limitations of diplomatic intelligence. Once General de Gaulle had pronounced upon Britain's continued exclusion from the Common Market no amount of information could alter that fact.[13]

Any evaluation of the extent to which governments have profited from the latest techniques of intelligence-gathering lies outside the scope of this brief survey. There is, however, evidently much truth in Walter Laqueur's observation that the

> more intelligence there is, the more difficult it will be to establish priorities, and the greater the danger that truly important developments and events will be lost in a tidal wave of information varying from the mildly interesting to the irrelevant.[14]

The appetite of governments for intelligence has rarely made the life of the resident ambassador any the easier. Its collection has involved professional diplomats in liaison with the security services of other governments, and, as in the case of revolutionary Iran, they have thereby run the risk of being identified with the forces of 'repression'. They have also had to learn to live with colleagues whose reports are dispatched to different masters, whose long-term predictions may contradict their own current and usually more prosaic assessment of events, and whose very presence in their missions may

194

compromise their relations with host governments. Moreover, the tit-for-tat expulsions of embassy staff which have often accompanied the unmasking of major spy rings can prove to be more than just diplomatic embarrassments. They have sometimes impeded the efficient functioning of missions and interfered with otherwise quite legitimate activities. In the meantime, foreign ministries have had to reckon with the emergence of agencies which have access to alternative sources of information on developments abroad, and which, in virtue of their constitution and the secrecy of their operations, may stand closer than themselves to heads of state and government. Both the making and the implementation of foreign policy have thereby been further entangled in webs of intrigue and suspicion. The gradual professionalization of intelligence communities has in this respect simply confirmed how myopic were those visionaries of 1918 who anticipated a new era in which nations would deal, not only more openly, but also more honestly, with each other.

THE UNITED NATIONS

Between 1939 and 1945 far less was heard of the shortcomings of secret diplomacy than during the First World War. Perhaps, because National Socialism seemed so inherently evil, and because the Axis Powers appeared so blatantly aggressive, it was more readily accepted by the public in Britain, the Dominions, and the United States that a premeditated war had been thrust upon them. Politicians and diplomats were blamed for their lack of foresight, and for having failed in the past to make a sufficiently firm stand against Hitler and his friends. And if the new diplomacy had in practice proved no more successful than the old in averting war, the League of Nations was not dismissed as a worthless experiment. Western statesmen and their advisers were more inclined to regard the war as evidence of the need for a wider and more effective system of collective security. There was also an echo of Wilsonian idealism in some of their pronouncements. The Atlantic Charter upon which Churchill and Roosevelt agreed in August 1941 proclaimed their commitment to the principle of national self-determination, to international economic co-operation, and to the idea of all states having access on equal terms to the raw materials of the world. Nevertheless, after the United States' entry into the war it soon became clear that the Americans would not be satisfied with just a revamped League. Roosevelt wanted an organization in which for several years to come executive power would be in the hands of Great Britain, the United States, the Soviet Union, and China. The two nascent superpowers, a declining world power, and a large Asiatic nation, would then constitute a global concert or directorate. It was, therefore, quite appropriate that the term 'United Nations' should first have been used in January 1942 to describe what was essentially an anti-Axis alliance.

195

Shape was given to the new organization by a team of American, British and Soviet diplomats at Dumbarton Oaks in August–September 1944, and its charter was eventually accepted in the following spring by the representatives of some fifty states at the San Francisco Conference. It bore an institutional resemblance to the League. The United Nations (UN) was thus provided with a Security Council, a General Assembly, a permanent secretariat, and a secretary-general. But this time the executive was equipped with the means to enforce its will. All UN members were obliged by the United Nations' Charter to accept and implement the Council's decisions, including those relating to the application of armed force. Its role as an instrument of collective security was, however, limited by the granting to its permanent members (Britain, China, France, the Soviet Union and the United States) of a veto on all but procedural matters. Effective action depended upon the maintenance of some semblance of harmony amongst them, and when the advent of the cold war finally destroyed any notion of the wartime allies collaborating to maintain peace, the organization evolved along very different lines to those originally conceived by Roosevelt. The Security Council was, in the absence of the Soviet delegate, able to authorize the use of force under the UN's banner in Korea (1950–3), and it has since assisted in the containment of conflict through the deployment of observer and peacekeeping forces in areas of tension and unrest. Nevertheless, prior to the end of the cold war, significant binding sanctions were only applied in the form of a general trade embargo against Rhodesia and a ban on arms sales to South Africa.

During the early post-war years the Security Council sometimes seemed less like an agency for consensus-building and mediation than a forum for confrontation and condemnation. In addition, the public broadcasting of the Council's proceedings gave a new dimension to the process of negotiation. Sir Gladwyn Jebb, who had participated in the drafting of the Charter, and whose appointment in 1950 as the head of the permanent British delegation to the headquarters of the UN at New York coincided with the outbreak of the Korean War, was pitched into an arena of media diplomacy in which his verbal duelling with the chief Soviet delegate was transmitted across North America by radio and television. For many Americans these Anglo-Soviet contests became compulsive viewing, and through his debating skills Jebb (later Lord Gladwyn) gave the lie to the jibe of Ernst von. Weizsäcker, who had once represented Germany at Geneva, that 'it was the representatives of dark-haired nations who gained most from conferences'.[15]

Professional diplomats were subsequently to grow accustomed to explaining their governments' actions and policies before television cameras. Indeed, the readiness of modern ambassadors to address large audiences and to submit themselves to journalistic scrutiny has been one of the most interesting developments in the conduct of international politics since the Second World War. It is, however, questionable whether the public sessions of the Security Council, which in the summer of 1950 ranked just below Bob Hope in American television's popularity ratings, could truly be said to have constituted diplomacy. Harold Nicolson, a staunch defender of traditional practices, was highly critical of the 'circus atmosphere encompassing these momentous deliberations'. Declamatory addresses and the scoring of propaganda points appeared to matter more than the achievement of compromises and the resolution of conflict. Yet in retrospect Gladwyn recalled that the televised Council debates helped to defuse controversy and to reduce international tension that might otherwise have reached explosion point. 'It was not', he noted, 'that a "solution" of the difficulty was likely to be found in this kind of proceeding. That would no doubt have to be worked out by others . . . It was the show itself that was the thing.'[16]

Much the same might have been said about the General Assembly. George Kennan, a seasoned American diplomat, was suspicious of a body in which all questions, 'regardless of whose responsibility [was] primarily engaged and of who must bear the main burden of execution', were decided by momentary majorities composed of states of unequal size and interests. And in November 1949 he warned the United States secretary of state against Assembly resolutions 'in which the stance is taken for the deed, and the realities are inferred rather than experienced'.[17] This did not, however, deter the United States from seeking to mobilize support in the Assembly against its enemies in the cold war. The geographical distribution of member states during the 1940s meant that Washington could count upon a sympathetic majority, and in November 1950 Truman's administration sponsored a 'Uniting for Peace' resolution with the object of circumventing deadlocks within the Council and transforming the Assembly's recommendations into actions. Yet, as Kennan had foreseen, parliamentary diplomacy could be a double-edged sword. Decolonization during the 1960s and the rapid growth in the number of independent Asian and African states profoundly altered the composition of the Assembly. By 1986 membership of the United Nations had grown to 158 states, two-thirds of whom spoke for less than 10 per cent of the world's population. Most of the new members were poor and weak, few of them embraced American political and social values, and many of them found in the Assembly a forum for venting their grievances against the United States and the existing international order. American delegates had therefore to accustom themselves to being in a minority in an Assembly whose decisions on important matters required a two-thirds majority. Deserted on some occasions even by their closest allies, they often had to face voting combinations of Third World countries and the Soviet bloc.

The true significance of these developments for the practice of diplomacy is debatable. The Assembly has frequently seemed like a talking shop in which the representatives of a frustrated and power-seeking nether world engage in empty rhetoric. Its sessions have been characterized by propagandistic shadow-boxing and the passage of resolutions which, since they are non-binding, have had only a limited impact upon the outside world. Nevertheless, the Assembly has provided the underprivileged with a platform. It has drawn international attention to some of their problems, and the near universality of its membership has conferred a certain legitimacy upon its deliberations. In an ideologically divided world it became an important arena in a continuing war of ideas as well as words. Debates in the Assembly and its committees led delegates to adopt techniques more usually associated with parliamentary tactics than diplomatic dialogue. Blocs and interest groups emerged within the UN, its agencies and sponsored conferences, and delegates have become engaged in the lobbies and caucuses of what has been compared to a quasi-legislative process. Moreover, long before the erosion of Soviet power brought an end to the cold war, the international system had grown more polycentric, and the East–West divide within the organization was supplemented, and in many instances superseded, by a complex structure of economic and political alignments.

Some of the largest blocs have, since their foundation, been dominated by new members. Typical examples are the Non-Aligned Movement (NAM), which dates from the Belgrade conference of 1961, and the Group of 77 (G-77), which consists of over 120 developing countries. The latter came into being as a result of the setting up in 1964 of the United Nations Conference on Trade and Development (UNCTAD), a forum whose original purpose was to consider the relationship between international trade policies and development in the Third World. The G-77's primary concern has been with economic matters, and more especially since the mid-1970s with the betterment of the lot of developing countries through its advocacy of the notion of a new international economic order (NIEO). But it is the methods by which it has tried to achieve consensus amongst its members, firstly at a regional sub-group level, and then amongst these sub-groups, and its mode of negotiating with other blocs and groups, which make G-77 interesting from the point of view of the evolution of diplomatic practice. Assisted by UNCTAD's secretariat at Geneva, it has utilized ministerial meetings, regional conferences, and consultations and co-operation between ambassadors of member states in foreign capitals, to draft and present comprehensive policy programmes. It has also contributed to what Gidon Gottlieb has termed 'parity diplomacy', by which groups of states (whether based upon shared ethnicity, geography or interest), rather than individual sovereign states, deal with each other on equal terms with the object of achieving accommodation through consensus.[18]

This form of international collective bargaining has helped to overcome some of the problems faced by the more highly industrialized powers in participating in those assemblies and conferences where, despite their size and strength, they have had to reckon with majorities made up of representatives of micro-states and the remainder of the less developed world. At the same time it has allowed smaller countries with limited diplomatic resources to have at least some say in the framing of accords on global matters. Indeed, the growth of group diplomacy in the 1960s and 1970s complemented a trend towards the geopolitical classification of members of the Assembly and institutions such as UNCTAD. Inter-group dialogue has, however, also masked very serious divergences in the economic and social aspirations of states which have combined solely with the object of exerting greater political leverage in multilateral negotiations. Ill-prepared and inexpert delegations of minor states have sometimes been all too ready to support policies advocated by leading members of their group. But group discipline cannot always be maintained. Separate alignments have emerged, as during the Law of the Sea conference when some landlocked countries in the G-77 found themselves at odds with their Third World neighbours over drafting an agreement on the future exploitation of the seabed. Consensus-seeking between groups can in any event be a long and tedious business and may yield only meagre results. And the disappointment felt by less developed countries in their failure to make headway in the promotion of the NIEO probably accounts for a tendency amongst them to resort to older modes of bilateral negotiation.

Another problem of multilateral diplomacy within the UN framework has been the politicization of several of the organization's technical agencies. The determination of some states and some groups of states to use them for ideological and propagandistic ends has diminished their efficacy and discredited their labours in the eyes of Western governments. Conferences set up to debate women's rights have expended much time and energy debating motions on Palestine, the West Bank and South Africa, and the Soviet bloc utilized the United Nations Industrial Development Organization to raise issues relating to disarmament and 'peace'. Reluctant either to pursue unpopular courses, or to risk isolation, American delegates in UNCTAD have acquiesced in consensus resolutions even when they have challenged Washington's free trade principles. But when, in 1982, the general conference of the International Atomic Energy Agency at Vienna voted to deny the credentials of its ally, Israel, the United States suspended its participation, and two years later first the Americans and then the British withdrew from the United Nations Educational, Scientific and Cultural Organization after having failed to change its anti-Western stance.

The United States might have fared better in the UN if the State Department had paid more attention to the peculiar requirements of a system in which success has depended on the applications of legislative, rather than strictly diplomatic, skills. Multilateral (or parliamentary) diplomacy at the UN demands a thorough grasp of the procedures and rules of debate, an understanding of the interrelationship amongst institutions as far apart as New York, Geneva, Vienna, Rome, Nairobi, Paris and Montreal, and an expertise in constructing and mobilizing political coalitions. The permanent delegations, which all but a very few states maintain at New York, and those which many governments appoint to the UN organs elsewhere, resemble other diplomatic missions in their size and composition. Their function is, however, an altogether more public one. They are the defenders not just of their country's national interest, but also of its national image. An adverse vote in the Assembly or the Security Council may not impede a state from persisting with a particular policy, but it can limit its ability to win and keep the sympathy of other powers. As was demonstrated during the Falklands conflict in 1982, governments are anxious for both national and international reasons to appear to have right on their side. The adept diplomacy of the British ambassador at New York in ensuring that the Security Council both condemned the resort to force as a means of resolving the dispute and demanded the withdrawal of the Argentinian invaders, bolstered Britain's moral position and helped it to maintain the support of its friends and allies in western Europe. On the other hand, it is conceivable that had wiser counsels prevailed in Buenos Aires the ruling junta still might have saved face and lives by accepting a UN-proposed compromise.

The permanent delegations at New York have also been active participants in the more traditional tasks of diplomacy. Some of the smaller states, which maintain only a few embassies abroad, have come to rely on their delegations as valuable sources of information on international developments, and use the UN as a forum for conducting bilateral negotiations with countries in whose capitals they are unrepresented. Even states which maintain a sophisticated network of diplomatic missions have taken advantage of formal and informal contacts amongst delegates to resolve disputes and explore the prospects for future co-operation. The permanent delegations have likewise been used as channels of communication between hostile states, between countries which have simply broken off diplomatic relations with each other, and at times when one government has not recognized the authority of another. Such links can, of course, be established by other means, such as special missions, the mediation of other powers, meetings between accredited agents in neutral capitals, and the maintenance of 'interests sections' in the embassies of countries not party to a dispute. But it may be easier to begin talks between delegates who have some familiarity with each other through their work in the UN, especially if, as is often the case, states are represented at New York by individuals of political or diplomatic distinction. Moreover, the customary presence of national leaders at the autumn sessions of the Assembly has provided, and continues to offer, opportunities for private discussion and negotiation at a ministerial level. There too ministers and delegates can avail themselves of the good offices of the secretary-general.

The UN Charter is rather more specific than was the League covenant in defining the functions of the secretary-general. It thus describes him as the 'chief administrative officer' of the organization, and article 99 attributes to him the right to draw the Security Council's attention to 'any matter which in his opinion may threaten the maintenance of international peace and security'. But successive incumbents of the office have sought, either on their own initiative or at the behest of the Assembly, the Council, or individual members, to act as intermediaries, investigators and mediators. Their diplomatic role has been conditioned by personality and political circumstance. It has also reflected the paralysis that has so often afflicted the Security Council, and the evolution of the UN as an instrument of persuasion, rather than coercion, in the amelioration and containment of domestic strife and international conflict.

The first two UN secretaries-general, Trygve Lie (1946–53) and Dag Hammarskjöld (1953–61), assumed distinctly high profiles in world politics. The former, who, in Alan James's words, displayed 'an utopian flamboyancy', attempted to assert himself almost as a semi-autonomous force, and the latter, whilst advocating 'quiet diplomacy', ended by adopting courses which divided the organization.[19] Indeed, neither was able to fulfil his mission without offending Soviet susceptibilities. Moscow's representatives resented Lie's attitude at the time of the Korean War, and during his last two years in office treated him virtually as a *persona non grata*. And Hammarskjöld's approach to the internal problems of the former Belgian Congo and the intervention there in the summer of 1960 of a UN peacekeeping force led the Soviet leadership to propose that in future the secretariat's actions should be dependent on the consent of a tripartite executive or *troika* representing the communist, Western and the non-aligned states. Even the self-effacing U Thant, who replaced Hammarskjöld, came a cropper in the eyes of some governments when on the eve of the 1967 Arab–Israeli War he sanctioned the withdrawal from Sinai of the eleven-year-old UN Emergency Force.

No UN secretary-general is likely to enjoy either the admiration or respect of all the member states. Nevertheless, to be effective during the era of the cold war, they had at least to be trusted by opposing power blocs and the majority of non-aligned states. Kurt Waldheim, a career diplomat, survived two terms in the post (1972–82) without incurring the obvious displeasure of the superpowers. Through private and public diplomacy he demonstrated how it was possible to win international confidence in the impartiality and reliability of his office and his representatives. Had he been less cautious and more adventurous the UN might have played a more prominent part in promoting peace and reconciliation in the Middle East. Critics of both his diplomacy and that of his successor, Javier Perez de Cuellar, argued that Iraq in 1980 and Israel in 1982 could have been restrained from resorting to military action if use had been made of Article 99, and the UN compelled to focus its attention upon the crisis zones in the Persian Gulf and the Lebanon. Yet, as was made apparent at the time of the Falklands

War, a secretary-general's ability to intervene in a dispute depends very much upon the readiness of contending parties to take advantage of his services. Other intermediaries and other options may be available. In addition, the resources of the secretary-general are limited. Nothing ever came of proposals, first made by Lie and repeated by Waldheim, for the stationing of UN ambassadors in the capitals of member states, and the secretary-general remains without any truly independent sources of information on world developments.

Perez de Cuellar and his assistants demonstrated the vitality of the secretariat by acting as intermediaries between otherwise non-communicating Afghan and Pakistani delegates in the negotiations which led to the Geneva accords of April 1988 on the Soviet withdrawal from Afghanistan. They likewise assisted in the peace-making process in the Persian Gulf and southern Africa. More recently the end of the cold war and improved relations amongst the permanent members of the Security Council have raised expectations of the secretary-general playing a more active and effective part in world affairs. The organization's peacekeeping operations have multiplied since 1988, and the imposition of sanctions upon Iraq, after its invasion of Kuwait in 1990, provided evidence of a collective will to maintain the 'new world order' proclaimed by President Bush. But the collapse of old hegemonies has also led to a revival of old enmities. Boutros Boutros-Ghahli, the Egyptian diplomat who became secretary-general in 1992, has the unenviable mandate of seeking to reform and repair mechanisms ill-adapted to dealing with conflicts whose origins seem so often to be domestic rather than international. He remains in any case only the servant of an organization whose role, in the words of Hammarskjöld, 'is to serve as a complement to the normal diplomatic machinery of the governments'.[20] The UN offers a framework for modern multilateral diplomacy, and sets standards of international conduct in a culturally and ideologically diverse world. Its secretary-general is, however, above all what de Cuellar has called a 'technician in international negotiations'.[21] He is a valuable accessory to, rather than an essential component of, a states system which still functions very largely outside the pale of the UN and its agencies.

MULTILATERALISM AND THE DIPLOMATIC SPECIALIST

At the time of the drafting of the UN Charter one view commonly held within governing circles in London and Washington was that international conflict had its roots in the malfunctioning of the world's economic and financial system. After all, without the industrial and monetary crises of the early 1930s Hitler might never have gained power in Germany, and some of the newer states of central and eastern Europe might have stood a better chance of survival. It was therefore quite natural that the UN should have been provided with an Economic and Social Council. And it was in the same spirit that in July 1944 an allied conference at Bretton Woods in New Hampshire laid the foundations of what eventually became the International Monetary Fund (IMF) and the International Bank for Reconstruction and Development (IBRD). These institutions were intended to assist in the achievement of international financial stability, the reconstruction of economies shattered by war, and an expansion of world trade on the basis of free exchanges. Yet, even before the IMF came formally into existence in 1948, the United States had perceived the need for more drastic measures if western Europe were going to be saved from economic collapse and the threat of Soviet domination. The result was the launching of the European Recovery Programme (ERP). The Marshall Plan, as it is more usually known, offered massive financial assistance to the ailing economies of Europe. It also offered fresh work to a new breed of specialist diplomats, some of whom the war had already schooled in the practices and language of international economic co-operation.

The Lend–Lease administration had set a precedent for the employment of trained economists on the staff of American diplomatic missions. Early in 1942 the administration sent to Ankara an agent charged with assessing Turkey's economic and strategic situation, and in time he and a colleague in the British embassy helped their ambassadors in advising on what Turkish imports should be permitted to pass through the allied blockade. Such specialists continued to operate alongside regular career diplomats in the aftermath of the war. But the implementation of the ERP also required an institutional response on the part of its European beneficiaries. The United States wished to encourage greater economic integration in western Europe, and the Organization for European Economic Co-operation (OEEC) was founded in 1948 with the express purposes of assisting in the distribution of American aid and of working out a code for the liberalization of trade and transactions among its sixteen member states. This was a novel venture in peacetime diplomacy, and it offered a model for other international agencies. It was thus provided with a council, which met frequently, either at ministerial or representative level, and which, in conjunction with specialists and expert committees, hammered out common policies for the co-ordination of economic development. As with the UN at New York, so also at Paris, where the OEEC had its headquarters, there soon emerged a separate diplomatic corps with ambassadors accredited specifically to the organization. The formation of the North Atlantic Treaty Organization (NATO), a military alliance which bound the United States and Canada to an arc of European states stretching from the Arctic to Anatolia, was followed by a similar rash of new diplomatic appointments. Its council of deputies eventually became a council of permanent representatives appointed by allied governments.

The politics of economic and military interdependence raised once more the problem of defining the relationship between the specialist and the generalist in diplomacy. The United States, which dispensed both aid and advice to its partners in Europe, created an elaborate structure of special missions dealing with the OEEC, NATO and individual governments. An Economic Co-operation Administration (ECA) was established at Washington, and its agents, many of whom were drawn from the worlds of commerce and industry, were in theory subordinate to heads of American diplomatic missions in host capitals. But Averell Harriman, who was appointed to Paris as a special representative for Europe (SRE), and whose task was to co-ordinate the work of the various American economic missions, had considerable independence of the United States ambassador to France. His staff, which was appropriately housed in the Hôtel de Talleyrand, had to see that the OEEC came up with proposals for economic recovery which fitted the pattern of legislation passed by congress. It was therefore largely composed of experts skilled in agricultural, manufacturing, fiscal and legal matters. Military specialists were added to their number when in 1953 the SRE was encompassed in the United States Mission to the NATO and European Regional Organizations (USRO). Meanwhile, a national security administrator was added to the president's immediate staff to co-ordinate all foreign aid programmes in Washington.

Aid could not, however, easily be separated from the more traditional aspects of foreign relations, and the existence of different American missions in a European capital was a recipe for ambiguity. A devaluation of the French franc might, for instance, be of obvious interest to USRO. But the question remained as to whether discussions on the matter should be the responsibility of the director of the office of economic affairs at USRO, or that of the economics counsellor in the United States embassy at Paris. In the end all came to depend on the heads of the separate American missions arriving, whenever possible, at a *modus vivendi* on an effective division of labour.

Similar problems of competence and bureaucratic demarcation were observable in the diplomacy of other powers. The increased involvement of governments in the management of national economies, and a widespread recognition of the need for international co-operation in the promotion of economic growth, were reflected in an intermeshing of external and internal policies and the presence abroad of ever growing numbers of experts and representatives from domestic departments. The transformation in 1960–1 of the OEEC into the Organization of Economic Co-operation and Development (OECD) typified this trend. The new body, which included Canada and the United States as full members, and which Japan joined in 1964, aimed at the closer co-ordination of economic policies amongst the principal developed countries of the non-communist world. Since then it has evolved into a sort of permanent international economic conference in which officials drawn from various domestic ministries meet their opposite numbers in committees and working parties in order to investigate and evaluate issues of mutual concern. It provides a forum, not so much for negotiation, as for consultation, amongst senior civil servants. Likewise, the Group of 10 (G-10), which dates from 1962, and whose membership is identical to the OECD's working party no. 3, has allowed representatives of the finance ministries of ten advanced industrial nations to discuss, monitor, and sometimes achieve an agreed position on, world financial developments.

A parallel expansion of specialist diplomacy accompanied the evolution of the European communities. The first of these, the European Coal and Steel Community (ECSC), which came into being in 1951, responded to the idealism of those who, like Jean Monnet, hoped for a federal Europe, and the pragmatism of other Frenchmen who wished to contain West Germany's economic recovery within an international framework. Its object was to establish and regulate a common market for coal and steel, and to this end it was provided with: a council of ministers, representing the six member states (Belgium, the Federal Republic of Germany, France, Italy, Luxemburg and the Netherlands); a high authority, which was supposed to represent the community as a whole; a parliamentary assembly to which the high authority was responsible; and a court of justice for the settlement of disputes. Six years later, after an unsuccessful attempt had been made to create a European Defence Community, the same states concluded the Treaty of Rome and thereby founded the EEC and the European Atomic Energy Community (Euratom). The constitutional structure of the former was similar to that of the ECSC. A Council of Ministers was to ensure that ultimate authority remained in the hands of the political representatives of the member states, and a Commission, which was nominated by their governments, but answerable to a parliament, was to initiate all community policies. A Committee of Permanent Representatives (COREPER) was also established to prepare work for the Council and to carry out tasks assigned to it by ministers. Henceforth matters which might previously have been the subjects of bilateral negotiations were regulated by a combination of supranational administrations and institutionalized multilateral diplomacy.

The institutions of the EEC, the ECSC and Euratom were merged in 1965, and it has since been customary to refer simply to the 'European Community' (EC). In the meantime the exigencies of integration led diplomats and politicians alike to explore and adopt new methods of bargaining. The Council of Ministers, whose membership may be drawn from domestic departments rather than foreign ministries, meets sixty to seventy times a year and decides policy either on the basis of a weighted voting system or through compromises reached in conjunction with the Commission. This has sometimes involved a lengthy process of give and take, and marathon sessions of the Council have assembled diplomatic packages covering a variety of contentious issues. In 1970 it took 72 hours of uninterrupted negotiation to put together arrangements which provided the Community with its own financial resources. Such sessions may be politically and psychologically essential if participants are to demonstrate to the public and the press that sacrifices have not been made without a fight. But on many occasions ministers have to do no more than sanction the proposals of the Commission or formalize agreements already worked out in COREPER. The latter has come to occupy a pivotal position in the administration of the Community, especially as its members, unlike, say, ministers of agriculture or finance, or commissioners with specific portfolios, have a truly integrated mandate. A permanent representative, who may rely on a staff recruited from several home departments, engages in a form of conference diplomacy which demands a detailed understanding of a multiplicity of topics. He also requires instructions which are broad enough to leave plenty of scope for manoeuvre. As one Dutch diplomat has put it, COREPER has to approach 'in an integrated way, the difficult task of reconciling the national interests of individual member states with the lofty goal of a more unified Europe'.[22]

It is, nevertheless, all too easy to exaggerate the significance of these confederal organs for the evolution of diplomatic practice. The EC has, after all, a good, if somewhat primitive, precedent in the shape of the Germanic Confederation. It too was composed of sovereign states, and its Federal Diet at Frankfurt was, like the Council of Ministers and COREPER, essentially a diplomatic congress with quasi-administrative functions. Indeed, the EEC of the original six seemed to combine the boundaries of Napoleonic France with the constitutional peculiarities of Metternich's *Bund*. And just as the governments of other powers found it expedient to maintain representatives at Frankfurt, so non-EEC powers have found it advantageous to be represented at the Commission's headquarters in Brussels. The EEC, which was empowered to negotiate commercial accords, constituted too important a trading area to be neglected by other states, and within ten years of its foundation there were 69 missions at Brussels accredited specifically to it. Since then their number has risen by more than half as many again. They engage in much the same kind of activities as embassies elsewhere. They observe, report, negotiate and attempt to influence the Community through its various institutions. But given the functional as well as the regional orientation of the EC and its successor the European Union (EU), they are much more likely to be made up of individuals with expertise in commercial, financial and fiscal matters than a traditional embassy.

One of the more bizarre aspects of the appointment of permanent representatives to international institutions relates to their status in the diplomatic hierarchy. Problems of precedence and protocol have arisen which in some cases match those of the courts of Renaissance Europe. Nowhere has this been more apparent than in Brussels where some countries now have ambassadors accredited to the Belgian government, the

EU, and NATO. In the early days of the EEC hosts and hostesses had to cope with the sometimes embarrassing question of how to arrange seating at a dinner table when the guests included the United States ambassadors to both Belgium and the Community. And if the ranking of ambassadorial carriages no longer gave rise to brawling in the streets, the numbering of license plates for diplomatic vehicles compelled the Belgian authorities to consider how honour might be done to separate diplomatic corps. The result was an ingenious solution. Diplomats accredited to Belgium were provided with plates which started with the lowest numbers (e.g., 1 for the Papal nuncio), and those appointed to the EEC began with the highest. There was also the question of who should receive the credentials of representatives to the Community? The French insisted that nothing should be done that might detract from the superior authority of the member states, and it was finally settled that new ambassadors should present their papers to the presidents of both the Commission and the Council of Ministers.

The French were equally reluctant to endorse the notion of the EC acting as a kind of superstate in world affairs. They opposed a single joint announcement in 1972 of an agreement amongst Community members and Britain to recognize the newly-formed state of Bangladesh. Nevertheless, the EEC has since its inception negotiated and concluded agreements on commercial matters with non-member states. It has also engaged in what has been termed 'associative diplomacy' with other trading blocs and regional groupings, such as the African, Caribbean and Pacific group (ACP), the Association of South East Asian Nations (ASEAN), and the Council for Mutual Economic Assistance (Comecon) which linked the economies of Soviet-dominated eastern Europe. Its representatives have participated in conferences and negotiations sponsored by the OECD, UNCTAD, and the General Agreement on Tariffs and Trade (GATT) – the Geneva-based agency which since 1947 has been endeavouring to establish a universal system for reducing barriers to international trade. The EU commissioner for external affairs has his own staff in Brussels and delegations in Geneva, Paris (where the OECD has its headquarters), New York (where the EC has observer status in the UN General Assembly), Tokyo, Washington, and Latin America. The Community did not, however, possess anything that might be equated with a diplomatic service. Its associative diplomacy was concerned primarily with trade and aid, and only indirectly with strictly political issues. Indeed, until the drafting of the Single European Act in 1986 such progress as had been made towards creating a framework for the co-ordination and harmonization of the foreign policies of member states occurred outside the formal treaty structure of the Communities.

During the early 1970s several factors encouraged EC countries to work more closely together in conducting their external relations. These included the admission of Britain, Denmark and Ireland to the Communities; the general multilateralization of international affairs; the challenge posed to the economies of western Europe by Japan's growing industrial might; the new-found strength of the Organization of Petroleum Exporting Countries (OPEC); and the desire of the United States to remodel its relations with its transatlantic partners. But the mechanisms devised in 1970–3 under the rubric of European Political Co-operation (EPC) contained little that might be described as truly novel in the history of diplomatic practice. In their essentials they simply formalized inter-governmental consultation within a non-military alliance. Thus EC foreign ministers have since met at three-monthly intervals; these conclaves are preceded by discussions amongst their senior officials; 'correspondents' are designated within the foreign ministries of member states to liaise on problems relating to EPC; and the missions of Community members consult and sometimes collaborate in non-EC capitals and international organizations. Moreover, the whole process of co-operation on international issues has been assisted by the institution in December 1974 of regular summit meetings of EC heads of state or government in the form of the European Council. Member states have also collaborated within the mechanisms of the Conference on Security and Co-operation in Europe (CSCE) in order to bridge cold war divisions, set guidelines for relations amongst peoples and states, and ensure respect for human rights. A representative of the Commission participated in the 1973–5 negotiations which resulted in the CSCE Final Act; and since then Community countries have, with a considerable measure of success, co-ordinated their policies in the review conferences and other meetings for which the Act provided.

EPC has none the less remained strictly inter-governmental. And although it acquired its own secretariat in 1987, it is still serviced by the foreign ministry of whichever state is presiding over the Council of Ministers, with continuity provided by a *troika* of past, present and succeeding presidencies. The representation of the Community's collective will has, in consequence, rarely been less than complex, a fact that has been more than adequately demonstrated by the EC's participation in the Middle East peace process launched by the United States in the aftermath of Iraq's withdrawal from Kuwait. At the Madrid conference in October 1991 the EC was represented at the conference table by its Portuguese presidency, and in the several stages of the multilateral talks which took place in Moscow in the following January it was represented by its Dutch presidency, the Commission and individual members states. Meanwhile, a special co-ordinating group was established and senior officials of the *troika* were present in Washington for the bilateral discussions which continued throughout 1992. Collective diplomacy on this scale has involved co-operation amongst representatives on several levels and at a variety of venues. It has also involved a certain rivalry amongst those representing the different elements of the Community. The extent to which this can be mitigated by the tighter structures of the Common Foreign and Security Policy, foreseen by the participants in the Maastricht summit of 1991, remains a matter for speculation.

In so far as its external relations are concerned, the greatest contribution of the EC to the evolution of diplomatic technique probably lies in the sphere of associative diplomacy. The Lomé conventions of 1975, 1980, 1985 and 1990 which the EEC concluded with the ACP countries, and which govern the latter's access to the common market and the provision of development aid, were a notable experiment in the multilateral management of relations amongst developing and industrialized states. They have resulted in the establishment of an EEC–ACP Council of Ministers which meets annually, an Ambassadors' Committee which meets every six months, and a Joint Assembly. Likewise the dialogue conducted between the EC and the Arab League in the wake of the 1973 Arab–Israeli War demonstrated the scope for mitigating conflict through committees and consultations amongst economic and financial experts. But these developments have also been indicative of a tendency, particularly in the developing and newly industrialized areas of the world, for countries to seek to better their international standing through the formation of functional and regional bodies equipped with a panoply of consultative and executive organs. Three obvious examples are: the Organization of American States (OAS), which dates from 1947–8; the Organization of African Unity (OAU), which emerged from a summit conference of thirty-one independent African states at Addis Ababa in May 1961; and ASEAN, a loose alignment of six south-east Asian states which was founded in 1967. All three have arguably made a modest contribution towards easing tensions amongst their members. In addition ASEAN has utilized methods not dissimilar to those applied by the EC in negotiating with other trading blocs and non-member states. Associative diplomacy, like bloc diplomacy at the UN, has sometimes been useful to smaller and poorer nations who have had neither the resources nor the time to acquire more than very rudimentary foreign services.

NEW-STATE DIPLOMACY

The nineteenth century witnessed the extension of the norms and practices of the European state system to the rest of the world. By 1914 most of Africa and a large part of Asia were under European domination, and those Asiatic polities which still retained their independence had either adopted, or adjusted to, the diplomatic methods of the West. In the Americas, the former colonies of Britain, Portugal and Spain continued to conduct their foreign relations largely according to the European model, and the British Dominions, which began to establish their own diplomatic services in the early years of this century, followed their example. Likewise, the redrawing of the map of Europe in the aftermath of the First World War did not in itself threaten existing modes of diplomatic behaviour. The new states had, however, to pay for their admission to the system. Not only had buildings to be purchased and leased for foreign ministries and missions, but suitable personnel had also to be recruited and trained. Where, as in Hungary and Poland, there existed a native aristocracy with cosmopolitan connections and some experience of diplomacy this was less of a difficulty than in those countries whose national leaders had only a limited cognizance of the outside world and whose nobility was of alien extraction. Individuals with a knowledge of international affairs and the ability not only to speak, but to negotiate in foreign languages were often in short supply. The Czechs chose, for instance, to avail themselves of the assistance of academics and publicists who had recently been engaged in propagating their national cause abroad. The Irish experience was similar. Indeed, the complaint of the Free State's first foreign minister that 'our representative in Berlin knows little German, our representative in Madrid is only learning Spanish, and our Rome representative does not know Italian' could doubtless have been echoed elsewhere in the Europe of the 1920s.[23]

Some of the new states of the post-Second World War era were better endowed for diplomacy. India, for example, already possessed a quasi-foreign service before the formal transfer of power from Britain in August 1947. It had been a member of the League of Nations, its nationals had assisted in staffing missions in neighbouring states and territories, and in October 1946 a ministry of external affairs and Commonwealth relations was established in Delhi. During the final years of empire Malaya was also represented in other Commonwealth countries. Yet of Britain's other colonial possessions only the Gold Coast (Ghana) and Nigeria benefited from an extensive preparation for the administration of foreign affairs. Ghanaians were thus included in a governor's advisory committee on defence and external affairs, which was established in 1954, and it sponsored the selection of diplomatic trainees. In the case of Nigeria an external affairs department was created four years before it achieved independence in 1960, and Nigerians had the opportunity to gain experience of diplomacy both in British missions and in the colony's offices in London and Washington and its consulates elsewhere in Africa. The acceleration of the pace of decolonization in the early 1960s was, however, to leave the imperial powers with precious little time in which to provide their precocious, and sometimes neglected, offspring with adequate apparatus for participation in world politics. In some instances the results were disastrous. The Belgians decided to dispose of their colony in the Congo (now Zaïre) only six months before proclaiming its independence, and in July 1960 departed from a land which was tottering on the brink of anarchy and patently incapable of managing either its own internal or foreign affairs.

Even those newly emergent states which possessed the bases of sophisticated administrative machines found diplomacy an expensive business. Ambassadors required residences, offices, teleprinters, ciphers and courier services. Some of the older British Dominions were able to assist newer and poorer Commonwealth countries with staff training and the transport of embassy mails. But diplomatic representation remains one of the clearest manifestations of state sovereignty, and governments, which were anxious to proclaim their national emancipation, were sometimes all too eager to invest in the trappings of diplomacy. Ghana opened 60 missions immediately after gaining its independence, and during its first year of full diplomatic representation Uganda spent 20 per cent of its foreign service budget simply on renting residential and office accommodation. The appointment of unsuitable political figures to posts in Europe and North America likewise proved a costly experience when nepotism was combined with incompetence and the pursuit of personal grandeur. It took only five months for one Ghanaian ambassador at Bonn to draw an advance on his expenses equal to five times his salary, thereby ensuring that he had at his disposal a Rolls Royce and two Mercedes. Such ambassadorial profligacy has not been limited to representatives of Third World countries. It has, however, been all the more difficult to justify when, as has so often been the case in the newer states of Africa and Asia, national leaders have concentrated foreign policy making in their own hands and bypassed or ignored their diplomats. Typical in this respect was Kwame Nkrumah, who was prime minister and subsequently president of Ghana between 1957 and 1966. Distrustful of his British-trained diplomats, he filled Ghana's embassies with non-career men, set up his own African affairs bureau, and left to his successors a thoroughly demoralized and corrupted foreign service.

Shortly after achieving their independence many African, Asian and Caribbean countries seemed to drift almost inevitably towards authoritarian systems of government. But the same forces which contributed so much to the destabilization of post-colonial democracies – poverty, domestic dissent and the social strains associated with industrialization – also fashioned the style and content of new state diplomacy. Most of the newer states were poorer states, and few of them were able to contemplate more than a very restricted representation abroad. This usually meant the maintenance of at least a permanent delegation at New York, an embassy or high commission in the capital of a former imperial power, and a mission accredited to one or more of the most important neighbouring states. Third World countries have thus been able to broaden their opportunities for participation in international affairs through representation in the General Assembly and its committees, and by maintaining a diplomatic presence in capitals like London, where the Commonwealth has its secretariat, Brussels and Paris. Multiple accreditation, such as the appointment of single missions to both the UN and the United States government, and the establishment of embassies at the seats of regional organizations, has also saved on ambassadorial costs. Of equal significance has, however, been the determination of many Afro-Asian leaders to engage in personal diplomacy, whether this be in the form of the grand tour, or attendance at regional summits and foreign ministerial conferences. Unencumbered by expensive diplomatic establishments, presidents and prime ministers of states large and small have sometimes sought to enhance their reputation at home by demonstrating their diplomatic talents abroad. Moreover, since much of the so-called North–South debate has been about aid and trade, it is hardly surprising that in many cases ministries of co-operation, development, education and finance have preferred to deal directly with equivalent agencies in Europe and North America.

Neither summitry nor bureaucratic rivalry has of course been peculiar to the diplomacy of new states. But the propensity of heads of government both to personalize the management of external affairs and to rely on the technocrats of domestic departments has naturally limited the growth and influence of professional foreign services in the Third World. Their role has also been circumscribed by shortages in many of the developing countries of qualified personnel, and, in particular, their lack of the financial and legal expertise that modern diplomacy so often demands. Another deficiency, itself the by-product of inexperience and low staffing levels, has been unsatisfactory liaison between foreign ministries and missions abroad. This has sometimes meant that African and Asian diplomats have been left with far more discretion than their modern European counterparts. At the same time, in the absence of a competent administrative machine, their reports may be neglected, their advice ignored, and such intelligence as they have gathered left uncollated and unutilized. An ambassador may in any case be extremely reluctant to act on his own initiative. By appearing to step out of line he may simply increase the risk of his being summarily dismissed by a paranoid dictator, or permanently exiled as the result of a *coup d'état* at home. Divided loyalties within a mission have on some occasions led to intramural violence and intervention by a host government. The overthrow of Prince Norodom Sihanouk's régime in Cambodia was followed in the spring of 1970 by a bitter power struggle in the Cambodian mission at Prague in which the second secretary attempted to seize the embassy building with the assistance of ten students. And at Paris a street battle ensued when the Cambodian military attaché tried to wrest his apartment from a pro-Sihanouk faction.

Diplomatic farce on this scale has fortunately been rare. Indeed some of the micro-states which emerged from the confetti of empire in the 1960s and 1970s possessed insufficient diplomats to mount an embassy squabble. The Indian ocean state of the Maldive Islands, which in 1967 applied for UN membership, could barely afford to pay its annual fees, let alone staff a qualified permanent delegation at New York. Western Samoa, with a population of 130,000, was even less ambitious. It preferred to rely on New Zealand for its overseas representation, and not until 1976, fourteen years after achieving independence, did it establish its first embassy in the form of a high commission in Wellington. Another island state, the phosphate-exporting republic of Nauru, with just 7,000 inhabitants, took the extra-ordinary step of advertising in the Australian press for an external affairs secretary, and chose to be represented in Australia, not by a diplomat in Canberra, but through an office in Melbourne, the headquarters of the phosphate commission. Such austerity has, however, been the exception rather than the rule amongst the more populous of the new states. In the first flush of independence many of them wished simply to be noticed, and scant attention was paid to balancing the costs and benefits of an extensive diplomatic network. As one Guyanan diplomat has indicated, their very desire to assert their non-alignment reinforced their inclination to establish diplomatic services on a par with those of the major powers.[24] Even those societies which could look back upon a tradition of pre-colonial diplomacy (and amongst these must be included not only the ancient polities of Asia, but also the kingdoms and tribal-based societies of west Africa) seemed readily to assume the mannerisms, methods and practices of the European states. There was, perhaps, nothing truly surprising about this. After all, sovereignty was a European notion and its acquisition and exercise meant acceptance of a code of conduct which the Europeans had evolved to fulfil the requirements of a system of sovereign states.

Nevertheless, the proliferation of new states has made international politics a more complicated and more costly business. The break-up of the Soviet Union and Yugoslavia, and the sudden emergence of twenty-one states where once there were only two, has strained the budgets of Western foreign ministries and encouraged them to envisage sharing mission premises with the representatives of like-minded countries. Such diplomatic inflation has also eroded that intimacy which once characterized the *corps diplomatiques* of the great capitals of Europe. Before the First World War when there were no more than 56 missions in London, and when a mere nine of these were fully-fledged embassies, it was still possible for an ambassador to be personally acquainted with all his *chers collègues*. But that is unlikely in Britain today, where, according to one estimate, there live 17,000 foreign diplomats, their families and staffs. Moreover, the new global order has been permeated by a spirit of diplomatic egalitarianism which has virtually eradicated the legations and ministers-plenipotentiary of yesterday. Between the world wars a number of British and French legations were upgraded to embassies, and in 1927 a commission of experts, appointed by the League, recommended that the heads of all missions should have the same titles and styles. The proposal was, however, opposed by the United States and the principal European powers on the grounds that it did not correspond either to the facts of international political life, or to the necessity for preserving a hierarchical structure within the diplomatic services of each state.

On the eve of war in 1939 France had only sixteen embassies abroad (ten in Europe), as compared with thirty-eight legations (twenty-two outside of Europe). Yet within three decades this situation was profoundly altered. The new states of Africa and Asia were determined to assert both their sovereignty and their equality of status, and the notion of ranking missions according to standards appropriate to the defunct monarchies of Europe seemed anomalous to countries emerging from a century of imperial rule. The conservatively minded Swiss were, as ever, reluctant to change. Yet by the 1970s almost all permanent diplomatic missions appointed by one state to another were designated either embassies or high commissions (the title used to describe the missions which Commonwealth countries maintain in each other's capitals). Henceforth the head of mission of a west African republic with a staff of three ranked equal to a United States ambassador with an establishment of 100 or more.

The classification of missions is one of the subjects covered by the Vienna convention on diplomatic law. The product of almost five years' work by the UN's international law commission and a conference of 81 states at Vienna in 1961, the convention codified, and sought to clarify, the rules of diplomatic law as they had evolved in the past two centuries. Much of what had previously been accepted as diplomatic law was based on custom and bilateral agreements designed to facilitate the establishment of formal relations. Jurists and international institutions had ruminated upon its precise application and content and, in 1928, several Latin American countries subscribed to a multilateral convention governing diplomatic officials. But it was not until the 1950s, and then in response to the problems of the cold war and the exigencies of an expanding international system, that a successful attempt was made to achieve a global accord covering such matters as the involability and protection of mission premises and communications and diplomatic immunities and privileges. The resulting convention was followed by others on consular relations, special missions and representation in international organizations. The vast majority of Third World states, many of whom have criticized other aspects of international law as the relics of Western imperialism, have subscribed to their provisions. This is not to say that the principles they enshrine have been invariably respected. In the nineteenth century some writers optimistically believed that with increased public order and the acceptance by states of a legal obligation to protect aliens, diplomatic immunity and inviolability would eventually become unnecessary and lapse. They would have been sadly disappointed. Despite, or perhaps in some cases because of, the Vienna convention, diplomats have been limited in their movements, harassed by state security services, kidnapped by urban guerrillas, and become the victims of mob violence and terrorist attacks. In some instances governments have been unable or unwilling to afford protection, and in others they have deliberately conspired to denigrate and discredit foreign missions.

If diplomacy has become a more hazardous occupation this is in part due to the inflated size of modern embassies. Ambassadorial residences have been separated from chanceries, and to embassy staffs have been added a multitude of cultural and technical assistants. Some Afro-Asian and Latin American states have simply not had the means with which to provide adequate protection for the increased numbers of personnel claiming diplomatic status. Many countries are all too prone to civil conflict and unrest, and the very fact that their governments are under an obligation to safeguard the lives and property of foreign diplomats make the latter uniquely valuable hostages for dissident guerrilla groups. The abduction of an envoy and the consequent embarrassment of the host government enhances the bargaining position of the rebels. Moreover, embassies are peculiarly vulnerable targets for ideological, religious and political zealots who are anxious to punish the powers whom they believe responsible for their real, or more usually supposed, ills, sufferings and oppression. Yet from an international legal standpoint there is a considerable difference between the incidents perpetrated by bands of would-be revolutionaries, or those which result from a breakdown of public order, and those in which government agents and local police forces are complicit. Even the latter may, however, only represent a momentary expression of national outrage. The sacking of the British and Malaysian embassies in Djakarta in September 1963, and the subsequent refusal of the Indonesian government to make any reparation, was a clear breach of international law. Nevertheless, in retrospect this seems less like a threat to the precepts of Western diplomacy than a manifestation of regional instability. The same might possibly be said of the outrages committed against foreign diplomats during the cultural revolution in China and following the Shah's eviction from Iran.

Neither China nor Iran can of course be described as new states. But both the communist leadership in Peking and the Islamic theocracy in Tehran have identified with, and sought to direct, significant sections of the non-European world. Moreover, China's cultural revolution of 1966–7 was an amalgam of xenophobic nationalism and ideological fervour which specifically rejected the values of the West. The Chinese foreign ministry, which since the proclamation of the People's Republic in 1949 had been organized on the Soviet model, was taken over by ultra-leftists, who preached the universalist principles enshrined in the thoughts of Chairman Mao and denounced China's diplomats for having succumbed to western decadence. Over forty of China's ambassadors were recalled to Peking, diplomatic immunity was denounced as 'a product of bourgeois norms', foreign diplomats in China were humiliated and physically assaulted by Red Guards, and at the height of the troubles in 1967 the British embassy was gutted.

Once, however, the revolution had run its course and order had been restored, the authorities in Peking were prepared to apologize and make recompense. By 1971, when the People's Republic took China's seat on the UN Security Council, the events of six years before seemed like a temporary reversion to the spirit of the Boxers.

The most recent versions of militant Islam may on the other hand pose a more serious challenge to the peaceful conduct of international relations through resident missions and professional diplomats. The student invasion in November 1979 of the United States embassy compound in Tehran, and the 444-day hostage siege which followed, certainly represent one of the greatest offences against diplomatic immunity in modern times. Further-more, Khomeini's Iran offered itself as the only truly righteous model for the whole Muslim *Ummah* (community or world). The international stand-ards and conventions established by the impious majority are *ipso facto* false, and may therefore be flouted. Guided by these principles, the régime in Tehran has in the view of one author practised a 'violent diplomacy', seeking to extract specific advantages by using state-sponsored violence against the nationals of other countries.[25] Very often these have been diplomats. Pro-Iranian or Iranian-inspired terrorist groups were thus re-sponsible for car bomb attacks on the United States embassies in Beirut in April 1983 and in Kuwait in December 1985, and in 1987 the deputy head of the British mission in Tehran was attacked and abducted for 24 hours.

Other Middle Eastern governments have similarly ignored and abused the Vienna convention. Terrorists and assassination squads have been assisted and encouraged through diplomatic channels, and embassies have become mini-garrisons in conflict with migrant opposition groups. Matters were taken to an extreme in 1984, when, under the inspiration of Colonel Qadhafi, the Libyan leader, revolutionary students took over the Libyan mission (known since 1979 as the Libyan People's Bureau) in London. Subsequent attacks upon Libyan *émigrés* were followed by protest demon-strations outside the bureau, and on 17 April gunshots fired from a first-floor window of the building resulted in the wounding of several protestors and the death of a woman police officer.

One result of this tragedy was that the People's Bureau was closed and its occupants expelled. Another was that it gave a fresh stimulus to public demands in Britain and other Western countries for an ending, or re-striction, of diplomatic immunity from prosecution. Unpaid parking fines, one of the commonest offences by foreign diplomats, were irritating enough, but it seemed manifestly unjust that British courts should be unable to try or punish those responsible for killing a police officer. A similar sense of public outrage prevailed in France when in 1987 Wahid Gordgi, a locally engaged interpreter at the Iranian embassy in Paris, whom the police wished to question in connection with a series of terrorist bombings, was given sanctuary in the Iranian chancery. Matters reached crisis point when the Iranians responded by trumping up charges against a French diplomat in Tehran, and the affair was only resolved when each man was allowed to return to his respective capital. Diplomatic immunity was thus used to protect the export of violence. Some comfort may, however, be drawn from the fact that in claiming immunity both Libya and Iran insisted on the application of one of the basic tenets of Western diplomacy. It is in any case difficult to see how any kind of dialogue can be maintained amongst states without respect for the well-being of diplomats and their property. The oldest and probably the most effective sanction of diplomatic law remains reciprocity, and the non-observance of rules is likely to lead to retaliation and eventually isolation. Moreover, as the early Bolsheviks discovered, until a universalist creed achieves universal acceptance, the alternatives to diplomacy are few and dangerous. In a multicultural and interdependent world a Talleyrand is probably a more valuable asset than a Trotsky.

DIPLOMATIC INFLATION

The emancipation of the Third World, the spawning of international organizations and régimes, and the broadening of the agenda of diplomacy, have been matched by a corresponding and seemingly inevitable expansion of the foreign services of the superpowers and their European allies. Despite government attempts to cut personnel, and the closure of overseas posts, diplomacy has been one of the growth industries of the mid-twentieth century. Thomas Jefferson managed United States foreign policy with the aid of five clerks, two messengers and a part-time translator. But by 1979 there were some 10,500 American foreign service employees. Likewise the numbers engaged in the Quai d'Orsay leapt from 447 in 1945 to 2,699 in 1981 – a sixfold increase in less than 40 years. Individual missions have also grown in size and function. In 1914 the British embassies at Washington and Paris had respectively staffs of 8 and 11. By 1988 these figures had swollen to 82 and 40. And when ancillary and other staff are taken into account the number of individuals engaged at Britain's Washington mission is nearer to 300. Some embassy compounds are indeed, like that of the United States at Bonn, equivalent to small townships with shops, filling stations and leisure facilities. Diplomatic inflation has tended, however, to modify the role of the professional generalist. The pace of technological change, the speed of modern communications, and a heightened awareness of regional and global interdependence, have meant increased involvement in external affairs by domestic ministries, such as those concerned with agriculture, civil aviation, finance and health. The content of diplomacy has become altogether more technical, and many area and subject specialists have been drawn into inter-governmental dialogue. In some instances they have dealt directly with each other without the assistance of foreign ministries and diplomats, and in others they have been appointed to embassy and departmental staffs, or formed part of national delegations.

Almost everywhere this trend has been associated with a fragmentation of the administration and execution of foreign policy. In the United States the State Department has been more or less consistently engaged in competition with other executive departments and agencies since the earliest days of the cold war. This was in part due to the élitist subculture of its officials, who were reluctant to embrace the new specialisms. They clung to the notion that all the most important foreign policy decisions were essentially political, and that the skills required to handle them were derived from intuition and experience. The lateral entry into the department of reserve officers to perform administrative, cultural and economic tasks did little to alter its complexion, and other agencies emerged to provide expert advice and representation. Internal opposition to the assimilation of the research and analysis branch of the OSS thus resulted in the establishment in 1947 of the CIA as a separate institution, and the foundation in the same year of the National Security Council (NSC) seemed to ensure that the defence community would have a pre-eminent influence on the politico-military aspects of American foreign policy. Then in 1953 another void was filled with the creation and attachment to the State Department of the United States Information Agency (USIA) to deal with propaganda, educational and cultural matters, and in 1954 the Department of Agriculture was allowed to reinstate its own foreign service. Within twenty years less than a third of the staff of American foreign missions represented the State Department. The rest were appointees of the departments of agriculture, commerce, defence, justice, transportation, the treasury, the USIA, the CIA and the Agency for International Development (AID) – the principal arm of the International Development and Co-operation Agency.

A misconceived attempt to integrate the personnel of the State Department and the foreign service neither satisfied the career diplomats, who resented the dilution of their status, nor produced the specialists whom the department required to re-establish its influence. And although John F. Kennedy gave his moral support to the idea of the department as the chief co-ordinating body for foreign policy, this conflicted with personal inclinations towards both centralized decision-making in the White House and the employment of special presidential envoys. Richard Nixon made the NSC his primary foreign-policy-formulating agency, and Henry Kissinger, firstly as Nixon's national security adviser and then as his secretary of state, assumed a role in the making and conduct of policy which, in the words of one historian, left the State Department languishing 'in a condition of bureaucratic desuetude'.[26] In the meanwhile the position of American ambassadors abroad was formally reinforced by Kennedy's introduction of the 'country team' concept, which made heads of missions the single authoritative voice for all non-military activities. Regular meetings amongst ambassadors, their senior staff and the representatives of other agencies were intended to allow them to concert their actions. This may have fulfilled the vision of Chester Bowles, a former ambassador at Delhi, of American ambassadors as 'administrators and co-ordinators'.[27] But it also left them in the invidious position of having to arbitrate between agents pursuing divergent departmental aims. The desire of an agricultural attaché to dispose of the United States' surplus grain might not be easily reconciled with the endeavours of the representative of AID to promote local self-sufficiency in food production.

Even in a country like France, whose foreign ministry has long occupied a central and privileged position in the management of policy, career diplomats have had to reckon with new and powerful rivals. The Quai d'Orsay has been labelled the '*corps malade*' of the French administration. Its authority has been weakened by presidential intervention in the making and implementation of policy, the enhanced significance of economic and strategic issues in international negotiations, and the increased interest taken by other ministries in external affairs. Thus the ministry of co-operation, which was established to oversee French assistance to Third World countries, is actively involved in Africa, and the ministry of the interior, by virtue of its interest in international terrorism, cannot be excluded from dealings with the Arab world. Again, however, as with the State Department, the Quai d'Orsay's loss of political leverage may to some extent be attributed to the conservatism of the diplomatic profession. Since 1945 all entrants to the Quai d'Orsay, except for those specializing in difficult languages, have had to pass through the interministerial training school, the *École Nationale d'Administration* (ENA). Yet there has been a marked decline in personnel exchanges with other ministries, and little use has been made of the additional talents of those younger diplomats who have taken the opportunity to spend time in business and industry. Today's French foreign service has, indeed, a plethora of generalists, skilled in the traditional tasks of negotiation, representation and reporting. In 1987 there were 60 diplomats of ministerial rank awaiting promotion to a vacant embassy. At the same time the French mission in Tokyo had not a single Japanese-speaker amongst its diplomatic staff.

All this contrasted sharply with practice in the Soviet Union and Japan. Prospective Soviet diplomats had, after passing through a rigorous selection process, to spend five years at the foreign ministry's Institute of International Relations. There, besides studying history, international law, economics, Marxism–Leninism and foreign languages, they were encouraged to become area specialists. Experienced diplomats could also return for study at the higher diplomatic school, and many of the younger men appointed to Third World countries underwent additional training in such subjects as agronomy and hydraulic engineering. Japan's foreign ministry has likewise sought to equip itself with the necessary expertise for handling contemporary issues. Faced with competition from the formidable Ministry of International Trade and Industry (MITI), it has placed a high premium on the recruitment of economics specialists, and a diplomat's secondment to an economics ministry has usually improved his chances of promotion.

Both in its style and content Japanese diplomacy has seemed to mirror Japan's phenomenal economic growth in the past forty years. Critics of British diplomacy have on the other hand seen a remodelling of the foreign service as a way of helping to arrest Britain's industrial decline. In the 1960s and 1970s, when British governments often appeared to be more concerned with the balance of payments than the balance of power, the Foreign Office was urged to make economies in its essentially representational services and to concentrate more upon supporting British exporters in their search for contracts and markets. Already, as a result of reforms introduced in 1943, the Foreign Office, the diplomatic, the commercial diplomatic, and the consular services were amalgamated into a single foreign service. Then in 1968 relations with Commonwealth governments, which had previously been handled by a separate department, were brought under the purview of an integrated Foreign and Commonwealth Office (FCO). But two British government reports, those of the Plowden (1964) and Duncan (1969) committees, also underlined the service's need for specialized training, stressed the importance of its being better able to assist commerce, and argued in favour of cuts in overseas representation.

The contents of the Duncan report were much resented by some diplomats who felt that they were being reduced to the level of commercial travellers. Their criticisms were, however, mild when compared with the howls of anguish which greeted the publication in 1977 of a report by the British government's Central Policy Review Staff (CPRS). It recommended that, on the basis of Britain's diminished role in world politics, and from the viewpoint of a cost–benefit calculation, the diplomatic service should be merged with the home civil service and that all government departments with foreign interests should participate in the control of overseas representation. Furthermore, it contended that priorities should be reviewed in all diplomatic missions, that export promotion should take precedence, that political work (i.e., the regular conduct of political relations and the analysis of political developments abroad) should, as far as possible, be shifted from the embassies to London, and that most of the cultural work of the British Council was unnecessary. Some of the critics of the report were justly infuriated by the blatant naivety of such statements as that 'intellectual ability [was] not very important' for political work.[28] And Sir Geoffrey Jackson, a former British ambassador, pointed to what many diplomats must surely have regarded as one of the chief weaknesses of the report when he wrote that it gave the impression 'of not realizing that there is an enduring function which by any other name, is always diplomacy'.[29]

Therein, however, lay the problem. How was that 'enduring function' to be defined in an age when the distinction between domestic and foreign policy had become so blurred? The proposals of the CPRS, though never implemented, at least had the virtue of focusing attention upon this enduring problem of modern diplomacy.

SUMMITS, SHERPAS AND SHUTTLES

The role of the resident ambassador has also been more narrowly circumscribed by the increased propensity of political leaders to engage in ministerial diplomacy. The jet aeroplane has made the world a smaller place and few politicians have been able to resist the temptation to try their hand at international negotiation. After all, air travel and television cameras have made world statesmen of the humblest party hacks. But since the bleakest days of the cold war a peculiar importance has been attached to the notion of summit diplomacy. The term itself was coined by Winston Churchill when in an election speech in February 1950 he called for a 'parley at the summit' as a means of easing and overcoming East–West tensions.[30] What he evidently had in mind was a conference of the Soviet and Western leaders similar to those that had taken place at Tehran, Yalta and Potsdam. In the absence of a unified and sovereign German state no peace treaty had been signed with Germany, the conference which had met in Paris in 1946 to make peace with the lesser Axis Powers had been a gathering of foreign ministers, and the new United States president, Harry S.Truman, had shown little enthusiasm for continuing with his predecessor's personal diplomacy. Churchill thus conjured up the idea of reviving a wartime relationship to overcome the divisions of the peace. Nevertheless, neither the Geneva summit of July 1955, nor the Paris summit of May 1960, both of which brought together the political leaders of Britain, France, the Soviet Union and the United States, could be said to have made much, if any, progress towards bettering relations between the superpowers. In 1955 the two sides were still divided over the future of Germany, and the Paris conference collapsed in ignominious failure after the shooting down of an American spy plane over Soviet territory. Moreover, other gatherings of heads of state and government were soon being described as summits in a way that seemed to debase Churchill's original conception.

When in 1963 Donald Watt attempted to give some precision to the term, he insisted that to qualify as a summit a meeting must be multilateral and be amongst 'the recognized leaders of the great Powers'. By this definition neither the talks which took place between Nikita Khrushchev and President Eisenhower at Camp David in September 1959, nor those between Khrushchev and Kennedy at Vienna in June 1961, qualified as summits. It was equally wrong, Watt maintained, to refer to the gathering of NATO heads of government which had taken place in December 1957 as a 'Western summit'.[31] Summits were not for scaling by the leaders of lesser powers. This, however, was a tardy exercise in semantic containment. Politicians, the public and the press had already found in 'summits' and 'summitry' convenient metaphors to apply (or misapply) to almost any conclave of heads of government. As a result all subsequent conferences between American presidents and Soviet leaders, whether they were of an improvised kind, such as that between Lyndon Johnson and Alexei Kosygin at Glasboro in June 1967, or of the carefully staged variety, such as that between Nixon and Leonid Brezhnev at Moscow in May 1972, were labelled summits. And amongst the other powers all that now seems to distinguish summits from other meetings of heads of government is the degree to which they are either deliberately contrived for maximum public effect, or institutionalized on the basis of treaties or accords. Thus the regular meetings between French presidents and West German chancellors, the three-yearly gatherings of leaders of the non-aligned powers, and the annual economic conferences of Western leaders, have been dubbed summits by their participants and the media. Yet many purely ceremonial and less formalized encounters have so far escaped the epithet.

Of one thing there can be little doubt, and that is that since the Second World War presidential and prime ministerial diplomacy has been on the increase. Summits of the kind envisaged by Churchill have in fact been rare. Ten years passed between the Potsdam and Geneva conferences, and, apart from the abortive Paris summit, American and Soviet leaders met only twice during the whole of the 1960s. In the following decade the quest for *détente* and agreement on the limitation of strategic weapons gave superpower summitry a boost, and there were six such meetings, if the talks between Brezhnev and President Ford at the Helsinki conference (July/August 1975) are included in this figure. But within alliances and regional groupings, it has become commonplace for the election of a new president or appointment of a new prime minister to be followed by a round of visits and of talks. This is now part of a process by which the leaders of friendly, and sometimes not so friendly, states come to know each other, and it has a certain similarity with the way in which the sovereigns of nineteenth-century Europe reinforced family and political ties with visits to each other's courts. Indeed, Abba Eban, the former Israeli foreign minister, has referred to this upstaging of ambassadors by foreign ministers and heads of government as the constant 'monarchization' of government.[32] Yet summitry also responds to the requirements of democratic politics. It provides political leaders with instant media coverage, and allows journalists to wallow in dramatic verbiage. Superpower summits are very often public relations exercises. Not only are they accompanied by seemingly inevitable press conferences and interviews, but the terms of the final communiqués may be drafted beforehand and set the framework for discussions.

Summits are not, however, without their advantages. Henry Kissinger, by no means an uncritical participant in presidential diplomacy, pointed out that they allowed heads of government 'to gain an insight into the perception and thinking of their counterparts'.[33] This, he suggested, could assist them in their future decision-making, especially during periods of crisis. It has also been argued that summits have an educative function in so far as they compel political leaders to turn their attention from the domestic to the international implications of their policies. Summitry has in any case a symbolic value. It has been used both to signal policy changes and to set deadlines for the conclusion of protracted negotiations. The visits by the West German chancellor, Willy Brandt, to Moscow and Warsaw in 1970 were a public demonstration of the meaning of the new *Ostpolitik.* Likewise, the announcement of a superpower summit in the autumn of 1987 was a spur to those then engaged in negotiating an agreement on intermediate nuclear forces (INF). Nevertheless, few professional diplomats have ever shown much enthusiasm for summits. A resident ambassador may be able to profit from a visit by his president or prime minister in order to extend his personal contacts and enhance his own position. But his illustrious guests and their advisers may also confine him to the social periphery of the proceedings, and then leave him with the arduous task of repairing damage done by less experienced negotiators. Many an ambassador must have had cause to recall Philippe de Commynes's advice that two 'great princes who wish to establish good personal relations should never meet each other face to face, but ought to communicate through good and wise ambassadors'.[34]

One obvious weakness inherent in most forms of summitry is that while such meetings raise public expectations of success, they are usually too brief to allow sufficient time for true negotiation. It is in any event unlikely that a busy head of government will be able to master all the details of a particular issue, and, even if he can, he may be temperamentally or linguistically ill-equipped to engage in international dialogue. Moreover, one of the main attractions of summitry from a statesman's personal point of view is likely to be the political kudos which he may gain from posing as a world leader. Yet this may in itself make it all the more difficult for him to offer the kind of concessions which an international accommodation requires. On the other hand his desire for a personal triumph may lead him to concede far more than is really necessary. Public diplomacy at the summit thus leaves little scope for the kind of bargaining which is the essence of negotiation. Indeed, most superpower summits have only come at the end of months, and in some instances years, of diplomatic preparation. The meeting in Washington of Ronald Reagan and Mikhail Gorbachev in December 1987 and their signing of the INF agreement thus brought to a conclusion six years of discussions between Soviet and United States negotiating teams at Geneva. The preceding summit at Reykjavik in October 1986 seems, however, to have been an exception to the general rule. It was no mere formality, and American and Soviet negotiators appear to have made significant progress there in working out the basis of an understanding.

Summitry amongst other powers has been patchy in its results. Shielded from the prying eyes of the press, President Carter and the Egyptian and Israeli leaders met at Camp David in September 1978. There, after thirteen days of negotiation, they succeeded in drafting a peace treaty whose achievement might have been impossible at any other level. But the meeting of the French president, François Mitterrand, and Colonel Qadhafi on Crete in November 1984 was a very different story. Qadhafi failed to carry out his promise to withdraw Libyan troops from Chad, and Mitterrand needlessly exposed himself and France to embarrassment and humiliation. By contrast, Mitterrand's predecessor, Valéry Giscard d'Estaing, was the prime mover in a highly successful enterprise in institutionalized summitry. He, with the backing of the West German chancellor, Helmut Schmidt, took advantage of the presence of other Western leaders at Helsinki in July 1975 to propose the holding of an economic summit. Both he and Schmidt had previously been finance ministers. They had grown accustomed to working closely with each other in the early 1970s and the collapse of the Bretton Woods system and the oil crisis seem to have convinced them of the need for a more collective management of the world economy. As a result of their initiative the leaders of other Western governments and Japan were persuaded to participate in a conference at Rambouillet in November 1975. This was followed by further annual Western economic summits, which, despite their name, soon began to consider matters of mutual political concern.

Giscard had originally hoped that these summits would be informal and private gatherings. All preparatory work was to be done by personal representatives of the heads of government, who were soon to be aptly designated 'sherpas'. But even at Rambouillet it proved impossible to exclude other ministers and officials, and although press reporters were forced to stay 35 miles away in Paris, the conference was as much a media event as any other summit. Subsequent economic summits received even more publicity and became ever more political. Nevertheless, these meetings of the leaders of the most industrially advanced nations (often referred to as the Group of Seven or G-7) demonstrated one of the great virtues of this mode of diplomacy. By bringing together heads of state and government to discuss topics as diverse as agricultural prices, arms limitation and reduction, energy conservation, export credits, monetary stability, political co-operation and the transfer of technology, it has served an integrative function. Summitry encourages and permits a co-ordination of policy and a linkage in international bargaining which may otherwise be difficult to achieve in an age of specialist diplomacy and bureaucratic rivalry. The same might also be said of the European Council where a supposed overall grasp of national, as opposed to departmental, policies may better enable heads of government to adopt a common stance. To leave the EC's agricultural spending to farm ministers would, so theory has it, be to abdicate control to the representatives of entrenched sectional interests. Yet through their enthusiasm for summitry Europe's prime ministers and presidents have also condemned themselves to hours of boredom and haggling in order to arrive at understandings whose true meaning few of them but dimly perceive.

As summits have become more common so too have they lost some of their dramatic impact. The failure of presidents and prime ministers to agree is far less likely to have the deleterious effect on international relations today that it might have had just thirty years ago. A meeting of European heads of government is, after all, almost an everyday event. Likewise, the itinerant minister-diplomat is now the norm. The foreign ministers of the victorious wartime allies (Britain, the Soviet Union, the United States and formally China and France) continued to meet in council until the autumn of 1947, and foreign ministerial meetings became a vital element in the evolution of the NATO alliance and the other institutions of European co-operation. Ernest Bevin, the British foreign secretary from 1945 to 1951, emerged as a key figure in building the Western Alliance, taking with him to Paris in 1947 a bevy of Treasury officials to mobilize Europe's response to the offer of Marshall Aid. Eden, who returned to the Foreign Office in October 1951, also displayed a nomadic instinct. He spent only eight days in London during his first five weeks in office, and if he achieved little in the four-power conference at Berlin in 1954, his performance in the Indo-China conference at Geneva in 1955 is usually rated a success. A similar pattern was discernible elsewhere. During the first ten years of the cold war French foreign ministers engaged in more or less routine discussions with their British and American counterparts. And Maurice Couve de Murville, whose tenure of the Quai d'Orsay lasted from 1958 to 1968, accompanied de Gaulle on his several foreign visits and still found time to spend two days a week at the EEC headquarters at Brussels.

There was, of course, a long tradition of active involvement by European foreign ministers in both exploratory and treaty-making negotiations abroad. This was not, however, true of the United States, where Cordell Hull's work had taken him overseas on hardly more than half a dozen occasions. Yet Eisenhower's secretary of state, John Foster Dulles, participated in some 50 international conferences and travelled more than 56,000 miles during his six years in office. A quarter of a century later at the time of the Falklands War Alexander Haig engaged in a round of crisis talks which took him 34,000 miles in just five days. Clearly, the new role of the American secretary of state reflected the United States' rise to superpower status. But the personality of the secretary, his position within the administration, and developments abroad, have also helped determine the extent and frequency of his travels. Kissinger had, for instance, already exercised a considerable influence on the making and conduct of American foreign policy before he replaced William Rogers in August 1973. He had negotiated personally with the Chinese in Beijing, the Russians in Moscow and the North Vietnamese in Paris. Nevertheless, his mediation in the wake of the Yom Kippur War constituted a dazzling display of how modern technology could be harnessed to a diplomacy which was at once spectacular, secret and ministerial. Between November 1973 and January 1974 he utilized a Boeing 707, which had been converted into a veritable airborne communications centre, to shuttle back and forth between Arab capitals and Jerusalem in pursuit of agreements on military disengagement.

Kissinger's achievements both in reshaping American foreign policy and in promoting peace in the Middle East were considerable. 'Shuttle diplomacy' has not, however, been without its detractors. After all, as one ex-diplomat has observed, if a mediator were needed between Israel and its neighbours then surely it might have been more appropriate to seek the assistance of the UN. And why should a United States secretary of state involve himself personally in negotiating a settlement when he has at hand a corps of experienced and professional diplomats? Henry M. Wriston argued in the mid-1950s that the diffusion of powers and responsibilities in foreign policy-making in Washington made it all the more essential for a secretary of state 'to remain at home and maintain constant contact with the members of the Cabinet and with every agency by which he can keep in touch with the views of others'.[35] There is no reason to suppose that such advice is any less valid today. Moreover, ministerial diplomacy, whether it be in the form of shuttles or summits, has tended to depreciate the currency of international dialogue. It has encouraged the belief that successful negotiation depends ultimately on ministerial intervention. Not only does public opinion seem to require political leaders to act as quasi-diplomats, but governments themselves are inclined to assume that no bargain is worthy of completion until after a meeting of the appropriate ministers or secretaries of state. The ambassadorial function is not thereby negated, but it is undoubtedly reduced.

In 1977 George Ball turned down an offer from President Carter of an embassy. Ball, who in 1961 had succeeded Chester Bowles as an under-secretary at the State Department, felt that 'jet planes and the bad habits of presidents, national security assistants and secretaries of state had now largely restricted ambassadors to ritual and public relations'. He had no wish to end his days 'an innkeeper for itinerant congressmen'.[36] There was nothing particularly original or peculiarly American about Ball's opinion of an ambassador's role. Sixty years before, when aeroplanes were no more than vehicles for reconnaissance and war, British ambassadors at Paris and Washington had complained of the way in which they were being bypassed and ignored. Theirs was admittedly the plight of diplomats disorientated by the exigencies of total war. But their grievances were no less relevant, for war encouraged a ministerial diplomacy which modern communications made possible. It also expanded the scope and content of inter-governmental negotiations, occasioned the emergence of a new breed of specialist diplomats, and shattered the old European political and social order. In a global state system which has become more complex in consequence of the collapse of empire, and more interdependent as a result of scientific and technological advances, international organizations and multilateral diplomacy have flourished. And the transition from cold war to *détente* has been accompanied by summit and personal diplomacy, and a seemingly interminable process of bargaining amongst experts in arms control and disarmament. Diplomacy, like the system which it serves, has been transformed. The extent to which its professional practitioners have been transcended remains for further consideration.

PART III

CONCLUSION

7

DIPLOMACY TRANSFORMED AND TRANSCENDED

Now listen, Mother dear, the Foreign Service has had its day – enjoyable while it lasted no doubt, but over now. The privileged being of the future is the travel agent.
> (Basil in Nancy Mitford's *Don't tell Alfred* (1960)).[1]

The idea that travel agents might one day supplant diplomats has not been confined to works of fiction. Louis Einstein, a retired American career diplomat, speculated in his memoirs 'that an international tourist agency like Thomas Cook could, with great convenience to the general public and considerable economy in personnel, rent and time, carry out most of the routine work of diplomacy jointly for many nations'.[2] More recently the authors of a BBC investigation into the FCO have suggested that much of the work done by embassies in supplying assistance and information to businessmen and politicians could be subcontracted to neutral states such as Sweden and Switzerland. The latter have already made a 'minor industry' out of providing consular services in countries with which for political reasons the major powers have no dealings, and might be persuaded to tender for extra duties.[3] Such recommendations, like those made by previous advocates of reform, are based upon the presupposition that embassies are expensive appendages of the states system, whose functions, though far from superfluous to modern needs, could in many instances be performed more efficiently by other agencies. After all, presidents, government ministers, their assistants and advisers meet and negotiate with their foreign counterparts within a matter of hours; they and their senior functionaries confer and converse by telephone; in many missions satellite communications have superseded wireless and cable telegraphy; automatic computerized means of transmission have replaced the laborious cryptographic methods of the past; and information is stored, and dispatches drafted, on computers. The FCO is in constant teleprinter contact with other EU foreign ministries, and a simultaneous televisual link-up amongst officials in London, Paris and Bonn is technically feasible. Nearly two decades on, the assertion made by Zbigniew Brzezinski in 1970, that if foreign ministries and embassies 'did not already exist, they surely would not have to be invented',[4] appears more than ever appropriate.

GENERALISTS, SPECIALISTS AND MANAGERS

The question of whether or not ambassadors should be regarded as anachronistic relics, the eccentric survivors of the advent of electricity and steam, depends upon the activities ascribed to them. They have traditionally been perceived as intermediaries. 'The distinctive function of a diplomatist', observed Lord Lyons in December 1860, 'is to carry on political business by personal intercourse with foreign statesmen'. And, he added, since the principal reason for maintaining representatives abroad was the impossibility of conducting communications between nations satisfactorily by writing alone, the faculty of influencing others by conversation was the 'qualification peculiarly necessary to a diplomatist'.[5] In other words, the value of a diplomat lay not in any specialist knowledge he might possess, but in his ability to communicate, negotiate and persuade. Many of the issues which are nowadays subject to international discussion and bargaining demand, however, a degree of expertise which only departmental and subject specialists can provide.

The continued expansion of the diplomatic agenda has been accompanied by a diffusion in the processes of policy-making and implementation. Yet it is far from obvious that officials from domestic ministries, whether on secondment to embassies and other missions or dealing directly with their equivalents abroad, have proved any less adroit as negotiators than their foreign service colleagues. They may not have the professional diplomat's experience of a wide variety of postings, his mastery of foreign languages, or his intuitive grasp of circumstances – his *Fingerspitzengefühl*. But these they have matched with a thorough understanding of the complexities inherent in the handling of such matters as agricultural subsidies, arms control, and Third World debt. By dint of their very expertise they have become essential participants in such quasi-institutionalized negotiations as are characterized by the initials SALT, START, STOP, MBFR and CSCE. This *Buchstabendiplomatie* (acronym diplomacy) of *détente* was, perhaps because it focused upon the achievement of an armistice in the cold war, very often diplomacy amongst strategic experts.

The sheer size and heterogeneous composition of many modern embassies have meanwhile reinforced the ambassador's supervisory position. Embassies are no longer the tight families of career diplomats that they once were, and ambassadors have, in the words of one of their number, become 'more referees than managers'.[6] They have to achieve and maintain a *modus vivendi* amongst the representatives of competing agencies and departments, and to introduce a sense of common purpose into the several negotiations upon which they may have embarked. By contrast, the foreign ministries of the major powers have very often failed to retain even this co-ordinating function. Just as in Washington, where the White House and the NSC may provide such cohesion as there is in United States foreign policy, so in Paris the Quai d'Orsay has been *dépossédé*[7] and the Elysée Palace and the Hôtel Matignon (the presidential and prime ministerial residences) have emerged as the chief agencies of synthesis in the administration of France's external relations. Likewise in London it is in the Cabinet Office rather than the FCO that negotiating positions are very often decided. In 1982 the then British prime minister acquired her own foreign policy adviser, albeit a career diplomat, and subsequent criticism of the FCO was accompanied by press speculation about the possible attachment to 10 Downing Street of a separate foreign policy unit. The bureaucratic tendency to regard diplomacy as what Waldo Heinrichs has termed a 'composite of special skills and knowledges rather than as a substantive endeavor in itself',[8] has thus encouraged both the erosion of established distinctions between home and foreign services, and the inclination of political executives to involve themselves personally in the application and execution of policy.

Nevertheless, despite retrenchment, reform and the relative decline in the role of the professional generalist, the conventional mechanisms of diplomacy have survived. Ironically, the very expansion of the states system has tended to inhibit radical change. The UN and other international organizations have provided some poorer countries with an affordable, though primitive, means of maintaining diplomatic contact with the rest of the world. But many new states have come to regard the exchange of ambassadors or high commissioners as a symbol of their sovereignty. Older ones have been reluctant to close missions lest they thereby forego advantages which others may retain. Even those revolutionary régimes which have been the most fervent in their rejection of Western values and institutions, and which have shown scant respect for diplomatic immunities and privileges, have seemed anxious to maintain their embassies. The recall of ambassadors, the closure of missions and the demotion of relations to a consular level have rarely been considered as anything more than temporary measures. They have been gestures of disapproval, or the outcome of crises whose resolution has usually been followed by a resumption of full diplomatic relations. Moreover, even after formal communications have been broken off between states it has not been uncommon for them to keep diplomats in each other's capitals in the guise of 'interests sections' in third-party embassies.

In truth there are few satisfactory alternatives to the resident envoy. Summits, ministerial delegations and special missions are a useful means of reinforcing existing relationships, registering agreement on specific issues, and settling particular disputes; delegate conferences and other organs of international co-operation are essential for tackling subjects of technical and multilateral interest; and fax, telephone and telex permit immediate consultation amongst political leaders. These are, however, no substitute for that continuity of communication, negotiation and representation which is the great virtue of the permanent mission. 'Embassies', according to one former diplomat, 'keep the lines open in the intervals between international conferences.'[9]

An experienced diplomat in regular contact with foreign statesmen and officials is, if properly instructed and fully appraised of the political situation at home, probably better placed than anyone not just to transmit his government's messages accurately, but to do so in a manner calculated to achieve their intended effect. This, however, may ultimately depend on his ability to influence groups within and outside the governing élite of the host country. The good relations which the Iranians enjoyed with the United States during the 1970s were at least in part due to the assiduous efforts of Ardeshir Zahedir, their ambassador in Washington, to maintain a high profile in society. By his spectacular party-giving, his association with worthwhile charitable causes, and the part he played as a successful mediator in a Black Muslims terrorist action, he helped bolster Iran's image. But ambassadors, their press officers and other embassy staff have of late become ever more frequently involved in explaining their country's domestic and foreign policies to wider public audiences. The emergence of professional diplomats as media personalities has indeed been a comparatively recent development. Nineteenth- and early twentieth-century diplomats were, though sometimes wary of too close an association with propaganda work, accustomed to using the press in order to put pressure on foreign governments or to enhance their country's reputation. Nevertheless, during his thirteen years as British ambassador at Paris between 1905 and 1918 Bertie made only one public speech, and was reluctant to give any publicity to his opinions. Nowadays it is almost commonplace for envoys to appear on radio and television, and foreign ministries have their own studios in which diplomats are instructed in media techniques. Instant news requires instant comment, if possible at the highest level, and to decline it in democratic countries is to risk leaving the field open to one's critics and opponents. As a former British ambassador has noted, the media have now to 'be conciliated, not bought'.[10]

The press also represents an alternative to diplomacy. Governments have thus sought by parliamentary and public statement to warn and cajole other powers, and to appeal to the moral sentiments and revolutionary ardour of their subjects. James Monroe proclaimed his 'doctrine' in the United States Congress, as did Woodrow Wilson his Fourteen Points, and Adolf Hitler mastered a megaphone diplomacy by which he rallied the party faithful and waged psychological warfare against Germany's neighbours. But it was during the 1950s that John Foster Dulles transformed the press conference

234

into a medium of international communication. Modern summit conferences would be incomplete without their accompanying press battalions, and more significance seems sometimes to be attached to what their participants declare in public than to what they decide in private. For a United States ambassador a free press can, however, be a serious embarrassment. He may have to mollify a local ruler angered by criticism in an American newspaper, or he may find his negotiating position undercut when during the give and take of a departmental press briefing or a presidential press conference his official instructions are in effect modified, or even flatly contradicted. The problem, aptly summarized in Charles Thayer's aphorism, is that since 'publicity is often a deterrent to the reconciliation of conflicts, the diplomat attempts to conceal what the journalist strives to reveal'.[11] Moreover, for the ambassador and his staff there is also the prospect of their political masters disregarding their advice and information and taking decisions upon the basis of media reporting and analysis. French embassies are said to await the publication of Le Monde before drafting their telegrams so that they at least know what ministers have already read.

Media competition has led to a greater emphasis being placed upon prediction rather than reporting in American embassies. None the less, it has done little to stem the flow of correspondence between the State Department and overseas missions. The department's telegraphic traffic quintupled in the thirty-five years between 1947 and 1982, and like other foreign ministries it has become a vast storehouse of information on global affairs. Much of this will probably be of more value to future historians than to contemporary policy-makers. Only when embassies are involved in important negotiations, or when international developments thrust their host countries into the limelight of world affairs, are they in a position to exercise any consistent influence on policy. But in time of crisis, or when the unexpected occurs, intelligence gathered by diplomats and sifted, annotated and collated by their colleagues at home is there to brief presidents, ministers and cabinets. Moreover, in an effort to avoid superficiality in responding to events, foreign ministries have established sections and units devoted to identifying long-term international trends and defining policy options. The State Department has had a planning staff since 1947, and now the FCO has its policy planning staff and the Quai d'Orsay its more ambitiously named Centre d'Analyses et de Prévision. They and the diplomatic planners of other EC and NATO countries meet regularly to examine and share their analyses of future developments.

Sensible policy planning must to a large extent depend upon quality of information provided by embassies and the sources available to diplomats. In closed societies such as Stalinist Russia, where relations with the local population may be confined to purely formal contact with ministers and officials, all that a diplomat can hope to do is to gauge the political atmosphere and perhaps get to know some of the prominent personalities. He may even be able to predict what is unlikely to happen. Elsewhere the opportunity to socialize with the political and social establishment permits diplomats, whether generalists or seconded specialists, to make acquaintances and form friendships with politicians, officials and journalists, all of whom may at some time or other supply useful snippets of information. A good deal of diplomatic entertaining is, however, of an essentially representational kind, such as the celebration of national holidays and the birthdays of reigning monarchs, and such gatherings may only allow for superficial chatter. J.K. Galbraith, whom John F. Kennedy appointed United States ambassador to India, was in this and other respects scathing in his indictment of his fellow ambassadors and high commissioners at Delhi. They were, he claimed, a 'spectacular example of . . . disguised unemployment', and he went on to recall that he 'never learned anything at a cocktail party or dinner that [he] didn't already know, needed to know, or wouldn't have learned in the normal course of business'.[12]

Galbraith's somewhat jaundiced view of the diplomatic life was that of a political nominee. He was an outsider, whose professional staff doubtless assisted him in achieving the two-hour official working day of which he boasted. Nevertheless, it is in the nature of diplomacy that its practitioners tend to live and work within fairly narrow social confines. If a diplomat is to succeed as an intermediary, he needs to maintain the confidence of the government to which he is accredited, and that in some countries could be forfeited by attempts on his part to establish relations with individuals opposed to the existing régime, or disaffected groups within society. The honourable spy can all too easily become the distrusted subversive. This was the problem which faced Sir Anthony Parsons, the British ambassador at Tehran during the late 1970s. In a land which was soon to be overwhelmed by revolutionary Islam, he had to observe the political scene 'without arousing any suspicion of improper involvement in Iran's internal affairs or of making clandestine contacts, which, if discovered, would severely damage [Britain's] relationship with the Shah'.[13] Such discussions as his embassy had with the local police and intelligence forces were thus concerned with the threat to Iran from external subversion and the security of British and Iranian interests in the neighbouring states. His American colleague, William Sullivan, was possibly more adventurous in his attempts to gain some impression of popular feelings in the bazaars – the acknowledged barometer of Iranian political sensibilities. But in the end he had to admit that the bazaaris were not interested in meeting Americans or being seen with them, and that he too was 'unable to judge the true political ferment that permeated the bazaars by 1978'.[14] Except in so far as they can provide cover for locally based intelligence officers, embassies are, as a result of their association with the established order, not always the best instruments for observing and measuring political and social discontent.

One criticism levelled against the Western embassies in Tehran after the overthrow of the Shah was that their political reporting had suffered as a result of too great a concentration upon commercial work. In his own account of his mission Parsons argued that the British failure to anticipate the revolution was due not to any lack of information, but to a misinterpretation of events. Nevertheless, he admitted that he had reorganized his embassy to give priority to the seeking out of commercial and investment opportunities for British firms. Even his service attachés were absorbed less in the collation of military information than in the pursuit of arms contracts. All this was quite in line with what three separate review bodies had recommended in the 1960s and 1970s. As early as 1964 the Plowden report had insisted that Britain's representatives overseas must be increasingly dedicated to export promotion. Indeed, at a time when the British foreign service was under attack, its potential for economic analysis, commercial negotiation and the furtherance of trade was used to justify its extensive network of diplomatic posts. There was nothing particularly new about this. Trade and diplomacy had long been closely related, and early advocates of a career foreign service in the United States had stressed the value of diplomacy for business. Yet there have been doubts about both the quality of commercial reporting by diplomats, and the extent to which embassies of countries with free market economies should be actively involved in aiding individual firms. After all, other institutions more closely aligned to industry and with more clearly defined commercial mandates might be better suited to the task. Germany's industrial associations have, for example, their own foreign commercial service. Sweden has a trade commissioner service staffed by businessmen, Norway an export council with its own representatives abroad, and Canada a trade service which has opened and shut offices according to their cost-effectiveness.

The commercial sections of modern embassies vary in their size and functions. The role of their attachés and counsellors may be limited simply to providing information on economic developments and markets, and to assisting in the organization and sponsorship of trade exhibitions. On the other hand, in communist states, and in other countries with centrally organized or corporatist economies, they were almost bound to be involved in the arrangement of any bilateral contracts with local purchasing organizations. Elsewhere concessions and orders for goods may be linked to aid packages, loans and government guarantees, in whose negotiation commercial diplomats are likely to have a hand. Their services may also be of vital importance when company representatives are confronted with the prospect of bargaining with individuals of whose language, culture and commercial practices they have little or no comprehension. But visiting businessmen may likewise have recourse to an embassy's consular section. The amalgamation of consular and diplomatic services has in many cases meant the inclusion of consular officials on embassy staffs. In the United

States foreign service the consul-general in a capital city may thus have the diplomatic title of counsellor, or in the case of a consul, that of first secretary. Consular duties have meanwhile continued to centre upon providing aid and protection to fellow nationals and local expatriate communities. And although consuls are probably less likely than they once were to be concerned with the fate of shipwrecked mariners, the growth of tourism in the last thirty years has left them with the responsibility for easing the trials and tribulations of their destitute, drunken and imprisoned compatriots. There are indeed times when foreign service officers seem destined to replace travel agents.

Less needy, though hardly less troublesome (and on occasions no less inebriated) callers upon embassy assistance are the visiting presidents, ministers and other politicians for whose ventures in diplomacy resident ambassadors and their staffs may be expected to provide accommodation, entertainment and enlightenment. The analogy between ambassadors and innkeepers is commonplace. But their function as hosts is none the less important. Statesmen and official delegations usually require briefing as well as bed and board. The embassy can assist in arranging meetings, in explaining the current political and economic circumstances, and in advising guests on with whom and how best to tackle particular problems. In many instances the mission will already have been actively involved in preparing the groundwork for any discussions or negotiations which are due to take place between ministers. Moreover, in the aftermath of a presidential or ministerial visit the embassy may be left with the task of settling, or tidying up, the details of any agreement reached. It may also have to explore the prospect for future talks, and in the event of the visit having led to confusion, contretemps or misunderstanding between the parties, the ambassador may have to apply himself to restoring cordial relations. In these respects the comparison drawn by a recently appointed United States ambassador to London between his job and that of the air hostess is peculiarly pertinent. His purpose is to inform and reassure itinerant statesmen, and to clear up the mess after their departure. He is on the spot and presumably in the know, and may in time of unexpected crisis have to take decisions without reference to a higher authority.

ORDER, DISORDER AND DIPLOMACY

Diplomacy has historically been both a function and a determinant of the international order. Without independent and proximate political entities with a will to communicate amongst themselves it would be unnecessary. Without diplomatic intermediaries of some kind or other a states system would be almost unintelligible. The resident envoy, the most enduring feature of modern diplomacy, was the product of the collapse of Christendom with its hierarchical structures and common ethical code, and the emergence first in Italy and then elsewhere in Europe of polities whose rulers were beholden to no superior political institution. Meanwhile diplomacy helped fashion a pattern of international behaviour and law which formed the basis of the new system of sovereign states. The extension of that system through the growth of European influence overseas, the eventual erosion of Europe's pre-eminence, the rise of the superpowers, the birth of new states, and the challenge of universalist creeds and ideologies, each in their own way influenced the methods, style and content of diplomacy. The emancipation within barely thirty years of almost all of the colonial and dependent territories of Britain, France, the Netherlands and Portugal thus vastly inflated the world's *corps diplomatiques*, strained traditional diplomatic values, and transformed institutionalized multilateral diplomacy – or diplomacy by committee as it has been most appropriately termed – from a convenience into a necessity. But the means by which governments deal and negotiate with each other have also been shaped by, and in response to, three other factors: the threat, prevalence and changing nature of war; the evolution of the state, its governance and economic and social composition; and advances in science and technology, especially as they relate to transport and communications.

In addition to being an alternative and an antidote to war, diplomacy has been its godchild, servant and begetter. Permanent missions, like permanent armies, were the means by which the rival princes and republics of Renaissance Italy sought to achieve their ends. Negotiation, though it might carry with it the menace of war, was cheaper than armed conflict, and less uncertain than arbitration. But at a time when previous constraints on war were being rapidly eroded and when states could more swiftly mobilize their armies, resident envoys were appointed to report on the military strength of potential foes, and to seek political combinations with potential friends. They were also to become involved in conspiracy and subversion, and so suspect were their activities that during the Reformation and the wars of religion there was an almost complete breakdown in diplomatic relations between the Protestant and Catholic lands of Europe. Medieval notions of diplomatic immunity and privilege were eventually replaced by practices and theories of extraterritoriality which were both secular and pragmatic, and which provided a stabler basis for the exchange of envoys in a world divided in its beliefs. Diplomatic congresses were also utilized to make peace in the aftermath of wars, and within 200 years they had come to be regarded as a means of settling differences, minimizing the dangers of general conflict, and regulating the affairs of Europe.

The image of diplomats as licensed spies still, however, persisted, and seemed even to be confirmed when in the nineteenth century the first service attachés were appointed. The latter were, like the earliest resident envoys, a diplomatic response to the increased sophistication of war. Diplomats were in the meanwhile as busily engaged as ever in constructing military alliances and pacts. Indeed it was the failure of the concert of Europe to preserve peace, the division of the great powers into rival alliance blocs, and fears generated by arms races and international crises, which in the years before the outbreak of the First World War did much to encourage the search for new and more open forms of diplomacy. That search led ultimately to demands for the creation of an international organization to assist in the better management of world affairs and, after four years of war to the foundation of the League of Nations.

War has also had a catalytic effect upon the evolution of diplomacy, hastening rather than initiating change. It was, after all, Charles VIII's invasion of Italy and the subsequent preoccupation of the other European monarchies with the affairs of the peninsula that encouraged the extension of the Italian system of resident envoys beyond the Alps. The Napoleonic Wars likewise nurtured the development of a form of personal diplomacy amongst the sovereigns and ministers of the various coalition partners which, in the form of the short-lived congress system, persisted into the early post-war years. Much the same was true of the two world wars, both of which witnessed a heightened propensity on the part of allied leaders to engage in a ministerial and presidential diplomacy which after 1945 merged into the pursuit of cold war summitry. The all-embracing character of modern warfare has also engendered a rapid expansion in the subject matter of international relations. It required collaboration amongst allies in spheres which lay outside the traditional purview of embassies and legations, and fostered the growth of inter-allied administrations which in the aftermath of war gave way to new international agencies and commissions for reconstruction, reparation and development. Moreover, the onset of the cold war led to the creation of opposing alliances with their own councils, secretariats and permanent delegations. In these and other respects the exigencies of twentieth-century warfare contributed to a decline in the significance of established diplomatic missions, to the greater and more direct involvement of departments of state other than foreign and service ministries in international affairs, and to the rise of the diplomatic specialist. At the same time the origins and purposes of war had to be explained to civilian populations that were called upon to make ever greater sacrifices, and to neutral states that might possibly become allies. Diplomats were increasingly associated with propaganda work, and diplomacy itself became more open to public scrutiny and debate.

Open diplomacy, which in practice has often amounted to little more than the rhetorical display of moral indignation, has, despite its skilful exploitation by some distinctly undemocratic régimes, usually been linked to the advent of modern democracy. It was an element of that 'new diplomacy' which Harold Nicolson attributed to 'the belief that it was possible to apply to the conduct of external affairs, the ideas and practices which in the conduct of internal affairs, had for generations been regarded as the essentials of liberal democracy'.[15] In truth, the history of diplomacy cannot be divorced from that of the state, its institutions, responsibilities and political and social dogmas. The Greek city-states, whose political life revolved around the *agora*, relied on the oratory of their representatives when dealing with each other; the rulers of Byzantium sought to ensure respect for their imperial pretensions through ceremony, protocol and the formal management and training of their diplomats; and Venice, with its early preoccupation with trade, in effect transformed its mercantile agents into resident envoys. But it was the rise and consolidation of the great dynastic monarchies of Europe, with their increasingly centralized administrations based upon royal courts, chancelleries and cabinets, which led to the appointment of secretaries, clerks and eventually separate departments with specific responsibility for external relations. Nowhere was this more apparent than in seventeenth-century France, where diplomacy, like the armed forces, was organized to meet the needs of an expansive and potentially hegemonic power. Diplomacy also acquired its aristocratic ethos at a time when government was largely in the hands of the crown and the nobility, and when an envoy's title or ancient pedigree was an invaluable social, and therefore political, asset. This last assumption, the fact that ambassadors were regarded as the personal representatives of their sovereigns, and the special linguistic skills required of diplomats, tended to set them apart from other officials and functionaries of state. Nevertheless, the emergence of career civil services and the adoption by governments of bureaucratic methods and practices were paralleled by the gradual professionalization of diplomacy.

The same process was also observable in the United States. But there it was delayed and limited by a distrust of what was widely regarded as the deviousness of European diplomacy, a suspicion of the vested interest of permanent officials, and a reluctance on the part of incoming administrations to forgo the political advantages of the spoils system. There too a democratic tradition, which had developed in relative isolation from the European states system, encouraged faith in the good sense of public opinion and a belief in the virtues of moral exhortation as an instrument of foreign policy. It had its counterpart in the efforts of the early Bolsheviks to win sympathy and support abroad through public appeals to governments and peoples. Their initial concern was, however, less with advancing state interest than with the safeguarding and promoting of revolution. The later triumph in Italy and Germany of social-Darwinian ideologies further demonstrated how the purposes of open diplomacy could easily be distorted through its fusion with propaganda, subversion and terror tactics. Internal rivalries within Nazi Germany in the meanwhile bred a para-diplomacy which exemplified, albeit in an exaggerated and anarchic form, how in a modern state a plurality of individuals, agencies and groups may become engaged in the conduct of foreign relations.

By the 1930s foreign ministries and embassies had acquired, or were competing with, cultural, press and information services. Yet of greater significance in the long run has been the expanding role of government in the management of economic and social matters and the manner in which these have impinged on foreign relations. An enhanced awareness of the interdependence of domestic and external affairs has contributed both to the fragmentation of diplomatic competences and to the growth of functional as well as regional forums for international co-operation and dialogue.

'The classical world of bilateral and multilateral diplomacy' has, in the words of a senior State Department official, been 'progressively supplemented by transnational issues which may or may not involve government-to-government activity'.[16] Many such matters are dealt with officially, but at a subnational or non-central governmental level. In those countries with federal institutions, constituent states and provinces have grown accustomed to dispatching representatives abroad to promote and protect their interests, and elsewhere cities, municipalities and other agencies of local government have acted in a similar fashion. They have established transnational links and worked with and against each other in a variety of cultural, economic and environmental ventures. As with so much else in diplomacy little of this is truly new. Australian states and Canadian provinces have long maintained agencies-general and other offices in London, and in the first decade of the twentieth century lords provost and mayors of English and Scottish cities exchanged visits with their opposite numbers in France in order to take advantage of the latest entente cordiale. But during the past twenty years sub-state diplomacy has flourished and its growth has been encouraged by the globalization of what might once have been perceived as purely local issues. The desire to attract investment and tourism and the need to regulate migration have persuaded all but seven of the United States to establish offices abroad, and both Ottawa and Quebec have found it advantageous to maintain representatives in European and other North American cities. A shared sense of regional identity and interest has in other instances led to the formalization of cross-border relations in such bodies as the *Arbeitsgemeinschaft Alpen-Adria*, a working association of neighbouring provinces of Austria, Germany, Hungary, Italy and the former Yugoslavia.

Factions within governments and ruling parties and dissidents within states have also from time to time engaged, or attempted to engage, in unofficial diplomacy. Groups opposed to the existing status quo have sought international recognition and support, set up governments in exile, and claimed the right to speak and often fight on behalf of peoples whose lands may be under foreign occupation and rule. The 'non-state actor' is a new name for a not so very new phenomenon in international politics. James II, the exiled king of England, and his successors could be considered seventeenth-century non-state actors. The Czech and Polish national committees of the First World War, and the Free French of the Second, might likewise be regarded as the forerunners of contemporary national liberation movements, such as the South West African People's Organization (SWAPO) and the Palestine Liberation Organization (PLO). Established states and governments have, however, had to face the obvious problem of deciding when, whether and how to negotiate with non-state actors, the *ultima ratio* of whose diplomacy may well be the indiscriminate use of terrorism. Moreover, there is the question of what status should be granted to their leaders, representatives and other spokesmen. The UN has provided non-state actors with platform from which to address the world, and, as in other spheres of international life, it and its ancillary bodies have acted a sort of legitimizing agency. The PLO was thus granted observer status at the UN, its chairman, Yassir Arafat, addressed the General Assembly, and the 'Palestinian State', with the backing of other Arab countries, applied for membership of the World Health Organization. Much of this may be dismissed as make-believe diplomacy, for although the PLO may represent the aspirations of Palestinians under Israeli occupation it had until 1994 exercised no effective authority over any piece of territory. It is, however, diplomacy of a kind, and is evidence of the way in which not only the evolving, but also the would-be, state has helped shape diplomatic practice.

The disintegration of states from within has likewise posed peculiar problems for diplomacy especially when, as has so often happened, domestic conflict has been exacerbated by foreign intervention. The settlement of such issues has sometimes proved particularly difficult because the very act of agreeing to negotiate has meant conceding political legitimacy to rival parties. Thus in 1968 when an attempt was made in Paris to halt the war in Vietnam the Americans and their South Vietnamese allies were prepared to negotiate with a hostile North Vietnam, but reluctant to talk on equal terms with representatives of the Vietcong guerrillas who claimed to be waging a war of liberation in the South. The result was a distended dispute over seating arrangements and the position and shape of tables which seemed to resemble the squabbles over precedence and protocol that beset peacemakers of post-Renaissance Europe. More recently war amongst ethnic and religious factions in the Middle East has required a high-risk daredevil diplomacy on the part of neutral mediators. The efforts made by the Arab League in the spring of 1989 to bring an end to the civil war in the Lebanon between Christian and Muslim forces thus compelled the deputy chief of the League and a Kuwaiti diplomat to dodge shell and rocket fire in a dash by car across a divided Beirut. And Algerian and UN diplomats became intermediaries in a seemingly endless bargaining process between governments and guerrillas over hostages, their exchange and liberation.

The end of the cold war, the collapse of the Soviet Union, and strife and tension in the former communist countries of Europe and its borderlands, have meanwhile placed new demands on existing diplomatic structures. 'Preventive diplomacy', a term once used by Dag Hammarskjöld to describe UN peacekeeping operations and more recently applied by Boutros Boutros-Ghali to the prevention and containment of disputes, has become a prerequisite for the fashioning of a 'new world order'.[17] In practice, it has involved extending and redefining the competences of global and regional organizations.

During the autumn of 1990 the CSCE acquired its first professional bureaucracy in the form of a secretariat with its headquarters in Prague, a Conflict Prevention Centre in Vienna, and a Free Elections Office in Warsaw. A year later the disintegration of Yugoslavia and attendant friction amongst its constituent republics provided a powerful impetus to the setting up of CSCE mechanisms for mediation and intervention in the internal affairs of member states. Moreover, in June 1992, at the behest of the first summit meeting of members of the Security Council, the UN Secretary-General submitted an Agenda for Peace in which he explored how the organization could be made a more efficient instrument 'for preventive diplomacy, for peacemaking and for peace-keeping'.[18] His recommendations included new measures for confidence-building between potentially hostile parties and the improved diplomatic monitoring of international developments. Yet, as a former British ambassador to the UN has pointed out, these are only likely to succeed if they are buttressed by vigorous diplomatic action on the part of powerful states or groups of states.[19]

In the case of Yugoslavia, where diplomacy conspicuously failed to prevent fighting amongst republics and local and national militias, both the EU and the UN have assumed a prominent role in attempting to restore some kind of order. The result has been the institutionalization of a mediatory diplomacy, whose sponsors have been international agencies and whose focus has very often been the containment and resolution of conflict within, rather than between, sovereign states. International bodies have in some instances, complemented each other in promoting peace: the Geneva peace talks on the war in Bosnia, which were chaired jointly by EU and UN representatives, provide an obvious example. But agents of multilateral diplomacy have also seemed sometimes to compete and, in the absence of a clearly defined hierarchy of international institutions, belligerents have had the opportunity to regain in one forum what they have previously conceded in another. Established diplomatic procedures have, as in earlier periods of political upheaval and transition, been exploited for distinctly undiplomatic ends.

The ability of non-state actors and dissident or revolutionary factions to exercise an influence beyond their main zone of operations has been assisted by media coverage of their activities and actions. They have been the beneficiaries of that technological revolution which has facilitated the transformation, and in some instances the transcendance, of traditional methods of diplomacy. Meetings amongst sovereigns, chancellors and foreign ministers may have preceded the laying of railway tracks, and electric telegraphy was not solely responsible for the decline in ambassadorial authority and autonomy. Nevertheless, it seems reasonable to suppose that without the jet airliner, the telephone and television there would be less personal diplomacy on the part of political leaders and their minions. The world might have been denied the advantages of shuttle diplomacy, but it would have been spared the costs of much of the inconsequential summitry that has flourished under such rubrics as that of the G-7. There might also be fewer disgruntled professional diplomats, though those of Greece who, demoralized by neglect and poor pay, threatened to go on strike in the summer of 1988 seem likely to remain an exception. The diplomat is, after all, still a privileged being – too privileged, perhaps, when account is taken of those who abuse their immunities in order to shoot and loot for their country and themselves. Yet the diplomat remains at the same time a necessary being. The context, content and form of diplomacy have changed and in all probability will continue to change. But in the absence of world government or world revolution, it is difficult to conceive of any form of order without intermediaries between political entities, be they states, international organizations or even non-states. Richelieu's observation that 'to negotiate continuously, directly as well as in more devious ways, and in all places ... is absolutely necessary for the welfare of states',[20] remains as valid today as it was 300 years ago. A modern diplomat may, however, find it as advantageous to be as familiar with the ways of the servants of Mammon and mullahs as with the manner of negotiating with sovereign princes.

NOTES

1 THE OLD WORLD (pp. 7–28)

1 H. Nicolson, *The Evolution of Diplomatic Method* (Oxford, 1954), pp. 3–5
2 Quoted in F.S. Northedge, *The International Political System* (London, 1976), p. 40.
3 Y. Wang, 'The Development of the Nineteenth Century Chinese Diplomatic Service' (unpublished M. Phil., dissertation, Cambridge, 1990).
4 Before the outbreak of the Peloponnesian War, the Corinthians justified claims against Corcyra by reference to the common background. 'These, then, are considerations of right which we urge upon you – and they are adequate according to the institutions of the Hellenes' (Thucydides, 1. 41. 1).
5 D.J. Mosley, 'Diplomacy in Ancient Greece', *Phoenix*, 25 (1971), 4, 321 and 'Diplomacy in Classical Greece', *Ancient Society*, 3 (1972) for a more detailed treatment of the whole field.
6 Nicolson op. cit., pp. 3–5.
7 See H.D. Westlake, 'Diplomacy in Thucydides', *Bulletin of the John Rylands Library*, 53 (1970–1), 227–46.
8 See for example Demosthenes' sharp criticism of the system and its results contained in his attack on Aeschines' embassy to Macedon.

> Ambassadors have no battleships at their disposal, or heavy infantry, or fortresses; their weapons are words and opportunities. In important transactions opportunities are fleeting; once they are missed they cannot be recovered. It is a greater offence to deprive a democracy of an opportunity than it would be to deprive an oligarchy or autocracy. Under their systems, action can be taken instantly and on the word of command; but with us, first the Council has to be notified and adopt a provisional resolution, and even then only when the heralds and the Ambassadors have sent in a note in writing. Then the Council has to convene the Assembly, but then only on a statutory date. Then the debater has to prove his case in face of an ignorant and often corrupt opporition; and even when this endless procedure has been completed, and a decision has been come to, even more time is wasted before the necessary financial resolution can be passed. Thus an ambassador who, in a constitution such as ours, acts in a dilatory manner and causes us to miss our opportunities, is not missing opportunities only, but robbing us of the control of events. . . .
>
> (quoted in Nicolson, op. cit., p. 13)

9 M. Wight, *Systems of States* (Leicester, 1977), p. 56.

10 See Aeschines, *On the Embassy,* 115 for Amphictyonies, and Isocrates, *Panegyricus,* 4.43, for festivals.

11 Plato, *Laws,* 1. 626a.

12 See F. Millar, 'Government and Diplomacy in the Roman Empire during the First Three Centuries', *International History Review,* X (1988).

13 Tacitus, *Annals,* 11.24.

14 D. Obolensky, 'The Principles and Methods of Byzantine Diplomacy', in *Congrès Internationale D'Études Byzantines,* 1961, I (1963), 53.

15 Quoted in J. Shepard, *Byzantinsche Forschungen,* vol. X, *Information, Disinformation and Delay in Byzantine Diplomacy* (Amsterdam, 1985), p. 241. The power of these ideas was emphasized by their longevity – to a point where they ought to have been contradicted by the evident trend of contemporary events. In the fourteenth century, Basil I of Moscow omitted the emperor's name from the diptychs of the Russian Church, and was taken to task by the Patriarch of Constantinople:

> My son, you are wrong in saying, "we have a Church, but not an Emperor". It is not possible for Christians to have a Church and not to have an Empire.... The Emperor...is appointed *basileus* and *autocrator* of the Romans – to wit, of all Christians.

The insistence was effective. In the very last years of the Empire, his son Basil II of Moscow wrote to Constantine XI:

> You have received your great imperial sceptre . . . in order to establish all Orthodox Christianity in your realm and to render great assistance to our dominions of Russia and to all our religion.
> (from *Acta Patriarchatus Constantinopolitani,* II, pp. 190–2; quoted in E. Barker, *Social and Political Thought in Byzantium* (Oxford, 1957) pp. 194–6)

16 Quoted in C. Diehl, *Byzantium: Greatness and Decline,* trans. N. Walford (New Jersey, 1957), p. 59. The Russians gave an account of their own:

> We came to the Greeks and they led us to where they worship their God, and we knew not whether we were in heaven or in earth; for on earth there is no such beauty or splendour.... we know only that in that place God dwells among men, and their service is more beautiful than that of other nations: for we cannot forget that beauty.
> (*Povest'Vremennykh Let,* s. a. 987; quoted in Obolensky, op. cit., p. 60).

17 The most quoted evidence for Byzantine ceremonial is that given by an ambassador from the West, Liutprand of Cremona: see his *Antapodosis* and *Legatio.* The purpose was clearly set out by Constantine VII in the introduction to his *De Ceremoniis.*

18 Quoted in F.E. Wozniak, 'Byzantine Diplomacy', in *Dictionary of the Middle Ages,* 4 (New York, 1984), p. 196. The consequences could of course be enraging.

> When Valentinus, envoy from Justin II to the Turks of Central Asia, presented his credentials to the Khagan, he was met by an explosion of rage; putting his hands to his mouth, the Turkish sovereign exclaimed: 'are you not those Romans, who have ten languages and one deception?... As my ten fingers are in my mouth, so you use different languages to deceive sometimes myself, sometimes the Avars, my slaves. You flatter all peoples and you entice them with artful words and a crafty soul, you are indifferent to those who fall headlong into misfortune, from which you yourself derive benefit.... A Turk neither lies nor deceives'.
> (quoted in Obolensky, op. cit., p. 61)

19 S. Runciman, *Byzantine Civilisation* (London, 1933), p. 162.

20 Ibid., pp. 158–9.

21 Diehl, op.cit., p. 56.

22 See the general argument of Shephard (Shephard, op.cit.).

23 See Wozniak, op.cit., p. 196.

24 This section is based on M. Khadduri, *War and Peace and the Law of Islam* (New York, 1955); M. Khadduri, 'The Islamic Theory of International Relations and its Contemporary Relevance', in Jesse H. Proctor, ed., *Islam and International Relations* (New York, 1981); and F. Buckler, *Muslim Conduct of State*, New York.

25 M.A.R. Maulde la Clavière, *La Diplomatie au temps de Machiavel* (3 vols, Paris, 1892–3).

26 G. Mattingly, *Renaissance Diplomacy* (London, 1955), pp. 18–19.

27 *Legatus* was defined by Durandus thus:

> a legate is or can be called whoever has been sent from another. . . either from a ruler or from the pope to others. . . . or from any city or province to a ruler or to another. . . . or even from a proconsul. . . . On this account a legate is called a substitute for the office of another. . .
> (Durandus in V.E. Hrabar, ed., *De Legatis et Legationibus Tractatus Varii*
> (Dorpat, 1906) p. 32)

But as time went on, it is clear that legate came to be confined to representatives of the Pope, and a legate *a latere* had greater powers than any other papal representative (see D.E. Queller, *The Office of Ambassador in the Middle Ages* (Princeton, 1967) p. 65).

28 Mattingly, op.cit., p. 22.

29 See W. Roosen, 'Early Modern Diplomatic Ceremonial: Systems Approach, *Journal of Modern History*, 52 (1980), pp. 452–76.

30 It was possible for *nuncii* to be described in other words, although *nuncius* was the most frequently used. *Legatus*, which increasingly became limited to representatives of the Pope, *missus* and *mandatarius* were all possible. At the lower end of the spectrum of message carriers were *cursores, tabellarii, fanti, varletti* or *coquini*: all these were couriers of the simplest kind not entrusted with significant messages. Queller, op. cit., pp. 3–6.

31 Queller, op. cit., p. 23.

32 Queller, op. cit., p. 7, note 20.

33 For example, Henry III wrote to Raymond Berengar, Count of Provence, that the King's Council had agreed to the conditions for the treaty of marriage between the King and the Count's daughter Eleanor. Henry, therefore, was sending solemn envoys to conclude the marriage. Their letters of credence informed the count that he should believe in them without doubt and fulfil the pact just as if these things were treated and determined with the King himself present.
> (Queller, op. cit., p. 9).

34 Queller, op. cit., p. 10. The position of papal legates was just as clear, and in a ceremonial sense, because the papal ceremonial was more advanced, even clearer. Gregory VII said of a legate that one should 'see in the legate the Pope's own face and hear in his voice the living voice of the Pope' (Queller, p. 10, note 39). When it was said of a legate that he wore the Pope's mantle, this was literally true, as (it was that) he rode a white horse and wore the Pope's spurs.

35 See Hrabar, op. cit.; Baldo degli Ubaldi, *Commentaria* (Venice, 1515–16), p. 6, R. Sohm, *The Institutes: a Textbook of the History and System of Roman Private Law* (3rd edition, Oxford, 1907), p. 219.

36 Queller, op. cit., pp. 7–8.

37 Queller, op. cit., p. 225.

38 S. Anglo, *Spectacle, Pageantry and Early Tudor Policy* (Oxford, 1969), Chapter 4.

39 Nicolson, op.cit., pp. 42–3.

40 See F.L. Ganshof, *Le Moyen Age*, vol. I *Histoire des Relations Internationals*, ed. P. Renouvin, (Paris, 1953).

41 Queller, op. cit., p. 29.

42 D.E. Queller, in *Dictionary of the Middle Ages*, vol. 4 (New York, 1984), p. 204. See also D.E. Queller, 'L'Evolution du rôle de l'ambassadeur: les pleins pouvoirs et le traité de 1201 entre les Croises et les Venitiens', *Le Moyen Age*, LXVII (1961), 479–501.

43 Queller, *Office of Ambassador*, pp. 57–9, and notes 213 and 218, the latter giving the source for Hostiensis' remark that, provided the intention of the principal was clear, it did not matter whether the envoy was called an 'ass'.

44 Very broad powers were given to Venetian procurators (in these cases called *syndics*) in this respect in the early fourteenth century: see Queller, op. cit., pp. 44–5.

45 For example, Edward I of England explained to the Count of Hulcrath, who had asked about conventions apparently made on his behalf, that he did not yet know what his procurators had done, but would inform the Count when he did. Queller, op. cit., p. 46.

46 'In the marriage by proxy of Bona of Savoy to Galeazzo Maria Sforza, the procurator, Tristano Sforza, actually entered the marriage bed and touched her thigh' (Queller, *Dictionary of the Middle Ages*, vol. 4, p. 204).

47 There were some complications about this arising from the fact that it was felt more necessary that the fealty should be given in person than that it should be received in person: see Queller, *Office of Ambassador*, pp. 49–50.

48 See James I of Aragon's repudiation of part of the Treaty of Corbeil, and other examples in Queller, op. cit., pp. 54–5.

2 THE RENAISSANCE AND THE RESIDENT AMBASSADOR (pp. 29–54)

1 For du Rosier – and many others – see V.E. Hrabar, *De Legatis et Legotionibus Tractatus Varii* (Dorpat, 1906). The nature of the discussion changed at the end of the seventeenth century – see Chapter 5.

2 G. Mattingly, *Renaissance Diplomacy* (London, 1955), pp. 39–40.

3 See G.R. Elton, *The Tudor Constitution* (Cambridge University Press, 1965), p. 44.

4 Mattingly, op. cit., p. 59.

5 D.E. Queller, *The Office of Ambassador in the Middle Ages* (Princeton, 1967), p. 11.

6 A. Degert, 'Louis XI et ses Ambassadeurs', *Revue Historique*, CLIV (1929), 4–6.

7 Sir Thomas More, for example, negotiated on behalf of the Mercers Company in London with the City of Antwerp in 1509, and the Hanse, who were partly a commercial enterprise and partly a political authority, also regularly negotiated on their own behalf. Mattingly, op. cit., p. 29.

8 H. Nicolson, *The Evolution of Diplomatic Method* (Oxford, 1954), pp. 34–5.

9 Nicolson, op. cit., pp. 29–30.

10 Philippe de Commynes, *Mémoires* (Paris, n.d.), VI, pp. 198–9.

11 See Mattingly, op. cit., Chapter 2.

12 Nicolson, op. cit., p. 34.

13 Mattingly, op. cit., pp. 115–16.

14 Mattingly, op. cit., pp. 111–12, described the typical dispatch:

By 1500 the rules for ambassadors' dispatches were much alike in all the major Italian chanceries. Whatever their literary quality they had to satisfy certain formal requirements. Immediately after the salutation, the ambassador was expected to note, first, the official correspondence recently received, usually including pieces acknowledged in his last dispatch, and, second, the date of that last dispatch, which was represented either by a summary or by an enclosed copy. Then followed the body of the letter, supported by transcripts of relevant documents. Then, before the formal close, came the place and date of the dispatch, often with the exact hour of sending so that the speed of the courier could be noted. At the very bottom of the sheet the ambassador signed. Later this form was adopted throughout Europe.

15 Mattingly, op. cit., Chapter 11, note 5.
16 Nicolson, op. cit., p. 34.
17 Nicolson, op. cit., p. 31.
18 Mattingly, op. cit., pp. 67–9.
19 See Mattingly, op. cit., Chapter 6.
20 M. Wight, *Systems of States* (London, 1977), p. 53, also p. 141.
21 Nicolson, op. cit., p. 33; but see Mattingly, op. cit., p. 85 for a contrary view.
22 Mattingly, op. cit., pp. 76–7.
23 J. Hotman de Villiers, *De la Charge et Dignité de l'Ambassadeur* (Paris, 1604), f. 27vo.
24 Mattingly, op. cit., p. 155.
25 Mattingly, op. cit., p. 158.
26 Charles de Danzay, a professing Calvinist, succeeded Christopher Richer at Copenhagen in 1548 and served for forty years as the French representative in the Baltic area generally. Mattingly, op. cit., p. 178.
27 Mattingly, op. cit., pp. 176–7.
28 B. Picard, *Das Gesandtschaftswesen Ostmitteleuropas in der frühen Neuzeit* (Graz, Wien, Köln, 1967), pp. 50–4.
29 N.M. Sutherland, *The French Secretaries of State in the Age of Catherine de Medici* (London, 1962), p. 226.
30 After the Confession of Augsburg, 1555, which enunciated the principle of *eius regio, cuius religio.*
31 See p. 32 above.
32 Thomas Middleton, the early Stuart English playwright, wrote a play in 1625 which ran for nine consecutive days at the Globe theatre, on the theme of the public danger created by the representatives of Spain and the Pope. The Spanish ambassador, Gondomar, thinly disguised as the Black Knight, is caught and frustrated in a plot to subvert the White Kingdom. The play's plot was a tribute to the strength of anti-Spanish and anti-Catholic public opinion in England, but it also offered an exaggerated, but still interesting, view of the techniques that the resident enemy might employ. At one point Gondomar is made to mention various tricks of bribery, disguise and secret communication: 'letters conveyed in rolls, tobacco-balls', money carried 'in cold baked pastries'; but his real intention is espionage. His summer holiday was devoted to 'inform my knowledge in the state and strength of the White Kingdom'

> . . . No fortification
> Haven, creek, landing place about the White Coast,
> But I got draft and platform; learn'd the depth
> Of all their channels, knowledge of all sands,
> Shelves, rocks and rivers for invasion proper'st;

A catalogue of all the navy royal,
The burden of the ships, the brassy murderers,
The number of the men, to what cape bound:
Again for the discovery of the inlands,
Never a shire but the state better known
To me than to her best inhabitants;
What power of men and horses, gentry's revenues,
Who well affected to our side, who ill,
Who neither well nor ill, all the neutrality.
(*A Game at Chess*, at IV, ii, 60–73 in C.F. Tucker Brooke and N.B. Paradise, *English Drama, 1580–1642* (Boston, 1933), p. 968)

33 After 1534, England was not represented at Rome. The English embassy with the Emperor Charles V never firmly established its right to celebrate an Anglican communion, to the great detriment, almost termination of Anglo-Imperial relations. In Spain, the same problem put an end to the English residency. France maintained residents at Protestant courts, but their counterparts in Paris endured considerable discomforts and genuine risks (see Mattingly, op. cit., Chapter 2.

34 Mattingly, op. cit., pp. 48–9.

35 Durandus in Hrabar, op. cit., p. 32 and Queller, op. cit., pp. 175–7.

36 Queller, op. cit., p. 180.

37 Mattingly, op. cit., pp. 45–6.

38 Mattingly, op. cit., p. 48, for further material on the medieval limitations of ambassadorial immunities, see E. Nys, *Les Origines du Droit International* (Harlem, 1892), p. 347.

39 This proved to be a particularly clarifying incident. It caused the British Government to pass a special act through Parliament establishing legal protection for the immunities of ambassadors (7 Anne, cap. 12, 1709), and to a very clear statement from the Queen to the Tsar, who had broken off relations with England and demanded capital punishment for the ambassador's creditors.

And if any person hereafter. . .anyways violate the privileges of ambassadors and other foreign ministers, they will be liable to the most severe penalties and punishments which the arbitrary power of the judges shall think fit to inflict upon them and to which no bounds are given in this new act.
(E.R. Adair, *The Exterritoriality of Ambassadors in the Sixteenth and Seventeenth Centuries* (London, 1929), pp. 87, 91, 239–40.

40 E. Satow, *A Guide to Diplomatic Practice* (2 vols, London, 1922), I, pp. 264–8. Further episodes are discussed in Chapter 18.

41 Mattingly, op. cit., pp. 275–6.

42 Hrabar, op. cit., p. 130.

43 E.A. Adair, *The Exterritoriality of Ambassadors in the Sixteenth and Seventeenth Centuries* (London, 1929), pp. 251–9. The book provides a very complete list and evaluation of many examples and the way that theorists treated them. It also firmly concludes that it was not theorists or lawyers who brought about the general increase in diplomatic immunities, but the steady accretion of precedents.

44 For the inviolability of the ambassador's residence and *franchise du quartier* in general, see Adair, op. cit., Chapter 11, where it is exhaustively discussed.

45 Satow, op. cit., pp. 256–7.

46 For this and the following examples see Queller, op. cit., pp. 180–4.

47 Philippe de Commynes gives a description of a gala occasion in Venice:

After dinner all the ambassadors of the league met together in boats upon the water (which in Venice is their chief recreation); the whole number of their boats (which are provided at the charge of the Signory, and proportioned to every man's retinue) was about forty, every one of them adorned with the arms of their respective masters; and in this pomp they passed under my windows with their trumpets and other instruments of music. . . . At night there were extraordinary fireworks upon the turrets, steeples, and tops of the ambassadors' houses, multitudes of bonfires were lighted, and the cannon all round the city were fired. . . . there was great banqueting.

(de Commynes, op. cit., VI, pp. 227–9)

48 This could be taken to great lengths. When the son-in-law and envoy of Ludovico il Moro Sforza arrived on a mission to the King of France, he was led into the apartment where the royal mistresses resided, and was presented with one of them by the King personally. The King choosing another, they passed an agreeable two hours. This was reported back to Milan and much appreciated as a great honour. Queller, in the *Dictionary of the Middle Ages*, vol. 4, p. 212.

49 There is a thorough account of this expressed in sociological terms which overestimates the novelty of the point of view in W. Roosen, 'Early Modern Diplomatic Ceremonial: a Systems Approach', *Journal of Modern History*, 52 (1980).
    There are examples of the strains that questions of precedence engendered strewn across the centuries from the fifteenth until the mid-eighteenth. The best source for the fifteenth century was J. Burckhard *Liber Notarum*, which was published in ed. E. Celano, *Rerum italicarum scriptores*, (Rome, 1906–11). He was the papal master of protocol at the height of the fifteenth century and recounts, for example, the consequences of the demand made in 1488 by the French to supplant the ambassadors of the King of the Romans – the imperial heir – at the papal court and not therefore to stand below the orator of the King of the Romans at Mass. The French were refused, but persisted and were allowed to appear away from but still below their rival. Less than a month later, the French ambassador, the Bishop of Lescar, simply occupied the first place in a procession and when the German protested, attempted to ride him down on horseback. The German grabbed the Bishop by his hood and mantle and physically removed him from the place he had taken, occupying it himself with other Germans. The Bishop then demanded the excommunication of the German, which the Pope refused to pronounce then and there, wherewith the German delegation walked out while he was still speaking.

50 Particularly from du Rosier, in Hrabar, op. cit., pp. 4 ff. and Maulde la Clavière, *La Diplomatie au temps de Machiavel* (3 vols, Paris, 1892–3), II, pp. 176–201.

51 Extravagant clothing of one kind or another evidently played a great role in diplomatic nicety, both in the dress of both sides and among the gifts exchanged. Even the usually mean Venetians reckoned to clothe their ambassadors well and authorized gifts of clothing. Queller, op. cit., p. 203.

52 It is clear that during the reign of Galeazzo Maria Sforza Milan, 1466–76, a kind of competitive hospitality was being used as a weapon in foreign policy. See G. Lubkin, 'Strategic Hospitality: Foreign Dignitaries at the Court of Milan: 1466–1476', *The International History Review*, VIII (1986), 173–89.

53 Queller, op. cit., p. 195, gives a description taken from the Venetian ambassador Contarini's report of his audience with the King of France in 1492:

He and his colleagues were accompanied to their audience by a large number of *uomini di conto*. They were presented to the King in a hall about half the size of the Senate chamber of the ducal palace at home. At one end the King sat upon a dais, with a curtain behind his back and a canopy of Alexandrian velvet embroidered with the arms of France above his head. Along the side of the hall to the right of the King was a bench occupied by barons of the blood and on the opposite side one occupied by prelates resident in the court. These made up the secret council of the King. At the end of the hall opposite the King was a bench reserved for the ambassadors upon which the King wished that they sit and expose to him the purpose of their embassy.

54 Hrabar, op. cit., pp. 14–16.
55 Queller op. cit., p. 155.
56 Queller op. cit., pp. 184–90.
57 Generally, except for Venice, ambassadors were allowed to keep their gifts: Maulde la Clavière, op. cit., III, p. 373.
58 There were many thirteenth-century examples of rulers giving their envoys signed and sealed blanks to use at their discretion when a satisfactory conclusion had been arrived at, but this was at the extreme end of 'full powers', and became very rare as the much more tense atmosphere of the fifteenth century increased the self evident risks: Queller op. cit., pp. 130–6.
59 Full and written instructions became a feature of fifteenth-century diplomacy. In earlier periods they might be quite sketchy, and possibly not exist at all. In 1383, a Mantuan ambassador told his hosts that when he had asked for instructions, his principal had replied: 'You are a wise man. I send you to handle my affairs. It is not necessary that I should tell you what is to be done.' Queller op. cit., p. 122.
60 Du Rosier used by Mattingly, op. cit., Chapter 3.
61 Nicolson, op. cit., p. 40.
62 Queller op. cit., p. 200, note 139.
63 For ratification, see Queller op. cit., Chapter 8.
64 There is at least one example of an envoy representing both principals: Count Florence of Holland appears to have represented both Edward I of England and Adolf of Nassau in arranging a treaty. D.E. Queller, in *Dictionary of the Middle Ages*, vol. IV (New York, 1984), p. 209.
65 Certainly the expenses of defending embassies was resisted by Venice from an early date (1265), see Queller, *Office of Ambassador*, pp. 161–2.
66 For the financial side of embassies, see Queller, op. cit., pp. 163–74. Most information came from Venice and particularly from the 'Traité du gouvernement du cité et seigneurie de Venise, printed in P.-M. Perret, *Relations de la France et Venise* (2 vols, Paris, 1896), II, pp. 239–304.
67 For personnel generally, see Queller, op. cit., pp. 149–62.
68 Nicolson, op. cit., p. 29.
69 There were examples of the Venetians appointing local residents – generally merchants – as sub-ambassadors in England, on account of the appalling journey: Nicolson, op. cit., p. 34.
70 see Burckhard, *Liber Notarum*, 1, pp. 294–5.
71 G. V. Vernadsky, *The Mongols and Russia, A History of Russia*, 3 (New Haven, 1953), p. 68.
72 Governments were not very specific about what was to be reported to them: a Florentine ambassador of the late fifteenth century was told:

During the period of your legation you should observe and investigate diligently all those things you esteem not only to be pertinent to our particular affairs but all that should generally occur day by day. You should

give to us in detail and often news of every event, frequenting the court
and following continually his excellency the Duke, when he goes to any
place to stay, in order that you can communicate and relate from this
everything that happens day by day. And above all, you should write often
and specifically about everything.

Queller, op. cit., p. 138.

73 Queller, op. cit., p. 140.
74 Nicolson, op. cit., p. 38. Mauroceno also complained that gifts he had promised
were not being supplied. The network of gifts extended beyond the official
arriving and departing presents into a shadowy area in which the fine line
between giving agreeable tokens, perhaps of gratitude, and bribery was regularly
crossed. See Queller, op. cit., pp. 94–5.
75 The classic account of this is in D.E. Queller, *Medieval Diplomacy and the
Fourth Crusade* (London, 1980), Chapter 8, 'The Development of Ambassadorial *Relazioni*'.
76 See Charles H. Carter, 'The Ambassadors of Early Modern Europe: Patterns of
Diplomatic Representation in the Early Seventeenth Century', in *From the
Renaissance to the Counter-Reformation*, ed., Charles Carter (London, 1966).

3 THE EMERGENCE OF THE 'OLD DIPLOMACY'
(pp. 55–83)

1 In 1466 the Venetians regularized this attitude by forbidding its representatives
from receiving any allowances or payments in kind from their hosts, and refusing
to make any themselves. D.E. Queller, *Early Venetian Legislation on Ambassadors*
(Geneva, 1966), p. 22.
2 See E.R. Adair, *The Extraterritoriality of Ambassadors in the Sixteenth and Seventeenth
Centuries* (London, 1929).
3 For example, a bill of exchange for 300 sent to the British resident at Madrid
in October 1561 did not arrive for seven months. G.M. Bell, 'John Man: the last
Elizabethan Resident Ambassador in Spain', *Sixteenth Century Journal*, VII, 2
(1976), 77.
4 Richard Pace needing funds on a mission from Henry VIII to the Swiss Cantons
suggested it be sent sewn into the coats of couriers 'after the manner of Italy'.
J. Wegg, *Richard Pace, a Tudor Diplomat* (London, 1932), pp. 71, 82.
5 G. Mattingly, *Renaissance Diplomacy* (London, 1955), pp. 146–50.
6 In one case, it went even further. Sir Robert Wingfield sent as English resident
to the Emperor Maximilian actually lent *him* money – no doubt a further example
of Wingfield's notoriously optimistic disposition. Mattingly, op. cit., p. 166.
7 M.-N. Baudoin-Matuszek, 'Un Ambassadeur en Ecosse au XVIe siècle: Henri
Clutin d'Oisel', *Revue Historique*, 569 (1989), 94, 97. For other examples of this
kind of result, see M.A.R. Maulde la Clavière, *La Diplomatie au temps de Machiavel*
(3 vols, Paris, 1892–3), I, pp. 341–2.
8 Mattingly, op. cit., p. 148.
9 See, for example, D.B. Horn, *British Diplomatic Service 1689–1789* (Oxford, 1961),
Chapter 3.
10 Mattingly, op. cit., p. 234.
11 See F. de Bassompierre, *Memoirs of the Embassy of the Marshal de Bassompierre to the
Court of England in 1626: translated* (London, 1819). For more discussion of this
particular embassy see unpublished Cambridge M. Phil., dissertation (Seeley
Library) by Jocelyn Woodley, *The Development of the French Diplomatic System under
Richelieu, 1624–42* (1989).

12 See I. Vinogradoff, 'Russian Mission to London, 1569–1687', *Oxford Slavonic Papers*, New Series, XIV (1981), and 'Russian Missions to London, 1711–1789', *Oxford Slavonic Papers*, New Series, XV (1982). Vinogradoff noted that Potemkin's 1681 embassy was the last one to end with the presentation of a gift in the traditional style, and also, interestingly, that he instantly converted it into cash (XIV, p. 51). This same Potemkin had earlier been in Denmark where his behaviour was a marked example of the famous Russian determination to obtain the maximum privileges. The Danish King being ill, the ambassador would not withdraw, 'but demanded (and obtained) a bed on which to lie side-by-side with the ailing monarch so that they might hold discourse' (XIV, p. 52).

This source is also full of useful evidence about the expenditure that Russian embassies caused the English Court and the successful resistance offered to what were anachronistic demands.

13 See, for example, W.J. Roosen, 'The True Ambassador: occupational and personal characteristics of French Ambassadors under Louis XIV', *European Studies Review*, 3 (1973), 136.

14 Apart from the dangers of attack, burglary and disease, journeying, particularly in Eastern Europe was simply physically unpleasant. Antonio Possevino, who was a Jesuit, went to Russia in 1582, sent by the Pope to mediate in a Russo-Polish war and left an account of his journey. The traveller needed a tent, since rooms were unlikely to be available. Everybody, including horses, might have to be accommodated together, so dividing curtains should be taken and beds needed to be like mosquito-netted sleeping bags so as to be protected from falling soot, 'as happens in Muscovy and Lithuania', and 'from the flies, which bite fiercely and, unlike elsewhere, are active at night, working their way through the linen to cause intense discomfort'. H.F. Graham, ed., *The Moscovia of Antonio Possevino, S.J.* (Pittsburg, 1977), p. 40.

15 Mattingly, op. cit., p. 150.

16 Particularly in England, service abroad could lead to subsequent preferment at home: see G.M. Bell, 'Elizabethan Diplomatic Compensation: its Nature and Variety', *Journal of British Studies*, 22, 2 (1981), 1–25.

17 Mattingly, op. cit., p. 238.

18 See Horn, op. cit., Chapter 5; and, for an amusing Austrian example, D.E.D. Beales, *Joseph II* (I, Cambridge, 1987), p. 426, where it is explained how the wrong Count Cobenzl represented the Habsburgs at the negotiations for the Peace of Teschen in 1779.

19 Mattingly, op. cit., p. 224.

20 For Spanish developments particularly see Mattingly, op. cit., Chapter 15, and Chapter 26.

21 Mattingly, op. cit., pp. 246–7.

22 Mattingly, op. cit., pp. 220–1, 261 and note 7 to Chapter 24, which gives the Latin text of Wotton's remark: *legatus est bonus vir peregre missus ad mentiendum Reipublicae causa.* There is no pun in the latin: the ambassador is sent abroad to tell lies for the sake of his country. In Stuart English to lie also meant to live – hence the pun in the English translation.

23 See the account of Wolsey's treatment of ambassadors and their papers in Mattingly, op. cit., pp. 274–6, particularly the celebrated case of de Praet, the Emperor's resident in England whose courier was stopped, his papers read, de Praet himself then arraigned before the royal council for derogation of duty as an ambassador, declared in a more modern phrase, *persona non grata*, and detained at the King's pleasure.

24 For codes and ciphers generally, see Mattingly, op. cit., pp. 247–50; see also Maulde la Clavière, op. cit., III, pp. 133ff.

25 For example, the termination of the English residency in Spain after investiga-
    tions by the Inquisition of the ambassador's religious practices. The ambassador
    was a particularly awkward Anglican Bishop, John Man, Bishop of Gloucester.
    Mattingly, op. cit., p. 202.

26 Mattingly, op. cit., p. 253.

27 There is an exhaustive and exhausting account of the evolution in nomenclature
    and classification in O. Krauske, *Die Entwickelung* (Leipzig, 1885) pp. 150–87,
    leading up to the final formalization agreed at the Congress of Aix-la-Chapelle
    in 1818. This listed in order of status: ambassadors, legates, nuncios followed by
    envoys extraordinary, ministers plenipotentiary, followed by ministers-resident,
    and finished with chargés d'affaires.

28 W.J. Roosen, *Early Modern Diplomatic Ceremonial*, p. 464.

29 J. Rousset de Missy, *Mémoires sur le rang et la préséance entre les souverains de l'Europe*
    (Amsterdam, 1746), Introduction, quoted in Anderson M., *Europe in the Eighteenth
    Century* (London, 1967), p. 163.

30 H.F. Graham, trans and ed., *The Moscovia of Antonio Possevino, S.J.* (Pittsburg,
    1977), p. 128.

31 'Le Congrès finit par declarer que les titres prit ou omis, de part et d'autre, ne
    pourront ni nuire, ni préjudicier à qui que ce soit'. H. Vast, *Les Grands Traités
    du Regne de Louis XIV* (3 vols, Paris, 1893), p. 33. This evidently only produced
    a limited improvement, since Vast observed on the same page, after discussing
    the protocol of visiting wives: 'Ainsi les difficultés de protocole prennent plus
    de temps que les discussions d'affaires'.

32 'When one evening in 1698 the King (Louis XIV) asked the Earl of Portland
    to hold his bedroom candlestick, the episode resounded through the chan-
    celleries of Europe as a highly significant, and perhaps portentous, event'
    (Nicolson, op. cit., pp. 60–1.)

33 C.G. de Koch, and F. Schoell, *Histoire Abrégée des Traités de Paix entre les Puissances
    de l'Europe depuis la paix de Westphalie* (4 vols, Brussels, 1838), I, p. 204.

34 E. Satow, *A Guide to Diplomatic Practice* (London, 1922), p. 2 (trans. Richard
    Langhorne).

35 For further discussion of this material see R. Langhorne, 'The Development of
    International Conferences, 1648–1830', *Studies in History and Politics*, 1981–2,
    pp. 67–75.

36 At the Congress of Ryswick in 1697, for example, the peculiar yet declining
    significance of the Holy Roman Empire provoked the imperial ambassador to
    demand, and to succeed in his demand, that he not be seated opposite any other
    representative. He was allowed to enter the room first and then accommodated
    by being placed opposite a large mirror, in which naturally, he was faced or
    outfaced only by himself. O. Weber, *Der Friede von Utrecht* (Gotha, 1891) p. 203.

37 Mattingly, op. cit., p. 108.

38 The way in which the emphasis changed can be discovered from surveying the
    extracts from many commentators collected and reprinted in V.E. Hrabar, *De
    Legatis et legationibus tractatus varii* (Dorpat, 1906).

39 A. de Wicquefort, *L'Ambassadeur et ses Fonctions* (2 vols, the Hague, 1680–1).

40 François de Callières in, M.H.A. Keens-Soper, and K.W. Schweizer, eds, *The Art
    of Diplomacy* (New York, 1983), p. 27.

41 Nicolson, op. cit., p. 62.

42 See F.H. Hinsley, *Power and the Pursuit of Peace* (Cambridge, 1963).

43 Keens-Soper and Schweizer, eds, op. cit., pp. 33–4.

44 Mattingly, op. cit., p. 222.

45 A. Pecquet, *Discours sur l'art de négocier* (Paris, 1737).

46 Keens-Soper and Schweizer, eds, op. cit., pp. 38–9.

47 M. Carmona, *La France de Richelieu* (Paris, 1984), p. 144. 'Richelieu, en laicisant la nature des rapports entres les états, impose la notion de l'équilibre européen comme principe directeur des relations internationales'.

48 'J'ose dire hardiment, négocier sans cesse ouvertement en tous lieux, quoiqu'on n'en reçoive pas un fruit présent, et celui qu'on peut attendre à l'avenir ne soit pas apparent, est un chose tout à faire necessaire', A.J., du P. Richelieu, *Testament Politique* (Paris, 1947), p. 347).

49 'Les Rois doivent bien prendre garde aux traités qi'il font: mais quand ils sont faits, ils doivent les observer avec religion' (Richelieu, op. cit., p. 355).

50 'Il est tout à fait nécessaire d'être exact au choix des ambassadeurs et autre négotiateurs, et on ne saurait être trop sévére à punir ceux qui outrepassent leur pouvoir, puisque par telles fautes ils mettent en compromis la réputation des princes et le bien des Etats tout ensemble' (Richelieu, op. cit., p. 355).

51 '. . . personnes qui connaissent le poids des paroles et qui sachent bien coucher par écrit' (Richelieu, op. cit., p. 352).

52 Nicolson, op. cit., pp. 51–3.

53 *Etat Numerique des fonds de la correspondence politique de l'origine à 1871* (Paris, Archives du Ministère des affaires Etrangers).

54 The *Règlement* of 1626 explained:

> Le Roy, jugeant qu'il est à propos et très expédient pour le bien de ses affaires que les provinces Estrangers soient toutes entre les mains d'un seul de ses Secretaires d'Estat, pour faire les déspêches et expéditions qui luy seront demandées, S Majesté a résolu de changer les départements suivant lesquels ils ont travaillé justques à présent.
> (O.A. Ranum, *Richelieu and the Councillors of Louis XIII*, (Oxford, 1963), p. 191)

55 > Considérant que les affaires du Roi demeurées aux mains de ceux qui les reçoivent se confondent parmi les papiers de familles particuliers en telle sorte que la mémoire s'en perd au grand préjudice de l'Etat, il ordonne qu'il sera tenu un régistre de ces actes, et que les originaux de dits actes, tant du passe qu'à l'avenir, serond protes au trésor des Chartes et ajoutes à l'inventaire d'iceluy.
> (C.S. Blaga, *L'Evolution de la Diplomatie* (Paris, 1938), p. 26)

56 Ranum, op. cit., pp. 55–6.

57 Although the title of Secretary of State first emerged at the Vatican only in 1644, the office had been preceded by early sixteenth-century examples both of a new department, the *Secretaria Apostolica* and an official, the *secretarius papae*.

58 See Horn, op. cit.

59 Nicolson, op. cit., p. 55.

60 By 1713, it would have probably taken some twenty coaches to move the then foreign minister, Torcy, and his staff from Versailles, and from Paris to Fontainebleau. J.C. Rule, 'King and Minister', in R. Hatton and J.S. Bromley, eds, *William III and Louis XIV: Essays 1680–1720 by and for M.A. Thomson* (Toronto, 1968), p. 216.

61 M. Anderson, *Europe in the Eighteenth Century* (London, 1961), p. 156.

62 See *Ocherk istorii Ministerstva Inostrannykh Del', 1802–1902* (St Petersburg, 1902). I am indebted to Professor V. Matveev of the Moscow State Institute of International Relations for information from this source. See also B. Meissner, 'Die zaristische diplomatie, A. Der Gesandtschafts-Prikaz (Posolskij Prikaz)', *Jahrbucher für Geschichte Osteuropas*, Neue Folge, Band 4 (1956).

63 E. Matsch, *Geschichte des Auswartigen Dienstes von Österreich (Ungarn), 1720–1920*, (Wien, 1980), pp. 72–6.

64 Matsch, op. cit., pp. 76–7.
65 C.V. Findlay, 'The Legacy of Tradition to Reform. Origins of the Ottoman Foreign Ministry', *International Journal of Middle East Studies*, 1 (1970).
66 P. Fraser, *The Intelligence of the Secretaries of State and their Monopoly of Licensed News, 1660–1688* (Cambridge, 1956), p. 65.
67 Anderson, op. cit., p. 162.
68 Anderson, op. cit., p. 161.
69 Horn, op. cit., pp. 45–6.
70 *Ocherk istorii Ministerstva Inostrannykh Del*, p. 70.
71 In England where in-service training continued to be favoured, an attempt was made to improve what was provided at the universities. The Regius chairs of history established at Oxford and Cambridge in the early eighteenth century had 'the express intention of providing a "constant supply of persons in every way qualified for the management of such weighty affairs and negotiations" as need might occasion'. Maurice Keens-Soper, 'The Practice of a States-System', in *The Reason of States*, ed. Michael Donelan (London, 1978) pp. 33–4.
72 Anderson, op. cit., pp. 159–60. See also H.M.A. Keens-Soper, 'The French Political Academy, 1712: A School for Ambassadors', *European Studies Review*, II, 4 (1972).
73 This consideration had begun to improve both recommendation, for example, both Wicquefort and de Callières, and practice by the early eighteenth century.
74 See F. Dickmann, *Der Westfälische Frieden* (Munster, 1959).
75 C.G. de Koch, and F. Schoell, op. cit., IV, p. 108.
76 M. Prior, *History of His Own Time* (London, 1740), p. 33.
77 H. Vast, *Les Grands Traités du Règne de Louis XIV* (3 vols, Paris, 1893), II, p. 203, note 1.
78 J.W. Zinkeisen, *Geschichte des Osmanisches Reiches in Europa* (Gotha, 1857), p. 209.
79 G. de Lamberty, *Mémoires pour servir à l'histoire du XVII Siècle* (14 vols, Amsterdam, 1735–40, VII), pp. 8–12. O. Weber, *Der Friede von Utrecht* (Gotha, 1891), p. 203. Koch and Schoell, op. cit., I, p. 204.
80 Koch and Schoell, op. cit., I, p. 313; see also p. 311 for a new order of signature. Each ambassador took a copy he had signed first.
81 Koch and Schoell, op. cit., III, pp. 280–1. d'Angeberg (L.J.B. Chodzko), *Le Congrès de Vienne et les Traités de 1815* (Paris, 1863), p. ix. C. Metternich, *Mémoires, Documents et Ecrits Divers*, (Paris, 1879), I, pp. 175–6.
82 C.K. Webster, *The Foreign Policy of Lord Castlereagh* (2 vols, London, 1931), I, p. 199.
83 Webster, op. cit., I, p. 200.
84 Webster, op. cit., I, p. 209.
85 Webster, op. cit., I pp. 212–13.
86 d'Angeberg, op. cit., I, pp. 362–4 (trans. Richard Langhorne).
87 E. Hertslet, *The Map of Europe by Treaty* (4 vols, London, 1875–91), I., p. 317.
88 To facilitate and to secure the execution of the present Treaty, and to consolidate the connections which at the moment so closely unite the Four Sovereigns for the happiness of the world, the High Contracting Parties have agreed to renew their meetings at fixed periods, either under the auspices of the sovereigns themselves, or by their respective Ministers, for the purposes of consulting upon their common interests, and for the consideration of those measures which at each of those periods shall be

considered the most salutary for the repose and prosperity of Nations, and for the maintenance of the Peace of Europe.

(Treaty of Alliance and Friendship between Great Britain, Austria, Prussia and Russia. Paris, 20 November, 1815. E. Herstlet, *The Map of Europe by Treaty* (London, 1875))

4 THE 'OLD DIPLOMACY' (pp. 89–135)

1 Vicomte de Chateaubriand, *Le Congrès de Vérone*, vol. II (2nd edition, Paris, 1838), p. 246.

2 Cited in Lamar Cecil, *The German Diplomatic Service, 1871–1914* (Princeton, 1976), p. 244.

3 C.K. Webster, *The Foreign Policy of Lord Castlereagh* (2 vols, London, 1931), I, pp. 225–32.

4 Michael Hurst (ed.), *Key Treaties for the Great Powers, 1814–1914* (2 vols, Newton Abbot, 1972), I, pp. 13–14.

5 C.K. Webster, *The Congress of Vienna, 1814–1815* (5th edition, London, 1950), p. 61.

6 Ibid., p. 74.

7 Hurst, op. cit., pp. 96–7.

8 C.K. Webster, *British Diplomacy, 1813–1815: Select Documents Dealing with the Reconstruction of Europe* (London, 1921), p. 383.

9 Hurst, op. cit., p. 123.

10 G. de Berthier de Sauvigny, *Metternich and His Times*, trans. P. Ryde (London, 1962), p. 119.

11 Ibid., p. 256.

12 Louis Einstein, *A Diplomat Looks Back* ed. L.E. Gelfand (London, 1968), p. 5.

13 N. Rich and M.H. Fisher (eds), *The Holstein Papers* (4 vols, Cambridge, 1955–63), III, p. 567.

14 P. Bury, 'La Carrière Diplomatique au temps du Second Empire', *Revue d'histoire diplomatique* (1976), 283.

15 House of Commons Parliamentary Papers (1861), vol. VI, pp. 412–13.

16 R.A. Jones, *The British Diplomatic Service, 1815–1914* (Gerards Cross, 1983), especially Chapters I, II, VIII and IX.

17 De Sauvigny, op. cit., p. 89.

18 Jules Cambon, *The Diplomatist*, trans. C.R. Turner (London, 1931), pp. 112–14.

19 Harold Nicolson, *Diplomacy* (3rd edition, London, 1969), p. 125.

20 For the full story see: H.J. Bruce, *Silken Dalliance* (London, 1946), pp. 127–30.

21 R.H. Werking, *The Master Architects: Building the United States Foreign Service, 1890–1913* (Lexington, Kentucky, 1977), p. 14.

22 William Barnes and John Heath Morgan, *The Foreign Service of the United States: Origins, Development and Functions* (Washington, 1961), p. 92n.

23 D.C.M. Platt, *Finance, Trade and Politics in British Foreign Policy, 1815–1914* (Oxford, 1968), p.XIII.

24 Nicole Carcan-Chanel, '*Rôle des intérêts et des ambitions économiques de la Belgique dans l'histoire des relations diplomatiques, 1870–1914*', *Agents diplomatiques belges et étrangers aux xix*^e *et xx*^e *siècles*, Centre d'histoire économique et sociale, université libre de Bruxelles (1968), pp. 101–2.

25 Platt, op. cit., p. 32.

26 K.A. Hamilton, 'An attempt to form an Anglo-French "Industrial Entente"', *Middle Eastern Studies*, XI (1975), 59.

27 Alan Palmer, *The Chancelleries of Europe* (London, 1983), p. 112.

28 Cecil, op. cit., p. 128.
29 Ibid., p. 142.
30 de Sauvigny, op. cit., 105.
31 Alan Palmer, *Metternich* (London, 1972), p. 60.
32 Henry Contamine, *Diplomatie et Diplomates sous la Restauration, 1814–1830* (Paris, 1970), p. 295.
33 Kenneth Bourne, *Palmerston: the Early Years, 1784–1841* (London, 1982), p. 481.
34 D.J. Grange, 'La découverte de la presse comme instrument diplomatique par la Consulta', *Opinion publique et politique extérieure*, vol. I (Rome, 1981), p. 493.
35 Paul Gordon Lauren, *Diplomats and Bureaucrats: The First Institutional Responses to Twentieth-Century Diplomacy in France and Germany* (Stanford, California, 1976), p. 185.
36 Ibid., p. 523.
37 Michael Balfour, *The Kaiser and His Times* (London, 1964), p. 257.
38 R.A. Jones, op. cit., p. 173.
39 Keith Hamilton, *Bertie of Thame: Edwardian Ambassador* (Woodbridge, 1990), p. 60.
40 Lord Vansittart, *The Mist Procession: The Autobiography of Lord Vansittart* (London, 1958), p. 53.
41 Centre National de la Recherche Scientifique, *Les Affaires Étrangères et le Corps Diplomatique Français*, vol. II (Paris, 1984), p. 190.
42 Ibid.
43 Albert Sorel, *Essais d'histoire et de critique* (Paris, 1913), pp. 273–82.
44 Muriel Chamberlain, *Lord Aberdeen: a Political Biography* (London, 1983), p. 487.
45 Lord Newton, *Lord Lyons: A Record of British Diplomacy* (London, n.d.), p. 59.
46 Ministère des Affaires Étrangères (Paris), Archives des Archives, Commission des Archives Diplomatiques, Procès-verbaux des séances, vol. II, ff.22–7.
47 *5th Report of the Royal Commission appointed to inquire into the Civil Service, 1914–16* (Cd. 7749), XI, p. 57.
48 Lord Ribblesdale, ed., *Charles Lister: Letters and Recollections* (London, 1917), p. 129.

5 THE 'NEW' DIPLOMACY (pp. 136–182)

1 George Young, *Diplomacy Old and New* (London, 1921), p. 15.
2 Ministère des Affaires Etrangères (Paris), Pierre de Margerie papers, J. Cambon to de Margerie, 24 March 1905.
3 J. Cambon, *The Diplomatist*, trans. C.R. Turner (London, 1931), p. 142.
4 J.D. Shand, 'Doves Among the Eagles: German Pacifists and their Government during World War I', *Journal of Contemporary History*, X (1975), 97.
5 F.L. Carsten, *War against War: British and German Radical Movements in the First World War* (London, 1982), pp. 29–30.
6 E.D. Morel, *Morocco in Diplomacy* (London, 1912), p. 201.
7 George W. Egerton, *Great Britain and the Creation of the League of Nations: Strategy, Politics and International Organization, 1914–1919* (London, 1979), p. 31.
8 Roberta M. Warman, 'The Erosion of Foreign Office Influence in the Making of Foreign Policy, 1916–1918', *Historical Journal*, XV (1972), 133–59.
9 T. Bentley Mott, *Myron T. Herrick. Friend of France: An Autobiographical Biography* (London, 1930), p. 155.
10 Arno J. Mayer, *The Political Origins of the New Diplomacy, 1917–1918* (New Haven, Conn., 1959), p. 17.

11 K.A. Hamilton, 'The Pursuit of "Enlightened Patriotism": the British Foreign Office and Historical Researchers during the Great War and its Aftermath', *Historical Research: the Bulletin of the Institute of Historical Research*, LXI (1988), 323.

12 S. Gwynn, ed., *The Letters and Friendships of Sir Cecil Spring Rice* (2 vols, London, 1929), II, pp. 239, 320–1.

13 Lord Hankey, *Diplomacy by Conference: Studies in Public Affairs, 1920–1946* (London, 1946), pp. 12–15.

14 Keith Hamilton, *Bertie of Thame: Edwardian Ambassador* (Woodbridge, 1990), p. 384.

15 Gwynn, op. cit., II, pp. 366–7, 374.

16 T.H. von Laue, 'Soviet Diplomacy: G.V. Chicherin, People's Commissar for Foreign Affairs, 1918–1930', *The Diplomats, 1919–1939*, ed. Gordon A. Craig and Felix Gilbert (2 vols, 8th edition, London, 1974), I, p. 235.

17 Ibid.

18 Richard K. Debo, *Revolution and Survival: the Foreign Policy of Soviet Russia, 1917–18* (Liverpool, 1979), p. 38.

19 Jane Degras, ed., *Soviet Documents on Foreign Policy, vol. I, 1917–24* (Oxford, 1951), pp. 1–3.

20 David Lloyd George, *War Memoirs* (popular edition, 2 vols, 1938), II, pp. 1510–17.

21 Mayer, op. cit., pp. 353–67.

22 Harold Nicolson, *Diplomacy* (3rd edition, London, 1969), pp. 125–6.

23 Keith Eubank, *The Summit Conferences, 1919–60* (Norman, Oklahoma, 1966).

24 *The Treaty of Peace between the Allied and Associated Powers and Germany* (HMSO, London, 1919), p. 203.

25 Esme Howard, *Theatre of Life* (2 vols, London, 1935–6), I, pp. 292–3.

26 K.A. Hamilton, 'A Question of Status: British Diplomats and the Uses and Abuses of French', *Historical Research: the Bulletin of the Institute of Historical Research*, LX (1987), 128–9.

27 F.P. Walters, *A History of the League of Nations* (Oxford, 1960), pp. 48 and 54.

28 Paul Cambon, *Correspondance*, ed. H. Cambon, (3 vols, Paris, 1940–6), III, pp. 327–8.

29 Walters, op. cit., p. 50.

30 James Barros, *Office without Power: Secretary General Sir E.R. Drummond* (Oxford, 1979), p. 15.

31 Alan Sharp, 'Lord Curzon and the Foreign Office', *The Foreign Office, 1782–1982*, ed. Roger Bullen (Frederick, Maryland, 1984), p. 72.

32 Jon Jacobson, 'The Conduct of Locarno Diplomacy', *Review of Politics*, XXXIV (1972), 71.

33 Ernst von Weizsäcker, *Memoirs*, trans. John Andrews (London, 1951), p. 106.

34 Zara Steiner and M.L. Dockrill, 'The Foreign Office Reforms, 1919–21', *Historical Journal*, XVII (1974), 131–56.

35 D.C.M. Platt, *The Cinderella Service: British Consuls since 1825* (London, 1971), p. 241.

36 R.D. Schulzinger, *The Making of the Diplomatic Mind: the Framing, Outlook and Style of United States Foreign Service Officers, 1908–1931* (Middletown, Conn., 1975), p. 15.

37 Alan Cassels, *Mussolini's Early Diplomacy* (Princeton, 1970), p. 9.

38 David Irving, *The War Path: Hitler's Germany, 1933–39* (London, 1978), p. 166.

39 Franz von Papen, *Memoirs*, trans. Brian Connell (London, 1952), p. 400.

6 TOTAL DIPLOMACY (pp. 183–227)

1 Cited in Warren Christopher, 'Normalization of Diplomatic Relations', Modern Diplomacy: the Art and the Artisans, ed. Elmer Plischke (Washington, 1979), p. 41.
2 Robert Dallek, Franklin D. Roosevelt and American Foreign Policy, 1932–1945 (London, 1979), p. 532.
3 Robert Sherwood, ed., The White House Papers of Harry L. Hopkins (2 vols, London, 1948–9), I, p. 233.
4 Ibid., p. 237.
5 Ibid., pp. 268–9.
6 Earl of Halifax, Fulness of Days (London, 1957), p. 236.
7 David Kelly, The Ruling Few or the Human Background to Diplomacy (London, 1952), p. 313.
8 Documents Diplomatiques Français, 1871–1914, 2ème série, vol. I, no. 147.
9 Christopher Andrew, Secret Service: the Making of the British Intelligence Community (London, 1985), p. 298,
10 Christopher Andrew and David Dilks, eds, The Missing Dimension: Governments and Intelligence Communities in the Twentieth Century (London, 1984), p. 6.
11 Ibid., p. 10.
12 One of the most recent examples of this occurred in 1985 when the American constructors of the new US embassy building in Moscow discovered belatedly that metal beams supplied by Russian contractors, and already in place, were riddled with sophisticated eavesdropping devices. In 1988 the cost of demolishing and rebuilding the structure was estimated at $300 million. In the meanwhile the Russians were not allowed to occupy their long-completed new embassy building in Washington. The Daily Telegraph, 28 Oct. 1988.
13 Peter Wright, Spy Catcher: The Candid Autobiography of a Senior Intelligence Officer (London, 1987), pp. 110–13.
14 Walter Laqueur, A World of Secrets: the Uses and Limits of Intelligence (New York, 1985), p. 36.
15 Ernst von Weizsäcker, Memoirs, trans. John Andrews (London, 1951), p. 75.
16 Lord Gladwyn, The Memoirs of Lord Gladwyn (London, 1972), pp. 232 and 240.
17 Foreign Relations of the United States 1946, II, pp. 15–23.
18 Gidon Gottlieb, 'Global Bargaining: The Legal and Diplomatic Framework', Law-Making in the Global Community, ed. N.G. Onuf (Durham, N.C., 1982), pp. 109–30.
19 Alan James, 'The Role of the Secretary General of the United Nations', International Relations, I (1959), 620–38.
20 Ibid.
21 David Charlton, The Little Platoon: Diplomacy and the Falklands Dispute (Oxford, 1989), p. 219.
22 Jan Hendrik Lubbers, 'New Horizons in Postwar Diplomacy', The Washington Quarterly, X (1987), 18.
23 Dermot Keogh, 'The Department of Foreign Affairs [Ireland]', The Times Survey of Foreign Ministries of the World, ed. Zara Steiner (London, 1982), p. 280.
24 Robert J. Moore, Third-World Diplomats in Dialogue with the First World (London, 1985), p. 29.
25 Alex von Dornoch, 'Iran's violent diplomacy', Survival (May/June, 1988), 252–65.
26 Hugh de Santis and Waldo Heinrichs, 'The Department of State and American Foreign Policy', The Times Survey, p. 595.
27 Christopher, op. cit., p. 41.

28 Ernest Albert, 'Axing and Pruning Britain's Oversea's Services?', *Aussenpolitik* [English edition], XXIX (1978), 17–27.

29 Geoffrey Jackson, *Concorde Diplomacy: The Ambassador's Role in the World Today* (London, 1981), p. 225.

30 Martin Gilbert, *Winston S. Churchill*, vol. VIII, '*Never Despair*' (London, 1988), p. 510.

31 D.C. Watt, 'Summits and Summitry Reconsidered', *International Relations*, II (1963), 493–504.

32 Abba Eban, *The New Diplomacy: International Affairs in the Modern World* (London, 1983), p. 361.

33 Henry Kissinger, *The White House Years* (London, 1979), p. 781.

34 Charles W. Thayer, *Diplomat* (London, 1960), p. 113.

35 Henry M. Wriston, 'Ministerial Diplomacy – Secretary of State Abroad', in *Modern Diplomacy*, ed. G. Plischke (Washington, 1979), p. 160.

36 Eban, op. cit., p. 332.

7 DIPLOMACY TRANSFORMED AND TRANSCENDED
(pp. 231–45)

1 Nancy Mitford, *The Nancy Mitford Omnibus* (London, 1986), p. 561.

2 Louis Einstein, *A Diplomat Looks Back*, ed. L.E. Gelfand (London, 1968) p. 211.

3 Simon Jenkins and Anne Sloman, *With Respect Ambassador: An Enquiry into the Foreign Office* (London, 1984), pp. 131–2.

4 *The Times*, 7 Jul. 1970.

5 *House of Commons Parliamentary Papers* (1861), vol. VI, p. 442.

6 David D. Newsom, *Diplomacy and the American Democracy* (Bloomington, 1988), p. 5.

7 An expression used by a French diplomat, Thierry de Beaucé, *Le Monde*, 5 Sept. 1987.

8 Waldo H. Heinrichs, 'Commentary', *Instruction in Diplomacy: the Liberal Art Approach*, ed. Smith Simpson (Philadelphia, 1972), p. 90.

9 Michael Palliser, *Britain and British Diplomacy in a World of Change* (London, 1975), p. 11.

10 William Hayter, *A Double Life* (London, 1974), p. 170.

11 Charles W. Thayer, *Diplomat* (London, 1960), p. 70.

12 J.K. Galbraith, *A Life in Our Times* (London, 1981), pp. 391–2.

13 Anthony Parsons, *The Pride and the Fall: Iran, 1974–1979* (London, 1984), p. 5.

14 William H. Sullivan, *Mission to Iran* (London, 1981), p. 102.

15 Harold Nicolson, *The Evolution of Diplomatic Method* (London, 1953), p. 84.

16 *American Foreign Policy Current Documents, 1989*, ed. N.L. Golden and S.B. Wells (Washington, 1990), p. 18.

17 *Report of the Secretary-General pursuant to the statement adopted by the Summit Meeting of the Security Council on 31 January 1992*, SC Doc. S/24111, 17 June 1992.

18 Ibid.

19 Anthony Parsons, 'The United Nations in the Post-Cold War Era', *International Relations*, II (1992), 189–200.

20 Cited in Maurice Keens-Soper, 'The Liberal Disposition of Diplomacy', *International Relations*, V (1975–7), 911.

BIBLIOGRAPHY

The literature on diplomacy and its history is vast and the monographs listed below represent only a selection of those works which have proved particularly useful in the preparation of this study. Those seeking a glossary of diplomatic terms should consult Sir E. Satow's *Guide to Diplomatic Practice* (2 vols, London, 1917), the latest revised edition of which was published in 1979. It remains an indispensable aid to the study and practice of diplomacy.

THE THEORY AND PRACTICE OF DIPLOMACY

Adair, E.A. *The Extraterritoriality of Ambassadors in the Sixteenth and Seventeenth Centuries* (London, 1929)

Adcock, F. and Mosley, D.J. *Diplomacy in Ancient Greece* (London, 1975)

Anderson, M.S. *The Rise of Modern Diplomacy* (London, 1993)

Andrew, C. *Secret Service: The Making of the British Intelligence Community* (London, 1985)

Andrew, C. and Dilks, D. (eds) *The Missing Dimension: Governments and Intelligence Communities in the Twentieth Century* (London, 1984)

Andrew, C. and Gordievsky, O. *KGB. The Inside Story of its Foreign Operations from Lenin to Gorbachev* (London, 1990)

Armstrong, D. *The Rise of the International Organization: A Short History* (London, 1982)

Ashman, C. and Trescott, P. *Outrage: The Abuse of Diplomatic Immunity* (London, 1986)

Barber, P. *Diplomacy: The World of the Honest Spy* (London, 1979)

Barros, J. *Betrayal from Within: Joseph Avenol, Secretary-General of the League of Nations, 1933–1940* (London, 1969)

—— *Office without Power: Secretary-General Sir E.R. Drummond* (Oxford, 1979)

—— *Trygve Lie and the Cold War: The UN Secretary-General Pursues Peace, 1946–1953* (DeKalb, Illinois, 1989)

Barston, R.P. *Modern Diplomacy* (London, 1988)

Berman, M.R. and Johnson, J.E. (eds) *Unofficial Diplomats* (New York, 1977)

Berridge, G.R. and Jennings, A. (eds) *Diplomacy at the UN* (London, 1985)

Bull, H. and Watson, A. (eds) *The Expansion of International Society* (Oxford, 1984)

Busk, D. *The Craft of Diplomacy: Mechanics and Development of National Representation Overseas* (London, 1967)

Cambon, J. *The Diplomatist* (trans. C.R. Turner, London, 1931)

Cardozo, M.H. *Diplomats in International Co-operation: Stepchildren of the Foreign Service* (Ithaca, NY, 1962)

Carsten, F.L. *War Against War: British and German Radical Movements in the First World War* (London, 1982)

BIBLIOGRAPHY

Cassels, A. *Mussolini's Early Diplomacy* (Princeton, 1970)

Clark, E. *Corps Diplomatique* (London, 1973)

Contamine, H. *Diplomatie et diplomates sous la Restauration* (Paris, 1970)

Craig, G. and Gilbert, F. (eds) *The Diplomats, 1919–1939* (Princeton, 1953)

Debo, R.K. *Revolution and Survival: The Foreign Policy of Soviet Russia, 1917–1918* (Liverpool, 1979)

Denza, E. *Diplomatic Law: Commentary on the Vienna Convention on Diplomatic Relations* (London, 1976)

Egerton, G.W. *Great Britain and the Creation of the League of Nations: Strategy, Politics and International Organization, 1914–1919* (London, 1979)

Eubank, K. *The Summit Conferences, 1919–1960* (Norman, Okla., 1966)

Frodsham, J.D. (ed.) *The First Chinese Embassy to the West: the Journals of Kuo Sung T'ao, Liu Hsi-Hung and Chang To Yi* (Oxford, 1974)

Grahame, R.A. *Vatican Diplomacy: A Study of Church and State on the International Plane* (Princeton, 1959)

Johnson, E.A.J. (ed.) *The Dimensions of Diplomacy* (Baltimore, 1964)

Jones, R.A. *The British Diplomatic Service, 1815–1914* (Waterloo, Ont., 1953)

Hankey, Lord, *Diplomacy by Conference: Studies in Public Affairs* (London, 1946)

Headrick, D.R. *The Invisible Weapon: Telecommunications and International Politics, 1851–1945* (Oxford, 1991)

Hoffman, A.S. (ed.) *International Communication and the New Diplomacy* (London, 1968)

Horn, D.B. *The British Diplomatic Service, 1689–1789* (Oxford, 1961)

Iklé, F.C. *How Nations Negotiate* (New York, 1964)

Ilchman, W.F. *Professional Diplomacy in the United States, 1779–1939* (Chicago, 1961)

Jackson, G. *Concorde Diplomacy: The Ambassador's Role in the World Today* (London, 1981)

Kaufmann, J. *Conference Diplomacy* (Leiden, 1968)

Kertesz, S.D. and Fitzsimons, M.D. (eds) *Diplomacy in a Changing World* (Notre Dame, 1959)

Laqueur, W. *A World of Secrets: The Uses and Limits of Intelligence* (New York, 1985)

Lemoine, Y. *La Diplomatie française pendant la Révolution* (Paris, 1989)

Mak, D. and Kennedy, C.S. (eds) *American Ambassadors in a Troubled World: Interviews with Senior Diplomats* (London, 1992)

Mattingly, G. *Renaissance Diplomacy* (London, 1955)

Maulde la Clavière, M.A.R. de *La Diplomatie au temps de Machiavel* (3 vols, Paris, 1892–3)

May, E.R. (ed.) *Knowing One's Enemies: Intelligence Assessment before the Two World Wars* (Princeton, 1984)

Mayer, A.J. *The Political Origins of the New Diplomacy, 1917–1918* (New Haven, Conn., 1959)

Merlini, C. (ed.) *Western Summits and Europe: Rivalry, Co-operation and Partnership* (London, 1984)

Mitchell, J.M. *International Cultural Relations* (London, 1986)

Moore, R.J. *Third-World Diplomats in Dialogue with the First World* (London, 1985)

Newsom, D.D. *Diplomacy and the American Democracy* (Bloomington, Ind., 1988)

Nicolson, H. *The Evolution of Diplomatic Method* (London, 1954)

—— *Diplomacy* (3rd edn, London, 1969)

Northedge, F.S. *The League of Nations, its Life and Times, 1920–1946* (Leicester, 1986)

Picard, B. *Das Gesandtschaftswesen Ostmitteleuropas in der frühen Neuzeit* (Graz, 1967)

Plantey, A. *De la Politique entre les États: Principes de la Diplomatie* (2nd edn, Paris, 1991)

Platt, D.C.M. *Finance, Trade and Politics in British Foreign Policy 1815–1914* (London, 1968)

265

—— *The Cinderella Service: British Consuls since 1825* (London, 1971)

Plebwe, F.K. von *Internationale Organisation und die Moderne Diplomatie* (Munich, 1972)

Plischke, R. (ed.) *Modern Diplomacy: the Art and the Artisans* (Washington, 1979)

Putnam, R.D. and Bayne, N. *Hanging Together: The Seven-Power Summits* (London, 1984)

Queller, D.E. *The Office of Ambassador in the Middle Ages* (Princeton, 1967)

Roberts, A. and Kingsbury, B. (eds) *United Nations, Divided World: The UN's Roles in International Relations* (Oxford, 1988)

Roosen, W.J. *The Age of Louis XIV: the Rise of Modern Diplomacy* (Cambridge, Mass., 1976)

Russell, J.G. *Peacemaking in the Renaissance* (London, 1986)

Sen, B. *A Diplomat's Handbook of International Law and Practice* (The Hague, 1979)

Schulzinger, R.D. *The Making of the Diplomatic Mind: the Training, Outlook, and Style of United States Foreign Service Officers, 1908–1931* (Middletown, Conn., 1975)

Schwabe, K. (ed.) *Das Diplomatische Korps, 1871–1945* (Boppard/Rhein, 1985)

Seydoux de Clausonne, F. *Le Métier de Diplomatie* (Paris, 1980)

Shepard, J. and Franklin, S. (eds) *Byzantine Diplomacy: Papers from the Twenty-fourth Spring Symposium of Byzantine Studies* (Aldershot, 1992)

Simpson, S. (ed.) *Instruction in Diplomacy: the Liberal Arts Approach* (Philadelphia, 1972)

Taylor, P.M. *The Projection of Britain: British Overseas Publicity and Propaganda, 1919–1939* (Cambridge, 1981)

Thayer, C.V. *Diplomat* (London, 1960)

Vagts, A. *The Military Attaché* (Princeton, 1967)

Virally, N. et al. *Les missions permanentes auprès des organisations internationales* (4 vols, Brussels, 1971–6)

Walters, F.P. *A History of the League of Nations* (London, 1952)

Watson, A. *Diplomacy: the Dialogue between States* (London, 1982)

Whitcomb, E.A. *Napoleon's Diplomatic Service* (Durham, N.C., 1979)

THE ADMINISTRATION OF DIPLOMACY

Barnes, W. and Morgan, J.H. *The Foreign Service of the United States* (Washington, 1967)

Boyce, P.J. *Foreign Affairs for New States: Some Questions of Credentials* (St Lucia, Queensland, 1977)

Bullen, R. (ed.) *The Foreign Office, 1782–1982* (Frederick, Maryland, 1984)

Calvert, P. *The Foreign Policy of New States* (Brighton, 1986)

Cecil, L. *The German Diplomatic Service, 1871–1914* (Princeton, 1976)

CNRS *Les Affaires étrangères et le corps diplomatiques français* (2 vols, 1984)

Destler, I.M. *Presidents, Bureaucrats and Foreign Policy* (Princeton, 1972)

Dickie, J. *Inside the Foreign Office* (London, 1992)

Doβ, K. *Das deutsche Auswärtige Amt im übergang von Kaiserreich zur Weimarer Republik – Die Schülersche Reform* (Düsseldorf, 1977)

École française de Rome *Opinion publique et politique étrangère* (3 vols, Rome, 1980–5)

Estes, T.S. and Lightner, E.A. *The Department of State* (New York, 1976)

Ferraris, L.V. *L'amministrazione centrale del Ministero degli Esteri italiano nel suo sviluppo storico (1848–1954)* (Florence, 1955)

Findley, C. *Bureaucratic Reform in the Ottoman Empire: The Sublime Porte, 1789–1922* (Princeton, 1980)

Hayne, M.B. *The French Foreign Office and the Origins of the First World War, 1898–1914* (Oxford, 1993)

Hilliker, J. *Canada's Department of External Affairs vol.* I, *The Early Years, 1909–1946* (London, 1990)

Hocking, B.L. *Foreign Relations and Federal States* (Leicester, 1993)

Jacobsen, H.A. *Nationalsozialistische Aussenpolitik, 1933–1938* (Berlin, 1968)

Jenkins, S. and Sloman, A. *With Respect Ambassador* (London, 1985)

Jones, R.A. *The Nineteenth Century Foreign Office* (London, 1971)

Lauren, P.G. *Diplomats and Bureaucrats: The First Institutional Responses to Twentieth-Century Diplomacy in France and Germany* (Stanford, Calif., 1976)

Middleton, C.R. *The Administration of British Foreign Policy, 1782–1846* (Durham, NC)

Moscati, R. *Il Ministero degli Affari Esteri, 1861–1870* (Milan, 1961)

Palmer, A. *The Chancelleries of Europe* (London, 1983)

Plischke, E. *Microstates in World Affairs: Policy, Problems and Options* (Washington, 1977)

Seabury, P. *The Wilhelmstrasse: A Study of German Diplomats under the Nazi Regime* (Berkeley, 1954)

Steenbergen, J, De Clerq, G. and Foqué, R. *Change and Adjustment: External Relations and Industrial Policy of the European Community* (Dordrecht, 1983)

Steiner, Z. *The Foreign Office and Foreign Policy 1898–1914* (Cambridge, 1969)

—— (ed.) *The Times Survey of Foreign Ministries of the World* (London, 1982)

Twitchett, K.J. (ed.) *Europe and the World: The External Relations of the Common Market* (London, 1976)

Uldricks, T.J. *Diplomacy and Ideology: The Origins of Soviet Foreign Relations, 1917–1930* (London, 1979)

Wallace, W. *The Foreign Policy Process in Britain* (London, 1975)

Wank, S. (ed.) *Doves and Diplomats: Foreign Offices and Peace Movements in Europe and America* (London, 1978)

Werking, R.H. *The Master Architects: Building the United States Foreign Service, 1890–1913* (Lexington, 1977)

West, R. *The Department of State on the Eve of the First World War* (Athens, Georgia, 1978)

Zametica, J. (ed.) *British Officials and British Foreign Policy, 1945–50* (Leicester, 1990)

INDEX

Printed in the United States
88678LV00001B/148-171/A

9 780415 104753